THE LIVING HOUSE

THE LIVING HOUSE

An Anthropology of Architecture in South-East Asia

Roxana Waterson

WHITNEY LIBRARY OF DESIGN
an imprint of Watson-Guptill Publications / New York

Original edition © 1990 Oxford University Press Pte Ltd

This paperback edition © 1997 Roxana Waterson
First published in Great Britain in 1997 by Thames and Hudson Ltd,
London

This edition first published in the United States in 1998 by Whitney
Library of Design, an imprint of Watson-Guptill Publications, a division
of BPI Communications, Inc., 1515 Broadway, New York, NY, 10036.

Library of Congress Catalog Card Number: 97-61150

ISBN 0-8230-2835-6

Manufactured in Singapore

First U.S. printing, 1998

1 2 3 4 5 6 7 8 / 03 02 01 00 99 98

Contents

Preface and Acknowledgements

Since this book first appeared in 1990, its main thesis – that the kinship systems of island South-East Asia could be profitably reanalysed as house-focused systems – has been amply confirmed by dozens of excellent new ethnographic studies, particularly of previously little-known areas of eastern Indonesia. More and more of these recent works have chosen to focus upon the house as a key institution central to an understanding of how social relations are organized. As a result we are now moving toward a new synthesis in Indonesian kinship studies. The chance to republish this book therefore comes at an opportune moment and I hope will make the work more accessible to a wider audience than was possible formerly.

Although intended principally as a work of anthropology, the book also set out to cross disciplinary boundaries. At the original time of writing, the whole topic of indigenous vernacular architectures, and their intimate interconnections with patterns of social relations, was still a grossly neglected subject in anthropology. That is far less true today. New publications from all parts of the world, by both anthropologists and architects, have provided valuable documentation and confirmed the usefulness of a closer collaboration between the disciplines. Ironically, though, while these works bear witness to the genius of indigenous builders, the survival of the architectures they record is in many cases more threatened today than ever by the rapidly increasing pace of globalization and homogenizing development.

The Living House pays homage to Claude Lévi-Strauss, whose suggestively sketched concept of 'house societies' (*sociétés à maison*) provided part of the inspiration for the analysis. But it originally grew directly out of my earlier research on the Sa'dan Toraja people of highland South Sulawesi. In the course of two periods of fieldwork with the Toraja, I became increasingly interested in the role of houses within their bilateral kinship system. It was, in fact, impossible to understand this system without a consideration of how people traced their relationships to and through houses. Looking at the astonishing architectures of other Indonesian peoples, as well as the apparently irresolvable difficulties in a conventional analysis of their kinship systems, I became convinced that a cross-cultural investigation was called for. Thanks to the Cambridge University Evans Fellowship and a British Academy Southeast Asian Fellowship, I was able to spend two years, 1985–6, pursuing my researches in South-East Asia. I am deeply grateful to both these bodies for their sustained and generous support. Thanks to them I was also able to spend two months in pursuit of domestic architecture in Sumatra, in May–June 1986. My debt to them goes back beyond this, since they also supported my second period of fieldwork in Tana Toraja in 1982–3. I am also grateful to the Institute of Southeast Asian Studies, Singapore, which offered me its hospitality as a Visiting Fellow during 1985–6. My thanks go particularly to ISEAS's Southeast Asian Cultural Research Programme (SEACURP), and its then Honorary Director, Datuk Lim Chong Keat, for the chance to work on the Dorothy Pelzer Collection, a unique archive of photographs of South-East Asian architecture, and for permission to reproduce some of her photographs here.

Dorothy Pelzer was an American architect who spent much of the 1960s travelling through both mainland and island South-East Asia, recording domestic architecture. Tragically she died in 1972, before she had a chance to write the book she had planned. Her enthusiasm for the subject was clearly infectious to those who knew her, and is still inspiring to anyone reviewing her travels, which were often undertaken under much more difficult conditions than those of today. Although I have approached the subject from a different background and perspective, I hope that she would not disapprove of the result.

In researching the illustrations for the book, I have drawn on a wide range of historical material. Every effort has been made to clear copyright, but in some cases copyright-holders proved untraceable. Wherever

I could I have also tried to date the photographs, but this is not always possible. For this new edition, I have made no alterations to the text, though inevitably there are some parts that I might write differently now. In the analysis of cosmology, for instance, new studies are enabling a more dynamic approach that avoids seeing architecture simply as a reflection of cosmological ideas, but points to the possibility of built forms, or the rituals enacted within them, as themselves serving to generate a cosmology. I have become increasingly interested in the house as a vehicle for history and memory, but rather then rewrite this book, I shall pursue those themes elsewhere.

I owe a special debt of gratitiude to the late Professor Sir Edmund Leach, who gave me his encouragement and support from the very beginning of the project, lent me rare books, and reviewed portions of the manuscript. Others who have generously shared their criticism at various phases are Stephen Hugh-Jones, Geoffrey Benjamin, James Fox, Marilyn Strathern, and Vivienne Wee. I am forever grateful to my husband, Garth Sheldon, for all he has taught me about architecture and for his unfailing support. Finally, special thanks go to all those Indonesian acquaintances who helped me in the field, especially my Toraja friends and informants.

National University of Singapore ROXANA WATERSON
May 1997

Colour Plates

1. Bugis house with carved gable-finials on the island of Kalao near Bonerate, South Sulawesi, 1987. (Photograph: Roxana Waterson)

2. Rice barn in the Sasak village of Sade, southern Lombok, 1987. The shaded platform beneath the barn provides a comfortable place to work or rest during the day, and complements the enclosed interior space of the house, which has no windows. (Photograph: Garth Sheldon)

3. Karo Batak house at Lingga village, 1986. (Photograph: Roxana Waterson)

4. Carved and painted ring-beam of a Karo chief's house at Lingga village, 1986. (Photograph: Roxana Waterson)

5. Street of Hilisimaetano village, South Nias, 1986. (Photograph: Roxana Waterson)

6. Detail of the façade of the chief's house, Bawömataluo, South Nias, 1986. In the centre is the carved head of a protective monster or *lasara*. (Photograph: Roxana Waterson)

8. Carved stone seat at the head of the steep flight of steps which leads up from Orahili to the village of Bawömataluo. South Nias, 1986. (Photograph: Roxana Waterson)

7. Huge flight of stone steps leading to the village of Hilimaetaniha, South Nias, 1986. (Photograph: Roxana Waterson)

9. Sumbanese clan house at Prai Goli, West Sumba, 1987. (Photograph: *Roxana Waterson*)

10. Noble origin-house (*tongkonan*) at Lemo, Tana Toraja, 1983. (Photograph: Roxana Waterson)

11. Toraja origin-house at To' Kaluku Mataallo, near Kesu', under construction in 1983. The almost completed façade is already in position, prior to completion of the roof. (Photograph: Roxana Waterson)

12. Clan origin-houses in the Savunese village of Namata, Seba district, 1987. (Photograph: Roxana Waterson)

13. Beehive-shaped Atoni house in the mountain district of Soa'e, West Timor, 1987. (Photograph: Roxana Waterson)

14. Toba Batak village of Tolping, Samosir Island, Lake Toba, 1986. (Photograph: Roxana Waterson)

15. Paintings on the wall of an old Toba house at Lumban Binaga village show spirit figures on horseback. 1986. (Photograph: Roxana Waterson)

16–17. Pictures executed by a local artist in the 1940s decorate many of the houses at Sibadihun on the eastern shore of Lake Toba. These two panels present a local view of colonial Dutch life and mores; others depict scenes from World War II with Dutch and Japanese aeroplanes, ships, and soldiers. (Photographs: Roxana Waterson)

19. Mausoleum (*tugu*) at Tolping, Samosir Island, Lake Toba, surmounted by an older stone urn beneath which may be seen painted concrete figures of clan ancestors, 1986. Such monuments commemorate all the ancestors of a given clan, and are a recent invention frequently sponsored by migrant members of Toba clans. (Photograph: Roxana Waterson)

18. Stone sarcophagus of Raja nai Batu Sidabutar at Tomok, Samosir Island, Lake Toba, 1986. The curved lid echoes the roof shapes of Toba houses; its front end terminates in a finely carved *singa* or protective monster. The figure beneath is said to represent an Acehnese mercenary who came to Tobaland to advise the Raja on ways of resisting the Dutch, and subsequently died there. (Photograph: Roxana Waterson)

20. Minangkabau house in the village of Kampai, near Payakumbuh, West Sumatra, 1986. (Photograph: Roxana Waterson)

21. Minangkabau house owners relax on their front steps in the cool of the afternoon at Kampai, near Payakumbuh, West Sumatra, 1986. (Photograph: Roxana Waterson)

22. Guests gather to dance at a funeral before a Toraja house built in the new two-storey style, 1982. The lower storey has a square plan, with large doors and windows, while the upper storey retains the shape of the traditional Toraja house. Such 'transitional' styles represent the desire both for increased comfort and modernity, and for the high prestige which continues to be attached to the traditional style. (Photograph: Roxana Waterson)

23. Newly built Toraja origin-house with modern concrete bungalow alongside, 1983. The construction was funded by a wealthy migrant who lives in Jakarta. Migrants frequently invest a great deal of money in maintaining or rebuilding houses in their homeland, and return long distances to participate in ceremonies there. (Photograph: Roxana Waterson)

24. A new house, in traditional style, under construction at Cupak, Minangkabau, 1987. The construction was being funded by a wealthy migrant who lives in Jakarta. (Photograph: Anton Alers)

Figures

Introduction

ARCHITECTURE involves not just the provision of shelter from the elements, but the creation of a social and symbolic space—a space which both mirrors and moulds the world view of its creators and inhabitants. This book is an attempt to look closely at the social and symbolic aspects of indigenous architecture in one particular part of the world, South-East Asia, whose anonymous craftsmen have produced some of the most spectacular and beautiful wooden buildings anywhere in the world.

Most architectural studies have dwelt on the monumental and the formal; it is only relatively recently that vernacular architecture has come to be viewed as worthy of admiration and study. Yet only a tiny fraction of the world's population live in buildings with which architects or planners have had anything to do.[1] Among architects, Bernard Rudofsky (1964, 1977) has been foremost in promoting an aesthetic appreciation of the powerful, often 'organic' qualities, the ingenuity and the appropriateness of what he has aptly dubbed 'architecture without architects'. In the last twenty years or so, indigenous architectures have become the subject of a growing literature by both architects and anthropologists.[2] It is noticeable, however, that these works, although ranging far outside the normal confines of Western architectural history, have tended to concentrate on particular regions of the world—namely, Africa, India, and the Middle East. Paul Oliver could still lament in 1971 the extraordinary neglect of the subject in African studies (for which he blames, in the nineteenth century, the condescension of Western observers and in the early twentieth century, the unpopularity among anthropologists of studies of 'material culture') but by now a wealth of new research has helped to improve the situation (Oliver 1971: 8–12). All the same, his latest wide-ranging survey, *Dwellings: The House across the World* (1987) still raises many pertinent and as yet unanswered questions about indigenous architectures.

Work on Islamic architecture, especially such projects of research and practical application to new designs as those funded by the Aga Khan, have likewise expanded the understanding of functional, aesthetic, and social aspects of building traditions in the regions mentioned above. From time to time, these studies extend into South-East Asian countries like Malaysia and Indonesia, which have large Muslim populations; but their architectures are not Islamic in origin and the distinctive building traditions of the many non-Muslim groups inhabiting the region have remained outside their scope. Some works which have covered a more global field—such as Guidoni's *Primitive Architecture* (1978) or Duly's *The Houses of Mankind* (1979)—have done so in limited space, and are in any case intended to be primarily visual presentations, so that within them the South-East Asian region has received only cursory treatment. Although great temples and monuments in stone, such as Cambodia's Angkor Wat or Java's Borobudur, have attracted much attention among both indigenous and Western scholars, the remarkably rich vernacular traditions of South-East Asia have been undeservedly neglected. It is these traditions which form the subject matter of this book, which aims to show what can be learnt from them about the social worlds of their creators.[3]

For the anthropologist, the study of inhabited space, its construction and daily use, can provide a 'way in' to a whole culture and its ideas. Anthropologists' attention to this subject, though it can be traced back to the very beginnings of the discipline, has none the less been intermittent. There was a promising beginning with the publication in 1881 of Lewis Henry Morgan's *Houses and House Life of the American Aborigines*, a novel and wide-ranging attempt to analyse house forms in terms of kinship structures and social organization. Morgan paints a picture of Indian longhouse organization and its concomitant 'communism in living', where members shared food and resources and freely offered hospitality to strangers. He himself viewed the work as intrinsic to the development of his theories concerning the nature of the 'gens' (or lineage organization) and the stages of 'cultural evolution' through which mankind had passed. He had originally intended it to form a fifth volume of his much longer work, *Ancient Society* (1877), whose influence on Engels and Marx is well known. After this, however, interest in house and settlement forms appears to have been slight until the development of structuralism in the 1960s and 1970s stimulated a new spate of analyses of the layout of space in terms of indigenous cosmologies and symbolic ideas. The origins of this approach must be traced not only to French theoreticians, such as Durkheim and Mauss, but to Dutch writers on Indonesian societies. An early but seminal article was van Ossenbruggen's 'Java's Monca-pat: Origins of a Primitive Classification System' (1918), in which the author analysed the interrelations of Javanese villages arranged in patterns of four with a central fifth community. He pointed out the linkage between these arrangements and the Hindu cosmological conception of the world, arranged around the four cardinal points with a central fifth point, the centre being regarded as superior to the periphery and balancing the combined power of the four subordinate points.[4] Similarly, proto-structuralist approaches were pursued by a number of other writers, such as van Wouden in his analysis of eastern Indonesian societies.[5] Although this work was generally ignored by British anthropologists, it had its influence in France, as Lévi-Strauss (1963) acknowledged in his important paper on the analysis of settlement patterns, 'Do Dual Organizations Exist?', in which he paid tribute to the work of J. P. B. de Josselin de Jong.[6] Since then, there has been a slow growth in anthropological analyses of spatial organization (Cunningham 1964, Ortiz 1969, Douglas 1972, Bourdieu 1973, Tambiah 1973, Humphrey 1974, S. Hugh-Jones 1985, to name a few). Rather more recently, new and detailed South-East Asian ethnographies have begun greatly to increase our knowledge, not only of the power of the house as symbol, but of its vital role in kinship structures of the region (Barraud 1979, Forth 1981, Clamagirand 1982, Izikowitz and Sorensen 1982, McKinnon 1983, and Traube 1986). Very recently there appears at last to be a growing momentum in studies of indigenous architectures, with some interesting new works on South-East Asia emerging from architects too

(Domenig 1980, Gibbs 1987, Lim 1987, and Jumsai 1988).

The richness of house symbolism revealed by these studies should not be viewed as something extraordinary or unique to South-East Asia. Inhabited spaces are never neutral; they are all cultural constructions of one kind or another. Any building, in any culture, must inevitably carry some symbolic load. One has only to read Le Corbusier, for example, to discover a whole world view embodied in the supposedly strict functionalism of the Modern Movement's 'machines for living', only to view his designs for public spaces to read the messages they contain about political relations. Whatever the expansiveness of some of his visions, the authoritarianism of Le Corbusier's politics is as well documented as his autocratic personal behaviour.[7] The tower blocks of Britain's 'new barbarism' (which, to be fair, represented only a fragmentary adoption of those elements of Le Corbusier's vision which were found to be economically profitable) unquestionably contained messages to the users about the social distribution of power, and the authority of planners to decide people's life-styles. Users none the less found a way to respond, if only through vandalization, successfully resulting in the subsequent demolition of many of these structures. Rapoport, who has made major contributions over the past two decades to the understanding of meaning in built form, makes the pertinent observation that meaning resides not in things but in people: people want their environment to mean certain things. Even in architect-designed environments, users will try to personalize their own territories by endowing them with symbolic meanings—those meanings which Rapoport characterizes as by nature latent and associational, rather than manifestly 'functional'. For the architect who perceives his work as a statement of his own personality and aesthetic, the process by which users attempt to impose their own meanings may be viewed with disdain, if not outright hostility. This can lead to an 'overdesigning' of spaces in an attempt to exclude the possibility of users' adaptations. In Rapoport's view (1982: 22):

The entire modern movement in architecture can be seen as an attack on users' meanings—the attack on ornaments, on 'whatnots' in dwellings and 'thingamabobs' in the garden, as well as the process of incorporating these elements into the environment.

Actually it is not obvious that the architect's desire for

control over design is something uniquely to be blamed on the modern movement, but the remark does serve to illuminate the coexistence of at least two very different systems of meaning in the world of Western architecture. The separation between designers and users which has developed here is clearly not a feature of the societies I shall be considering. However, these brief comments should be enough to establish the point that we can never assume built form to be free of symbolic meanings, whether in 'modern' industrial societies or 'traditional', non-industrial ones.

In the Western world, the house is invested with meanings every bit as powerful as in the supposedly remote and exotic societies studied by anthropologists. One has only to reflect on the connotations of the English word 'home', with all that it implies about the structure of the family, to see this. In an earlier work, Rapoport quotes Steinbeck, who observed: 'Home—the very word can reduce my compatriots to tears.' In America, he goes on, the all-important idea of home *ownership* centres on the image of a free-standing house, preferably surrounded by trees and grass. He adds that since relatively few Americans actually live in houses like this, and most of them also move house every five years, what is represented is in fact 'not a real need but a symbol' (Rapoport 1969: 132).[8] The house, then, as he puts it, is in some sense the expression of an 'ideal environment', reflecting social ideologies and an ethos of living. The potent idea of 'home' doubtless coloured the impressions of many European observers of indigenous dwellings in South-East Asia, as it did elsewhere. The discordance between their expectations and the observed reality provides, as we shall see, a number of clues to the distinctive functions and significance of the house in this part of the world.[9]

The house, then, is a microcosm, reflecting in its layout, structure, and ornamentation the concept of an ideal natural and social order. Houses and settlements always offer themselves as a useful means of encoding such information. Though in no sense exclusive to South-East Asia, this aspect of architecture is highly elaborated in many societies of this region, as I shall show.[10] Schulte Nordholt (1971: 432), writing on the Atoni of Timor, expresses the relationship between the house and the world in literary terms: 'The house and the [communal meeting house] are for the Atoni—lacking a script as he does—a book in which the order of his world is recorded. They are the reflection and embodiment of his thinking.' Such representations, however, are rarely entirely systematic. What exactly constitutes a 'microcosm' has recently been critically analysed by Ellen in relation to the symbolism of the house among the Nuaulu of South-central Seram, in the Moluccas. Ellen expresses some suspicion of what he sees as the overly coherent analyses by some writers of house and village layouts in eastern Indonesia. He questions the assumption that the house somehow has primacy in providing what Forth (1981: 23), in the context of Sumba, has termed 'a comprehensive presentation of orderly universal forms and relations', or that it thus presents the observer with a code which has only to be cracked in order to explicate social relations in their entirety. Ellen prefers to view the Nuaulu house as but one of many symbolic domains which serve different symbolic purposes in different contexts. The house thus draws its imagery from other symbolic microcosms (the village, the body) between which there is a continual interplay, and within which particular sets of symbolic oppositions may appear to contradict each other. He takes as an example the symbolic opposition between 'male' and 'female', which is aligned, in the context of Nuaulu village layout, with a contrast between centre (the men's ritual house) and periphery (women's gardens and menstruation huts), while in terms of house layout the same opposition seems to be expressed in a contrast between east and west (or north-east and south-west). On still another level, villages themselves may be contrasted with each other as 'male' and 'female' as a way of giving expression to their mythic or historical relationship (Ellen 1986: 24). Personally, I do not think that Ellen's analysis differs very markedly in its essentials from that of Forth (1981: 41), who also recognizes the shifting, contextual nature of symbolism in his description of the Sumba house and village. But Ellen's discussion of some other aspects, such as the ritual importance of the house-building process itself, are of especial interest and I shall return to them again later.

The imagery of the house as 'book' is used again by Bourdieu in his analysis of the Berber house (1973, 1977). Like Schulte Nordholt, though in much more complicated language, Bourdieu draws attention to the manner in which inhabited space, and above all the house, may serve as an embodiment of cultural messages in the absence of a literary tradition. More than this, however, Bourdieu's concern is to demonstrate some mechanism whereby such encoded messages might be said to be absorbed and internalized by individuals growing up in the society. 'The "book" from which the children learn their vision of the world is read with the body, in and through the movements and displacements which make the space within which they are enacted as much as they are made by it' (Bourdieu 1977: 90). Speaking of the division of space in terms of the symbolism of gender in Berber society, he goes on to suggest (1977: 92) how complicated the interaction between body symbolism and house symbolism may be:

All the symbolic manipulations of body experience, starting with displacements within a mythically structured space, e.g. the movements of going in and coming out, tend to impose the *integration* of the body space with cosmic space by grasping in terms of the same concepts (and naturally at the price of great laxity in logic) the relationship between man and the natural world and the complementarity and opposed states and actions of the two sexes in the division of sexual work and the sexual division of work, and hence in the work of biological and social reproduction. For example, the opposition between movement outwards towards the fields or the market, towards the production and circulation of goods, and movement inwards, towards the accumulation and consumption of the products of work, corresponds symbolically to the opposition between the male body, self-enclosed and directed towards the outside world, and the female body, resembling the dark, damp house, full of food, utensils and children, which is entered and left by the same inevitably soiled opening.

Just how different patterns of gender symbolism, and their implications for the style of relations between the sexes, may be in the cultures of South-East Asia will be the theme of a later chapter; yet Bourdieu's approach to the analysis of the use of space is a challenging one. His analysis of symbolic oppositions in Berber society is basically structuralist in style, but he criticizes structuralism's failure to indicate how such systems are really learned, used, and perpetuated by the people themselves. Bourdieu himself postulates a dialectical relationship between habitat, the socially structured environment, and what he terms the 'habitus'—that collection of schemes of perception, attitudes, and behaviour which shapes the cognitive world of individual actors in a society and lends order to experience.

In the chapters that follow, I shall show how houses may be viewed as part of a 'set' of built forms which may include a number of other structures such as granaries, tombs, head-houses, public buildings, temporary ritual structures, and even boats. In island South-East Asia, other objects such as textiles and jewellery commonly belong to the house as heirlooms, providing complementary fields of symbolism and performing a dynamic role (for example, as objects of exchange) in articulating social relationships. Recent works by Gittinger (1979) and Rodgers (1985) have done much to deepen our understanding of how textiles and jewellery function within these societies, and this book is in some ways complementary to theirs; it aims to give a similarly cross-cultural view of the role of houses in South-East Asian patterns of social organization.

I begin by trying to trace the origins of recurring elements of architectural style, and go on to examine the technological and cosmological considerations behind them. I shall examine ideas and beliefs about buildings which are regarded as powerful, sacred, or alive. The 'house', also, must be regarded as consisting not merely of a physical structure, but of the group of people who are its members. I devote one chapter to the idea that kinship systems in South-East Asia—which have frequently puzzled anthropologists because of their apparent failure to fit comfortably within conventional anthropological categories—can better be understood when the house is viewed as the real focus of these arrangements. I go on to examine how social relations define the uses of space within the house, and how rules about space in turn oblige individuals to act out these relations in their own movements. Even the dead must have their dwellings; the frequency with which tombs echo house shapes, and the elaborateness of mortuary rituals (often involving secondary treatment of the bones of long dead ancestors) provide us with important insights into the indigenous ancestor-focused religions of South-East Asia. A final consideration is the effect of rapid social change on the architectural traditions of present-day South-East Asian societies, and the questions this raises for the survival of indigenous architectural forms.

1. No one knows how many dwellings there are in the world, though Oliver (1987: 7) offers an estimate of eight or nine hundred million, of which probably less than 5 per cent have been built with any professional or official involvement. Those actually designed by architects represent a still tinier proportion: 1 per cent 'might well be an over-estimate'.

2. See, for example, Rudofsky (1964, 1977), Fraser (1968), Rapoport (1969, 1982), and Oliver (1969, 1971, 1975, 1987) for some general approaches to the study of architecture.

3. Although I have been unable to avoid using the word 'tradition' in this book, it is not intended to imply something rigidly unchanging and only now under threat from processes of modernization. Like all other aspects of culture, built form is subject to continuous change and evolution over time, although rates of change differ and there is evidence for the considerable antiquity of certain South-East Asian architectural forms. Some attempt to treat the subject of what the peoples involved *themselves* mean by 'tradition' is made in the concluding chapter.

4. The influence of Hindu cosmological ideas in Indonesia, and their incorporation into already existing cosmologies, is treated more fully in Chapter 5.

5. Papers by van Ossenbruggen, van Wouden, and other Dutch scholars have been reprinted in English translation in P. E. de Josselin de Jong's *Structural Anthropology in the Netherlands* (1977).

6. Dutch and French anthropologists have apparently paid more attention to each other than the British anthropological establishment at one time paid to either of them, as evidenced by the fact that J. P. B. de Josselin de Jong had already presented (in English) a survey of Lévi-Strauss's *Les Structures Elémentaires de la Parenté* in 1952, a mere three years after its first appearance in French, whereas it took twenty years for an English translation to be published in Britain.

7. See R. Walden, *The Open Hand: Essays on Le Corbusier* (1977).

8. The symbolism of 'home' perhaps reached its most vivid expressions in a number of Hollywood films of the post-War era.

9. See Chapter 2 for an exploration of this difference of ideas.

10. See, for example, Griaule (1965), Bourdieu (1973), Ortiz (1969), and S. Hugh-Jones (1985) for discussions of the house as microcosm in Africa, North and South America, etc.

Map 1: South-East Asia showing Distribution of Ethnic Groups

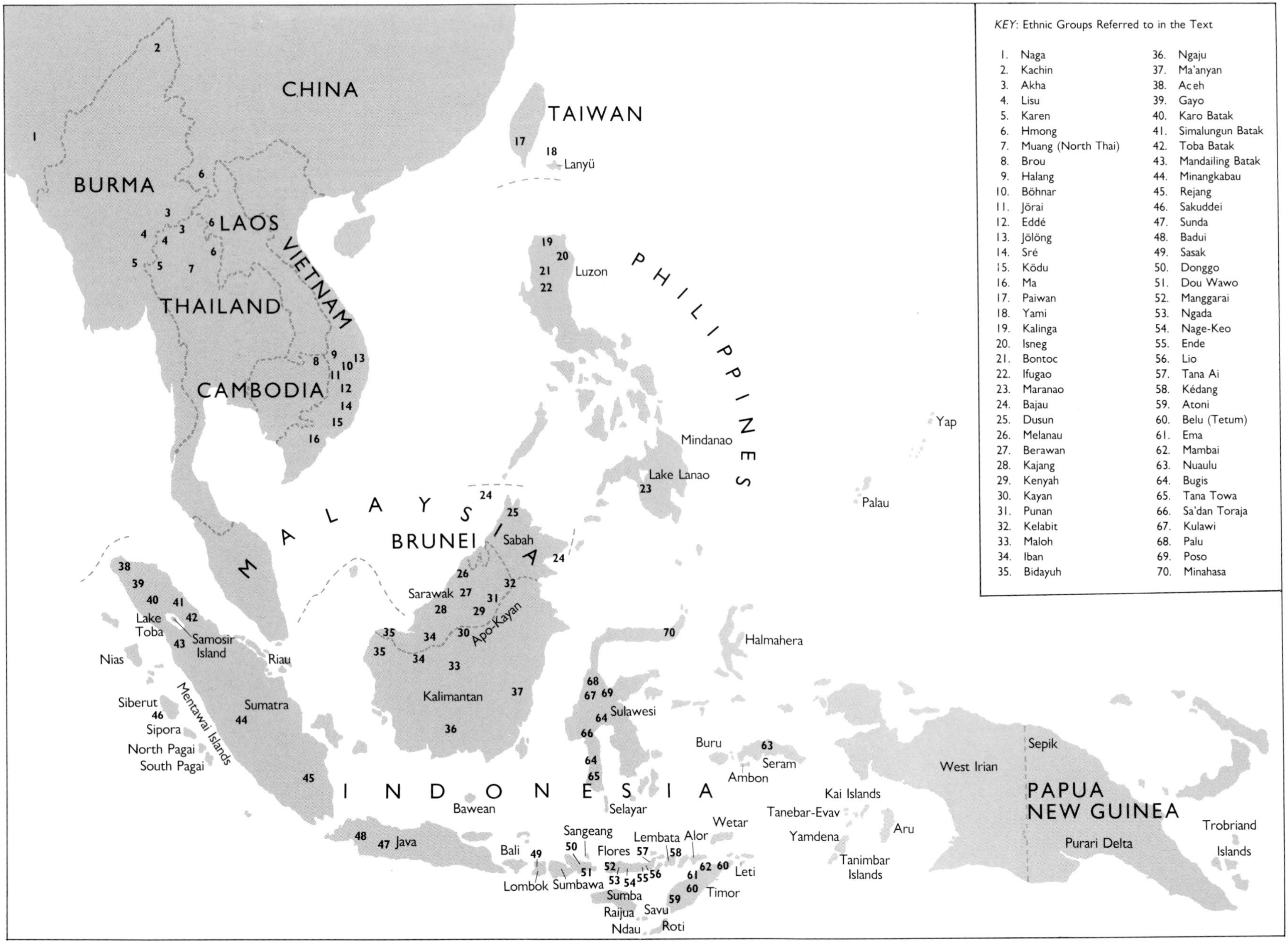

KEY: Ethnic Groups Referred to in the Text

1. Naga		36. Ngaju	
2. Kachin		37. Ma'anyan	
3. Akha		38. Aceh	
4. Lisu		39. Gayo	
5. Karen		40. Karo Batak	
6. Hmong		41. Simalungun Batak	
7. Muang (North Thai)		42. Toba Batak	
8. Brou		43. Mandailing Batak	
9. Halang		44. Minangkabau	
10. Bôhnar		45. Rejang	
11. Jörai		46. Sakuddei	
12. Eddé		47. Sunda	
13. Jölöng		48. Badui	
14. Sré		49. Sasak	
15. Ködu		50. Donggo	
16. Ma		51. Dou Wawo	
17. Paiwan		52. Manggarai	
18. Yami		53. Ngada	
19. Kalinga		54. Nage-Keo	
20. Isneg		55. Ende	
21. Bontoc		56. Lio	
22. Ifugao		57. Tana Ai	
23. Maranao		58. Kédang	
24. Bajau		59. Atoni	
25. Dusun		60. Belu (Tetum)	
26. Melanau		61. Ema	
27. Berawan		62. Mambai	
28. Kajang		63. Nuaulu	
29. Kenyah		64. Bugis	
30. Kayan		65. Tana Towa	
31. Punan		66. Sa'dan Toraja	
32. Kelabit		67. Kulawi	
33. Maloh		68. Palu	
34. Iban		69. Poso	
35. Bidayuh		70. Minahasa	

CHAPTER 1

Origins

A great chain of islands stretches between the Pacific and Indian Oceans for a distance of 5,630 kilometres, making up the present-day nation of Indonesia. Indonesia's more than 13,000 islands, of which nearly 1,000 are permanently inhabited, form one of the culturally richest and most diverse regions of the world. More than 350 different ethnic groups maintain their own languages and traditions in this country whose aptly chosen motto is 'Unity in Diversity'. But although Indonesia was the starting-point for this book and remains its major focus, its scope has become wider. In attempting to trace the distant origins of architectural styles, and the similarities in the social and symbolic uses to which buildings and inhabited spaces are put, we find ourselves following clues that lead not only back into mainland South-East Asia, but as far afield as Madagascar, Japan, and the islands of Oceania. Moreover, for the purpose of this book, it is useful to consider the Indonesian archipelago in more purely geographical rather than national terms as encompassing also the islands of the Philippines and those which form part of Malaysia, so that references to 'the archipelago' may be taken to refer to this wider area; in terms of prehistory at least, New Guinea and the Melanesian islands form a natural extension of this region, and they too enter into the picture—if briefly, for reasons of space. Map 1 shows the locations of ethnic groups referred to in the text. Movements of population and the consequent meeting and fusing of cultural traditions have been a constant feature of the region's history and prehistory. It is no surprise, then, that this book both begins and ends with the theme of migrations.

For a glance at the range of architectural styles which have developed in the communities of island South-East Asia quickly reveals some startling similarities, which are strongly suggestive of a perhaps distant, but common, origin. Although my chief concern will be with the social significance of architecture rather than with modes of construction, let us begin by looking at some of these shared physical features. Perhaps the most obvious of them is the use of pile foundations. This is a very general feature of built form in both mainland and island South-East Asia, as well as Micronesia and Melanesia, though as we move further east it seems to fade out in Polynesia, where buildings are more often set upon raised stone platforms.[1]

In very few parts of island South-East Asia are buildings set directly on the ground; a notable exception today is Java, yet here, too, temple friezes of the ninth-fourteenth centuries in Central and East Java (Figures 1 and 2) provide illustrations of a number of different kinds of pile-built dwellings, with people sitting or standing under them, which indicate that in earlier periods of Javanese history, pile construction may have been the norm. In Sunda (West Java), low piles are a feature of the few surviving examples of an older style of village architecture. The adoption of ground-built structures is generally attributed to Indian influence; in Bali, which remains Hindu, most household structures (but not granaries) are likewise built on the ground, generally set upon a raised stereobate or platform. Examples of Balinese architecture may be found also in western Lombok, which from the early eighteenth century was ruled over by the Balinese kingdom of Karangasem. The indigenous Sasak population of Lombok, interestingly, build houses set upon the ground and enclosing an interior raised platform about 1 metre high, made of clay mixed with dung and straw, and polished to a smooth surface. This platform forms the floor of the main room, and is surrounded by an interior wall of woven bamboo with a pair of wooden doors in front. Their barns, however, are pile built, resembling those of the Balinese with their convex roofs. In all the rest of Indonesia, excepting some highland regions of West Irian and Timor, only the tiny island of

1. Pile-built structure from a frieze on the north side of the first gallery of the Borobudur temple, Central Java, ninth century AD. Note the extended gable line, the circular rat guards on the piles, and the use of the space beneath the floor for daily activities—all features which remain typical of many domestic buildings in Indonesia today. (Photograph: Jacques Dumarçay)

2. Building with extended gables depicted on a frieze from the south side of the first gallery of the Borobudur temple, Central Java, ninth century AD. (Photograph: Jacques Dumarçay)

Buru appears to lack a tradition of pile building (Nguyen 1934: 112, Map). In most parts of mainland South-East Asia, buildings are likewise raised on piles. In the mountains of northern Thailand, for example, houses with earth foundations are found only rarely as a response to cold at high altitudes or, as among the Yao, as the result of Chinese influence. Another variation of the raised floor structure which appears to be of equal antiquity is the method of building on foundations of logs laid in a square and crossing each other at the corners, a method which is still in use today in various widely scattered parts of the region we are considering.

In a tropical environment, pile building confers a number of distinct advantages, which will be considered more fully below. But this fact in itself would hardly be sufficient to explain its occurrence, and some attempt must be made to trace its historical develop-ment as well, although the evidence available to us is of necessity fragmentary and somewhat inconclusive. Already fifty years ago, the broad distribution of South-East Asian pile building caught the attention of one author, Nguyen Van Huyen, who made it the subject of a cross-cultural survey (Nguyen 1934). Nguyen compiled information from ethnographic reports then available on a wide range of societies in Indonesia, the Philippines, the Malay Peninsula, and Indo-China. However, he chose to restrict his investigations to a study of floor plans, the result being a series of tantalizingly incomplete glimpses into the place of houses in the social life of the peoples concerned. More recent explorations of pile building in mainland South-East Asia are to be found, among others, in the work of Clément and Charpentier (1974, 1975a, b).

A more distinctive element of style which recurs most widely in Indonesia is the saddle-backed roof,

3

with an extended ridge-line often resulting in outward-sloping gable-ends, and sometimes highly exaggerated points to the eaves, soaring up like buffalo horns among the Minangkabau of West Sumatra (Figure 3), or supported by huge free-standing posts among the Sa'dan Toraja of Sulawesi (Figure 4).[2] In other places, the saddle-backed roof has developed a whole range of variations, as among the Karo Batak of North Sumatra, some of whose finest structures are topped by a pyramid of multiple gables (Figure 5). Even in New Guinea, whose languages and cultures largely differ markedly from those of island South-East Asia, we find many remarkable similarities in architectural style. Domenig (1980: 44–7) illustrates a number of pile-built, saddle-roofed 'spirit houses' or ceremonial houses, with char-

acteristically extended ridge-lines, from different cultures of the northern coast of Papua New Guinea, but the style is by no means restricted to this area. Viewing the forms of the great men's ceremonial houses constructed by the peoples of the Sepik River (Figure 6), or of Kamari and Orokolo on the south-east coast (Figure 7), it is impossible not to see a further evolution of the saddle roof on a grand—almost a fantastic—scale. In Micronesia, the Palauans, too, once constructed low-piled, saddle-roofed ceremonial houses with magnificently decorated façades, whose general form, to be seen in old prints, bears an extremely close resemblance to that of, for example, Toba Batak houses (Figure 8). A point of interest about Palauan styles is that buildings were sometimes raised on low stone or wood piles set

3. Typical Minangkabau house in the village of Kampai near Payakumbuh, West Sumatra, 1986. (Photograph: Roxana Waterson)

4. Noble origin-houses at Lemo, Tana Toraja, Sulawesi, their gable-ends supported by free-standing posts, 1983. (Photograph: Roxana Waterson)

5. Karo chief's house with multiple decorative gables, 1936. A *geriten* or head-house, in which ancestors' skulls were stored, stands in front of it. (VIDOC, Koninklijk Instituut voor de Tropen, Amsterdam)

6. Men's house in the Middle Sepik region of Papua New Guinea. (Musée de l'Homme, Paris)

7. Men's ceremonial house (*ravi*) from Kamari in the Purari delta area of Papua New Guinea. The gable-ends of these structures may reach heights of 80 feet. (Haddon Collection, Cambridge University Museum of Archaeology and Anthropology)

9. Men's house in the village of Atiliu, Yap Island, Micronesia, after a photograph by Clarence Wong. (From Poirier 1972: 1203)

8. Decorated façade of a men's house in Melekeiok, Palau Islands, Micronesia, from a watercolour by A. Kramer in *Report of the South Seas Expedition*, 1908–10. (From Poirier 1972: 1205).

on top of the stone platform foundation commonly found in Polynesia, thus combining these two elements (see, for example, the illustrations in Domenig 1980: 37, 184–91). In the Caroline Islands, besides Palau, one may find numerous examples of the saddle-roofed, pile-built house, in Yap (Figure 9), Fais, Woleai, and Lamotrek (Domenig 1980: 29). Clearly, although not all pile buildings need have saddle roofs, one cannot help noticing how frequently these two elements appear in combination throughout the archipelago. A unique, indeed perhaps the strangest, development in the art of pile building is to be found in the Marianas Islands. Here, there survive groups of huge stone uprights, carved of coral or volcanic rock and topped with rounded capstones, and commonly arranged in double parallel rows. These are called *latte*, and are believed to have been house piles. The tallest are 5.5 metres in height, with some rows as long as 22 metres. Early Spanish accounts speak of houses with stone pillars, and some of the larger ones may have been men's houses or boat houses. The earliest carbon-14 date for these stones is AD 900, and they were in use from that

time until the seventeenth century, when local societies were much disrupted by the Spanish and most of the population was resettled on Guam. 'In basic principle,' notes Bellwood (1978: 283), 'the form is simply a translation into stone of the raised pile houses of Island South-East Asia.'

Another repeatedly recurring feature in South-East Asian architecture (both on the mainland and among the islands) is that of decorative gable-finials in the form of crossed horns. These may be formed simply from extensions of the rafters (as, for example, among the Bugis or Malay), or they may be elaborately carved. Names for these finials very often are derived from words for 'horns', and sometimes their likeness to buffalo horns is very explicit, as in the case of the Naga of North-east India, in North Thailand, among the Batak of Sumatra (the Karo even place dramatically modelled heads of buffalo at the eave-points of the house, and these are believed to serve a protective function for the inhabitants), or formerly in parts of Central Sulawesi. In other instances (as formerly was the case on the island of Roti, in Manggarai (West Flores) and in Poso (Central Sulawesi)), the horns are carved in the shape of birds or *naga* (the mythical water-snake of the underworld in South-East Asian cosmologies); or again, they may be likened to 'open scissors' (the *silang gunting* of the Malay house, now rarely seen) or to the prow- and stern-boards of boats (the *kora* of Tanimbar in the southern islands of the Moluccas)

(Plate 1; Figures 10–14). I. H. N. Evans (1951), writing on the occurrence of house horns among the Dusun and other Borneo peoples, including the seafaring Bajau, remarked on their existence also among the Sema and Angami Naga of North-east India and still further afield, among the Hova (Merina) of Madagascar. The horns of a buffalo being its chief weapons of offence and defence, he guessed that house horns might serve a symbolically protective function, though the majority of his informants in the 1950s had little to say about them beyond that they were ornamental. His guess is, none the less, quite a reasonable one, particularly if we take into account the example of the Karo, where both the appearance of the horns and their stated function are quite explicit. The Mandailing Batak, too, whose gables are topped with modelled buffalo heads, state that the horns have a protective value (Kartomi

1981: 9). Evans also noted that, although the horns were sometimes formed simply from projections of the rafters, wealthy Dusun liked to have them more elegantly carved in a branching form.

The choice of horns as a motif doubtless reflects the great importance of the buffalo in many South-East Asian societies, where it is a major form of wealth and its sacrifice is often a central feature of ceremonies (Figures 15 and 16). Kartomi (1981: 9) notes that the buffalo, in its sacrificial role, provides a link between earth and heaven; according to traditional Mandailing religion, as among many other peoples of the archipelago, the dead are also believed to ride to the upper world (or the afterlife) on a buffalo. Evans's observation that wealthier houses had more elaborate horns also points to the potential of these decorative elements to serve as a sign of rank or status. In Tanimbar, only

10. Fisherman's hut with buffalo-headed gable decoration near Balige, Lake Toba, Sumatra. (VIDOC, Koninklijk Instituut voor de Tropen, Amsterdam)

11. Gable-finial in the form of a *naga* or water serpent, on a Buginese house near Teteaji, Sidenreng, South Sulawesi, 1965. (Dorothy Pelzer Collection, courtesy of ISEAS, Singapore/Smithsonian Institution, Washington)

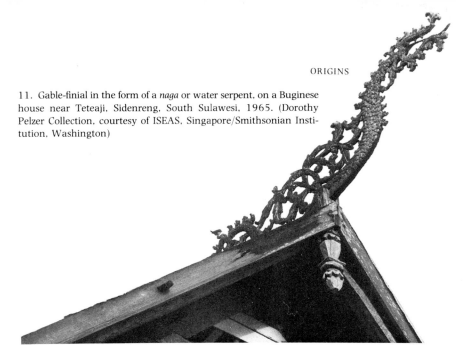

12. Hexagonal house typical of the Galela region of Halmahera in the Moluccas, with an elaborate ridge ornament in the form of a *naga* from which hang bird-shaped pendants. (VIDOC, Koninklijk Instituut voor de Tropen, Amsterdam)

13. Horn-shaped ridge decorations, called *kora*, on a house in Tanimbar. The same word is used to refer to the carved prow- and stern-boards of a ceremonial boat. (From Drabbe 1940: Pl. 50, courtesy of SOAS, London)

14. The tall roof peak of this Fijian chief's house echoes the forms of houses in eastern Indonesia. Here the extensions to the ridge are made from fernwood covered with shells. (Bernice P. Bishop Museum)

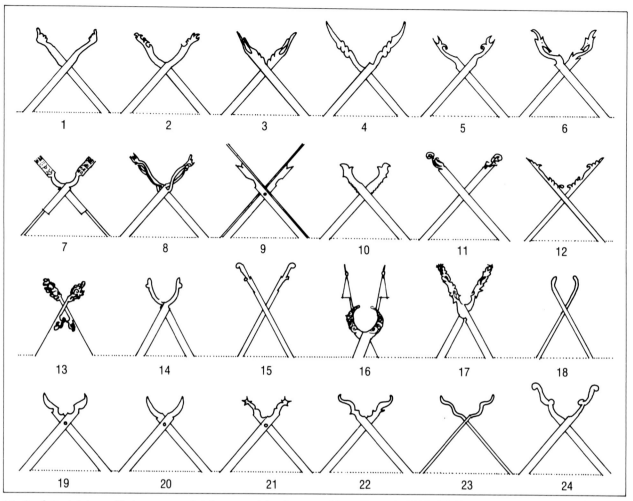

15. South-East Asian gable horns, compiled from a variety of sources. (From Domenig 1980: 20) Key to provenance: 1-6: Kalimantan; 7: Central Sulawesi; 8: South-east Sulawesi; 9-10: South Sulawesi; 11: Flores; 12: Singapore; 13: Riau; 14: West Sumatra; 15: West Java; 16: Tanimbar; 17-18: Roti; 19-22: Laos (Yuan); 23: Thailand; 24: Kampuchea.

important named houses of the nobility used to carry the finely carved ridge ornaments recorded in Drabbe's photographs of the 1930s (Drabbe 1940; McKinnon 1983). Among the Konyak Naga, horns are added to the ridges of noble houses only after the holding of an appropriate feast, one of a series of 'feasts of merit' by which families may raise their social status (Fürer-Haimendorf 1976: 16). In the more distant regions of Austronesian influence, the status element seems to have become of still greater importance. For example, in Japan, only the sacred Shinto shrines of Ise and Izumo, together with the imperial palace, were per-

mitted to have crossed-horn finials. The Sakalava of Madagascar applied a similar prohibition to pile building, which was traditionally reserved for royal store houses and council houses (Feeley-Harnik 1980: 567).[3]

The Austronesian World

Where did this style of building, with its raised floor and elegantly curved roof-lines, come from? To trace its origins we must look briefly at South-East Asian prehistory. Language provides us with one of our most important clues to the underlying historical and cul-

16. Gable ornaments of 'temples' (*lobo*) in South-east Central Sulawesi. (From Kaudern 1944: 28)

A, after Grubauer; B—E, after P. and F. Sarasin.

tural ties which bind the peoples of this region. The languages spoken in most of island South-East Asia form part of the world's largest language family, known by linguists as Austronesian. Map 2 shows the vast extent of the Austronesian language family, which stretches more than half-way round the world's circumference from its westernmost point of distribution, Madagascar, to the easternmost, Easter Island, and encompasses the whole of island South-East Asia, Micronesia, and Polynesia, as well as parts of the Malay Peninsula, South Vietnam, Taiwan, and coastal pockets of New Guinea. Even the Japanese language, which is currently classed as belonging to the Altaic family, is considered by Japanese linguists to possess an ancient substratum of Austronesian (Domenig 1980: 80), and the linguist Paul Benedict has recently propounded a

new theory reclassifying it altogether as belonging to the Austronesian family (Benedict 1986). Altogether there are an estimated 700–800 Austronesian languages spoken today. These have been classified by linguists into over fifteen district subgroups. The extent of the Austronesian language family is illustrated in Map 2.

All these languages have developed out of an original language (or more probably a group of dialects) which linguists term Proto-Austronesian, and which probably existed by at least 6,000 years ago. The evidence of linguistics co-ordinates rather well with that of physical anthropology and archaeology to give us a picture of early migrations through the archipelago in the Neolithic era. The fullest analysis of these developments is provided by Peter Bellwood (1978, 1985), who has done very important work in pulling together the multiple strands of evidence. Since I can only deal very briefly with the topic here, the reader who desires a fuller picture is recommended to the above works, on which I have largely depended for what follows.

Physically the populations of South-East Asia and the Pacific belong to two main phenotypes: the Australoid and the Mongoloid. The Australoids comprise the people of Australia and New Guinea. Isolated pockets of 'negritos' in parts of the Malay Peninsula and the Philippines used also to be regarded as Australoid, but most recent researches suggest that they are more probably Mongoloid. Broadly speaking, the Mongoloid peoples speak Austronesian languages, whereas the Australoids do not. It appears that Mongoloid populations, probably originating from a homeland in southern China, have moved southwards to displace an earlier Australoid population in a process that may have begun as long as 10,000 years ago. The Australoid life-style was one of hunting, fishing, and gathering, whereas reconstructions of Proto-Austronesian clearly show that its speakers were cultivators. Bellwood (1985: 97) rightly stresses that these movements were not simple 'waves' of migration as older theorists liked to postulate; instead, we must envisage a much more complex situation with continual gene flow between two populations which were already highly varied in themselves. The assumption of earlier theorists that movement of Mongoloid populations into the archipelago was via the Malay Peninsula has also been shown to be mistaken. Linguistic reconstructions of Proto-Austronesian point strongly to Taiwan as a linguistic 'homeland'. From Taiwan, speakers of Proto-

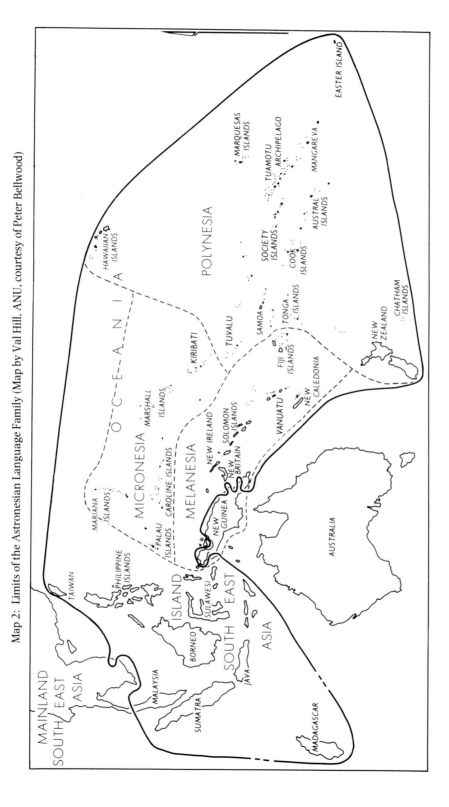

Map 2: Limits of the Astronesian Language Family (Map by Val Hill, ANU, courtesy of Peter Bellwood)

13

Austronesian languages most probably began to move into the Philippines around 3000 BC and thence into western and eastern Indonesia. The colonization of Oceania probably began some time after 2000 BC according to most recent estimates, while the Malay Peninsula and Vietnam were reached by Austronesian speakers in a movement back from the western islands of the archipelago, some time after 1000 BC. Madagascar was reached considerably later, around AD 400, at about the same time that, thousands of kilometres away, other Austronesian-speaking people were setting out from the Tahitian islands towards New Zealand.

Reconstructions of Proto-Austronesian vocabulary give us important indications about the life-style of its speakers. Initially cultivating colder climate species such as rice, millet, and sugar-cane, as they moved south into a more truly tropical zone they began to cultivate taro, yams, and other tubers, breadfruit, bananas, coconuts, and sago. Words for these plants appear in reconstructions of ancestral Malayo-Polynesian languages but not in the Formosan languages which split off at an early date to form a separate subgroup within the Austronesian family. They had pigs, and probably dogs and chickens, and they supplemented their agricultural activities with hunting, fishing, and collecting shellfish. They had tools of wood, bone, and shell, and had mastered a number of different fishing techniques, as well as the making of pottery and the sailing of outrigger canoes (Pawley and Green 1975; Blust 1976; Bellwood 1985: 114–15). It is interesting to note that many of the plants which became the most important cultigens in Polynesia—such as the breadfruit, banana, and taro—all have their wild distribution within Indonesia, and must have been introduced into the Pacific islands in domesticated form by Austronesian settlers.

What kind of houses were the early Austronesians inhabiting? Might they, for example, already have started to build on piles? Here, we have to accept that archaeology alone may never be able to answer this question fully. A house built of perishable materials is likely to leave at best only the marks of post holes and perhaps of ash deposits from fires (if it has an earth floor), and nothing much can be deduced from such evidence about what its overall appearance was like. Linguistic reconstruction, which has become such an important tool for prehistorians, can however provide us with some important clues. There is, in fact, some evidence that pile construction in both mainland and island South-East Asia could have been a development

of the later Neolithic. Blust (1976), in his reconstruction of the earliest form of Proto-Austronesian (including the Formosan languages), lists only one word relating to built forms—that meaning 'house/family dwelling', but terms reconstructed for the Malayo-Polynesian subgroups (that is, for a period after the splitting of these latter from the Formosan subgroup, when movement into the archipelago had already begun) include those for ridge-pole, rafter, thatch, house post, storage rack above the hearth, notched log ladder, hearth, and public building. From his reconstructions of these forms and their probable meanings, Blust concludes that Proto-Austronesian speakers were occupying settled villages which may have included both dwelling houses and some kind of public structure; that their houses were raised on posts, the floor being reached by means of a ladder; and that the roof (since it had a ridge-pole) must have been gabled, perhaps covered by an inverted log or bamboo rain-shield (for which cognates exist in several Philippine and Bornean languages), and thatched (probably with sago leaf). A hearth was built on the floor with one or more storage shelves for pots and firewood above it.

Archaeological evidence from Thailand offers some proof of a Neolithic development of pile building here too. Some important pottery assemblages from western Thailand have been grouped together as the Ban Kao culture, with dates between the late third and mid-second millennia. This culture is now thought to represent the southern extension of speakers of Mon-Khmer, a language grouping which once extended over much of mainland South-East Asia. At the related site of Nong Chae Sao, in 1966, the post holes of a house were excavated, 9.5 metres in length, with two burials and a group of four pots placed beneath the floor. This is the earliest excavated prehistoric house site in South-East Asia. A possible reconstruction of the house shows it with raised floor and rounded ends, in form not dissimilar to the dwellings of many of the present-day hill tribes of Thailand (Henriksen 1982) (Figure 17).

Although Neolithic assemblages of artefacts in Thailand show this region to have had a quite distinct cultural development from that which was taking place in the islands, we cannot discount the possibility of a still more ancient tie between these people and the Austronesians. The linguist Paul Benedict has put forward a theory that very early ancestors of the Austronesians in mainland South-East Asia spoke a language ancestral to both Austronesian and Thai, the latter

17. One proposed reconstruction of the neolithic house excavated at Nong Chae Sao, western Thailand. The house was about 9.5 metres long and dates to the late third–mid-second millennium BC. (From Henriksen 1982, courtesy of P. Sørensen)

having subsequently diverged to become monosyllabic and tonal. To this proto-language he has given the name Austro-Thai. Benedict's reconstruction of Proto-Austro-Thai also includes words such as 'platform/storey', 'house post', and 'ladder/steps leading up to house' (Benedict 1975). Although some linguists regard Benedict's methodology as idiosyncratic, the theory appears to be well grounded and has received widespread acceptance; indeed, some would extend the family even further to include the Austro-Asiatic languages.[4] All these developments give us increasingly strong indications of the great antiquity of links between island and mainland peoples.

Southern China and Japan

Even more significantly, Benedict has most recently published the evidence for his theory that Japanese is actually an Austronesian language, and this could have an important impact on our understanding of architectural development in the Austronesian world, since Japan is one region where the chances seem good for new archaeological findings which might help to fill gaps in the picture. Japanese linguists have for some time recognized the existence of an ancient 'substratum' of Austronesian in the language, but this now appears to be an understatement of the case. Further-

more, some features of traditional Japanese architecture are so strongly South-East Asian that some kind of historical link has long been assumed on these grounds alone. Attention will probably now focus on the Neolithic Yayoi people (see below) as the most likely bearers of Austronesian language and culture into Japan.

The possible origins of an 'Austronesian' style of architecture have been pursued in a highly interesting work by Domenig (1980), and it is significant that much of his evidence is already drawn from the work of Japanese archaeologists on the Neolithic and early Metal Ages in Japan. Domenig stresses the potential importance of southern China as a source of cultural influence in both Japan and South-East Asia. We must note that southern China at this period was not culturally 'Chinese'; Domenig points out that the origins of 'Chinese' (Han) culture are to be sought in the valley of the Huang Ho in northern China, but the Neolithic cultures of southern China, concentrated around the Yangtze River basin, are better regarded as belonging in character to the South-East Asian world. It was not until the Han period (206 BC–AD 220) that the peoples of this region began to be strongly influenced by northern Chinese culture. Domenig postulates that pile building could have developed in southern China during the Neolithic period. He notes that this area was most likely also a key region in the development of rice cultivation, and that it had an important influence not only on the subsequent Bronze Age culture of Dong Son, which had its epicentre in North Vietnam, but also on developments in Japan (Domenig 1980: 78).

Domenig's theory is that both pile building and the saddle roof could have developed simultaneously by a progression from a primitive tepee-shaped structure of poles set in the ground and overlapping at the top. This idea is based on reconstructions by Japanese archaeologists of Neolithic pit dwellings excavated in Japan. His scheme is reproduced in Figure 18.[5] Engraved pictures on the back of a fourth-century bronze mirror (Figure 19) show four distinct kinds of structure, three with piles and one without, but all with variations of a roof form which most logically could have developed from that of the ground-built structure (Domenig 1980: 70). It seems natural to conclude that these different styles of building all coexisted at the time the mirror was made, and from the evidence of other excavations, the ground-built form at least must by that time have already been in existence for a long time.

Archaeological evidence from southern China itself,

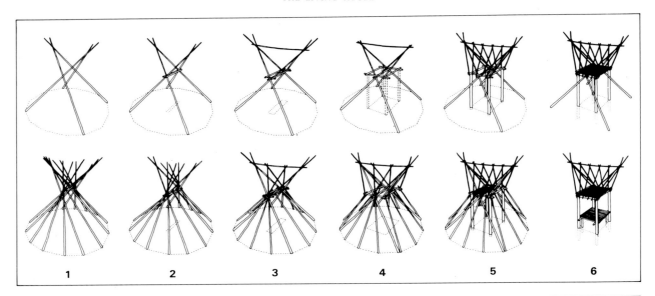

18. Domenig's proposed reconstruction of the development of pile building and the saddle roof from prehistoric pit dwellings in Japan. (From Domenig: 1980: 105)

which might help to fill in the picture of early Neolithic developments, is still unfortunately rather limited. A single isolated find from Ying-P'an-Li in south-easterly Kiangsi Province may be the earliest representation in East or South-East Asia of a saddle roof, and possibly of a pile structure. It is the house-shaped lid of a pottery vessel, dating at the earliest to around 1500 BC. The single stem of the vessel may be a simplified representation of what was really a four-pile structure—perhaps a granary (Domenig 1980: 85). Domenig's hypothesis becomes increasingly interesting in the light of the linguistic evidence for Japanese as part of the Austronesian family. There is still, however, an urgent need for new archaeological work in southern China, which should bring further major developments in our understanding of South-East Asian prehistory in general. Also, given their geographical position and the physical appearance of their present-day inhabitants, the Ryuku Islands of southern Japan might be expected to provide evidence of Neolithic contacts between Japan and South-East Asia, but so far they have not produced any (Bellwood 1978: 155).

The development of gable-roofed pile structures from pit dwellings in Japan is associated with the late Neolithic and early Metal Age Yayoi people. The Yayoi are so-called after an archaeological site in South-west

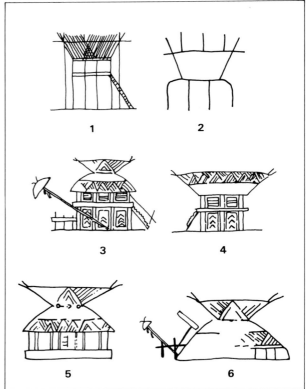

19. Pictures of houses incised on objects of bronze, Japan. 1: from Kagawa prefecture, first–second centuries AD; 2: from Fukui prefecture, first–second centuries AD; 3–6: from the back of a bronze mirror found in Nara prefecture, fourth century AD. (From Domenig 1980: 65)

16

Honshu, where remains of this culture were first excavated. The Yayoi are thought by Japanese scholars to have been an immigrant people who reached Japan, perhaps via Taiwan, from a homeland somewhere in southern China. Earliest Yayoi sites in Japan date to around 300 BC. They brought with them a knowledge of rice cultivation, and their development of pile building may have been intended originally for the construction of granaries, which would thus have provided improved storage conditions for grains, always vulnerable to rats and mould. Over time, their society became increasingly stratified, with considerable differentiation of wealth. Model houses and store houses of clay, placed in the tombs of the ruling class of the third–seventh centuries AD, show saddle roofs, sometimes with gable horns, and pile structure. These are also illustrated in pictures on clay tablets and the backs of mirrors (Figure 20). While residual traces of this distinctive built form may still be found in the architecture of some rural areas, the outstanding example of it is to be seen in the Shinto shrines of Ise and Izumo in southern Honshu. The shrine of Ise (Figure 21) is the holiest Shinto centre. Every twenty years the buildings of the shrine complex, built of Japanese cypress, are demolished and rebuilt in exactly the same detail. This custom started in the reign of the Emperor Temmu (seventh century AD), and to date they have been renewed sixty times. Interestingly, the gable horns, a distinctive architectural feature which, as mentioned above, is to

21. Ise Shrine, Japan: the *shoden* or main building. The pile structure and extended gable horns are clearly related to South-East Asian styles. The shrine has been ceremonially reconstructed in identical form every twenty years since the reign of the Emperor Temmu (seventh century AD); to date it has been rebuilt sixty times. Some details have however been added since that time, such as the bronze ornaments on the balustrade, and probably the veranda itself. (Courtesy of Ise Shrine)

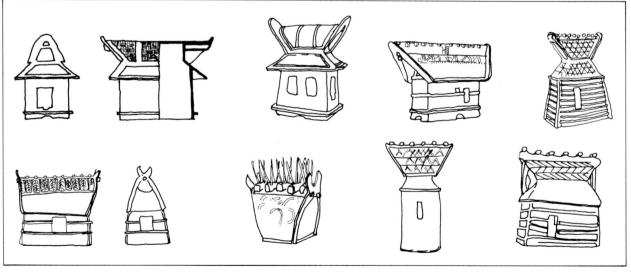

20. *Haniwa* clay models of houses and barns, found in Japanese tombs of the early Metal Age, AD 300–600. (From Domenig 1980: 64)

be found all over South-East Asia, in Japan became associated with imperial status and were reserved only for imperial architecture and Shinto shrines. The Emperor is custodian of certain precious objects symbolizing the presence of the deities, such as the Sacred Mirror of Ise, and serves as the chief intermediary between his people and the spirits (Drexler 1955: 23).

The Dong Son Culture and Its Influence

As we move into the early Metal Age we find the earliest clear representations of what archaeologists have termed an 'Indonesian-type' house, with pile structure and saddle roof (Bellwood 1978: 193). These are engraved images on bronze drums of the Dong Son culture, whose heartland was in North Vietnam and which flourished from some time between 600 and 400 BC till the first century AD (Figure 22). Antecedent sites with bronze have recently been excavated by Vietnamese archaeologists, and date back to 1500 BC, proving the great importance of this region in the development of bronze metallurgy. Through trade contacts and movements of people, the influence of the Dong Son culture extended to the populations of the archipelago. The drums were traded all over the islands (though they were never made there), and have been found as far to the east as the Kai Islands, just south of West Irian in Indonesia. Two other famous examples come from the islands of Sangeang (near Sumbawa) and Salayar (to the south of Sulawesi) (Figure 23). The Sangeang drum is of interest in that it shows a pile dwelling with a saddle roof occupied by people wearing what appear to be Chinese Han-dynasty costumes (Heine-Geldern 1947; Bellwood 1985: 282). The structure of the house, with its under-floor level occupied by animals (a pig, two chickens, and a dog), the main floor by humans, and partitioned attic containing what appear to be valuables (chests and a drum), already shows the three-tiered division of inhabited space which is so typical of dwellings in many present-day Indonesian societies.

The Dong Son drums are associated with weapons and other artefacts of bronze (as well as iron in the later Dong Son period), and a number of other important cultural features, including wet rice cultivation and megalithic practices. Bellwood (1985: 275) notes:

...this culture was centrally involved in a transition to a highly stratified and partly urbanised society with an economy based on intensive rice production, presumably in

22. Rubbing of the tympanum of a Dong Son bronze drum from Yunnan, showing saddle-roofed, pile-built houses with peacocks above, dancers with head-dresses, and people playing drums. (From Bellwood 1978: 184; Bernatzik 1947)

rainfed or irrigated bunded fields with ploughs and buffalo traction.... The intensified production supported an upper ruling echelon whose wealthy burials have been found in many sites, and who in turn were able to support a degree of craft specialisation associated in many other areas with literate civilisations. It is therefore not surprising that such professionally-made items as the magnificent bronze drums, and perhaps Vietnamese techniques for the manufacture of lesser bronze tools and weapons, would have had such an impact on the contemporary societies of Indonesia and Malaysia.

Older archaeological theorists, such as Heine-Geldern (1966) and Vroklage (1936), saw in the Dong Son culture the origin of many features of societies occupying the supposedly remote interiors of islands in the archipelago. They posited the arrival of Dong Son migrants in distinct 'waves', dominating and displacing already existing populations with a less advanced culture. The idea of 'cultural waves' sweeping into Indonesia was developed by these writers and others in the 1930s, probably building on earlier theories of racial 'layering' proposed by the Sarasin brothers around the turn of the century.[6] It was most fully formulated by Heine-Geldern, who was also among the first to describe and name the culture of 'Dong Son', which he called after its most important site in North

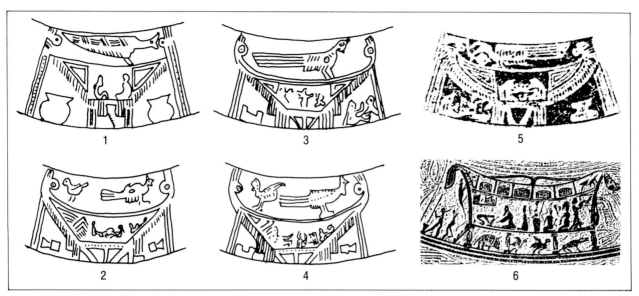

23. Houses represented on Dong Son drums. 1–4: from North Vietnam; 5: from the Moulie drum, North Vietnam; 6: from the Sangeang drum, eastern Indonesia. (From Domenig 1980: 33)

Vietnam. Heine-Geldern posited the existence of an 'older' and 'younger' megalithic tradition originating on the South-East Asian mainland and having a powerful impact on Indonesia. The 'older', Neolithic tradition introduced menhirs, dolmens, and stone seats, terraces, pyramids, and meeting places, and favoured a 'monumental' art style of simple, straight-lined forms. With this tradition Heine-Geldern associated also a number of other cultural traits, including head-hunting, the use of forked wooden posts, perhaps as offering stakes (still found today in Flores and Timor, and among the Naga, as well as in the forked forms of Nias ancestor figures), and motifs of buffalo heads and horns (Figures 24 and 25). For this culture, which he judged reached Indonesia during the second millennium BC, Heine-Geldern claimed an Indian origin, but there is no archaeological (or linguistic) evidence to support such a thesis. Heine-Geldern's own method depends almost entirely upon the tracing of similarities in art motifs, from which assumptions are drawn about diffusion from presumed centres of superior culture. His second, 'younger' or 'ornamental' style belongs to the early Metal Age and is associated with the Dong Son culture. To this second 'culture wave', Heine-Geldern attributed the introduction of cist and dolmen graves, stone sarcophagi, and a number of decorative elements, with an emphasis on curves and

24. Forked wooden ancestor figure (adu hörö) in a house in the village of Bahodarara, Central Nias. These figures served a protective function for the occupants. They echo the form of forked wooden posts erected as memorials of 'feasts of merit' among the Naga of North-east India. (From Schröder 1917: Pl. 10)

19

25. Local chiefs standing before a forked offering stake (*peo*) in the village of Boa Wae, Nage district, West Flores. Buffaloes offered to male clan ancestors are tied to the post before being slaughtered. Photograph taken *c*.1920; the post is still standing today. (VIDOC, Koninklijk Instituut voor de Tropen, Amsterdam)

Vroklage's thesis was that the curved roofs with their pointed ends actually symbolized the boats in which bearers of this culture reached the Indonesian islands (Figures 27 and 28). He called this roof style the 'ship roof', as better designating its 'true' meaning.[8] In support of this, he cites numerous examples of Indonesian societies who compare their houses or villages to boats, who use boat vocabulary to name parts of these, or who, for example, call village heads and other dignitaries by titles meaning 'ship's captain', 'steersman', etc., who believe that the souls of the dead travel by boat to the afterlife (which is conceived to lie in the probable direction of the land from which their ancestors indeed set sail to colonize new islands), and who bury their dead in boat-shaped coffins or in stone urns or graves to which are given the name 'boat'. He also notes the frequency with which houses or other structures are provided with projecting carved beam-ends which curve upwards like the prow of a boat. Of course, not all Indonesian societies show all, or even some, of these features, although boat symbolism does appear to be very important in some of them (Vroklage elaborated in more detail on the situation in Flores in an article of 1940; and see, for example, Barraud (1979: 57–8) on Tanebar-Evav, and McKinnon (1983: 144–6) on Tanimbar). Forth, on the other hand, has recently suggested that the evidence has, in some cases, been exaggerated by anthropologists eagerly searching for 'boat' associations.[9] He points out that words cited as referring to parts of boats are often generic terms whose primary meaning is more neutral. To give a simple example, a word claimed to mean 'mast' may have the primary sense simply of 'post'. Vroklage treats as a unity the occurrence of 'ship' architecture, buffalo horns, and a wide range of burial practices, which he sees as originating from the same 'culture wave'. The possibility of dating most of the stone structures which he discusses is unfortunately as limited today as it was when he was writing. Nor does he explain why the 'older' megalithic culture, which must also have reached Indonesia by sea, should have shown such a remarkable *lack* of interest in boat symbolism.

The nature of Vroklage's theory leads him to postulate the existence of an 'original', pure form from which deviations can only be explained as evidence of 'degeneration'. Thus, straight ridge-lines are a 'degeneration' from curved ones, adopted when peoples grew 'lazy' because straight ones were easier to execute; there is always the temptation to conclude that

spirals, typified in the ornamentation of the famous bronze drums.

Vroklage further elaborated this hypothesis in an interesting but now dubious article of 1936 on 'The Ship in the Megalithic Cultures of South-East Asia and the South Seas'. The article is worthy of note here since it represents an early attempt to draw far-reaching conclusions about observed similarities of architectural style in South-East Asia, Melanesia, and Oceania, with reference also to links with Japan and Madagascar.[7] He collected dozens of examples of building styles incorporating pile foundation, saddle roofs, and gable horns, which he associated with Heine-Geldern's 'younger megalithic culture' (Figure 26). The article also contains lengthy discursions on the different types of stone tomb and of secondary burial practices.

26. A collection of structures showing saddle roofs and gable horns, drawn by Vroklage. The author interpreted saddle roofs as imitations of the boats in which ancestral Indonesians reached the archipelago. The examples are drawn from various parts of eastern Indonesia (Nos. I–VII), East Java (VIII), Sumatra (IX–XII), Vietnam (XIII), North-east India (XVI), and Micronesia (XV). (From Vroklage 1936: 722)

27. Ceremonial launching of a new boat among the Yami of Lanyü Island, off the southern coast of Taiwan. Note the shape of the upturned prow and stern. Some authors have theorized that boat shapes have influenced the form of saddle roofs in Austronesian architecture. (From Kano and Segawa 1956: 345)

people who do not see their houses as boats have simply forgotten what they should have remembered. In the same way, stone cist graves are a 'degeneration' from stone burial urns, since they represent a less troublesome alternative (Vroklage 1936: 714, 755). Furthermore, the manner in which small boatloads of newcomers are supposed to have brought their culture intact from the mainland and established themselves in their 'boat' communities in already long-settled areas may now be viewed as simplistic and improbable. Most recently, Gittinger (1976) and Manguin (1986) have proposed much more convincing explanations of the recurring use of boat symbolism simply as a convenient organizing metaphor for expressing various ideas of social order or representing moments of transition. A further major problem with the older approach

28. During the launching ceremony for a Yami boat, members of the crew, wearing silver heirloom helmets, take their seats and pray for the prosperous future of the vessel. Sitting positions in a boat are sometimes used metaphorically by Austronesian peoples as a means of representing a hierarchical social order. (From Kano and Segawa 1956: 337)

lies in the very notion of anything so coherent as a 'megalithic culture' in Indonesia. Currently archaeologists, while acknowledging that Heine-Geldern's formulation represents 'an imaginative attempt to wrest order from the data', dispute that such an entity can be said to exist, given the huge diversity of stone structures in Indonesian societies (Glover 1979: 181; Glover, Bronson, and Bayard 1979: 253–4). Indeed, the temptation to label any use of stone 'megalithic', which certainly says something about the romantic appeal of the word to Europeans, may be misleading in terms of analysis.

Above all, the diffusionist theories of writers like Heine-Geldern and Vroklage are objectionable on the grounds that they attempt to explain everything in

South-East Asia as deriving from somewhere else (usually either India or China).[10] In fact, the archaeological evidence amply demonstrates that South-East Asia has had its own distinct cultural development and forms of expression since Neolithic times. Bellwood, therefore, draws an important and useful distinction between Dong Son *culture*, centred in North Vietnam itself, and the Dong Son *style*, which spread over a huge area and need not always have been the product of the same culture group. The old idea of distinct 'waves' of migration from the mainland into South-East Asia is almost certainly wrong, and trade more likely accounted for much of the contact and absorption of cultural features. The process could thus have occurred piecemeal among the many small communities of island South-East Asia, without their necessarily ever having been aware of the total cultural system from which the new objects had originated. Given the dominance of the sea as a means of travel and communication in the archipelago, one social anthropologist, James Urry (1981), has indeed suggested that trade and exchange had *already* provided the essential motives for Austronesian expansion through the islands during the Neolithic period. He posits a great deal more two-way travel between islands (and also contacts with the mainland initiated from the islands), than is assumed even in Bellwood's model of Austronesian migration and colonization of the islands. From this perspective, Bellwood would seem to give too much weight to agricultural expansion as the impetus behind Austronesian dispersal. Urry's hypothesis, like everyone else's, contains a large element of speculation, but given what we know of the importance of trade and exchange networks throughout the archipelago in historical times, it has an appealing logic. It helps to make sense of the incredible mobility of the Austronesians, which can hardly be accounted for solely by factors such as population pressure; it also reinforces the picture of the Austronesians as actively innovative populations always in search of new trade goods, and not merely the passive recipients of external influences.

A second Metal Age culture of the mainland which may have had a shaping influence on the islands of South-East Asia is the Sa Huynh culture of southern Vietnam. This culture is thought to have belonged to a Chamic-speaking (Austronesian) population who probably originated from Malaya or Borneo, and having acquired new metal working techniques on

the mainland, would have been well-placed to introduce them in a reverse movement back into the islands.
Significantly, they practised jar burial, a custom which
they may have brought with them from the islands,
since dates for jar burials in Borneo and the Philippines
may go back to the second millennium BC. Almost
identical types of pottery, stone ear-rings of an open
oval shape, and ear-rings or pendants with a pair of
animal heads have also been found in both Borneo,
the Philippines, and Vietnam.

The influence of Dong Son culture spread not only
to the east but also north into southern China, where
it had a particularly immediate impact on a second-
first century BC Metal Age civilization centred on Shih-
Chai-Shan in Yunnan. Here, Dong Son drums were
valuable imports (a total of twenty-seven have been
found) and were often converted by the rulers to make
lidded chests for the storage of cowrie currency (Bellwood 1978: 189; Domenig 1980: 86–9). The lid of
one of these drum/containers, illustrated by Domenig,
is decorated with an elaborate three-dimensional
bronze model of a pile-built house or granary structure
surrounded by people and drums (Figure 29). The
structure has a raised open platform and a saddle-
roofed enclosed upper storey, and bears a remarkable
resemblance to present-day barns of the Toba Batak or
Toraja. A number of similar free-standing bronze
model scenes of people and houses were found, some
with crossed-horn finials. Fragments of engraved
pictures from the sides of still another drum/container
from Shih-Chai-Shan show people storing sheaves of
grain in tall saddle-roofed barns. These barns are
apparently not built on piles but are constructed from
interlocking crossed logs (much like a log cabin)
(Figures 30 and 31).

Interestingly, crossed-log foundation structures
can still be seen in buildings today in parts of Sumatra
(Karo and Simalungun Batak; see Sargeant and Saleh
1973; Sargeant 1977), Central Sulawesi (Kaudern
1925), and South Sulawesi (as an older, and almost
vanished, mode of construction among the Sa'dan
Toraja) (Figure 32). Hauser-Schäublin (1985: 80)
notes that a variant and possibly distantly related
form of this construction, in which the joints are bound
with lianas, may be encountered in Papua New
Guinea. Some of the most impressive examples of this
form of construction are to be found in the Trobriand
Islands off the south-east tip of Papua New Guinea,
where the technique is used for the construction of

29. Bronze drum converted into a container for cowrie currency,
found at Shih-Chai-Shan in Yunnan, second-first century BC. The lid
is decorated with bronze figures surrounding a pile-built, saddle-
roofed house or granary structure. (From Domenig 1980: 87)

magnificent tall yam store houses in which yam
harvests are put on display. The discovery at Shih-
Chai-Shan seems to indicate that this manner of building may have coexisted with pile building in the
Austronesian world from a very early date.

Because of the pictures on bronze drums, it has
been almost universally assumed that the origins of the
'Indonesian-style' house are to be attributed to the
Dong Son period. As we have seen, material evidence
for earlier periods is hard to come by. However, there
are some logical problems about the attribution, and
indeed it seems likely that the importance of Dong Son
in this respect has been overestimated. If we discount
the idea of massive migration 'waves' into island
South-East Asia at that time, how was the new technology spread? After all, only a few of the drums
actually illustrate houses, and of those for which I have
found illustrations, five were found in Vietnam

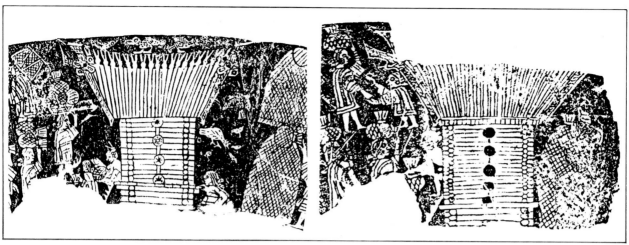

30. Engraved images from the side of a bronze drum found at Shih-Chai-Shan, Yunnan, showing sheaves of grain being stored in granaries with saddle roofs and crossed-log construction. The drum dates to second–first century BC and is evidence of Dong Son influence in the area. (From Domenig 1980: 88–9)

31. A yam store house on Kiriwina, Trobriand Islands. Compare the crossed-log structure to that of the Bronze Age granaries in the previous illustration. (Photograph: Peter Bellwood)

32. An old-fashioned Toraja house with crossed-log foundation structure in Sareale district, Tana Toraja, 1982. (Photograph: Roxana Waterson)

(Domenig 1980: 33) and one in Yunnan (Bernatzik 1947). Apparently, the only drum with a house image on it to be found in Indonesia is that from Sangeang. As Domenig (1980: 34) points out, traders moving through the islands bringing pictures, or even verbal descriptions, of such houses would hardly have been sufficient to achieve the introduction of a new style of architecture. Furthermore, Dong Son influence was not so widespread that it can be called upon to account for the appearance of the style in Melanesia and western Oceania; by this time the northern coast of New Guinea and the islands of Micronesia had prob-

ably been settled by Austronesian speakers for at least 1,000 years. Evidence from these areas must thus be regarded as especially significant for the tracing of culture traits of possible Austronesian origin.[11] It thus seems much more logical to conclude that what has been called the 'Indonesian-type' house would actually be better viewed as a genuinely 'Austronesian' creation, pre-dating the Dong Son period, and that the saddle-roofed buildings represented on the Dong Son drums were examples of a style which was already well developed by this time.

1. Such platforms were also to be found until the mid-nineteenth century among the southern Pingpu tribes of Taiwan. Their distribution is charted by Li (1957), who notes the prevalence of pile building in western Austronesia and platform building in eastern Austronesia. He includes the Bontoc of the Philippines in his examples of platform building, but this may be the result of misinterpretation of a photo showing a raised stone-paved courtyard used as a men's meeting place, together with the adjoining wall of an (actually ground-built) men's house. Bontoc build their actual dwellings (fayu) on piles. Palau, included by Li as an example of platform building, is of interest in that here both techniques were combined, with pile-built structures commonly placed on top of platforms. Following a theory proposed by Buck in the 1940s, Li suggested the occurrence of platform building might be used as evidence of migratory routes into Polynesia via Micronesia. Unfortunately, this idea is not borne out by archaeological and linguistic evidence, which points strongly to Melanesia as the more important route of migration eastward (Bellwood 1978: 281–2).

2. Dumarçay (1981) gives a brief review of the distribution of the saddle roof, but some of his conclusions, for example, on matters of dating, seem unsupported.

3. Pile building is none the less common in some other parts of Madagascar, especially where heavy rains create dangers of flooding.

4. Geoffrey Benjamin (personal communication).

5. See also Drexler (1955: 9–21) for an account of these developments.

6. The Sarasins were the first to coin the expressions 'proto-' and 'deutero-Malay' as a way of labelling perceived physical differences in Indonesian populations (Sarasin and Sarasin 1905–6).

7. Another author who pursued the theme of house styles in Oceania was Tischner (1934).

8. See Adams (1974) and Lewcock and Brans (1975) for recent revivals of Vroklage's thesis. The assumption of a Dong Son origin for South-East Asian house styles is uncritically maintained in a more recent brief work by Dumarçay (1985).

9. Forth (1981: 53 and personal communication).

10. Indeed, Heine-Geldern (1966: 211) at times went further and attempted to claim that the 'megalithic complex', as manifested everywhere in the world from Africa to Hawaii, must have derived from a single source somewhere in the Mediterranean.

11. Alkire (1972) has made a similar point in his examination of shared concepts of order and space in South-East Asia and Micronesia. Certain cosmological and conceptual patterns have been widely attributed (again, notably by Heine-Geldern) to Hindu influence, reaching South-East Asia from around AD 100–200 onwards. Alkire, however, demonstrates not only that some of these ideas differ significantly in their details from Hindu conceptions, but that they are also to be found in Micronesia; since later diffusion from Hinduized South-East Asia to this region is judged unlikely, they can thus more reasonably be explained as belonging to a more ancient, pre-Hinduized—that is, Austronesian—culture.

CHAPTER 2

Perceptions of Built Form:
Indigenous and Colonial

It is easy to feel impressed by the power and grace of architectural forms in the island South-East Asian world, by the skill of their construction, and their harmonious sense of scale and proportion. At the same time, the very unfamiliarity of these building styles to a stranger's eye leads us to suspect that on closer investigation, the ideas behind the forms may likewise prove unfamiliar. How do—or did—the builders view their constructions, and what social conceptions are expressed in these forms? My purpose in this chapter is to examine how foreigners first reacted to these new styles of architecture. I draw my main examples from the experiences of the Dutch in Indonesia. The disjunction which clearly existed at times between their perceptions and those of the house owners helps us to gain some insight into the principles governing South-East Asian styles of construction. This will lead on to a closer look at symbolic elements of architecture and at indigenous cosmologies in the following chapters.

Europeans who first came to the Indies in search of spices gained many of their initial impressions of local cultures through their experience of the region's large trading centres. Reid's analysis (1980: 237) of the structure of South-East Asia's cities in the fifteenth-seventeenth centuries shows that a number of urban centres (such as Melaka, Ayutthaya, and Demak in the sixteenth century, and Aceh, Makassar, Surabaya, and Banten in the seventeenth century) were extremely large by European standards of the time, having populations which probably fell within the range of 50,000–100,000—bigger than almost any European city of the time with the exceptions of Naples and Paris. At the same time, the style and layout of these urban centres was very unfamiliar to Europeans. Reid notes that a 'rural' pattern of life was continued in the city, with airy, pile-built wooden houses half-concealed within their own yards of coconut, banana, and other fruit trees—a pattern which to some extent is still favoured by South-East Asians today. Cities—consisting of a conglomeration of compounds—spread out over wide areas without any clearly defined boundaries such as typified the walled towns of the Mediterranean or China. Early travellers were delighted by the rural appearance of the city of Aceh, which one described as 'very spacious, built in a Wood, so that we could not see a house till we were upon it. Neither could we go into any place, but we found houses and great concourse of people: so that I think the town spreadeth over the whole land.' A Jesuit priest describes 'an incredible number of houses made of canes, reeds and bark' set in 'a forest of coconut trees, bamboos, pineapples and bananas'. 'When one is at anchor,' he adds, 'one sees not a single vestige or appearance of a city, because the great trees along the shore hide all its houses.'[1] Reid identifies the most important assets of citizens here not as land, houses, and furniture, but fruit trees, manpower, and heirloom valuables. Anyone could collect materials from the forest to build his own house, or even transport a house from one site to another; the ever-present danger of fire was balanced by the relatively small amount of labour necessary to construct a new dwelling. The main purpose of warfare was to gain manpower in the form of slaves, and if a city was attacked it would simply be abandoned by its inhabitants, the chief losses which an enemy could inflict being the destruction of the fruit trees which formed a vital part of the household economy. Many seventeenth-century rulers reserved to themselves the right to build in stone, for fear that powerful nobles or European traders might create for themselves impregnable strongholds; indeed the Portuguese in Melaka and Maluku, and the Dutch in Jakarta, were never able to be dislodged once they had built their forts in these cities (Reid 1980: 246). Although at times the open cities of South-East Asia became lawless and violent places, Reid (1980: 241) notes how well, in some ways, they were adapted to local conditions. By contrast,

...the treeless, congested quarters which the Chinese built of stone or brick beside the Southeast Asian market centres, and which Europeans began to emulate in Manila after the 1583 fire and in Batavia in the mid-seventeenth century, were stuffy, exposed to the sun, and unhealthy. By building on the ground, they suffered from problems of flooding and of drainage and waste disposal from which the typical elevated pole house of maritime Southeast Asia was immune. Eventually, these alien urban models became pestilential and were abandoned to the poorest urban inhabitants.

Batavia, in particular, up until the early nineteenth century, was such a breeding-ground of disease that it has been described by one author as 'the most notoriously insalubrious place in Southeast Asia, and possibly the world' (Savage 1984: 160). It was built in the middle of a malarial swamp, and in imitation of Dutch cities, was threaded by canals and ditches (Figure 33). These, however, received much of the city's waste and were allowed to become stagnant. According to the theories of the time, malaria was caused by 'miasmas' or noxious vapours given off by rotting and decomposing matter, and Batavia's unhealthiness was attributed not only to the smells of surrounding marshes but to such factors as the exposure of the river's mud banks at low tide and the fact that the trees lining the banks of canals impeded the circulation of air and caused the miasma to become 'suspended'. An estimated 87,000 soldiers and sailors died in Batavia's hospitals between 1714 and 1776, and while there were rarely more (and usually less) than 1,500

33. A lane of tightly packed buildings in the Chinese quarter of old Batavia, backing on to one of the canals which the Dutch built to remind them of their native Holland. The congestion of such buildings and stagnation of the waterways, coupled with the location of the city in a malarial swamp, for long made Batavia one of the world's unhealthiest cities. (Photograph: Jean Demmeni, c.1911, courtesy of Times Editions, Singapore)

European troops there at any one time, the registers of one military hospital over sixty-two years of the eighteenth century record an average of 1,258 deaths a year. No wonder Savage (1984: 161–2) comments that for the Dutch soldier of this period, a military posting to Batavia was the equivalent of a death sentence. It was not until the early years of the nineteenth century that the city was transformed by the filling in of canals, cleaning of rivers, drainage of the swamps, and the shifting of the new city to a more elevated site some kilometres from the original fort.

Jean Gelman Taylor, in a fascinating analysis of the social life of Europeans and Eurasians in Batavia from its founding in the early seventeenth century, notes the centuries-long refusal of Dutch men in the service of the East India Company to adopt such South-East Asian habits as frequent bathing and changes of clothes, resting in the heat of the day, or the building of airy, well-ventilated houses. They were scandalized by the sight of their mistresses bathing in full public view in the River Ciliwung, and stuck to their wigs, layers of clothing, afternoon office hours, and heavy drinking. In the British interregnum (1811–16), under Raffles, essays were written in a newly formed weekly paper, the *Java Government Gazette*, by Britons anxious to reform Dutch habits and end the devastating unhealthiness of old Batavia. Gelman Taylor (1983: 101) records:

'Benevolus', a prolific letter-writer, spoke of 'the narrow streets, small windows, cramped living quarters and thickly curtained beds' that prevented the circulation of air, and argued that Dutchmen had only to change their habits for Batavia to be a safer place to live. Such opinions drew a derisive response from one Dutch inhabitant, who wrote that sea breezes and 'noxious vapours' were the true causes of Batavia's high mortality rate.

Ironically, most of these men were married to Eurasian women who were Indies-born, spoke Malay, liked Asian food and entertainments, and wore a form of Indonesian costume; moreover, once they came to the Indies many of them never set foot in Holland again. Gelman Taylor's analysis (1983: 101, 136) reveals that it was precisely in the late nineteenth century, when improved communications at last meant that those in the colonial service could maintain meaningful ties with the homeland, and when changing colonial policies brought larger numbers of marriageable Dutch women out to the colonies, that the Dutch began enthusiastically to adapt to the trop-

ical environment with the wearing of colonial whites for work and batik pyjamas at home, the eating of a version of Indonesian food in the form of the *rijsttafel*, and the taking of siestas. Now that they had theatres, libraries, clubs, and imported pianos, they could however maintain Dutch tastes in entertainment, and the author adds somewhat caustically (1984: 130) that 'the attitude they now displayed towards Indonesians was one of scientific interest when it was not one of humorous contempt.'

The late nineteenth and early twentieth century was a period, too, when the Dutch were extending their control over the outer islands. Some regions of Indonesia—including parts of northern Sumatra, Sulawesi, Bali, Lombok, Sumbawa, Sumba, and Flores—now came under colonial administration for the first time. This territorial expansion was accompanied by an important change in colonial policy, as for the first time economic exploitation and profitability ceased to be the main justifications for Dutch rule, being replaced by what was termed the 'Ethical Policy', with its official professions of concern for Indonesian welfare and improvement.[2] The relatively new interest in hygiene becomes a prominent feature of administrators' reports on hitherto isolated areas which had now come under Dutch control. Certainly, some of these areas were never to be economically very profitable to the Dutch in any case, though it must be added that the Ethical Policy also failed to live up to all of its promises. A journal of the period, *Nederlandsch-Indië Oud en Nieuw* (*Netherlands Indies Old and New*), whose first issue appeared in 1916 and which ran until around 1935, reflects in the comprehensiveness of its subtitle both the increased 'scientific interest' referred to by Gelman Taylor, and the new concern for development. It reads: 'Monthly magazine devoted to: Architecture—Archaeology—Geography and Ethnology—Arts and Crafts—Trade and Transport—Plantations—Mining—Hygiene.' This all-embracing definition of scope, with its suggestion of the simultaneous excavation of archaeological and mineral wealth, none the less posits a two-way flow of knowledge in which the colonial authorities (and, vicariously, readers of the magazine in Holland) will both study local cultures and aid in their improvement. In practice, articles on cultural matters dominated successive issues, far outweighing any contributions on the development of mines or plantations. The concern with hygiene, however, recurs in administrators' accounts of local architectural styles, and in a number of cases it became a reason for active intervention, with resultant changes not only to built forms themselves but to the patterns of interaction of the people who used them.

Let us now look more closely at some of the characteristics of building styles in island South-East Asia, in order to see why it was that they should at times have seemed so strange to a European observer. One of the most striking features of architectural style in this part of the world is the enormous predominance of roof over wall. Whereas in the history of Western architecture, the wall is an essential element of built form, many of the buildings of Indonesian societies have no walls at all, but consist entirely of roof, enclosing a pile-built platform. The house itself, in several of these societies, may sometimes be referred to as 'floor' or 'platform'. Where there are walls, they may be very insignificant in proportion to the roof; among the Karo, for example, proportions of pile : wall : roof may be as little as 1 : 1 : 9, and houses may reach heights of over 14 metres (Singarimbun 1975: 55) (Figure 34). The

roof, then, is unquestionably the dominant expressive element in South-East Asian built form.

A surprising feature of some of these structures is that the impressive and apparently huge exterior does not necessarily enclose a proportionately large interior space. The origin-house of an aristocratic Sa'dan Toraja family, for example, is visible from afar with its great upward-sweeping eaves, yet the interior consists generally of three very small rooms affording not much more living space than the bamboo house of a poor commoner may do. It is clear that most of the effort has been dedicated to creating an imposing exterior (Figures 35 and 36). Volkman (1980: 95) expresses this contrast well when she describes the Toraja house interior as

a private, family, unadorned, dark, even dingy, but well-liked space, for which Toraja constantly apologized to us as Western guests, while proudly directing our attention to the impressive exterior form, lavish carving, or quantities of buffalo horns hung from the central house post.

34. Karo Batak village of Batukaran, Sumatra, date unknown. Note the variations in roof forms, the absence of windows, and the dominant proportions of the roof in relation to the rest of the building. (VIDOC, Koninklijk Instituut voor de Tropen, Amsterdam)

35. Façade of an old Toraja origin-house belonging to a noble family in the village of Tampan, Sa'dan district, 1983. In spite of their impressive exteriors, the interiors of such houses tend to be small and dark. (Photograph: Roxana Waterson)

36. Ornately carved panels of the house façade at Tampan, 1983. The wooden buffalo head commemorates the holding of a funeral ceremony of the highest rank and expenditure. (Photograph: Roxana Waterson)

Many Dutch colonial officials and missionaries were close observers of the societies they administered or sought to transform; they left us valuable accounts of them, and described beliefs and customs which the present-day members of these cultures have in many cases now forgotten. The most outstanding among them also began to produce novel and startling analyses of the cosmological and social worlds of the peoples they observed, analyses whose impact on the development of anthropological theory is still acknowledged today. As we might expect, they also shared some of the prejudices of their times, and it must be admitted that, when they allowed expression to their personal feelings, Dutch visitors to remoter parts of Indonesia tended to view indigenous habitations in a somewhat unfavourable light. These buildings, typical-

ly occupied by a number of related families, where open hearths often provided the only source of light and heat, and where the residents disposed of all kinds of waste by simply allowing it to fall through the floor, could hardly have failed more dismally to conform to a European notion of cosiness. Accustomed to expecting from a house above all a comfortable interior space, Westerners were taken aback by the absence of furniture or interior partitions, and judged the houses to be dark, smoky, overcrowded, and unhygenic. Interestingly, disapproval of multi-family living arrangements does not appear to have been framed in terms of arguments about promiscuity, although this was a prominent anxiety among missionaries in other parts of the world, notably South America and to some extent also North America.[3] But at times the concern of some ob-

31

servers with interiors seems to have led them completely to overlook the impressive beauty of the exteriors; they did not see that it was the outside, rather than the inside, which was intended to have meaning.

Edwin Loeb (1935: 23), for example, quotes a late nineteenth-century description of Karo Batak habitations by Neumann. I have been unable to trace the original of this passage, and it remains unclear whether the author is J. B. Neumann, an administrative official writing in the 1880s, or perhaps H. H. Neumann, a missionary with the Nederlandsche Zendelinggenootschap (Dutch Missionary Society) who arrived in the Batak lands in 1899. At any rate, the author clearly suffered a particularly extreme reaction to the architecture of the Karo. He writes:

No matter what Batak building one sees one obtains a feeling of repugnance. The houses are all equally unclean. Soot covers the walls and ceiling, the corners are full of cobwebs, the walls are smeared with chalk, and the floor is covered with sirih [betel-nut] chews and chicken excrement. The houses are like caves into which the openings in the walls scarcely admit a ray of light. When the houses are filled with smoke one asks oneself how human beings can live in them. It is almost impossible for a human being to spend a night in one of them, for centipedes and scorpions wander about freely, ants build their runways and make their way across the natives, cockroaches fly around unmolested, and lice lurk over all. One really cannot sleep in such a house. The Bataks themselves are accustomed to their environment.

Loeb adds that from the point of view of Europeans, the liberties taken by domesticated livestock were scarcely less disagreeable: chickens nested within the house and pigs scavenged freely around the village. Matters, he claimed, improved with the introduction of Dutch sanitary measures. The Dutch also discouraged the stalling of buffaloes in the space beneath the house. This was customary, particularly among the Toba and Toraja, and in other places where a foundation structure of interlocking posts and beams creates a convenient and strong enclosure beneath the house floor, where animals could be kept safe at night. More peaceful conditions no doubt obviated the need for such security measures; yet we might note that living above one's cattle is a custom not unknown among European peasant farmers also.

The interior darkness of the house is something frequently noticed with surprise by foreign observers. From a practical point of view, they rarely appeared to note that the inhabitants spent little time inside the house during the day, and that other spaces—the sheltered area beneath the house, the platform under a rice barn, or even a purpose-built open-walled pavilion (as in Bali) or a simple roofed platform (as among the Sasaks of Lombok or among the Yami of Lanyü Island, off the southern coast of Taiwan)—might all in different cultures complement the enclosed space of the house and form an essential extension of it (Plate 2; Figure 37). Cederroth (1981: 44) gives a good picture of the importance of these outside spaces in the following description of the layout of a typical Sasak mountain hamlet:

There are ... two rows of houses (bale), flanked by a number of rice barns (lumbung) with a row of pavilions (berugaq) in between. The latter are rectangular constructions, supported by six wooden pillars and without walls, but with a matted sitting platform about one metre above the ground.... The houses are large, square wooden constructions with bamboo walls and thatch of grass. They have no windows, are thus dark and are mainly used for sleeping and cooking food and as a storage for the heirlooms of the family. The daily social intercourse of the family does not normally take place inside the house but on the pavilion which is thus an indispensable appendix to the house. These pavilions are used for all kinds of social activities, and sometimes for sleeping as well, but they also have important ritual functions and serve as the place where deceased persons are put to rest before being carried to the graveyard. Their functions are thus much more diversified than those of the houses and they are truly ingenious constructions, admirably fitted to the climate and to the lifestyle of the people.

If for the pavilion we substitute the platform beneath a rice barn, many of these observations would hold true for the Sa'dan Toraja, or the Ema of Timor (Clamagirand 1975: 39). The granary (lako) of the Ema is a versatile building, whose open lower section can even be walled in to transform it into a house. But in general it functions as a sheltered open space for meetings, as a women's work place, and a place to receive guests at ceremonies. The enclosed upper part may be used for the storage of musical instruments as well as grains. In Sumba, as well as the undercroft of the house (which is used for weaving, tethering animals, etc.), there is also an open gallery or veranda at the front and back of the house, which provides an airy, open space to complement the dark interior. The latter, as in the Sasak case, serves the important function of providing storage for highly valued heirlooms (a point to which I shall return below) (Forth 1981: 31).

In the case of the Yami, whose island is frequently swept by typhoons, architecture responded (as in another fiercely windy place on the far fringes of the Austronesian world—Easter Island) by going half-underground. Houses are dug into the hillsides which rise steeply from the coast, and topped with extremely thick thatch. Here, too, the house is the storage place for heirlooms, including gold and silver disks, jars, ancient carnelian beads, and most important of all, the large silver helmets which men wear on ceremonial occasions, such as the inauguration of a new house or the launching of a boat. Completion of a new helmet is celebrated by a ritual feast, after which it is revered as an animate object and is stored in a special basket at the back of the house (Beauclair 1969: 126). Although dark, the house is complemented by a pile-raised resting platform called *tagakal* (Figure 38).

37. Unwalled pavilion, or perhaps a granary with an open platform beneath the upper storey, depicted on a frieze from the north side of the Visnu temple at Prambanan, Central Java, ninth century AD. (Photograph: Jacques Dumarçay)

38. Coastal village of the Yami of Lanyü Island, southern Taiwan. The heavily thatched houses are half-dug into terraces in the hillside to shelter them from typhoons. A resting platform (*tagakal*) can be seen in the foreground; these structures provide pleasant places to sit during the day. (From Kano and Segawa 1956: 36)

According to Kano and Segawa (1956: 70),

almost every Yami family owns a resting-platform which is erected in front of the main dwelling. It is built on four piles with the plank flooring raised about three metres above the ground. The roof is thatched and access is by a ladder. Resting on the platform even in the heat of midday is refreshing and the refreshing cool sea breezes make it possible to forget the unbearable heat of the tropics. From this vantage point one can also see the incoming boats with their catches of fish.

The absence, or minuteness, of windows was generally dictated in practical terms by defensive requirements or the desire for protection against cold and bad weather in high mountain regions; we may note that in hot and humid coastal areas where ventilation is the dominant consideration for comfort, houses generally incorporate large windows, enclosed only by shutters and often reaching from floor to ceiling on all sides of the house—as among the Malays, Bugis, and Acehnese, for example. By contrast, the Karo, living at an altitude of 1,200 metres on their wet and wind-swept mountain plateau at the northern end of Lake Toba, have developed a style of architecture which well protects them against the elements, and indeed they believe the wind to be harmful. The imposing and rather severe forms of Karo architecture, with their symmetrical shape, heavy over-hanging eaves, and few and small openings for doors and windows, are well adapted to Karo requirements (Plates 2 and 3).

Symbolically, the dark house interior appears to be of significance in a number of societies. Cunningham notes the contrast elaborated in Atoni thought between the darkness of the house with its hearth as an artificial source of light and heat, and the exterior brightness of the sky and the sun. Among another Timorese people, the Tetum, the house has no windows and its dark interior is compared to the body.[4] More particularly, the main rear room, focus both of everyday domestic life and of ritual, is called 'the womb of the house' (uma lolon), the symbolically female rear door being known as the 'house vagina' (Hicks 1976: 57-60). Volkman (1985: 47) draws attention to the fact that in Tana Toraja, house beams must always be arranged with their 'root' ends to the south, which is referred to in the Sesean area as the 'root' of the house. Sacred heirloom cloths and swords are sometimes stored in the southernmost room of the house because, as a priest explained, the 'roots' must be 'fertilized' so that the 'branches and leaves' (the carved and decorated façade of the house, symbolic of family rank) will

be beautiful. The dark house interior, then, is a source not only of nourishment (the hearth, where food is prepared) but of 'fertilizer' (the heirlooms, associated with the house's ancestors, who have the power to promote the fertility and good fortune of their descendants). In Sumba, storage of heirlooms inside the tall roof peak of the clan house makes the house sacred and represents the presence of the founding ancestor's spirit in the house. The house peak is sometimes lined with buffalo hide to keep out any chink of light, and the treasures themselves are stored within many nested baskets or in a sealed box. Some of these items, largely comprising gold and silver ornaments or other objects of metal associated with the founding ancestors, are thought to be so powerful that they have a light of their own, and are capable of causing natural disasters if handled indiscriminately; the oldest of them may not be viewed at all (Forth 1981: 95; Rodgers 1985: 216).[5]

Clearly, one must have somewhere to store valuable objects; even if the house is scarcely used during the day, this remains one of its most irreducible functions. But the intimacy of association between houses and heirlooms goes further than this. Traube (1986: 75-6) provides a vivid example in her study of the Mambai of eastern Timor. Here sacred, agnatically inherited heirlooms constitute a particular class of exchange valuables (separate from the valuables exchanged in marriage), which circulate among houses related through males. Just as houses do, heirlooms have their own names, personalities, and histories, and the memorizing of their movement from house to house (called 'the walk of sacred objects') is frequently used as a substitute for genealogical reckoning:

Whereas individuals would often give markedly different genealogical accounts of interhouse relations, there was an equally marked tendency to reach consensus regarding the distribution of sacra. Upon entering unfamiliar cult houses, my assistants would orient themselves by inquiring as to the names of the house's sacra, and not its ancestors. On several occasions, they went on to deduce genealogical connections from the sacra, reasoning that if an object which by tradition had once belonged to one of their own houses now resided in this one, then it must have been brought here by some distant descendant of their own line.... Members of junior houses will say that they participate in the rites held by a senior house because their own sacred objects 'first went out from that house', or conversely because objects retained by the senior house are 'mother and father' to their own.... Some people would personify sacred objects and describe them as so eager to participate in the festivities at their origin place that they set out on their own, dragging their human owners along behind them.

Clearly, there are aspects of the functions and uses of space in these societies which, because they were unfamiliar, were often overlooked by Dutch observers. The absence of architectural features familiar to a European could be disturbing, too, from an aesthetic point of view, even if objections were more often voiced in practical terms. Wetering, for example, writing of the Rotinese house with its massive, all-enveloping roof almost touching the ground, and its absence of decoration, compares it unfavourably with the houses of the Bataks or Niassans (Figure 39). The most flattering word he can choose to describe the structure, he says, is 'barn', and even this would be a 'very euphemistic' use of the term (Wetering 1923: 445). He goes on:

From the outside, the appearance of the Rotinese house is neither inspiring nor beautiful. One asks oneself how it is

possible for people to live in such a 'haystack'. Seen from the outside, it is nothing but a huge roof of *alang-alang* [grass] or lontar palm leaves....

A curious passage from Drabbe's account (1940: 50) of the culture of the Tanimbar Islands in the southern Moluccas is even more indicative of disquiet:

The houses are built next to each other with a certain regularity; the whole nonetheless strikes one with a deathlike appearance, chiefly because the houses themselves look so dead, on account of their form of roofs-on-legs.[6] One sees such roofs-on-legs in four more or less regular rows of five to twenty, depending on whether one is in a larger or smaller village.

One may surmise that what disturbed Drabbe about the Tanimbar house was the absence of windows, or to be more precise, of walls with windows in them (Figure 40). The house looks 'dead' because it has no eyes, even if in this case it does have legs. Drabbe's reactions suggest to us that Europeans, too, conceive of the house as a body, albeit on a far less conscious level

39. Traditional Rotinese house in the village of Sanggaoen, Baa, 1987, its roof of lontar palm leaves almost reaching the ground. Almost none of these houses now survive, since the local administration in the 1970s encouraged their demolition on the grounds that they were unhygienic and old-fashioned. (Photograph: Garth Sheldon)

40. Village of Sangliat Dol on Yamdena Island, Tanimbar. In the foreground is a boat-shaped stone plaza used as a ceremonial and sacrificial site. Tanimbar houses are typical of Austronesian architectural styles in their absence of windows and the predominance of roof over wall, features which were apparently disturbing to some European observers. (VIDOC, Koninklijk Instituut voor de Tropen, Amsterdam)

than many of the peoples they observed in South-East Asia. The building's possession of 'legs' at least, one might argue, gave it a human feature lacked by European buildings, but limbs cannot redeem the absence of a face, and anyway the choice of words (*daken-op-pooten*) suggests an animal rather than a human, for *pooten* really means the paws or legs of a creature such as a hare, a fox, or a dog. There is a mocking and derogatory tone in Drabbe's tag of 'roofs-on-legs'; Tanimbar architecture is a strange beast which defies classification according to European canons of construction.

The implication that Tanimbar architecture was primitive was not one that was drawn by every visitor to the islands, however. On the contrary, at least one other observer had been impressed by the degree of artistry manifested by the Tanimbarese. The British naturalist Forbes (1885: 319) made a number of detailed observations about the interior of Tanimbar houses, including the ancestral altars they contained, and concluded:

Their houses, though little more than floor and roof, are very neat structures.... After seeing how elaborately covered

almost everything they used was with carvings, executed with undoubted taste and surprising skill, we began to ask ourselves, first, Can such artistically developed people be savages?—and, next, the more difficult question, What is a *savage?*

Turning to Flores, we find in Nooteboom's account of ridge decorations on the houses of Manggarai, in the western part of the island, a particularly interesting account of the changes brought about in Manggarai society by the Dutch administration. The author, writing in 1934 after a stay of eleven months in Manggarai, discusses both his own interest in the house as representative of a social and cosmological system, and the more practical concern of the administration to improve the health of the local inhabitants.[7] The houses of Manggarai used to be of two types, having either a circular or an elliptical plan (Figures 41 and 42). The great conical roof of the former kind rose to a point at the top, while the latter had a short ridge. Ridges were often decorated with carved ornaments in the shape of buffalo horns or crossed finials ending in bird or *naga* heads; these form the principal subject of Nooteboom's article. The roof itself, thatched with

36

41. Conical houses of Cumbi village, Manggarai, West Flores. The circular roof reaches to the ground, enclosing a separate platform within. (VIDOC, Koninklijk Instituut voor de Tropen, Amsterdam)

42. One of the huge multi-family houses of Manggarai which were capable of housing hundreds of people and which the Dutch administration demolished on grounds of hygiene. (VIDOC, Koninklijk Instituut voor de Tropen, Amsterdam)

alang-alang grass, descended almost to the ground enclosing a platform built on short piles only a metre or less in height. Nooteboom tells us that these enormous houses might contain 'several dozen' families, and that often an entire village lived in a single house. He goes on (1939: 222):

This type of house, which was inhabited by a crowd of people sometimes as many as several hundred strong, was the cause of a very high incidence of hookworm disease, while the outbreak of other sicknesses such as dysentery could quickly bring catastrophic results. The very low space beneath the house floor served as the depository for human faeces and all kinds of refuse, and simultaneously as the customary abode of dogs, pigs and children. Sunlight could not penetrate into this hotbed of disease. Besides, many parts of this country are frequently shrouded in mist or blocked from the sun by thick clouds. Furthermore the high, thick grass-thatched roof had no openings to let out the smoke from the many hearths. In such a house it was still pitch dark even in broad daylight, and the air was always close from the smoke of the fires and the presence of so many people. The people whose everyday dwellings these were, were consequently much weakened and prone to all kinds of illnesses. From the hygienic point of view the existence of these buildings was unjustifiable.

On the other hand there was the fact that this house-type was intimately bound up with the religious conceptions of its inhabitants, that it functioned not only as a dwelling but also as a sacred place for the community in general. Some of the most important religious performances in Manggarai ritual took place within the house and were functionally closely bound up with it. In spite of this very important objection, which speaks for itself, the Government, in consultation with the Public Health Service, took the decision to have all these houses pulled down and to have them replaced with model houses of strictly controlled maximum dimensions and a maximum number of occupants. In addition all houses were provided with a model latrine, consisting of a pit in the ground of established dimensions, covered by a well-sealed floor and with a simple rectangular hut built over it. These measures, in addition to more direct action in combating disease, resulted in a dramatic reduction of hookworm disease, and when other epidemic illnesses broke out it was with much less virulence than formerly.

Nooteboom states that during his stay in Manggarai, he found it extremely difficult to learn very much about indigenous religious beliefs. Missionaries working in the area had the same experience. He goes on to speculate whether this was due to the extreme reticence of the Manggarai towards outsiders, particularly anyone connected with the government, or whether it might rather be attributed to the fact that Manggarai culture

was already in an advanced state of decay due to their centuries-long domination by more powerful neighbours. Manggarai had paid tribute to the Makassarese kingdom of Goa, and subsequently to the kingdom of Bima (eastern Sumbawa), prior to the coming of the Dutch. Governmental interference had undermined traditional social organization, and then the Catholic mission began what Nooteboom, with some vehemence, calls its 'culture-crushing work of Christianisation', meeting with great success.[8] Recent events, one might imagine, would be quite enough to explain the unwillingness of the people to reveal any more of their original beliefs, though Nooteboom finds added evidence for the thesis of cultural decay in the observation by Stapel (1914) that many of the Manggarai showed no concern to define the characteristics of their supreme deity, Moeri Kraeng. The lack of coherent theology is actually rather typical of indigenous South-East Asian religions, whose focus tends to be ritual action rather than metaphysical speculation. But it was clearly puzzling to some Dutch observers of this period.[9]

Whatever the causes of decline, Nooteboom notes that now, in 1934, the old *adat* houses were a thing of the past, and that the few elderly people who retained knowledge of traditional Manggarai religion were simply not prepared to discuss it with outsiders.[10] Unfortunately, this means that Nooteboom himself is unable to elaborate for us on how exactly the huge houses functioned within the Manggarai social and religious system, though his observation that they were the foci of the community's ritual life certainly gives us a clue as to their importance. He can, however, tell us about the effects of their replacement. He describes the dimensions of the new, government-introduced houses, which were of two kinds, either round or square. A minimum distance was established between one house and another, and not more than three families were to live in a single house. The house piles were to be higher, so that the sun could strike beneath the floor for at least part of the day and help to disinfect the unwholesome waste area beneath. He adds (1939: 224–6):

Due to a misguided idea on the part of some of the lesser officials entrusted with the execution of the plan, initially only the square house was introduced as a model. People however had a poor understanding of the construction of such a four-sided building, with the result that houses were often blown over by the wind. Besides which, the square house

43. Manggarai house of circular plan, Pongkor village, 1965. (Dorothy Pelzer Collection, courtesy of ISEAS, Singapore/Smithsonian Institution, Washington)

had absolutely no connection with the adat. Then when people considered the possibility of building a round house of fixed dimension, they often undertook the construction of these on their own initiative. This accorded much better with tradition. Admittedly they were too small for the old adat ceremonies, but they could at least accommodate the performance of some kind of substitute. In the rebuilding which has take place in most recent years (1932 and 1933) almost no more square houses have been erected. In our travels we saw entire villages with houses of the circular type.... The overall improvement in the health of the people has been very marked and is fully acknowledged by various leading Manggaraiers. On the other hand the loss of the great adat house is certainly mourned. But people refuse to commit themselves as to what precise cultural loss this has entailed....

Nooteboom adds that, in spite of the loss, the new houses appeared to have found a place in Manggarai culture, evidence of which was the way they continued to be given the variety of ridge decorations which he describes in his article (Figure 43). The Catholic Father van Bekkum, however, writing only a few years later in 1946, states that the art of woodcarving had virtually disappeared since the destruction of the old *adat* houses. He illustrates a number of carved pillars and door posts from the houses of Todo and Pongkor. The great house at Todo, which belonged to the ruling noble clan of that village, was left standing after the change to smaller dwellings, and is still there today, though in a state of disrepair. The ruler of Todo in the past, with the support of the Sultan of Bima, claimed nominal authority over those of other districts and a Todo chief was subsequently chosen by the Dutch to become the first 'raja' of Manggarai under a system of self-rule (Gordon 1980: 49).

Nooteboom's account gives us some sense of the dislocation of Manggarai culture in the early twentieth century. In spite of the 'secretiveness' and apparent passivity which he describes, however, we might conclude that the Manggarai actually showed both initiative and a fair degree of tolerance towards the Dutch. By reducing their own architecture to a smaller scale, they made an active attempt to reach a compromise over the housing issue, and then quietly dropped the alien model which had proved such a flop. Their reticence in explaining what had been lost is not after all so surprising, for this must have been as much as anything an atmosphere, a feeling of unity produced by so many people living together—albeit in unwholesome conditions. Clearly, the old huge houses also

44. Mentawaians standing before their *uma* or longhouse, date unknown. During the 1950s attempts were made to resettle the people in coastal villages of single-family dwellings. (VIDOC, Koninklijk Instituut voor de Tropen, Amsterdam)

represented in a more obvious way the community's ritual unity. The ceremonies performed there would have been intended to safeguard the community's wellbeing, and did so in a way which, even if ineffectual in the view of the public health service, must have been spiritually satisfying. Even here, Nooteboom's account hints that attempts were made to adapt Manggarai rituals, too, to fit within the new structures.

distribution of food aid, since the disruptions caused to East Timor's fragile subsistence economy by civil war resulted in widespread famine. The model for the new villages is basically a Javanese one, with rectangular houses built on the ground. Whether or not these concentrated larger settlements can ever become self-sustaining remains to be seen, for the land is extremely arid, and a great deal of marginally cultivable land at higher altitudes is now out of bounds to the population (Weatherbee 1981). A further example may be taken from Cambodia, where Matras-Troubetzkoy (1975: 205) reports that the Brou, a highland people of Cambodia, used to construct their villages on a circular plan, with houses arranged like spokes of a wheel around a central communal house. By the 1970s they were being obliged by the Khmer administration to abandon these settlements and shift to more accessible sites. Some hamlets were made to agglomerate at roadsides, resulting in the formation of interminable linear villages. What has become of the Brou today is impossible to say.

Introduction of new house forms may sometimes occur as part of a 'Development' package in less dramatic circumstances than the Timorese or the Cambodian; Ellen (1978: 58) notes that one such programme carried out among the Nuaulu of Seram in the Moluccas included an attempt to enforce a new style of house, built on the ground, in place of local pile dwellings. Conversely, Javanese transmigrants unaccustomed to pile-built dwellings have sometimes proved reluctant to live in pile houses prepared for them by local people in Sumatra. One Indonesian group who suffered particularly heavy-handed attempts at 'modernization' by government authorities in the 1950s and 1960s are the Sakuddei of Siberut (Mentawai Islands), who have been extensively studied by Reiner Schefold (1980, 1982; see also Kis-Jovak 1980) (Figure 44). The traditional religion was outlawed, and people were given the choice of conversion to either Islam or Christianity, and were made to wear clothes and cut their hair. They were obliged to abandon their upriver longhouses in order to be resettled in new tracts of single-family housing on the coast, which had disastrous effects both on coastal ecology and on the ability of the Sakuddei to sustain themselves, since they were then too far removed from the fields they had formerly cultivated upstream, while plans for the development of local industries were largely unrealistic and failed to materialize (Wagner 1981a, b). There

Sometimes resettlement by colonial authorities had the more immediate aim of 'pacification'. In Central Sulawesi, for example, they obliged the people to move from fortified hilltop villages to valley settlements where they could be easily reached by roads. At the same time, they created a new administrative structure of districts and sub-districts, to which they appointed headmen; the old kin-based structure of small villages must have been considerably altered. To choose a more modern example, the military take-over of East Timor by Indonesia has been followed by resettlement of at least a third of the population in larger and more accessible villages, both for purposes of control and to aid the

has since been a considerable moderation of attitudes, and commendably the government started work in 1979 to set up a nature reserve and assist the Mentawaians in preserving some of their traditional way of life and, most importantly, offering them some chance to choose their own path of development.

The open hearths within most traditional houses and the resultant smokiness of interiors, about which outsiders so often complained, were another feature which colonial authorities often sought to change. In Tana Toraja, for example, the hearth is traditionally positioned in the central room of the house, on the east side, the side associated with the rising sun, life, and the life-enhancing 'Rituals of the East'. Women, as the preparers of food, have an obviously close association with the hearth. The Dutch encouraged the moving of the kitchen into a lean-to or separate shed, and now this pattern is virtually universal. The hearth has thus been displaced as the focus of the household. Interestingly, Feeley-Harnik (1980: 571), writing of Madagascar, points to a similar pattern among the Sakalava, where the French colonial authorities likewise insisted on the moving of the hearth out of the house into a separate kitchen building. This was ostensibly because of the danger of fire and the unhealthiness of smoke, though incidentally it had the result of obliging the Sakalava to buy a number of new products, including lamps for light, blankets for warmth, and mosquito-nets for protection against insects. It also, in changing the focus of the house, resulted in an increased separation of men and women. Nowadays, men and circumcised boys eat together inside the house, while women and children eat outside at the back of the house or in the kitchen (Feeley-Harnik 1980: 572). A final example of such changes may be drawn from Sumbawa, this time due to new religious ideas. Peter Just (1984: 46) discusses changes in the house forms of the Donggo people of the highlands of eastern Sumbawa, where a trend toward building larger dwellings on the model of lowland houses has occurred at the same time as the introduction of Islam. These changes are resulting in new definitions of space within the home. In place of the former undifferentiated, hearth-dominated space of older houses with their single, small room, houses now have a front and a back room; the tendency increasingly is for the front to be viewed as the place of men and the rear of women. As we come across examples of such changes in built form, we become aware, too, of the resulting shifts which take place in the form of social relationships. Built forms and social forms are continually acting upon each other, and an alteration in one is likely to be reflected in changes, subtle or dramatic, in the other. From the reactions of outsiders to the architecture of island South-East Asian communities, we gain some clues about the extent of the conceptual differences which lay behind these creations. In the following chapters, I move on to a more detailed examination of the practical and symbolic considerations which have helped to shape the architecture of South-East Asia.

1. A. Markham (ed.) (1880), *Voyages and Works of John Davis, the Navigator*, London, p. 147; Y. M. H. de Querbeuf (ed.) (1780-83), *Lectres Edifiantes et Curieuses, écrites des missions étrangères (de la Compagnie de Jésus)*, Vol. 16, Paris, pp. 344-5. Both quoted in Reid (1980: 241).

2. See Ricklefs (1981) for a succinct account of the history of this period.

3. Stephen Hugh-Jones (personal communication); Etienne and Leacock (1980).

4. See Chapters 6 and 8 for further discussion of the Tetum house.

5. See also S. Errington (1983b) for a description of how ancestral power is believed to accumulate in heirloom ornaments and textiles among the Bugis.

6. '... het geheel doet echter doodsch aan, vooral omdat de huizen zelf er zoo doodsch uitzien wegens hun form van daken-op-pooten.'

7. The article was actually published a few years later, in 1939.

8. 'Toen het sloopingswerk zoover gevorderd was, begon de R. K. Missie haar cultuurvermelend Christianiseeringswerk en had succes, veel success.' (Passages from the Dutch in this chapter are my own translation.)

9. Missionaries had a vested interest in identifying 'supreme deities' in traditional religions, since they provided the peg on which to hang the Christian concept of God, and solved the problem of how to translate the word 'God' in preparing editions of the Bible in local languages. In more than one instance, this concern has had a traceable impact on the careers of particular deities who formerly were part of a complex pantheon, but who in response to Christianity have assumed a new importance even within surviving indigenous belief systems. The Toraja deity Puang Matua is a case in point.

10. *Adat* ('custom, tradition') is a term widely used throughout the Malay and Indonesian world. In the broadest sense it refers to all those principles of order, and their expression in ritual, which according to indigenous perspectives are essential for the maintenance of proper harmony and balance in the cosmos.

CHAPTER 3

The Interrelation of Built Forms

INDIGENOUS habitations, then, might certainly confound the expectations of a European visitor. Not only are some of their functions unfamiliar—as storage place for heirlooms, for instance—but so too is the manner in which a variety of functions may be distributed between the house and other structures (such as open-walled pavilions), so that to understand one type of structure it has to be viewed in conjunction with others. Clearly, there is more to be said about a range of South-East Asian built forms—boats, granaries, graves, pavilions, ritual structures, or public buildings—in their relation to the house. Debates concerning boat symbolism in the Indonesian world have already been touched on in Chapter 1, while granaries will receive further mention in Chapter 8, and both graves and 'head-houses' are discussed in Chapter 9. Here I want to focus on how ritual and public functions are distributed between buildings in a variety of different ways. Looked at cross-culturally, we find that there is something of a continuum between public and private buildings, and between 'temple' and 'house'. Sometimes these functions may be fused within a single structure. Rather than a too hasty categorizing of the structures themselves, therefore, I prefer to start by looking at the functions and their distribution.

The House as Ritual Site

Whereas in the Western world the house's function as a dwelling place takes precedence over everything else, the South-East Asian house is not always primarily, or even at all, a place of residence. Some houses, although all-important as places of origin for the kin groups which claim descent from them, may actually be left uninhabited. Enormous effort and expense may be put into maintaining the unoccupied building, which remains above all a *ritual* site and as such should not be allowed to disappear. Certain clan origin-houses in

Sumba, for example, are more like temples than houses, and have even been described as such by some investigators. Adams (1974), for example, uses the term, but this should not be allowed to disguise the fact that the buildings to which she refers are really houses which have accumulated sacred power.[1] As was mentioned in the previous chapter, they contain the sacred heirlooms of the clan, powerful items used in rites as a medium through which contact with the ancestors may be established. These houses have become so surrounded by prohibitions that living in them is too much of a burden for the owners, who prefer to install family slaves as caretakers while themselves residing in more profane ordinary dwellings elsewhere. But they still remain the ritual centres for the clans, and it is these houses which individuals will name as 'theirs', even if they reside elsewhere (Forth 1981: 255).[2] The sacredness of the origin-house makes it 'hot', while ordinary houses are thought of as 'cool'.

Among the Sa'dan Toraja, too, it is not uncommon to find a newly restored *tongkonan* or origin-house left empty, its descendants all preferring to live in more spacious modern houses nearby but still prepared to expend large sums on the traditional house, with its fine carving, which alone is regarded as the proper site for ceremonies. Certain ritual offices, important for the performance of communal ceremonies, are also vested in particular noble houses rather than being inherited by individuals. Whoever is resident in the house will be the current holder of the title, and this may be either a woman or her husband, depending on whether the house belongs to her family or his. Since men most often move to live with their wives at marriage, it is common for a woman to be the office-holder, though her husband will assist in carrying out particular duties, such as pig slaughtering, which are considered to be masculine tasks. Should a house burn down or fall into disrepair, the ritual offices will be temporarily attached to a related house, but they will shift back again if the original house is restored. The house symbolizes family rank, and the rituals performed there enhance the family's social prestige. The word for origin-house, *tongkonan*, is derived from the verb *tongkon*, 'to sit', for this is the place where kin gather and sit to discuss family affairs, such as the arrangement of a marriage or the division of an inheritance. It is the origin-house, rather than the house one lives in, that is the source of an individual's pride and feelings of identity. Ordinary houses are sometimes referred to as mere 'huts' (*lantang-lantang*) by comparison. Toraja migrants in distant cities often content themselves with very poor living conditions in order to be able to save and remit money home, but they will speak with pride of their real 'house' in their village of origin (Nooy-Palm *et al.* 1979; Waterson 1984b).[3]

In parts of Indonesia, one may encounter whole villages of origin-houses which are left uninhabited, save for occasions when the descendants gather there to perform rituals. I visited one such ceremonial village, Lewohala, on the north coast of Lembata, in November 1987. It lies high up on the slopes of the volcano Ileape,

looking down towards the sea (Figure 45). The community of Ileape actually lives in a village down below, on the seashore, but each clan has its origin-house in the upper village, where they come together for an annual ceremony at the end of the dry season. Only one or two families reside as caretakers on the fringes of the origin-village. The clan houses are low, open-walled structures with overhanging thatched roofs, containing sacred clan heirlooms such as elephant tusks and bronze drums. Traube (1986: 71) provides a rather similar account of origin-villages among the Mambai of Timor:

Origin villages vary in size and scale, according to the status of the groups affiliated with them. Some are imposing stone-walled structures, perched high on mountain slopes and containing several interrelated cult houses. Others are little more than fenced enclosures built around small stone altars and rather ramshackle cult houses. All origin villages are practically deserted during ordinary time. They are visited only by an appointed 'master' (*ubun*), who is regarded as the eldest member of the group. He tends the cult house and maintains a private residence near the origin village. But when a birth or a death occurs within the group, when it is

45. Lewohala origin-village on the slopes of the Ileape volcano, northern Lembata, 1987. Each clan has a house in this village, which is almost deserted except at times of ceremonies. (Photograph: Roxana Waterson)

time to perform the yearly agricultural rites, or when the 'master' judges it time to rebuild the cult house, then the scattered members of the group return to their origin place.

In Kédang, almost all villages have an 'old village' (*Léu Tuan*) or hamlet considered as origin-site. These villages have strong associations with the ancestors. Clans have their origin-houses there, used as ritual sites, and there are also stone altars, a village temple, and miniature houses called *huna lélang* or 'ancient house', which represent the houses of female ancestors (Barnes 1974: 51) (Figure 46). This latter feature is of particular interest, since it appears to recur in the Ngada region of Flores; in a clan village of West Sumba, too, I came across a miniature house structure erected on a stone platform, which I was told had the same significance. Kédangese 'old villages' tend to be only partially occupied, often by very old people and those who adhere most strongly to traditional custom. Some have become depopulated because the Dutch, and later Indonesian, governments obliged people to settle in

46. Miniature houses of female ancestors in a Kédangese 'old village'. (From Barnes 1974: 62)

lower-lying villages close to new roads (Barnes 1974: 44).

Empty houses are an equally common sight in villages of the Merina of Madagascar, described by Bloch (1971). Great importance is attached by the Merina to the maintenance of land, tombs, and houses within one's village of origin, even if one lives elsewhere. These houses, palatial by Malagasy standards, are 'used occasionally for holidays or family ceremonies such as burials, marriages, etc, which are held in the [ancestral village]'. To build such expensive houses, of brick with two or three storeys and glass windows, generally requires a joint venture by a close family group; conspicuous spending in this context is socially approved and thus free from the threat of witchcraft accusations by envious neighbours. Bloch (1971: 131) goes on to comment on the rarity with which these buildings are occupied:

Like all other ancestral property a share which is inherited in such a house should not be alienated. This means that a lot of these houses now belong to very many heirs. Unlike the tomb, however, there seems to be no system allowing for segmentation, and quarrels about the management of such a house are very common. This means that repairs cannot be done and many of these massive buildings start to decay as soon as they are finished, which gives an odd appearance to some of the villages near Tananarive. Indeed, villages of old Imerina have a very strange appearance to European eyes. There are a number of massive houses in construction, but the ones that are finished are all shut up and often in decay. The peasants tend to live near these pompous structures in pitiful dwellings. This is because they are rarely the *tompo-tany* ('owners of the land') of the villages where they live.

Among the Nuaulu of Seram, notes Ellen (1986: 6), traditional pile-built houses are called *numa mone*, or 'sacred houses', the emphasis being not so much on the building itself as on its contents, the heirlooms stored in it. The house is properly to be viewed as 'a depository for sacred objects, rather than a sacred structure in its own right, and even less a habitation for human beings, *which is virtually incidental*. More than this, it becomes a physical incarnation, literally an "embodiment" of the clan, its customs and sacra' (emphasis added). Houses are continually in process of construction, but are rarely actually finished, the process of building itself, with its attendant rituals, being more important. By the time a clan house is finished, it may be taken down and replaced almost immediately. In Ellen's words (1986: 26):

The building of the house is therefore one of the eternal ceremonial cycles and a focus of ritual which regulates the Nuaulu conception of time. It is a series of fixed points. So, there is a notion of an ideal house which is only temporarily realized, but which people are always striving toward.

In longhouse societies, such as the Iban of Sarawak, or the Sakuddei of Siberut, rituals play an important part in keeping the longhouse community together. During times of the year when people are busy tending their crops in sometimes distant hill gardens, individual households tend to disperse and enjoy the relative privacy of life in their small field huts. These periods provide some relief from the very intensive interaction which characterizes longhouse life, and which inevitably creates its own tensions. But after harvest they will be sure to return to the longhouse for the ensuing celebrations, when the atmosphere of excitement and bustle is again appreciated. Freeman (1970: 116) says of the Iban: 'It is in ritual terms that the longhouse community attains its real unity.' As well as communal ceremonies, many life-crisis rites of individuals, and shamanic performances, involve the whole community in the observance of taboos or in ritual participation. When a woman is giving birth, during the treatment of cottons with mordants prior to dyeing, and on a number of other ritual occasions, no stranger is allowed to enter the longhouse, and a banner will be displayed in order to alert passers-by to the fact (Freeman 1970: 125).[4] All these occasions, as well as the great festivals, must serve strongly to enhance a sense of community. For the Sakuddei, too, custom demands that all attend rituals held in the longhouse, and it is this communal participation in rites more than anything else that binds the members of the house together and helps to overcome the frictions that arise in the course of daily life: As Schefold (1982: 127) says:

The major uma (longhouse) ceremonies, performed collectively and with the greatest possible splendour, are an attempt to allay the constant threat of internal dissension and a consequent split; recurrent and strong emphasis on the necessity of remaining tightly-knit and close together shows clearly how disconcerting the possibility of the disintegration of the uma is to its members.

In Roti, people are divided into patrilineal clans called leo. Most clans have an origin-house called the uma leo or uma nitu (nitu = ancestral spirits), built and maintained by all the members of the group. Only one family actually lives in the house, and has charge of the sacred heirlooms stored in the attic (which in Rotinese houses is also the granary). This house is the site of yearly feasts at which all clan members congregate (Wetering 1923; Fox 1987: 176).[5] Here, as in Toraja, we find particular houses acting as the focus for kin group rituals, and inhabited by a single family representing the rest of the house descendants. In spite of the marked differences in the kinship systems of Toraja and Roti (and hence in the composition of the group belonging to the house), the functions of the origin-house in each case appear to be indistinguishable. In another eastern Indonesian society, the Atoni of Timor, the association of houses and ritual functions is if anything even more explicit. Cunningham (1964: 35) writes:

The house is a ritual centre for prayer, sacrifice and feasts. Ritual of the life-cycle is conducted normally at the house of those immediately involved, and sacred heirlooms are kept there. A house (with its sacra) should endure; an heir should maintain and eventually inhabit it. Prayers may be directed from the house to the Divinity (Uis Neno), the Powers (pah meni), the ancestors (nitu), and to special tutelary spirits; and diviners (mnane) normally work at the house of a client. Agricultural ritual begins and ends at the house.

Ethnographies of South-East Asian societies thus provide abundant evidence that ritual functions are inseparable from the house's identity. What are sometimes referred to in older literature as 'temples' were, in fact, simultaneously inhabited houses of a kin group. Kruyt, writing of the 'West Toraja' of the Palu and Kulawi regions of Central Sulawesi, describes a Kulawi village which contained three 'temples'. One, the howa (Figure 47), was used for the celebration of head-hunting rites and the death feasts of nobles, a large ramp being erected for carrying the buffalo-headed coffin in and out of the building. Kruyt witnessed the last such great feast held in the village of Lamba in Napu. A second structure, called tombi maa or 'great house', was inhabited by a noble family of the village, but thrown open to all on the occasion of special feasts held in honour of the spirit of the house. The third type, dusunga, was also inhabited by a noble family, and offering rites were held here for the spirit of this house. These two latter 'temples', then, formed the sacred part of a noble 'house', according to Kruyt (1938: 39). They were large buildings, supported on many piles,

47. Village temple (*howa*) of Lamba in Napu (West Central Sulawesi), used for the celebration of head-hunting rites and the death feasts of members of the nobility. The height of the building may be judged from the man standing beneath the floor. (From Kruyt 1938: Pl. 79)

sometimes high enough, to judge from his photographs, for a man to stand upright underneath, and surmounted by a very steep high shingled roof with carved gable horns at the ridge-ends.

Separate and uninhabited religious buildings appear to have been a more typical feature of villages of the eastern 'Bare'e Toraja' of the Poso region (Figure 48). These buildings, which were known in most districts by the name *lobo*, are described by Kaudern (1925: 96) as taking the form of 'a big house, used for several purposes the most important of which was to serve as a dwelling for the spirits. In this house numerous religious feasts were celebrated. For this reason we must call it a temple.' He adds:

About twenty years ago these temples were found in every village of importance all over Central Celebes, but nowadays we only find them in the distant mountain districts of the N. W. part. All the temples of the eastern part have been razed to the ground for some reason or other, without being subjected to any closer study.

Although Kaudern provides no further information, one must suspect that the destruction of these buildings was due to the influence of Protestant missionaries in the region and their hostility to many aspects of the indigenous religion. Kaudern (1925: 393) notes that the temple might also be used for conferences, and as a sleeping place for travellers. He suggests that originally, the Poso region very likely resembled the rest of Central Sulawesi in having no special temple structures; the house of the chief or priest would have been used instead.

48. Village temple (*lobo*) of Lembongpangi, Poso district (East Central Sulawesi), photographed by the brothers P. and F. Sarasin, *c.*1895. (VIDOC, Koninklijk Instituut voor de Tropen, Amsterdam)

Temples, Altars, and Temporary Architecture

The fusing of habitation and ritual site partly explains the absence, in many societies of the region, of buildings set aside for sacred purposes. Most indigenous South-East Asian religions do not make use of separate temples or places of worship, although there are exceptions.[6] Bartlett (1934) recorded the existence of some permanent ritual structures (called *parsuroan*) among the Toba Batak of the 1920s, though they were already rare at the time he was writing (Figure 49). He describes the *parsuroan* as a 'temple', dedicated to the gods and deified ancestors, which served as a place for the performance of certain communal rites. These structures had an enclosed upper part and an open platform below, intended as a resting place for the spirits of the ancestors. Drums were often hung here, and Bartlett (1934: 8–9) suggests that the name *parsuroan*

itself is etymologically related to Malay and Minangkabau *surau*, which designates an Islamic prayer house. The habit of summoning the faithful to prayer by means of a drum rather than from the minaret in these areas is suggestive of the possibility that the *surau*, as a place of ceremonial drumming, pre-dated Islam in Sumatra. The Batak also planted ceremonial enclosures, containing sacred plants such as betel, areca, and Cordyline, either separately or in some cases surrounding the temple. (The Karo Batak, many of whom still adhere to their old religion, still make such enclosures; I saw one in front of the old chief's house of the village of Lingga in 1986.) The peoples of Flores also maintained various types of small 'cult houses' associated with worship of the ancestors (Figures 50–53). The Nage, for example, had a male cult house (*bo hĕda*), containing the horns of buffaloes sacrificed to male clan ancestors, and a female cult house (*sao*

48

49. Batak temple (*parsuroan*) with its stockaded sacred enclosure, at Ihat Pane, Asahan. Bartlett's original caption notes: 'The people of this place have entered Islam, and have allowed animals to destroy the sacred plants. Probably the structure no longer exists, since this photograph dates from 1918.' (From Bartlett 1934: Pl. 1)

waja), in which heirlooms and wooden ancestor figures were stored. A few of these structures still exist, although much of the population today is Catholic. The peoples of Lio, Ende, and Sikka, in the more easterly parts of the island, all have their cult houses too. Unfortunately, there is a great lack of up-to-date ethnography on Flores, so that it is difficult to say a great deal about these structures. There are two kinds of cult houses in Lio, but only one in Ende. The latter is called *sao kedah*, and is also used for the secondary placement of the bones of the dead. Sikka's cult houses are called *woga*, and are used for men's circumcision rites.[7] Further east, in Alor, some villages still maintain their ancestral cult houses (Figure 54). A number of eastern Indonesian societies also make use of ancestral stone altars, sometimes in combination with forked posts (as among the Sumbanese, the Nage of Flores, or the Atoni of Timor). Forth (1981: 118) writes that Sumbanese altars are always associated with both a male and a female spirit, referred to as the 'Lord' and 'Lady', which unite as aspects of a single supernatural presence. Where altars consist of both wood and stone, the wood

is regarded as the male element and the stone as the female one.

In the centre of villages in the Tanimbar Islands (southern Moluccas) stood a ship-shaped stone structure (called *natar* in Jamdena and *didalan* in Fordata), which sometimes incorporated a carved wooden 'prow-board' and 'stern-board'. This formed the ritual centre of the village. In each village, the boat had its own name; ritual officials of the village had their stone seats on it, and on it stood also the main altar to the supreme deity, Ubila'a. At ceremonies held for the renewal of inter-village alliances, members of the visiting village performed a boat-shaped dance on it. Nowadays, village sites have often been moved from defensive cliff-top positions to the shore, and the stone boats abandoned, or their stones used as foundation-stones for churches, so that today most villages have as their centre a soccer field instead (Drabbe 1940: 50; McKinnon 1983: 22, 24). Altars are (or were) also a feature of villages among the Austronesian-speaking Paiwan of southern Taiwan. Ling (1958: 49, 51) records that slate-covered house courtyards might

contain a raised slab platform with a sacred tree planted in the middle, which he describes as an 'altar for the earth'.

On the whole, however, it is true to say that use of specialized structures for regular worship is associated, throughout the region, with the world religions—Buddhism, Hinduism, Islam, and Christianity—which have taken root here over the centuries. Indigenous religions, by contrast, centre on periodic participation in rituals which serve to maintain relations with the deities and ancestors, and ensure cosmic harmony. One is more likely, therefore, to find that ritual structures belong to a category of temporary architecture erected for the performance of particular ceremonies,

50. Cult house (*bo hĕda*) in the village of Boa Wae, Nage district, West Central Flores, date unknown. The horns of buffaloes slaughtered at the *peo*, or forked stake commemorating male clan ancestors, were stored here. Forth found that present-day inhabitants of the village could no longer offer any explanation of the wooden horse figure whose rider, according to some earlier writers, represents an ancestor. (VIDOC, Koninklijk Instituut voor de Tropen, Amsterdam)

51. Village of Bolonga, Ngada district, West Central Flores, date unknown. Around the edge of the plaza are houses with pig pens beneath, while in the centre are three *ngadu* or slaughter stakes (topped with conical thatched roofs) symbolizing male ancestors, and behind them *bhaga* or miniature houses symbolizing female ancestors. (VIDOC, Koninklijk Instituut voor de Tropen, Amsterdam)

52. Village of Roga, Lio district, South-east Flores, 1921. The thatched building is probably a cult house (*kedah*) dedicated to the ancestors, while the structure to the left is described by Vroklage (1940: 263) as containing a corpse. In the village of Nduria, Lio, which I visited in 1987, a similar low structure (with simple zinc roof) on the edge of the plaza was called *bale* and contained two coffins belonging to the founding ancestors of the village, a husband and wife. There was also a well-maintained *kedah*, closely resembling the one seen here. (VIDOC, Koninklijk Instituut voor de Tropen, Amsterdam)

53. Interior of the cult house (*kedah*) at Nduria, Lio, 1987, showing a hearth for the making of offerings, buffalo horns, and snakes and birds carved on pillars and beams. (Photograph: Roxana Waterson)

springing up as required and disappearing again. Among the Toraja, some of these structures imitate house shapes, while others represent a tree—perhaps the 'world tree' which holds the three layers of the cosmos together; their exaggerated height at the same time symbolizes the purpose of the rites, which is to bridge the world of humans and of the supernatural— as, for example, in rites of renewal, whose aim is to make contact with the deities and draw them down to earth (Nooy-Palm 1980: 174; Zerner 1983).

Temporary architecture has also reached great heights (both literal and artistic) in Balinese Hinduism. At funerals, in particular, which may exceed even Torajan mortuary celebrations in their lavishness, the

54. Pair of ancestral cult houses (called 'black' and 'white' houses), Takpala village, Alor, 1987. They have recently been rebuilt after having been allowed to fall into decay when the people first accepted Christianity in the 1950s. The villagers have now reached a new accommodation which allows them to maintain the largely agricultural rites associated with the cult houses, in conjunction with their new faith. (Photograph: Roxana Waterson)

dead are cremated in animal-shaped sarcophagi after being borne to the cremation ground in huge towers built of wood and bamboo and elaborately decorated with coloured paper, cotton-wool, tinsel, and mirrors. Covarrubias's description (1937: 371) of the tower reveals it to combine 'house' imagery with a model of the three-layered cosmos itself:

Shaped like the temple gates and the sun altars, the tower represents . . . the Balinese conception of the cosmos: a wide base, often in the shape of a turtle with two serpents entwined around its body, the symbol of the foundation upon which the world rests, supporting three gradually receding plat-forms—the mountains, with bunches of paper flowers and leaves on the corner of each platform to represent the forests. Then comes an open space, the *bale-balean*, 'rather like a house', the space between heaven and earth. This consists of four posts backed with a board on one side, and with a protruding platform to which the bodies are fastened. The *bale-balean* is topped by a series of receding roofs like a pagoda to represent the heavens. These are always in odd numbers which vary according to the caste of the family: one for

Sudras, from three to eleven for the aristocracy, and none [*sic*: 'nine'?] for the Brahmanic priests. The back of the tower is nearly covered with a gigantic head of Bhoma, the Son of the Earth, a wild-eyed, fanged monster with enormous out-stretched wings that spread some ten feet on each side of the tower. This mask and the wings are covered with bright-coloured cotton-wool. As many as seventy-five men are often required to carry the great tower and its complementary bridge, a tall bamboo runway by which the upper stages of the tower are reached.

Ritual architecture periodically brings added life to more permanent sites, such as temples or ceremonial grounds; in it are demonstrated many of the same skills, such as the working of bamboo, which go into the building of more ordinary dwellings. These are skills which, generally speaking, all adult men are able to demonstrate, and on ceremonial occasions they are often produced by communal labour. Ephemeral by nature, yet constantly being re-created, Zerner suggests that these forms might perhaps, ironically, stand a better chance of surviving the vicissitudes of history and the forces of tropical decay than many apparently more durable monuments of stone. Whether his prediction is proved correct, however, clearly depends a great deal on the continued vitality of the religious motivations behind the structures. In Tana Toraja itself, for example, certain life-enhancing community rituals are now rarely performed, since they are deemed unsuitable for the participation of members of the Toraja Church. Once a part of the community becomes Christian and opts out of these rites, ritual cohesion is lost and it becomes difficult for the remainder to afford the expense involved. By contrast, the temporary structures built for funerals are more likely to endure, since these rites continue to be celebrated with great enthusiasm. The Balinese, unattracted by conversion to other religions, will doubtless maintain their high levels of artistry in temporary architecture, in the same way as they constantly replace the crumbling stones of their temples.

The Granary: Sacred and Practical Functions

Another structure which is frequently characterized by having a sacred aspect is the granary. Rice, the staple of so many South-East Asian societies (though not some of the more arid eastern Indonesian islands where maize and millet are the main crops), is treated with the greatest reverence and widely associated with a female deity, called Dewi Sri in Java and Bali. (The association of women, rice, and the granary is so pronounced that I shall have occasion to refer to it again in Chapter 8.) In northern Thailand, the goddess of the rice is likewise revered. Here, the granary is sometimes attached to the house, but is commonly a separate building placed in an auspicious position in front of the house. It is built on heavy piles, which slope inwards slightly, in order, it is said, the better to support the weight of the building and its contents. The floor level of the granary is higher than that of the house, as a sign of respect to the rice goddess. In order not to disturb the goddess, rice is only put into or removed from the granary on certain auspicious days, but a bin on the balcony may contain rice which can be taken at any time, in case of sudden need. The importance of the granary is reflected in the fact that it is often more elaborately carved and decorated than the house itself (Krug and Duboff 1982: 76–8). In Bali, the granary may be known by various names, depending on its size and shape. The largest type is called *lumbung*. Situated

in the southern part of the house courtyard, near the kitchen, the barn is raised on four wooden pillars, sometimes resting on stone columns, and it often has an open platform beneath the enclosed part where the rice is stored. Covarrubias (1937: 81) notes in relation to the Balinese granary: 'Custom demands the respectful handling of rice. It must be fetched in silence and only in the daytime. A person who climbs into a granary should be in a normal state of physical and spiritual health and may not chew betel-nut.'

Among the Ifugao of northern Luzon (Philippines), the house itself is really an enlarged granary in form, with added hearth and shrine; here house, granary, and shrine are all fused into one (Conklin 1980: 6) (Figures 55 and 56). A similar fusion is evident in parts of Indonesia, for example, Alor (Figure 57), where a single structure combines an open platform for daytime activities (sometimes with its own hearth), an upper room for sleeping and cooking, and above it, two lofts, for storage of grains, and of heirlooms such as the precious bronze drums called *moko*. In nearby Kédang, Barnes (1974: 65) observes that the granary is called by a name which means 'great house'; he says that 'it is not separable from the ordinary dwelling, and is actually of more importance'. Some of his informants stated that in former times, people used to live in their granaries, apparently for reasons of defence. Most of the symbolically important rules about construction of the granary are also applied to the house, though unlike the former, Kédang houses are today built on the ground and not on piles (Figure 58). Another example comes from eastern Sumbawa, where the highland Donggo people customarily built simple A-framed houses called *uma leme*, raised on four heavy teak piles, with a single doorway and no windows (Figure 59). One wall of the single main room is taken up with the hearth, and opposite it is a shelf for offerings to ancestral spirits. A compartment along one side provides storage for grains, mats, and other possessions, while an attic storey above might be used not only for storage but as a sleeping place for unmarried girls. Beneath the house floor, a bamboo platform was sometimes lashed to the tie-beams linking the house piles, providing space for daily activities, relaxation, or the reception of guests (Just 1984: 34). In 1983, Just found only three examples of the *uma leme* surviving, one of them having been the former residence of a high priest of the old religion. Although unoccupied, it was still being preserved because the traditional spiritual

55. Ifugao village at Puitan, Banaue, northern
Luzon, 1968. (Dorothy Pelzer Collection, courtesy
of ISEAS, Singapore)

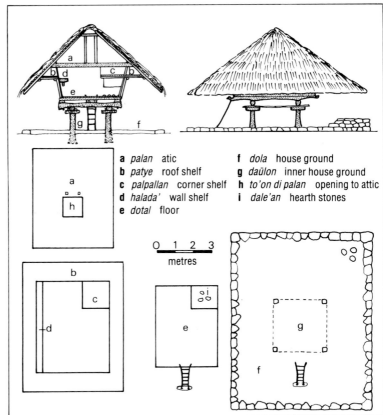

a *palan* atic
b *patye* roof shelf
c *palpallan* corner shelf
d *halada'* wall shelf
e *dotal* floor
f *dola* house ground
g *daūlon* inner house ground
h *to'on di palan* opening to attic
i *dale'an* hearth stones

0 1 2 3
metres

56. Storage and living space in an Ifugao pile
dwelling (*bale*). (After Conklin 1980: 6)

54

57. Frame of a granary, Kédang. In the past, the granary sometimes also served as a house. (From Barnes 1974: 62)

58. Donggo house (*uma leme*), highlands of eastern Sumbawa, date unknown. (VIDOC, Koninklijk Instituut voor de Tropen, Amsterdam)

59. Houses in Takpala village, Alor, 1987. The house incorporates an open platform for daytime use, an enclosed upper floor for cooking and sleeping, and two attic levels for storage of grains and heirloom valuables, such as the prized bronze drums called *moko*. (Photograph: Roxana Waterson)

leaders of the community felt that such a house was the only proper site for the holding of the most import-ant annual cycle of rituals, performed on behalf of the whole community (Just 1984: 32). We see here once more the fusing of house, granary, and ritual site into a single structure. Even where house and granary are separate, the form of the latter is often a close imitation of the house, as is the case in Toraja.

As well as their occasional use as dwellings, barns may serve some other practical social functions, as we saw in the last chapter. Where they are built with an open platform beneath the storage area (as among the Toraja, the Toba and Karo Batak, or the Ema of Timor), this space becomes an important public area for re-laxing, chatting, or the performance of various tasks. On ritual occasions, the Toraja granary platform also becomes a privileged sitting place for high-ranking guests, and if a dispute is to be settled by the village council, the speakers likewise seat themselves upon this platform. Toba Batak barns (called *sopo*) have a similar platform which may be used as a meeting place. In the past, Toba gave the name *sopo* (or *sopo bolon*, 'great *sopo*') to another similar but larger structure, which served as an open-walled communal meeting place, and also as the place where young unmarried men would sleep at night. These buildings fell into disuse, however, a few generations after Dutch con-tact in the late nineteenth century. Vergouwen (1964: 109) states that they were already a rarity at the time he was writing, in the 1920s, and Viner (1979: 105) suggests that none exist today. I was therefore very surprised, on a visit in June 1986, to find a magnificent *sopo bolon* still standing in the village of Lumban na Bolon on the eastern shore of Lake Toba. Its fine dec-orations are old and mellowed and its proportions are very impressive (Figures 60 and 61). Local villagers

60. Toba Batak *sopo bolon* or 'great *sopo*' at Lumban na Bolon, on the eastern shore of Lake Toba, Sumatra, 1986. This is almost certainly the only surviving example of this type of building. It faces the house of the village chief and was formerly used as a village meeting place. (Photograph: Roxana Waterson)

61. Detail of the façade of the *sopo bolon*. Note the relief carvings of double pairs of breasts (symbolizing fertility) with lizards, representing the deity of the earth, Boraspati ni Tano; *singa* or 'lion' figures on either side of the upper floor beam (though generally interpreted as 'lion', *singa* may really be a contraction of *si inga*, meaning '[protective figure] of the corner'), and in the centre of the façade, a so-called *gaja dompak* or protective horned monster, 1986. (Photograph: Roxana Waterson)

58

say that the building is 200 years old, and so far as I could ascertain it is the sole surviving example of this kind of structure. It stands directly opposite the house of the chief, and I was told that in the past, its enclosed upper part was used for the storage of valuables belonging to this house.

Karo rice barns (*jambor*) are three-storeyed structures fulfilling a number of purposes. The open-walled platform which forms the lowest level is used as a men's meeting place during the day; the middle section houses the stored rice, and has a heavy floor to support the necessary weight; above this is an attic, used as a sleeping place for young unmarried men and male guests. Access to the central storage level is from above, through this attic. Singarimbun (1975: 19) mentions that in Liren—one of the villages he studied—there was also a '*jambor* of women', which the women used as a meeting place, but he states that this is unusual. In a pattern which seems similar to that of some other Sumatran societies (in particular, Aceh and Minangkabau), the sexes do not mingle very much among the Karo. Their pattern of family relationships requires parents and their adult children of the opposite sex to avoid one another, and they cannot stay alone in the same room together without being accused of an impropriety; males from a fairly young age tend to spend a great deal of their time hanging around the *jambor*, returning home only to take meals.

In the above examples, we see that the rice barn, while certainly not a 'public' building (for it belongs to a particular house), is none the less a rather versatile structure, whose cool, sheltered platform may fulfil the function of public space within the village. Simultaneously, in most of these societies, the size, number, and quality of workmanship of a house's granaries serve as highly visible indicators of their owners' wealth and prestige. This is particularly true for the Toraja, where the same rules about rank govern the amount of carving permitted on granaries as on houses. Some renowned noble origin-houses (such as those at the village of Nanggala) are faced by a long row of rice barns. The storage of rice has here become an almost secondary purpose, for these barns have been built by different branches of a house's descendants chiefly so that when they congregate at ceremonies they will have their privileged sitting places, where their most distinguished members will be seated. Not to have a barn on these occasions could give rise to embarrassment at not 'knowing where to sit', or the

risk of humiliation at having to sit in an unsuitably humble spot.[8] Even where family members are living outside of Toraja, perhaps holding government posts in other parts of the archipelago or engaged in business, the barns may still store the harvest from inherited rice-fields—rice which will eventually be used to meet expenses and feed guests at some future ceremonial occasion.

Communal Structures

'Public' functions, then, may be fulfilled by buildings or spaces which are not constructed specifically for that purpose; at the same time, where public buildings do exist, we find considerable variation in function. A good example of a society which does without any such structures would be the Iban of Sarawak. An Iban longhouse satisfies all the necessary functions of both public and private space within a single structure. Individual family apartments provide not only sleeping and cooking space, but also storage for heirloom valuables, such as gongs and large Chinese jars, as well as a bin for rice. Enemy heads used to be hung from the rafters in the communal gallery outside the apartment. Each household has responsibility for the maintenance of its own section of the gallery. The gallery is the place for sitting, socializing, pounding rice, and working at various chores during the day, and serves as a sleeping place for young men and guests at night. Dances and rituals are held here, as are meetings to discuss village affairs, in which all adults of both sexes participate, from the age of fourteen or fifteen (Komanyi 1972: 81).

Although a similar pattern holds good for most Borneo longhouse peoples (Figure 62), Hudson (1972) records that some Ma'anyan communities also build a 'ceremonial hall' called *balai*. This is sometimes used for discussion of village disputes, but its chief use is for the performance of the great *idjambe* rites connected with secondary burials (see Chapter 9). The Bidayuh (formerly known as Land Dayak) also built a special structure, the *pangah*, adjoining the longhouse, which was characterized by extremely tall piles and could be round, square, or octagonal in shape, with a high peaked roof (Figures 63 and 64). Although one or two of these structures survived until recently, it appears that by now they may all have fallen into disrepair or been demolished. Although these buildings contained enemy heads and have commonly been referred to in the literature as 'headhouses', Geddes (1957: 51)

62. Gigantic longhouse village of Long Nawang in the Apo-Kayan region of Central Borneo, photographed in 1900 by Jean Demmeni, official photographer of the Nieuwenhuis expedition. (Tillema Archiv, Rijksmuseum voor Volkenkunde, Leiden)

points out that the various terms by which they are known more accurately have the meaning of 'hall' or 'bachelors' residence'. Boys and unmarried men sleep here at night, and village meetings and ceremonies are also held here. Geddes (1957: 48–50) provides a vivid description of the head-house:

The headhouse is always the most elevated building in the village. Sometimes, in villages of little spirit, it is built just off the outer edge of a longhouse verandah and only a little above it. . . . But frequently the spot chosen for it is immediately above sharply sloping ground, so that the sensation one gets on first looking out from it is of a shockingly celestial suspension. For instance, in the village of Temong only eight or nine steps were needed to take one into the headhouse, yet when one crossed its expanse to the far side—it was magnificently wide—the nearest visible point of the globe was a stony stream bed at least a hundred and fifty feet below. . . . [Inside] the walls sloped inwards very steeply to meet at a point below the stars. The house was big by day, the smoke-blackened rafters giving a greater age, and the spider-web curtains an ampler perspective, to the roof. But if it was big by day, at night it vastly expanded, as the glow from the hearth in the centre and from the wicks of a few unglassed lamps made the corners remote and the roof an indefinite extension.

63. 'Head-house' or ceremonial hall (*pangah*) of a Bidayuh longhouse at Mungo Babi, Sarawak. Note the hornbill decoration on the ridge. (From Beccari 1902: Fig. 22)

64. Portion of a Bidayuh longhouse, Sarawak, with the communal
room or *pangah* projecting. (Musée de l'Homme, Paris)

61

Large and finely built community houses are likewise a feature of several of the hill peoples of southern Vietnam, particularly the Böhnar, Eddé, Jölöng, and Halang, and the Austronesian-speaking northern Jörai (Figures 65–67). The name for these community houses is *rong*, or variants thereof (Dournes 1971). The Brou of Cambodia formerly built circular villages in which the houses were arranged like spokes of a wheel around the central community house, called *roong* (Matras-Troubetzkoy 1975) (Figure 68). These structures all seem to share various functions. From puberty, boys sleep in the *rong*, which in the past, in times of war, served as a guard house for the village at night. The square in front of the building is used as market place, sacrificial site, and place for meetings and the reception of guests. Guests also sleep in the *rong*. Other societies where the 'men's house' is an even more developed institution are the Naga of North-east India and the Bontoc of northern Luzon. Naga villages are divided into wards based on patrilineal clans or lineages, each

centring on its men's house or *morung*. The *morung* serves as combination guard house, council house and meeting house, dormitory, and focus of head-hunting rites. Captured heads are stored on shelves inside the building, and fed with rice-beer once a year at the spring festival (Fürer-Haimendorf 1976: 100). Jenks (1905: 52), writing on the Bontoc, noted that their men's houses, the *pabufunan* and *fawi*, served remarkably similar functions. The *pabufunan* is a stone and thatch structure which functions as a sort of men's club during the day, and a sleeping place for unmarried men and guests at night (Figure 69). The *fawi*, a building similar in appearance, is the council house, frequented by older men, and also contains the skulls of head-hunting victims.[9]

In both these societies, war and head-hunting were important male occupations, and men were required to defend the village at night, which no doubt accounts in part for the prominence of the institution (though the same might be said of some other groups, such as

65. Böhnar community house (*rong*) at Kon So Tiu, Kontum (highlands of South Vietnam), 1964. (Dorothy Pelzer Collection, courtesy of ISEAS, Singapore/Smithsonian Institution, Washington)

66. Community house of the Eddé (or Rhade) at Buon Kram, Ban Me Thuot (highlands of South Vietnam), 1964. (Dorothy Pelzer Collection, courtesy of ISEAS, Singapore)

67. Interior of the Eddé community house at Buon Kram, 1964. (Dorothy Pelzer Collection, courtesy of ISEAS, Singapore)

68. Community house (*roong*) of the Brou of Cambodia. The Brou used to build their houses in a circle around the community house, which served as guard house, meeting house, and accommodation for guests. (Musée de l'Homme, Paris)

the Iban, Ifugao, or Kalinga, who had no men's houses). Looking at the Naga and Bontoc men's houses, some writers have attempted to extend the comparison to a variety of Indonesian societies, specifically to those that have buildings called *balai* or *bale*, used as meeting houses, as, for example, in Nias, Minangkabau, Bali, or among the Malays. The Dutch scholar Rassers, in particular, constructed an elaborate and highly speculative theory according to which all such buildings, and also elements of the Javanese shadow play, pointed to the previous existence in Indonesia of men's secret societies such as typify the cultures of New Guinea and Melanesia (1959: 197ff.) Although admitting that such societies are actually unknown in Indonesia, except for a part of the island of Seram (geographically very close to New Guinea), this, according to Rassers, was only because they had all died out, leaving only vestigial traces in the existence of buildings such as the *sopo* of the Toba Batak, the *bale* and *osali* of Nias, or even the Mentawaian longhouse, which he claimed

is really dominated by the men who congregate in the front half of the building.[10] Rassers also cites the division of the audience into male and female groups at a Javanese shadow play, when this is held at a family's house. The women sit in the 'inner' part of the house and the men in the outer courtyard, which is also the side occupied by the *dalang* or puppeteer. Rassers' assumption that the *dalang*'s side is the more privileged is however mistaken: the shadow side is the more sacred, and according to Gunawan Tjahjono (1988: 8), only the women have the honour of watching the shadows.[11] In common with other Dutch theorists of the 1930s, who were much influenced by the work of Durkheim, Rassers was in search of a supposed original dualism in Indonesian social organizations, which he sought to relate to a system of totemism on the model of Australian aboriginal societies; these speculations, although they gave rise to some interesting studies of social symbolism, have not stood the test of time very well. The kind of sexual segregation which Rassers

69. *Ato* or public meeting place of a Bontoc village, northern Luzon, Phillippines, 1968. Before the men's house (*pabufunan*) stand carved fernwood figures decorated with horns, commemorating old head-hunting raids; formerly they would have had human heads attached to them. (Dorothy Pelzer Collection, courtesy of ISEAS, Singapore/Smithsonian Institution, Washington)

claims must originally have been a part of Austronesian social organization is, in fact, highly untypical of Indonesia, as is the Melanesian emphasis on exclusion of women from ritual. On the contrary, in perhaps the majority of indigenous Indonesian religions, not only is the participation of women essential, but women also act as shamans or ritual specialists, and the symbolism of male and female is one of creative complementarity and fusion.[12] Rather than leaping to the conclusion that all public buildings (where these exist at all) are really 'men's houses', we should look more closely at the exact range of functions which these buildings serve. It then becomes obvious that we are not dealing with a single, easily defined category. An examination of the range of meanings attributed to the word *balai* provides further evidence of this.

Blust (1976), in his reconstructions of Proto-Austronesian, gives the word *balay* as meaning 'public building'. The word recurs frequently in present-day Austronesian languages as *bale*, *balai*, and related forms. Although it quite commonly carries the sense of a public building, used for discussion of village affairs, Blust himself also notes its applications to some other types of buildings, and, in fact, a range of referents can be drawn up for the term. I would therefore query whether it is correct to assume that the Proto-Austronesian word necessarily had this meaning. Gonda (1952: 79) defines *balay* as 'an Indonesian word for "an unwalled house"'. For both the Ifugao, and the Sasak of Lombok, *bale* refers to the dwelling house, and cognates such as *fare* (Tahiti) and *fale* (Samoa) also have this meaning. The Sasak use another term, *berugaq*, for their pavilions (which, however, are not 'public' buildings but belong to each house) (Cederroth 1981: 44). This latter term would appear to be a cognate of *baruga*, which occurs in a number of Sulawesi languages, where it does refer to an (often unwalled) 'meeting hall'. Balinese *bale* is defined by Covarrubias (1937: 409) as 'a pavilion, a house, a couch or bed'. Open-walled pavilions within the house courtyard are called *bale*; the meeting place of a village ward (mainly used by men) is called *bale banjar*. This, too, is an open-walled building, as is the meeting house for (male) village elders among the Minangkabau, which is called *balairung* (Figure 70), and the men's council house (*bale*) of Nias. The Ma'-anyan *balai*, as noted above, is principally a ceremonial hall; Hudson makes no mention of its being used as a men's club. Blust notes: 'Malay *balai*, "public building, in contrast to a private house; an unwalled or low-walled building where people met, public business was transacted, and strangers spent the night" ', but also: 'Puluwat (Western Carolines) *faal*, "boat house", 'Are (Southern Malaita) *hare* "house of retirement for women during menstruation and after childbirth", Arosi (Northern San Cristoval) *hare* "shed for yams; house with one side of roof only, made in gardens; shrine, small house on poles".' Leaving aside the diversity of meanings which appears to have developed in the Pacific, we may detect something of a continuum in meanings within the Indonesian archipelago, from

'house' to 'public building'. Intriguingly, *bale* even recurs in Temiar (a non-Austronesian language of the Malay Peninsula which has assimilated a number of Austronesian words), with the meaning of 'platform'.[13] Since South-East Asian architecture at its most basic essentially involves a roofed platform raised on piles, it is not surprising to find that the word 'platform' is quite frequently used in different languages as a synonym for 'house'. But perhaps the most interesting example of the meanings of the word comes from the Moluccas, where we find *baileu* (a cognate of *bale/balai*) used to signify 'a place for meeting to discuss village affairs' (Cooley 1962: 8). Cooley, however, goes on to give a rather detailed account of exactly what the *baileu* signifies in Ambonese communities, and it becomes clear that there is a point here, as in a number of other societies of the archipelago, where 'house', 'temple', and 'meeting-place' may all blend into one (Cooley 1962: 9):

Two answers are commonly given by an Ambonese to the question about what the baileu is. The more ready explanation is that it is the place of deliberation by the village elders

70. Minangkabau council house (*balairung*) at Singkarak, West Sumatra, 1965. (Dorothy Pelzer Collection, courtesy of ISEAS, Singapore/Smithsonian Institution, Washington)

on all matters having to do with village welfare.... As the matter is pursued more deeply, however, it will emerge that the baileu is referred to, or conceived as, the *rumah adat* (adat house). The writer, on several occasions when discussing this phenomenon with an Ambonese who knew him quite well, has even heard the baileu characterized as *geredja adat* (adat church). Either of these characterizations points to the fact that the baileu is the physical manifestation of the village as an adat community. One informant referred to the baileu as, in effect, the village rumah tua, the ancestral house of the clan where formerly all heirlooms and articles believed to have particular meaning and powers, because they were connected with the ancestors, were kept, and where all matters having to do with the welfare of the clan, or any individual in the group, were discussed, decided and carried out. If this be the case, it is evident why all adat ceremonies having to do with the village community as a whole must be carried out in the baileu....

Although the importance of the *baileu* faded in the early decades of the twentieth century, and in many places the buildings themselves have disappeared, Cooley was able to ascertain that they were traditionally regarded as the dwelling places of the ancestral spirits. Traditionally, the *baileu* was an open-walled building erected on piles in the centre of the village, and in order to enter it one had to dress in *adat* costume and behave in an appropriate manner, permission first being asked of the spirits by a special functionary who recited verses and blew upon a conch shell. Formerly, erection of a *baileu* required the holding of head-hunting ceremonies, and every single person in the community had to participate in the work of construction. Fixed responsibilities were allotted to particular clans to provide certain posts, and to families to provide sections of roof thatch. The health of the community was regarded as dependent upon the 'health' of the *baileu*, and should it be permitted to fall down, the result would be death. The *baileu* and its surrounding yard were regarded as sacred, and each *baileu* had a ritual name or title, which could only be uttered by authorized persons, during the course of particular ceremonies. Some even had myths associated with them, describing the extraordinary circumstances by which their location had been chosen (Cooley 1962: 10–12).

There are a number of points of interest in this account. The *baileu* is clearly a development from the clan ancestral house, which has come to represent the health and unity of an entire community. Reference to features such as its sacredness, its possession of heirlooms and of a name, its intimate association with the

ancestors, the necessity for its maintenance over time, and so forth, all remind us strongly of certain aspects of the house in other Indonesian societies, as well as of the features which Lévi-Strauss outlines as characterizing houses in 'house societies' (see Chapter 7). Another almost equally interesting case is that of the Nias *bale* or *osali*. Early accounts are confusing about what exactly these structures were; according to Schröder, *osali* was the term used in North and Central Nias, and *bale* in South Nias, to refer to a temple; but other authors indicate that the term *osali* was also known in the south (Suzuki 1959: 52n). Although early accounts are very confusing on whether the terms were interchangeable, or referred to separate structures, it seems that the *osali* may have been both a meeting house and a kind of temple; at any rate, missionaries chose this word to mean 'church' (Feldman 1977: 79, 102). A single published photograph of an *osali* by Schröder (1917: Pl. 79) shows an elliptical, pile-built structure with open walls and a conical roof (Figure 71). Only a single example of a *bale* now survives, in the South Nias village of Bawömataluo (Figure 72). Today, the building functions as a men's council house, and during the day there are usually a certain number of men hanging around in it. It also contains standard weights and measures for gold and pigs, each size of pig having its fixed equivalent in units of gold in Nias. Ancestor figures commemorating the village founders were formerly stored inside it, as well as enemy heads, and like the house of the chief, the taking of a head was necessary for its construction. The building provided a direct link with the ancestors, for during orations in the *bale*, their spirits were thought to be present (Feldman 1985: 76). In view of the conflicting nature of the available data, Feldman reserves judgement on whether the *bale* was formerly also a temple, although Suzuki definitely adopts this view. If he is correct (and we can now only speculate), then the present function of the building as a men's meeting place represents only a part of its original character, for in the past this was the place where the priestesses carried out their work and made contact with the deities. The use of the temple (or the open space around it—see Figure 73) for the discussion of *adat* affairs and settlement of disputes proves, according to this view, the formerly inextricable relation between custom and religious belief. Furthermore, the 'head' end of the building is said to be associated with Lowolangi, the deity of the upper world, and its 'foot' with Lature Dano,

71. *Osali* of Awa'aj village, North Nias. None of these structures survive today, and evidence is confusing as to whether they functioned as temples, meeting houses, or a combination of both. (Schröder 1917: Pl. 79)

72. Termination of a stone-dragging procession before the *bale* of Bawömataluo village, South Nias. The *bale*, today a men's meeting house, in the past apparently also functioned as a temple. (Schröder 1917: Pl. 206)

73. Formal oratory taking place at a distribution of sacrificial pigs in front of the *bale* of Bawömataluo. (Schröder 1917: Pl. 208)

deity of the underworld. Although there is not space fully to reproduce his argument here, Suzuki (1959: 53) sees the building as a microcosm symbolically uniting upperworld and underworld, noblemen and common folk, male and female, and functioning as the focus of the life of the village, under the care of the *ere* or priestesses (Figure 74).

In the meanings of *bale* and its cognates, then, we find a semantic range indicative of a continuum of functions differently distributed between houses and other structures in the societies of the archipelago. Some buildings appear to fall in between the Western definitions of 'public' and 'private', and others combine functions which one might have expected to be separate. House and temple, temple and meeting hall, may turn out to be a single structure, so that it is impossible to draw sharp lines between categories of building types. Physical characteristics of the *bale*, too, are variable. A feature shared by many of the buildings with this name is that they are wall-less, but even this is not universal. There are also some apparently rather similar structures which are known by different names.

The circular, open-walled meeting house of the Atoni, for example, is called *lopo*; Tanimbar men met to eat and drink palm wine (though for no more serious purpose) in open-walled buildings called *lingat* (Drabbe 1940: 40–2) (Figure 75). Rounded pavilion forms (like the Samoan *fale*) being likewise extremely widespread in Oceania, it is probably safe to conclude that pavilion architecture had well-established indigenous (Austronesian) precedents in the archipelago long before Hindu styles of construction had had their impact upon the architecture of Java and Bali (Austin 1988: 6).[14]

The Married and the Unmarried

Where meeting houses do exist, there is an observable tendency for men to dominate public discussions, but it would certainly be a mistake to assume that this dominance extends into the ritual arena (as Rassers did), or the economic one. Both Nias and Minangkabau societies, for example, have men's council houses, but the power and influence of women in Minangkabau

74. The assembled priestesses (*ere*) of Bawömataluo. (Schröder 1917: Pl. 235)

75. *Lingat* or open-walled building in which men gather to eat and drink palm wine, in a village in southern Jamdena, Tanimbar Islands. (From Drabbe 1940: Pl. 14, courtesy of SOAS, London)

matriliny, where they are automatically the owners of houses and ancestral lands, is well known. Men are here permitted to perform the roles of public spokesmen, while exercising very little authority over sisters or wives (Tanner 1982; F. Errington 1984). Even in Nias, where women's economic position is much weaker, they used to play a dominant role in ritual life in their highly important functions as priestesses (Suzuki 1959: 48–55).[15] A feature shared by a number of Sumatran societies is the tendency toward segregation of the sexes in their daily activities, with men spending more time in the 'public' arena, but again, the implications for women vary. It seems probable that this pattern pre-dated Islam, since it is shared by some non-Muslim groups such as the Karo, but in Muslim societies of Sumatra today the separation of men's and women's spheres of interest is further emphasized by the identification of men with Islam, with the mosque and the prayer house. In Aceh, the prayer house is called meunasah, and in neighbouring Gayo meresah—both words deriving from Arabic. The Minangkabau prayer house is called surau. Like the granary of the Karo, the prayer house doubles as a sleeping place for boys, young unmarried men, and guests at night. Gayo widowers, according to Loeb (1935: 250), also sleep in the meresah, which suggests that the significant contrast here is not so much with the house as male to female domain, but as the place of the unmarried or sexually inactive to that of the married. The house is the site and source of fecundity as represented not simply by women but by the married couple. Indeed, most of the communal structures discussed above are used as sleeping places for unmarried males. The existence in a few societies of some more unusual structures built especially either for unmarried girls or boys suggests that this symbolic dimension deserves some further investigation. Kis-Jovak (1980: 25), for example, reports that among the Sakuddei, adolescent boys sometimes built themselves a special house, in which they could develop some independence from their elders. Schefold's lengthy description (1976) of distinctions between married and unmarried statuses in the Mentawai Islands confirms that this contrast is a highly significant one in Mentawai societies. It is this, rather than simply a male/female opposition, which determines in what part of the longhouse a man sleeps. On Sipora and Pagai, a young couple may live together in a field house for several years before going through a formal marriage ceremony in the longhouse,

and being incorporated back into the longhouse community as an officially married couple. Loeb (1935: 56) mentions that among the 'southern Batak', young girls used to sleep in a communal house called bagas padoman, under the charge of an older woman. Unmarried men would come here to court them: 'They come in small groups, with lights burning, and speak with the young women, offer them sirih, and remain until the chaperon gives them a signal to depart.'

A unique example of a structure built for the unmarried comes from Tanimbar, in the southern Moluccas. Here, Drabbe (1940: 43) records the existence, at one time, of a type of building called kusali. This was a small structure built on very high piles, in which a very high-ranking girl might be secluded, surrounded by 'female' valuables, for a period before her marriage. Drabbe records that no one, in his time, could remember ever seeing one; but some said that only a girl who had ten brothers (or, according to others, eleven), and was the only daughter of the family, was confined in this way, and that, in the same way, an only son in a family of ten or eleven sisters might also be placed in a kusali full of 'male' valuables. In myths, the deity Ubila'a is said to have let down marriageable women, or sometimes other humans, to earth inside a small house called kusali, in order that they might marry earthly nobles (McKinnon 1983: 28).

*　　*　　*

This brief review of buildings and their functions reveals some interesting features of the uses of space in South-East Asian communities. I have argued that there exists a continuum between dwelling houses and public buildings, for sometimes the house itself may serve the functions of meeting place or temple without the development of separate structures for these purposes. Moreover, certain kinds of buildings have clearly developed as extensions of the house as sacred origin-place of a grouping of kin, as in the case of the Ambonese baileu. Although a few of the more warlike societies of the region have developed the 'men's house' as a useful institution, this is not so widespread a phenomenon as has sometimes been claimed, and the evidence tends rather to support the idea that it is the house itself which is the dominant structure in the organization of the community. Understanding the uses of 'public' and 'private' space requires several dimensions to be brought into play, for we have seen that contrasts such as male/female, married/ unmarried, sacred/profane may be woven together in a variety of ways, while some societies do without any structures designed specifically as 'public' buildings. If males appear to dominate a number of the communal structures we have described, we may begin to suspect, conversely, that the association of women with houses may prove an equally important theme, and it is one which I shall address more closely in Chapter 8.

We have seen in this chapter that the significance of the house extends far beyond the mere provision of shelter. In its role as origin-place and ritual site, the house may even cease to perform its function as dwelling, yet in these instances it still claims the allegiances, and the material resources, of those who belong to it, and its place in their lives and identities is, if anything, perhaps still more significant.

1. This is absolutely clear from Forth's description of such houses in Rindi, the domain of eastern Sumba which formed the locus of his study.

2. Forth names as an example Parai Yawungu, the chief village of Rindi.

3. The manner in which Toraja people trace associations with their houses of origin is explained more fully in Chapter 7.

4. The dyeing of cottons prior to *ikat* weaving is a highly specialized and difficult process surrounded by ritual. Weaving itself involves mystical dangers because of the power inherent in the designs. Dyeing is referred to by the Iban as 'the warpath of women', and women's achievements in this art are likened to those of war chiefs. A successful weaver was entitled to have her fingers tattooed in a manner similar to male head-hunters (Mashman 1986: 28–30).

5. Unfortunately, Fox, the major recent ethnographer of Roti society, does not in his published works to date discuss the role of houses in any great detail, though he hints at their importance within the kinship and alliance systems (1980: 115).

6. Some of these religions in Indonesia are under pressure to define themselves in terms of government definitions of what constitutes a 'religion', and thus find the need to stress the similarity between repeatedly used ceremonial sites (such as the Toraja *rante*, or funeral ground) and the places of worship used by world religions.

7. Suchtelen 1921; Lebar 1972; Gregory Forth and Signe Howell (personal communications).

8. See also Volkman (1985: 75, 164) on the significance of 'sitting places' as indices of prestige in Toraja.

9. Bontoc villages also have a dormitory for unmarried girls, the *olag*. Only the very young sleep at home with their parents; from the age of about five or six, brothers and sisters avoid each other, and even before this they have begun to spend the nights with their peers in their respective dormitory buildings.

10. See below for a fuller discussion of the Nias *bale* and *osali*. The impression that Rassers gives of Mentawaian society is a very different one from that to be obtained from more modern ethnography (for example, Schefold 1976, 1980, 1982), in which the complementary participation of the sexes in longhouse rituals, for example, is much more obvious. It is difficult to avoid the conclusion that Rassers was forcing his data in the search for comparisons with Melanesia.

11. See Chapter 8 for further discussion of the division of space in the Javanese dwelling.

12. For an exploration of the symbolism of gender in the Indonesian world, see Becker and Yengoyan (1979).

13. Geoffrey Benjamin (personal communication).

14. Austin (1987: 7) suggests that rounded forms, which perform better in high winds, are a regional adaptation in Oceania to areas where regular cyclones are a climatic feature. Many round-ended structures of Oceania have the lightly constructed roof built around an internal gable structure, while the ultimate development of the form, seen in the circular Samoan *fale tele*, consists simply of two rounded ends with the central gable structure eliminated: 'The ends become the building itself.' If one accepts this account of the progression from gabled to round-ended forms, it might be applied equally well to the elliptical forms of West Flores and Savu, and the circular ones of Timor. Climatic features, however, should not be seen as the only determinant of such choices; nor, according to Austin, the 'cultural' explanations favoured by anthropologists. He himself makes a plea for the consideration of aesthetic play as a significant aspect in the production of built form.

15. The coming of Christianity has meant the loss of women's prestigious role as priestesses, though they do appear to be active in a lay capacity in various church organizations.

CHAPTER 4
Technology and Symbolism

SOME analysts of architecture have striven to explain vernacular styles entirely in terms of practical considerations, as representing adaptations to local climate, geography, and environment, or in terms of the properties and limitations of the particular materials used in their construction. Others have gone to the opposite extreme in attributing every aspect of the design of small-scale communities to the pursuance of time-honoured principles of cosmology, handed down by the ancestors. The weaknesses of attempts to explain architectural form either in purely functional or in purely cosmological terms have been dealt with very concisely by Amos Rapoport in his book *House Form and Culture* (1969), and it is not necessary for me to reiterate his arguments here. But, as I have already argued, it would be a mistake to suppose that the societies which we are considering are essentially different from our own in the degree to which symbolic and functional considerations intersect. In this chapter, I begin by examining materials and techniques of construction, and some functional and adaptational aspects of built form in South-East Asia, but this discussion will lead on to a consideration of various totally non-functional features of buildings which are to be found in several of the societies we are considering. By 'non-functional' I mean that these features look like unnecessary additions from a constructional point of view, in spite of the fact that they may be essential to the local concept of the house and even of its structural viability. Although such features might easily be overlooked by the casual observer, they are particularly important in helping us understand how houses are thought about in these societies. For in the words of Daniel Coulaud (1982: 188), we find in the house the intersection of 'the visible and the invisible worlds'.

The fact that the architectural styles of the region are, to greater or lesser degrees, rather well adapted to local environments and make clever use of locally available materials, while in itself interesting, actually tells us very little about why buildings should take the exact form they do. The great variety of forms to be found in ecologically similar regions of South-East Asia is sufficient to suggest that climate, geography, or materials only dictate the outside limits to architectural design, without at all determining the end results. Another important factor determining architectural form is that of historical continuity. It is, of course, particularly difficult to assess, since the pressures toward conservatism or innovation differ from society to society; moreover, wooden buildings in the tropics cannot be expected to last much longer than 200 years at the maximum, and for many of the societies we are considering we face an absence of written records or recorded images which might help us to identify changes and developments in style. The discussion in Chapter 1 has, however, demonstrated that continuity can be surprisingly strong and must be significant in any attempt to explain house forms in the Austronesian world.[1] Such a basic feature as pile building, for example, while it can be argued to have various functional advantages, is also part of a very ancient method of building which has endured among South-East Asian peoples to the present day; while, in spite of these advantages, it has not necessarily been adopted by other settlers in the region such as the Chinese, who have an equally long tradition of building on the ground (Figure 76). The tenaciousness of 'Austronesian' roof forms, too, has been remarkable. The aesthetic satisfaction derived from these forms, and their uses as symbolic 'markers', even as shifts take place in the public perception of what exactly they signify, is a subject to which I shall give attention in my concluding chapter. I turn now to look at how buildings are put together, and at some of the potentials and limitations of the materials used in their construction.

76. Hilltop village of Betsimisaraca, Madagascar. Building on piles is an ancient and enduring feature of South-East Asian architecture, and its presence here is one of many cultural features which indicate Austronesian influence. Austronesian people reached here from Indonesia by *c.* AD 400. (Musée de l'Homme, Paris)

77. Skilful mortising and pegging of joints may be seen in this corner of a Toba Batak granary at Simanindo, Samosir Island, Lake Toba, Sumatra, 1986. Traditional architectures of South-East Asia make no use of nails. (Photograph: Roxana Waterson)

Materials and Technology

The traditional buildings of South-East Asia, while utilizing a range of locally available materials, tend to share one characteristic feature; they are held together entirely without the use of nails, by means of a variety of techniques of joining and mortising, sometimes reinforced by pegging, wedging, or binding (Figure 77). In some cases, timbers are simply lashed together rather than jointed, using rattans, strips of bamboo, or fibre cords. This method is particularly important in roof constructions. Sometimes members may be ingeniously shaped, notched, or scooped to form a joint. As we have already seen, the wall is generally not an important building element. Where walls do exist they are rarely load-bearing, but may consist rather of prefabricated screens attached to the main structure of posts and beams which carries the load of the floor and roof (Figure 78). Most of the built forms we are con-

74

sidering can be described as variants of a post-and-beam system of construction. They require relatively few secondary members, such as reinforcing wall studs. Posts may on occasion run right through the building, but in a number of cases, such as the Toba, Karo, or Toraja house, the system of foundation posts and beams is topped off by a heavy ring beam, and the actual inhabited space of the house (including the roof structure) sits on top of this, almost like a box. We can also find a number of examples of structures in which the floor and roof systems, instead of being integrated, are separate from each other, the roof bearing on to its own system of posts and forming an envelope around

the platform floor. The circular houses of Manggarai provide one example, and the houses of the Isneg of northern Luzon (Philippines) another (see Figure 79).[2]

The curved lines and pointed eaves of the 'Austronesian' saddle roof are not everywhere achieved by means of the same construction methods. The point is interestingly explored by Sherwin (1979) in an analysis of Toba Batak and Minangkabau roof constructions. These two Sumatran peoples both provide famous examples of the saddle roof, yet the structure and proportions of their houses are substantially different from each other. Proportions of roof to wall in the Toba house are about 3 : 1 and the structure of the roof, and the extent to which the gable triangles can be made to slope outwards and upwards, is integral to the way the whole building is put together (Figure 80). The major exterior columns of the Toba house carry longitudinal

78. House under construction at Prapadaeng, Thailand, 1967. The prefabricated wall screens are being hoisted into position on the post-and-beam framework. Where walls exist at all in South-East Asian dwellings, they are rarely load-bearing. (Dorothy Pelzer Collection, courtesy of ISEAS, Singapore)

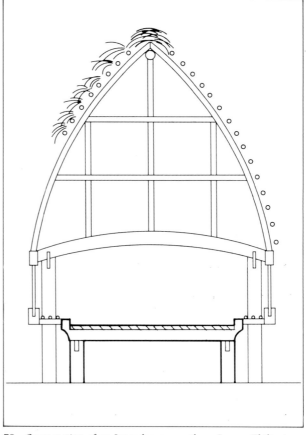

79. Cross-section of an Isneg house, northern Luzon, Philippines, showing the separation of floor and roof structures. (After Scott 1966: 188)

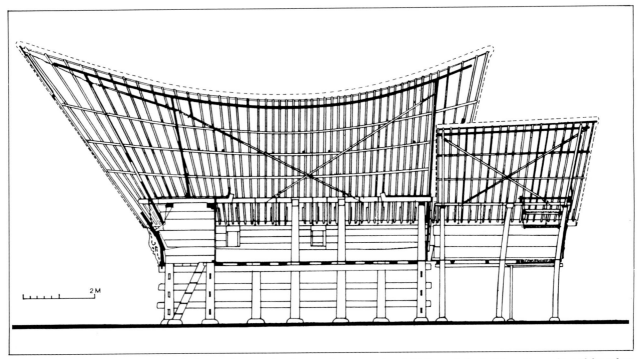

80. Longitudinal section through a Toba house, showing the absence of posts running right through the building, the angling of the rafters to produce the projecting gable, and the diagonal ties reinforcing the roof. (From Domenig 1980: 157)

beams (*labe-labe*) which run the length of the house at head height. The walls are light and lean outwards, lending added stability to the whole structure. The top of the wall, and the wall plate which joins the top of the wall and supports the rafters, is hung from the *labe-labe* beam by means of rattan thongs, while the bottom of the wall rests on a huge beam at floor level, whose upturned ends project (as in so many Indonesian houses) like the prow and stern of a boat. The rafters are straight poles springing from the wall plate, angled outwards to produce the curve of the roof. They are not braced by any horizontal battens, but some reinforcement is provided by diagonal ties which run back from the tip of the gable-end to the middle of the *labe-labe* (see Figure 80). There are no interior trusses to the roof, which forms an open and potentially usable space inside the house. By contrast, in the Minangkabau house the relation of the roof to the rest of the building is different. Walls may be of varying heights depending on the wealth and taste of the owners, and the roof sits on top of the habitable space rather than creating it. A truss and cross-beam structure is used for the roof and the roof peaks are built up by means of many small

rafters and battens. In the biggest houses, the ends (*anjung*) project up and out from the main body of the house in tiers (Figures 81 and 82). The roofing thatch of *ijuk* (sugar palm fibre) is tied on in bundles which can easily be made to fit the curves of the roof peaks. Sherwin analyses some changes which occurred in the style when Minangkabau migrants settled in Negeri Sembilan, on the Malay Peninsula. There, they adopted a Malay style of roof construction with a continuous ridge-piece, and palm-leaf thatching prepared in rigid lengths fastened to battens. These methods were simpler, and resulted in the roof having a much less pronounced curve than the original form and blunter ends to the eaves (Figure 83). Certain changes appear also to have taken place in the way that space is used inside the house, with women becoming more confined to the back of the house than is the case in Minangkabau.

One could probably find several other examples of contrasting methods of roof construction used to produce similar results, except that unfortunately such detailed architectural analyses as Sherwin's are hard to come by. In other parts of the archipelago, the roof

76

81. An outstandingly beautiful old house at Lima Kaum in the Minangkabau highlands, West Sumatra, with its rice barns in front of it, 1986. The roof peaks of the Minangkabau house are built up on a truss and cross-beam structure, and traditionally thatched (as here) with *ijuk* or sugar palm fibre, so tough that it may last up to 100 years. (Photograph: Roxana Waterson)

82. Detail of the woodcarving on the gable-end of the house at Lima Kaum, Minangkabau, 1986. (Photograph: Roxana Waterson)

83. An old Malay palace—the Istana Hinggap—at Seremban, Negeri Sembilan, Malaysia, 1969. Originally built in the 1860s, it has been dismantled and relocated several times, resulting in much alteration. Nevertheless, the adoption of elements of the Malay style of roof construction, leading to a greater rigidity in the roof form, is still apparent. (Dorothy Pelzer Collection, courtesy of ISEAS, Singapore/Smithsonian Institution, Washington)

form has developed its own unique features, as among the Sa'dan Toraja. Here, the dramatically extended eaves are built out by means of a cantilevered framework and given extra support by free-standing posts at either end of the house (Figure 84). Among the Karo, diagonal roof braces similar to those used by the Toba are exploited to the full to reinforce the taller and more elaborate developments of the extended-gable pattern. These are well documented by Domenig (Figure 85).

Sometimes a feature of construction which results from technological considerations may be exploited to symbolic effect. One such feature relates to the way beams are mortised into the posts. In the building styles of the Thai, Malay, or Acehnese, for example, a basic single-room unit can easily be expanded to form a number of rooms by adding on similar units at various angles, the floor beams of these extra units being jointed into the main house posts. Clearly, where a post holds more than one beam, they must be mortised one above the other, resulting in different floor levels in the finished house. The arrangement of levels does not, however, remain a neutral feature of the building: in all three cases, strict rules are applied about which floor should be the highest, and which the lowest, the most

important room always being given the highest floor. Thus, systematically imposed upon the technological feature, we find a pattern of symbolic meanings.

One advantage of the way buildings are fitted together without nails is that they are often capable of being dismantled and reassembled in a new location. A pile-built house can even, with enough helpers, be lifted intact from its foundation-stones and carried bodily to a new site (Figure 86). Once while staying in the Buginese district of Rappang in South Sulawesi, I met a party of villagers coming along a path towards me carrying a house in this manner. Given the levels of seismic activity which characterize the Indonesian archipelago, a perhaps more important consideration is that these jointed wooden buildings are well suited to withstand earthquakes. A major seismic belt curves the length of Sumatra and Java and on through the islands of Nusa Tenggara to the east, and another descends through the Philippines to northern Sulawesi. The entire region is dotted with dozens of volcanoes, many of which are active, and earth tremors are very common occurrences. Marsden, in *The History of Sumatra* (1811: 56), noted of the Acehnese house that its system of construction gave it the flexibility to

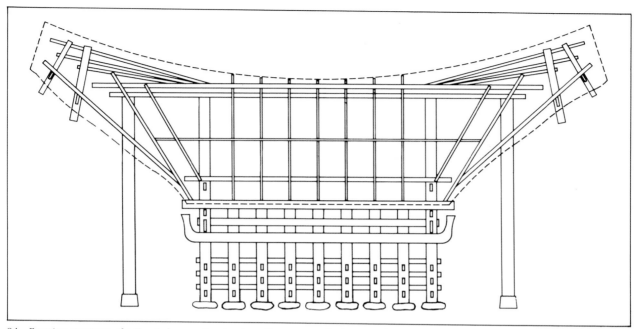

84. Framing structure of a Toraja house, showing how the eaves are built out and supported by free-standing posts.

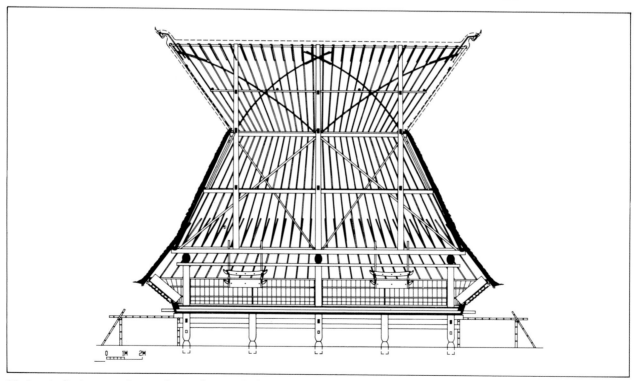

85. Longitudinal section of a Karo house, showing the heavy ring beam dividing the foundation structure from the inhabited portion, and the structure of the roof, reinforced by diagonal ties. (From Domenig 1980: 129)

86. Transporting a house at Bulukumba, South Sulawesi. (Photograph: Walter Imber)

withstand the frequent earthquakes and tremors characteristic of Sumatra. Snouck Hurgronje, in his famous study (1906: 42-3), made some further interesting observations:

The whole house belongs in Acheh to the category of movable property. Every peg is made much too small for its hole and is kept in its place by means of large wedges. For anyone who understands the uniform structure of the Achehnese house—and every native of the country is adept in this—the task of taking a house to pieces and setting it up again elsewhere is but the work of a moment.

So when an Achehnese sells his house, this means that the purchaser removes it to his own place of abode; a change of residence by the proprietor or rather the proprietress to another gampong (village) is quite a rare occurrence among the Achehnese....

It is to be understood that even the most solidly built Achehnese house shakes if anyone pulls at the posts. Thieves and burglars begin by shaking the house to discover whether the inmates are sound enough asleep to admit of their carrying out their nefarious purposes. If they hear from the

juree (inner room) or the front verandah the cry 'who is that shaking the house?' they know that the time is unfavourable for their task.

Men who have forbidden intrigues with the wife or daughter of the house make known their presence in the same way, so that the object of their affections may come out to them if opportunity occurs.

The same course is adopted by the revengeful, who seek treacherously to slay the master of the house. Having ascertained that the latter is sound asleep in the *juree* they can generally ascertain, as they stand underneath the house, on what part of the floor he is lying. Then follow one or two rapid spear-thrusts through the thin planks, and all is over.[3]

To force one's way into the house at night is difficult, as the doors are fastened with wooden bolts and besides every movement inside the house would be likely owing to the instability of the floor, to wake the inmates up.

Another architectural feature which seems well adapted to geological circumstances is to be found on the island of Nias (off the west coast of Sumatra). In the whole of island South-East Asia, it is perhaps in the

87. Chief's house at Hilinawalö, South Nias, 1986. Diagonal piles are a distinctive feature of Nias architecture, and serve to lend added stability to the house in a region of high seismic activity. (Photograph: Roxana Waterson)

88. House at Bawödesölö, North Nias, 1986. As in the south, diagonal piles are likewise a feature of the northern Nias style of house, with its oval plan. (Photograph: Roxana Waterson)
89. Undercroft of the house at Bawödesölö, North Nias, 1986, showing its structure of diagonal and vertical piles. Note how the piles rest on top of their foundation-stones, another common feature of South-East Asian architecture, which gives extra flexibility to withstand earth tremors. (Photograph: Roxana Waterson)

southern part of Nias that vernacular architecture has found its most monumental expression. Here huge ironwood piles, sometimes exceeding 1 metre in diameter, form the substructure of the house. A unique feature of Nias architecture is the use of diagonal as well as vertical piles (Figure 87). These diagonal piles, arranged in V-shaped pairs, give added resistance to earthquake stresses as well as lend stability to the structure as a whole, with its unusually high roof. The buildings of the northern part of the island, with their distinctive elliptical plan, also make use of diagonal piles (Figures 88 and 89).

Piles may either be set in the ground (as in the case of the huge ironwood trunks which form the foundations of Borneo or Mentawai longhouses, or the smaller piles of houses in the plain of Vientiane in Laos), or, more commonly, they may rest upon flat foundation-stones.[4] Nowadays concrete plinths may commonly be seen in place of stones, for example, in Thailand and

Malaysia. Where the piles are quite tall and simply rest upon stones, a system of beams mortised into the piles may serve to give the substructure added stability. Typical examples are the houses of the Toba Batak and Toraja peoples. Set above ground, the piles are less vulnerable to rot and termite attack, and in earth tremors the building can move on its stones without damage. Pile building has distinct advantages in a monsoon climate, lifting the inhabitants above the mud in wet weather and allowing excellent underfloor ventilation when it is hot. In hot and humid coastal areas, houses typically have openings under the roof and a rather open, slatted floor. The Buginese, Acehnese, and Malay styles all provide good examples (Figure 90). Warm air rises and passes out through the roof spaces, drawing a current of cooler air through the spaces between the floor-boards, which are frequently made of lengths of split bamboo. 'This sort of flooring,' wrote Marsden (1811: 56), 'has an elasticity alarming to strangers when they first tread upon it.'

The redoubtable traveller Isabella Bird observed of the Malays, as Marsden did of the Acehnese, that they also made use of this feature to drive away insects, by lighting small fires under the house at dusk. Smoke from the fires would be drawn through the house, dispersing mosquitoes and simultaneously providing relief for buffaloes tethered beneath, as well as fumigating the thatch. Returning from an excursion in the neighbourhood of Melaka, Bird remarks (1883: 141), 'The picturesqueness of the drive home was much heightened by the darkness, and the brilliancy of the fires underneath the Malay houses' (Figure 91). She noted that the open floors, 'though trying to unaccustomed Europeans', had the added advantage that debris from inside the house could easily be swept out through the gaps, and disposed of in these fires.

Very tall piles were sometimes adopted as a security measure, for example, in some Borneo longhouses. Roth (1896: 17–18) illustrates a Kenowit settlement on the Rejang River of Sarawak in the mid-nineteenth

90. Interior of a large Bugis house at Soraja Mannagae, Teteaji, South Sulawesi, 1965. Note the typical slatted floor made of split bamboo, allowing for excellent underfloor ventilation and easy disposal of rubbish through the cracks. (Dorothy Pelzer Collection, courtesy of ISEAS, Singapore)

91. 'Smoking the Mosquitoes', engraving from Isabella Bird's account of her travels in the Malay Peninsula in 1879. (From Bird 1883: 138)

century, whose longhouses tower above the river on enormously elongated piles (Figure 92). He quotes a number of descriptions of houses which were raised 20–40 feet above the ground, some of them being over 500 feet long. The longest Sea Dayak (Bidayuh) house on record, he states, was 771 feet. Sometimes a stockade of logs, or the dense trunks of the *nibong* palm, was added for further protection. Of the Melanau, Crocker (1881: 199) mentions that:

The (Melanau) houses were formerly built on posts of hard wood, raised about 40 feet from the ground, for protection against their enemies. Several of these houses still stand, but they are never replaced or rebuilt now, as, under Sarawak rule, peace and order have been restored.

Sir Spencer St. John (1862: 38) provides the following description of a Kenowit village:

The village consisted of two long houses, one measuring 200 feet, the other 475. They were built on posts about forty

feet in height and some eighteen inches in diameter. The reason they give for making their posts so thick is this: that when the Kayans attack a village they drag one of their long *tamuis* or war boats ashore, and, turning it over, use it as a monstrous shield. About fifty bear it on their heads till they arrive at the ill-made pallisades that surround the hamlets, which they have little difficulty in demolishing; they then get under the house, and endeavour to cut away the posts, being well protected from the villagers above by their extemporized shield. If the posts are thin the assailants quickly gain the victory; if very thick, it gives the garrison time to defeat them by allowing heavy beams and stones to fall upon the boat, and even to bring their little brass war pieces to bear upon it; the Kayans will fly if they suffer a slight loss.

Hudson (1972: 21), writing over a century later of the Ma'anyan of Paju Epat, describes a few houses built on very tall piles still surviving from the 1880s; being expensive and time-consuming to build, once the need for defence had ceased they had nearly all been re-

84

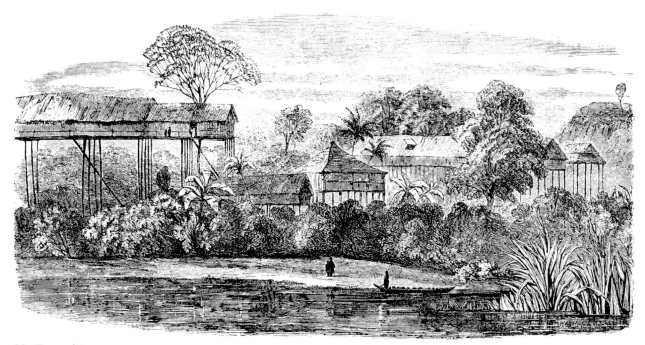

92. 'Town of Kenowit, Rejang River', 1849, engraving from Henry Ling Roth's *The Natives of Sarawak and British North Borneo*. Enormously high piles were a feature of some Borneo longhouses in the days when defence was an important consideration. (From Roth 1896, Vol. 2: 19)

placed by new ones with much lower piles. Incidentally, tall piles represented a distinct adaptational advantage in highly malarial regions of Borneo, one which was almost certainly not consciously articulated by the builders. A historian of malaria notes that sleeping more than 20 feet above the ground helps to keep one out of range of the night-flying female mosquitoes which carry the disease, and postulates that Borneo longhouses represent an adaptation to these conditions (Hobhouse 1985: 5). Nineteenth-century European observers, however, generally attributed the occurrence of fevers among the natives to other factors, such as their allowing all sorts of rubbish to rot underneath the houses, malaria at that time being believed to be caused by the vapours given off by decaying vegetable matter.[5]

The forests of South-East Asia provide a number of woods favoured for house building, foremost among which are the hardwoods such as teak and *cengal* (*Balanocarpus heimii*), a dark wood much used in Malaya and formerly also in Sumatra. These dense woods contain oils which make them resistant to termites. Ironwood (*Eusideroxylon zwageri*) is so hard

that it can endure for up to 150 years. Whole trunks are used for the main posts and beams of Borneo longhouses, and they may often be reused in a new building. Roth (1896: 18) notes:

In many of the villages they have them, descended, it is said, from a long line of ancestors, and these they remove with them wherever they may establish themselves. Time and wear have reduced many of them to less than five inches in diameter, the very heart of the tree, now black with age and exposure.

For temporary buildings, or where wood is expensive or in short supply, bamboo provides a highly versatile and readily available building material. Larger stems provide framing members; split and flattened, they can be used as flooring, or woven to make wall screens. Shorter lengths sliced in half make interlocking tiles, such as are used to roof the family origin-houses of the Toraja. A well-made bamboo roof of this type will last for forty years or so—much longer than its now popular substitute, zinc.

Equally versatile are the palms (which include the rattans or climbing palms).[6] *Nibung* (*Oncosperma tigillarium*) provides one of the hardest woods known, but coconut, sugar palm, and areca (betel-nut) palm may also provide posts or can be split to make floor-boards. Sailing ships from the Riau Islands, off the east coast of Sumatra, may still be seen arriving at Singapore with their cargoes of *nibung* poles, which are used as scaffolding for the construction of high-rise buildings. In the arid islands of Roti and Savu, in eastern Indonesia, where only limited agriculture is possible, a whole economy has developed around the fan-leafed *lontar* palm (*Borassus flabellifer*). The palms are tapped for their sugary juice, which forms an important part of the diet; whole leaves are made into buckets, or split and woven into all kinds of artefacts, including house walls, while the trunk provides wood for house building (Fox 1977) (Figure 93). Palm leaves form one of the commonest thatching materials throughout South-East Asia, the kind of palm used depending on altitude and ecological zone. Most important in coastal areas is the *nipah* (*Nypa fruticans*), whose fronds make a very durable thatch (called *atap* in Malay and Indo-

nesian). Inland, the sago palm (*Metroxylon sagu*), known to the Malays as *rumbia*, is used. *Rumbia* thatch can last for about seven years. Coconut fronds can be used but endure less well. In hilly regions, *bertam* (*Eugeissona tristis*) is often used. Foraging aboriginal peoples of the Malay Peninsula often use *bertam* to thatch their jungle shelters. By far the toughest of all thatches is made from *ijuk*—the rough black fibre found on the trunk of the sugar palm (*Arenga saccarifera*). This fibre, also used to make ropes, is the traditional thatching material of the Minangkabau house. It is so tough that it will endure for up to 100 years.

Grasses may also be used for thatching, though generally they will not last more than two or three years. This depends on the technique and thickness of the thatch, however, for Covarrubias (1937: 95) records that a really well-made Balinese thatch (which may be 0.45 metres thick) 'will last through fifty tropical rainy seasons'. The tough *Imperata cylindrica* species, called *lalang* in Malay, *alang-alang* in Indonesia, and *cogon* in the Philippines, is commonly used.

93. House made from leaves of the lontar palm, on the beach of Raijua Island near Savu, 1987. (Photograph: Roxana Waterson)

At altitudes above 500 metres in the Philippines, another species, *Miscanthus*, is used. In North Thailand, an ingenious roof covering can be made with the *tung* leaf—the broad leaf of a kind of bastard teak (Figure 94). One feature of thatch is that it requires a steep roof angle to provide a good run-off for the heavy rains of the tropics; changes from steep to shallow roof angles in Malay houses this century may be related to the advent of new materials, such as tile and zinc (Hilton 1956: 35). The distinctive style of older buildings, Hilton suggests, developed partly as a result of technical limitations, and when these are removed, the style too may disintegrate as utilitarian considerations of construction become uppermost; it becomes possible to save on materials by lowering the roof and constructing it at a shallower angle (Hilton 1956: 139). Although authors such as Hilton (and probably Westerners in general) find older styles aesthetically more pleasing and condemn such innovations as tasteless, the remarkable popularity of zinc in today's world perhaps deserves some further comment. There are certainly places where it is cheaper than traditional roofing materials, and the labour of installation is much reduced; but it rusts quickly, provides no insulation and so is unbearably hot in hot weather and cold in cold weather, and when tropical rains descend the noise brings conversation to a halt. It can fairly be said that, compared to local materials, it is less well adapted to climatic conditions. Yet, even in places where it is more expensive than traditional alternatives, it is often regarded as prestigious and is a most coveted item.[7] As early as 1907, its use had become popular with the Minangkabau (Kato 1982: 52), which certainly raises a question in the mind about when an item may properly be considered to have become 'traditional', if the word has any meaning at all. In the same way, ground-built houses of stone or concrete, though they may actually be less well adapted to local conditions, often come to be viewed as highly desirable and prestigious. In my concluding chapter, I shall illustrate how 'traditional' and 'modern' notions of prestige may coexist and result in the uniting of elements of old and new to

94. Wall panel made of leaves, Keng Kok, Laos, 1968. (Dorothy Pelzer Collection, courtesy of ISEAS, Singapore/Smithsonian Institution, Washington)

produce 'transitional' styles. But now let us move on from this consideration of the more functional elements of designs to examine the occurrence of some more unusual building elements, which are not essential to a building's structure and which can only be explained by reference to symbolic systems.

The Symbolic Significance of Building Elements

Where anthropologists have given us detailed descriptions of the physical structure of buildings in different South-East Asian societies, their accounts reveal a number of examples of building elements which can only be described as superfluous in terms of the building's structural viability. In symbolic terms, however, these elements may feature very prominently, and as such may be regarded by the builders themselves as essential to the house's strength and stability. An examination of them, as the following examples show, provides us with some valuable insights into conceptions of the house and its place in the scheme of things.

Cunningham, discussing the structure of the house among the Atoni of Timor, shows that its layout reflects a set of ideas about the universe, organized around cardinal points and the east–west 'way of the sun'. Opposed categories such as inner/outer, high/low, front/back, and right/left are used to embody statements about the relationships of those who live in the house (see Chapter 8). The inner/outer dimension appears to be of particular significance in cosmological terms. Informants say that the house must not face east–west, 'because that is the way of the sun' or 'because the sun must not enter the house'. These statements express the notion that the house is set in opposition to the sun, sky, or day (all called *neno* in Atoni). Windowless and dark, the house is segregated from all these external sources of light and heat, but has its own, internal source in the shape of the fire which is kept lit all the time by women. At the summit of the beehive-shaped house roof are two parallel ridge-beams, one above the other. The top one is the larger, and its ends project after the ridge-thatch decoration is tied. It is called the 'sun cranium' (*fuf manas*), while the lower one is called the 'fire cranium' (*fuf ai*). The beams are joined together at the middle by a rope in a figure of eight, which is called *mausak* (a kind of liana), whether or not it is actually made from this liana. The bottom edge of the roof is encircled by a pair of parallel spars called 'hold water' (*tnat oe*). Cunningham points

out that the naming of the two summit beams concerns an opposition or separation of 'heats', one of the hearth fire (*ai*) and the other of the sun (*manas*). The 'hold water' spars at the lower eaves further stress a separation of earth and heaven. They do not literally 'hold water', but symbolically keep rain water (for which most prayers to the Divinity are made) from touching the ground by the house. The word used to mean 'hold' really has the particular sense of 'to hold in giving or receiving in the ceremonial context when a formal gift is made', such as tribute, bridewealth, or food to a host at a feast. Other ritual acts and expressions further show that the house is supposed to be 'cool', and must be made so by means of ritual control of heat and water from the sky (sun and rain) (Cunningham 1964: 50). Gifts in Atoni thought represent the means of linking opposed spheres, and this idea emerges again in the name given to the rope (*mausak*, or *maus* for short) binding the two ridge-beams, of which Cunningham (1964: 52–3) writes:

This rope is *not essential structurally*, but it serves an important symbolic function. *Maus* has two meanings in Atoni: 'a type of liana' and 'things'. In ceremony, *maus* may refer to tribute, bridewealth, or an inheritance, all of which are 'things' which unite in political, affinal or descent contexts. Descent group ritual is termed *nono*, also a type of liana. Binding together, represented by a liana, is appropriate to house symbolism where the mode of opposition is complementarity, not separation (emphasis added).

We may note that the naming of the ridge-beams as 'crania' (and also of the wall posts as 'feet') reflects a conception of the house as body, an idea which we shall encounter again in a number of other societies. Some Atoni houses are even spoken of as having 'arms', 'top-knots' and 'ear-rings' (Cunningham 1964: 66n). Another example of functionally superfluous building elements comes from Sumba. By far the fullest description of the Sumbanese house is to be found in Forth's study of the domain of Rindi in eastern Sumba. Forth details the mode of construction of the house and the names of its parts, and notes that the rafters of the central roof peak are called 'bones'. He notes (1981: 29):

After an ancestral house is built, a piece of rotan twine is attached along the length of each of the *kamundu manu*, *rii ana*, and *rii bai* [the eight main rafters at the four corners and the centre of each side; *rii* means 'bone']. These eight cords are then called the *kalotu rii*, or more simply, the *kalotu*, 'sinews', of the house; and it was explained that just as a man could not endure without sinew, so it is with a house. *They serve no practical function.* Interestingly, the 'sinews', like the 'bones', appear precisely at those positions, or points of transition, which divide and hence articulate the major horizontal sections of the house: the front and back and the two named halves of the house floor (emphasis added).

A third example may be taken from the Sa'dan Toraja of Sulawesi. The most important origin-houses of the nobility, those which formerly were the seats of political power over their respective communities, have the title of *tongkonan layuk* or 'great origin-house'. They have a special feature which is omitted from all other houses, even those built in the same style. This is a large central post called the *a'riri posi* or 'navel-post'. This extra pile, although so prominently positioned, is not essential to the structure and is actually inserted after the house is finished. It symbolizes, however, the status of the ruling house. Sometimes these politically important houses are specifically referred to as *banua diposi* or 'house with a navel'. A significant comparison may be drawn with the concept of power centres as 'navels' among the neighbouring Buginese (see Chapter 6). In the western district of Saluputti, where I did much of my fieldwork, the post is personified as either male or female, depending on whether the main founding ancestor of the house was a man, or his wife. (Origin-houses are always founded by a married couple, but if the house is built on the family land of one of them it will be that individual who is regarded as the most important founder.) Occasionally, I was told, the choice of a 'male' or 'female' post is used to symbolize a 'paired' relationship between two related origin-houses: one will have a 'male' post and the other a 'female' one. The female post is carved with projecting breasts. There is a special ritual for installing the post, which is dressed in male or female garments and head-dress before being placed in position. The post is jointed into one of the main floor beams, and aligns with a pillar inside the house which becomes the focus of the most important fertility-enhancing ritual of the Toraja, the *ma'bua'*. This ritual, which involves many minor stages culminating in a huge communal celebration, takes an entire year to perform. During this year, a group of noble girls are secluded inside the house, and around the central pillar is built a figure of bamboo, grasses, and palm leaves, which is called the *ana' dara* or 'maiden' (Figure 95). Though obviously female, the

95. The figure of the *ana' dara* or 'maiden', built around the central pillar of a noble house when it sponsors the greatest of all Toraja life-enhancing rituals, the *ma'bua'*. The women, dressed in yellow (a colour associated with life), spend a year in seclusion inside the house prior to the climactic final celebration. During this period, the house itself is said to be 'pregnant'. Kalimbuang village, Sareale, Tana Toraja, 1982. (Photograph: Roxana Waterson)

ana' dara, with a complementarity typical of South-East Asian symbolism, also includes a symbolically male element in the form of a spear. For the duration of the period leading up to the final climactic ceremony, the house itself is considered to be pregnant.[8] For several years after the completion of the rite, the whole community is thought to go on benefiting from the enhanced fertility and good fortune which its celebration is supposed to bring.

The structural superfluity of the Toraja 'navel-post', then, contrasts with its obvious centrality in symbolic terms. Moreover, we begin to see from the examples above that such symbolic elements as these have their place within larger schemes in which the house serves as a representation of the cosmos, society, or the human body. In the next chapter, I turn my attention to these cosmological ideas and the way they influence the structure of both houses and settlements.

1. An indication of the potential length of time that commitment to a certain architectural style may last is to be found in Oliver's suggestion (1987: 159) that the circular forms of Navajo hogans in south-western USA, and the symbolic division of space within them, may well represent a continuity with the yurt forms of Central Asia. He points out that the Navajo originate from the main cluster of Athapaskan-speaking peoples who inhabit northern Canada, Yukon, and Alaska, close to the Aleutian land-bridge by which the Mongol peoples many millennia ago are believed to have crossed into the Americas.

2. An example from Micronesia comes from the atolls of Kiribati, where Woolard (1988: 9) suggests that the separate floor and roof structures serve to minimize damage to the lightweight structure from mechanical movement caused by wind and movement of the occupants. The roof structure rests on its own posts, which are here enclosed by the floor structure.

3. Pelras (1975: 63) notes that the greater height of house piles among the Bugis in former days was likewise designed to protect against spear-thrusts:

'The Bugis freely remark that the reason the old houses were built so high was to place the floor out of reach of enemy lance-thrusts. The protection thus offered was obviously partial at best, for the stairs were fixed in place and the roofs could very easily be set on fire' (my translation).

4. See Clément and Charpentier (1975b) for a description of both these types of construction in different areas of Laos.

5. It was not until 1897 that the British doctor Sir Ronald Ross first proved that malaria was transmitted by the anopheles mosquito.

6. For information on palms, see Whitmore (1977).

7. Regarding the prestige attaching to the climatically mal-adapted zinc, Rapoport (1969: 22) provides an amusing example from South America, where a local Andean community refused to collaborate in the construction of a school unless it were to be given a zinc roof. The architects did their best to overcome the resulting lack of insulation by installing a traditional thatch roof underneath the zinc one.

8. For fuller descriptions and analyses of the *ma'bua'* rite, see Nooy-Palm (1980), Waterson (1984a), and Volkman (1985: 56–8).

CHAPTER 5
Cosmologies

UNUSUAL features of buildings, serving symbolic rather than functional purposes, are merely a part of more complex patterns of symbolism which are woven into indigenous architectures, making them resonant with meaning. Human beings use built form as one means of creating for themselves a sense of place, and as such, the forms reflect the world views of their creators. South-East Asia offers an especially rich field for investigation of the influence of cosmological ideas upon house and settlement patterns. It would be impossible, for reasons of space, to do justice to all the published information on the subject; I have therefore chosen to restrict myself to discussion in this chapter of a few notable examples including Nias, Bali, Sumba, and the Badui of Sunda (West Java), in all of which the cosmological aspects of architecture are particularly elaborated.

The idea of 'place' deserves some further consideration here. The use of architecture to create bounded, organized spaces is after all not universal. There are cultures, including some in South-East Asia itself, in which people content themselves with the very simplest and most ephemeral of shelters, expending so little effort on their construction that one must pose the question (as Rapoport (1975) has for the Aborigines of Australia) whether they have any sense of place at all, and if so, from what is it derived? Such cultures in which shelter is minimal are essentially those of nomadic forest peoples who live by foraging, such as the Semang groups of the Malay Peninsula and the Punan of Borneo (Figure 96); one might include the so-called 'Sea Gypsies' who are nomads of the sea and live entirely in their boats.[1] Those who lead a foraging lifestyle must maintain an ideological commitment to non-materialism; they could have no use for elaborate houses since they are always on the move. Nor are houses necessary as a means of displaying rank or wealth, since these societies almost invariably are among the most egalitarian known to us. They depend directly upon the land (or sea) and its resources, their relationship to which is extremely intimate. Their sense of location thus embraces the entire environment and has almost nothing to do with man-made structures. Religion and myth reflect this attitude, in which humans see themselves as embedded in nature, co-operating with it, and maintaining reciprocal relations with its different elements. The cosmologies of many hunter–gatherer societies are as rich and elaborate as their material possessions are few.[2]

Historically, the invention of agriculture may be identified as a first step in the long process of human beings' alienation from nature. Only then did nature come to be seen as an antagonist—something to be dominated, owned, and exploited. House building, too, must have formed one of the earliest stages in this process, for it initiates a quite literal shift from a natural to a manufactured environment. The more effort is expended on built forms, the more architecture mediates our experience of the natural world, even as it may continue to mirror the social construction of cosmological ideas.[3] In modern industrial societies, the process has reached such an extreme that buildings maroon us inside gigantic bubbles of artificial climate, within which we might pass our whole lives without ever touching the ground or knowing where food comes from. Among the animist peoples of the Austronesian world, however, the fragmenting of a holistic world view appears to be deliberately resisted. In these cosmologies, humans still participate in nature on very much the same terms as everything else. Crops like rice have souls which have to be looked after and treated with respect; the Iban, for example, imagine the souls of rice to form a whole society, mirroring that of humans (Freeman 1970: 7). The house, too, vegetal like its surroundings, shares in the life force which animates the universe; like everything else in the en-

96. Punan shelters in the Borneo jungle. Simply constructed of branches and leaves, the habitations of these nomads are hardly distinguishable from the surrounding environment. Tillema (1938) suggests that such camouflage was partly deliberate, intended as a protection against raids by the head-hunting Iban. (From Tillema 1938: 245, courtesy of Rijksmuseum voor Volkenkunde, Leiden)

vironment, it is viewed as a subjective entity with which interaction and communication are possible.[4]

Houses and settlements, then, are but one of a number of possible elements which, in a given society, may contribute to the sense of location by which humans orient themselves in the world. They are, as I shall argue, for most South-East Asian societies particularly salient elements in a far from inanimate universe. Let us now look more closely at some of the organizing concepts of these cosmologies.

As a starting-point for an investigation of such ideas, it is interesting to reflect on the range of meanings of present-day cognates of the word *banua*, a word which has a very wide distribution in Austronesian languages. It is included in reconstructions of Proto-Austronesian, where it is given the meanings of 'continent, land, settlement, village, town, country' (Wurm and Wilson 1975: 44, 117, 183). Reconstructions of a Proto-Philippine language also give *banuwa* as 'sky' (Charles 1973). *Banua* (*wanua*, *benua*) has an equally wide range of referents in modern Austronesian languages, from 'house' or 'village' to 'continent' and 'cosmos'. Sa'dan Toraja *banua*, for example, means 'house' (Waterson 1986), while for their neighbours the Bugis, *wanua* refers to a 'territory' under the leadership of an elder or a noble lord.[5] In Minahasa (North Sulawesi), *wanua* means 'village' or 'locality' (Lundstrom-Bürghoorn 1981), while in the languages of Mindanao in the southern Philippines, *banwa* refers to a 'domain' (a district or group of villages).[6] In Nias, *banua* can mean 'village', 'world', and 'sky/heavens'; both early writings and more recent studies reveal the symbolic organization of the village around its own centre, forming a microcosm reflecting Nias concepts of the world in many of its organizational features (Suzuki 1959: 56–77; Feldman 1977). The Toba Batak, too, used the word *banua* to refer, in traditional cosmology, to the three 'levels' of the cosmos, the sky, earth, and underworld, which were called *banua ginjang*, *banua tonga*, and *banua toru*, respectively (Tobing 1956).

King states that among the Maloh of Kalimantan, *banua* refers both to the village and to the class of free commoners who make up the majority of Maloh society (King 1976b: 308; 1985: 126). Finally, in modern Indonesian, *benua* has the meaning of 'continent' or 'realm'. The same word recurs in Polynesian languages, for example, Tahitian *fenoa* ('island') and Fijian *vanua* ('land'). The range of meanings, particularly the combination of senses in the Nias and possibly the Philippine case, is suggestive of patterns of thought in which the layout of human settlements is regarded as reflecting in some sense that of the cosmos itself.

Given that the sea has always been such an integral and important element in island South-East Asian life, we may note here, too, that the commonest reconstructions of Proto-Austronesian words for 'boat' are *bangka* and *baranggay*, words which in contemporary Austronesian societies sometimes have the senses of boat/boatload and sometimes of house/household, or of some other small social unit (Wurm and Wilson 1975: 21–2; Manguin 1986). An example is Tagalog *baranggay* ('village'). Boats provide a convenient metaphor both for spatial order, and for ordered, hierarchical relationships—both essential on board ship. As Manguin (1986: 201) puts it:

Ship-like shapes may thus be seen as an essential organizing principle of an orderly society.... The traditional question of a Balinese enquiring about a person's rank: 'Where do you sit?', is accurately thought of, in neighbouring societies, in terms of places aboard a ship, thus providing a clear image of social order, as enacted in rituals.

Where symbolic parallels are drawn between boat and house or community, this need not be explained as some cultural survival of a literal boat community of the distant Austronesian past. The presence or absence of these ideas in different societies of the archipelago may be taken rather as evidence of how organizing concepts such as these 'are constantly being set aside, developed or reconstructed' over time (Manguin 1986: 188).

How is the world itself conceived? Most indigenous belief systems of the Indonesian archipelago share the concept of a three-tiered cosmos, consisting of a middle world inhabited by humans, sandwiched between an upper and a lower world. In Aceh, which was the first part of Indonesia to receive Islamic influences, Islam has fused with such older cosmological ideas (Wessing 1984: 39). Dall draws attention to the way the structure of the house may be seen to reflect the division of the cosmos into three layers; the sacred upper world, abode of the gods, the middle world inhabited by humans, and the nether world, abode of animals and lower deities. The area beneath the house is the most unclean part, where rubbish and faeces are thrown down from the kitchen and where animals are stalled. The house floor, raised above the earth on piles, is the part inhabited by humans, while the attic space—where heirlooms are stored—is the most sacred. In the Acehnese house, a heavily decorated skirting-board surrounds the whole house at floor level. Unlike the ring-beam of the Toba, Karo, or Simalungun house, this board is not a structural unit, but all the same it must not be omitted. Dall (1982: 51) suggests that it serves to accentuate the separation of the human living space from the profane underpart of the house. The same three-tiered division of the house has been remarked on by a number of ethnographers, for example, in Sunda (Wessing 1978: 62), among the Bugis (S. Errington 1979: 13), and on Roti (Wetering 1923: 471). It is indeed the norm throughout the archipelago, implicitly or explicitly reflecting cosmological ideas.

Houses and settlements may follow a variety of rules of orientation, either according to geographical features, such as an opposition between mountain and sea, as in Bali (Covarrubias 1937: 76) or Kédang (Barnes 1974), or upriver and down, as among the Ngaju (Schärer 1963: 66), or in relation to the cardinal points. In many such schemata the directions of east and west assume particular importance, with the common association of the rising sun with life and the setting sun with death. However, other directional concepts are much harder to grasp. Sometimes a whole set of co-ordinates is brought into play, as in Sumba where space is categorized not in terms of fixed cardinal points but of oppositions between 'upstream'/ 'downstream' and the 'head' and 'tail' of the island itself, as well as the rising and setting sun; these axes are defined independently of each other and relative to any given point of reference (Forth 1981:65). Forth notes several examples of societies where 'left' and 'right' are mapped on to the directional schema. The Rotinese and the Atoni both treat the east–west axis as the fixed one, north and south being expressed as 'left' and 'right'. In Ende (eastern Flores), the 'sea'–'land' axis is the fixed one, and 'left' and 'right' are defined in relation to this, when one is facing the sea (Forth 1981: 65). Whatever the points of reference may be, questions of orientation assume great importance and individuals are always aware of directions. In many local languages, for example, one typically greets a person by asking where they are coming from or going to; answers are given in terms of precise directions. In Sumba one answers in terms of upstream/downstream, etc. (Forth 1981: 58), while in Toraja words for 'going to' and 'coming from', as well as being in a particular location are modified depending on the cardinal directions involved. Either of these systems provides headaches for learners of the language who lack the necessary awareness of their orientation at any given moment. So strong is this awareness among the Balinese that an individual who has temporarily lost his bearings in relation to the 'mountain' direction, *kaja*, may become quite incapacitated by this disorientation, for example, a dancer becomes unable to dance (Bateson 1973: 89). A geographical metaphor is even applied by the Karo Batak to the interior of the house, where two raised floors run on either side of the central gutter or passage. The floors slope down somewhat from the walls towards the centre. The higher part is called *gunung* (mountain), and is the most honoured part, where people sleep, while the lower and least honoured part, near the centre, is called *sawah* (ricefield) (Sargeant and Saleh 1973: 3). This terminology creates a sort of landscape inside the house, which is thus a reflection of the natural world.

Commonly, too, rules of orientation are followed when lying down to sleep. Even the boat-dwelling Bajau follow a rule that one should always sleep crosswise, not lengthwise, in a boat, for the dead are buried lengthwise in a coffin made of a boat sawn in half.[7] The association of the 'wrong' direction with death is common elsewhere; Ellen (1986: 12n) reports that the Nuaulu sleep lying on an east–west axis and believe they will die if they sleep lying on the 'mountain'–'sea' (north–south) axis. The Toraja, too, sleep east to west. A corpse, at a certain point of the funeral ceremony, is turned with its head to the south (the direction of the land of the dead), and is only then considered fully dead; until this point, it has been referred to as 'the sleeping' or 'the sick' one, and has been regularly offered food and betel-nut at mealtimes. Even reed mats, within the house, are always laid out with their patterns running east–west, except when a funeral is in progress. Acciaioli records that the Bugis consider that to sleep facing the north is to be like a 'dead person', but they utilize this resemblance for magical purposes, believing that this orientation protects them from being struck by others' 'knowledge' (magic). If a Buginese sleeps facing the east, he should put his feet to the side so as not to 'step' on the direction of Mecca.[8] The Muang or Northern Thai sleep with their heads to the east, and regard the other directions as dangerous; the eastern wall of the bedroom is called 'the sleeping head' (Davis 1984: 50).[9]

Among the Toraja, houses always face north, the direction called 'head of the sky' (*ulu langi'*), which is associated with the 'heads' or sources of rivers. The south is called 'tail of the sky' (*pollo' langi'*) and the south end of the house is called *pollo' banua*. The north is the domain of Puang Matua, the 'Old Lord' of the sky, a major deity who created human beings. The south is the direction of the afterlife. East is the direction of life, the rising sun, deities, and life-affirming rituals, while west is associated with death, mortuary rituals, and ancestors in their deified form. In older houses, the hearth was always positioned in the central room on the east side, and the placentae of new-born babies are buried by the father on the east side of the house. Whenever offerings are made in or around the house, the direction in which they are laid out indicates whether they are intended for the deities or the ancestors. Even the four colours with which house carvings are painted have their directional associations, borne out in the use of colours in ritual; white is the colour of Puang Matua and the north; yellow of the deities and the east. Red, the colour of the setting sun, belongs to the west, and black to the south, to ancestors, and the dead. The structure provided by the cardinal points unites dimensions of both time and space, since it functions both in terms of geography and of a chronological sequence of rites, all of which in Toraja are associated either with the east or with the west. The course of human life itself parallels the passage of the sun from east to west.[10]

Most indigenous cosmologies named four cardinal points, though Hindu influence in some areas led to an elaboration of this basic schema. I mentioned in my Introduction van Ossenbruggen's pioneering analysis of the Hindu 4/5 pattern, representing the cardinal points with a fifth point at the centre, as it was applied to the layout of Javanese villages. There is, however, a strong possibility that rather than being an entirely novel idea, this Hindu schema was merely mapped on to already existing concepts, with which it happens to accord very closely. Shelly Errington (1983a: 547) comments that the traditional Buginese view of the universe includes seven dimensions: 'right, left, front, back, up, down, and the Datu (Ruler) in the pusat'. The Ruler is traditionally conceived of as occupying the navel (*pusat*) or still centre of the universe (an idea which is reflected in other Indonesian kingdoms which absorbed Hindu influence, particularly in Sunda (Wessing 1978, 1979), Java (Moertono 1968), Bali (Geertz 1980), and Timor (Schulte Nordholt 1971). Of the Bugis, Errington (1983a: 547) writes:

In traditional accounts, the navel of the polity was the navel of the world itself, the place where Batara Guru, a spirit from the upper world, descended to the middle world with his myriad of followers and retainers to become the first ruler of Luwu. The navel of the world was defined by the ruler, by the regalia or ornaments (inherited objects from the ancestors), and by their place of residence.

(Notice the emphasis upon house and heirlooms, featuring here as important attributes of the ruler.) The salience of the navel and of spatial 'navel-centres', in spite of these Hindu associations, is very likely to be a concept of older, Austronesian origin, especially in view of its very wide distribution and the fact that cognates of *pusat* itself occur in reconstructions of Proto-Austronesian (Wurm and Wilson 1975: 136).

The Toba Batak, whose language includes a significant proportion of Sanskrit-derived words (including *huta* for 'settlement' and *desa*, used to mean 'cardinal point'—a word which in Malay, Javanese, or Balinese has the sense of 'village' or 'territorial unit'; Gonda 1952: 81), under Hindu influence expanded their conception of the cardinal points from four to eight. The names in the eight-point system are clearly derived from Sanskrit (Parkin 1978: 200–15). The Batak calendar used for divination was also Hindu-derived. An eight-pointed design derived from Indian mandalas, which occurs with great frequency as a house-carving motif, represents the cardinal points and is called *bindu matoga* or 'powerful power-point' (Figure 97). This figure was also drawn on the ground at annual rites of renewal, with an egg placed at the centre, and the *datu* or priests would dance around it with their magic staffs. At the conclusion of the dance, one of the dancers would plunge his staff into the egg. The diagram itself thus served as a microcosm which could be used in ritual symbolically to destroy the cosmos in order to create it again, with the 'planting' of the *datu*'s staff, which symbolized the 'tree of life' of Toba mythology

97. Eight-pointed *bindu matoga* motif painted on the wall of a Toba Batak house, 1986. Derived from Indian mandalas, it represents the eight cardinal points. At the centre is the scorpion (*hala*), while the whole design is ringed by the *naga* or snake; both are associated with the underworld. According to pre-Hindu ideas, the *naga* controlled the four compass points; under Hindu influence, these became expanded to eight. The three-pronged motifs at the eight points represent the trident of Siva, who according to Hindu ideas controls the compass points (see Parkin 1978: 207 ff.) We can thus discern here a blending of indigenous and Hindu concepts, such as occurred widely throughout the archipelago. (Photograph: Roxana Waterson)

(Tobing 1956: 173).

The theme of the powerful centre which stands in complementary opposition to the periphery is a typically South-East Asian example of what Lévi-Strauss (1963: 135ff.) has termed 'concentric dualism'. This hierarchical representation of space is used as an expression of political relations as well as giving shape to the world view of the people concerned. The layout of many ancient South-East Asian capitals reflects the concept of a powerful centre, channelling power from the cosmos and dispersing it to the periphery. The influence of kings was strongest at the centre of their polities and tailed off towards the indeterminate boundaries of their kingdoms (Heine-Geldern 1942; Tambiah 1976; Geertz 1980). It is not my intention to discuss these ideas at greater length, since my major concern is not with centralized states and their achievements of monumental architecture, but with the smaller-scale societies of the region and their more perishable vernacular architectures. However, as we have seen, these Hindu conceptions also reached and were absorbed by quite distant communities of the archipelago (sometimes at second or third hand), where they were integrated with already existing world views.

The Badui

A strangely elaborate interweaving of settlement, geography, and cosmology is to be found in the case of the Badui of Sunda (West Java), of whom a brief account is provided by Wessing (1977). The Badui live in the mountains of South Banten, the westernmost province of Sunda, where they have steadfastly resisted Islamization. In an earlier period, they are said to have resisted Hindu influence as well, and until today they retain their own beliefs and maintain their distinctiveness as a group by means of numerous taboos on things regarded as 'modern'. Their territory is prohibited to outsiders, and among the cultural items they reject are wet rice agriculture, writing, the use of money, and glass windows.

There is an 'inner' and an 'outer' Badui territory, the 'inner' (which in Sundanese patterns of thought generally also implies 'higher' in status) being the most sacred. Here there are three villages, the total number of households in which must always be kept constant by moving people in and out of the 'outer' villages when necessary. Within the 'inner' territory, all taboos must be strictly followed and transgressions can be punished by exile to the 'outer' villages. The inner Badui wear white robes, while the outer wear black (indigo). The outer Badui do have some contact with outsiders, so that over time some Islamic ideas have, in fact, been absorbed into Badui thought even in the inner area.

At the centre of the inner Badui territory is an area called *Artja Domas*, which is conceptually the sacred centre of the Badui (and perhaps also the Sundanese) world. It consists of a series of thirteen terraces topped by a tall stone column and is said to be regarded as the place where souls go after death. This powerful centre

is thought to draw power from the cosmos for the benefit of the periphery. Thus, to the Sundanese as a whole, the existence of the Badui territory serves to maintain cosmic harmony, and its people, since they rigorously maintain old traditions, are regarded as the true guide to *adat* customs. Not just their own exclusiveness, suggests Wessing (1977: 301), but also the fact that they serve this reassuring function for the Sundanese as a whole, explains why the Badui continue to exist as a discrete entity today. In fact, the Indonesian Government had, by 1978, succeeded in resettling some landless 'Outer Badui' in new villages where they were given land, houses, and communal facilities including health services. This was done as part of a wider government programme to resettle its 'isolated tribes' (*suku terasing*), although there appears to be no attempt to force change upon the 'Inner Badui' (Djauhari Sumintardja 1979).

The Badui are not the only Indonesian community to maintain this unusual relationship with the outside world. There were definitely other such communities in Java, though the customs of the Badui are the best known and best preserved.[11] A brief but vivid account of another group, who inhabit an area called Tana Towa in Bone, South Sulawesi, is provided by Hanbury-Tenison (1975: 126–36). Accompanied by the anthropologist Christian Pelras, this author was allowed the honour, unprecedented for a European, of a visit to the inner territory of Tana Towa, where he was granted an audience with the *Ama Towa* himself. As in the Badui case, there is an inner and an outer territory of Tana Towa. The *Ama Towa*, who resides in the inner region and must never leave it, is the spiritual leader of both the inner and outer regions, while the *Arung* is the temporal leader of both regions, and resides in the outer one. The people wear home-woven clothes of dark indigo or black, speak an archaic form of Makassarese, and build houses of a distinctive pattern, supposedly based upon that of the first house, which came into being miraculously near the heart of Tana Towa territory. Humans, too, are also said to have originated here.[12] Like the Badui, the people of Tana Towa resist all modern and manufactured goods. Though they officially became Muslim, like their neighbours, in the early seventeenth century, they maintain that their old religion encompasses much more and therefore cannot be changed. Hanbury-Tenison observes that the people of Tana Towa are regarded by the Buginese with much the same awe as are the Badui by the Sundanese and Javanese, and they fulfil the same functions as mystic oracles and suppliers of talismans; the highest-ranking officials may seek their advice. Not surprisingly, very little is known by outsiders about these communities; but their relationship to the surrounding peoples, as the bearers and guardians of older cosmological traditions, is a specially intriguing one.

Orientations in Bali

Bali presents us with a particularly fertile field of exploration in terms of the application of ideas about orientations to the layout of settlements and dwellings. A considerable literature exists on this topic (see, for example, Covarrubias 1937; C. Geertz 1959; Swellengrebel 1960; Tan 1967; Soelarto 1973; Lansing 1974; Geertz and Geertz 1975; Soebadio 1975; Hobart 1978; Howe 1983; Lovric 1987). C. Geertz (1959) stresses the great diversity of Balinese village forms. Though based on common principles of organization, no one village is quite like another. Villagers share certain obligations, for example, to worship at and maintain certain temples. Each locality has three main types of temple—an origin-temple, *Pura Puseh* (literally, 'navel-temple'), supposedly the temple built when the village was first founded; the *Pura Dalam* or graveyard temple, for spirits of the dead; and the *Pura Balai Agung* or 'great council' temple of the gods, chiefly concerned with agricultural fertility. There are many other types of temples as well, with membership based on caste, kinship, associational, or political affiliations. Every adult villager has duties to a number of associations, those concerned with the *banjar* or hamlet (which is the main rural political and territorial unit); the *subak*, or irrigation society; groups concerned with the upkeep of temples, as well as voluntary groups of many kinds who co-operate in various economic and artistic endeavours. Memberships of all these groups cut across each other—for example, an irrigation society nearly always has members from several different *banjar*. A man and his wife, as a couple, have their duties in several of these organizations; if a man has no wife, he must have a female relative to act as his partner in order to participate (Geertz and Geertz 1975: 90). A 'village', then, is not so much a clearly bounded unit as the intersection, in C. Geertz's terms, of all these different 'planes' of social organization; each village has its own idiosyncrasies, with some organizational principles assuming greater prominence than others.

The Balinese are highly conscious of orientations, both in their everyday life and in the construction of buildings. According to early Dutch ethnographers, whose formulations have been repeated in numerous later publications, central to their view of the world is the opposition between mountains and sea, *kaja* and *kelod*. The mountains (particularly the great volcanic peak of Gunung Agung) are the home of the gods, while the sea is the habitation of demons. To the South Balinese, the mountain direction is to the north and the sea to the south; for North Balinese, the situation is reversed and south becomes the auspicious, mountain direction. This view has recently come under criticism from Lovric (1987), however, as being an overly simplistic and rigid version of Balinese cosmology—a kind of 'conceptual straitjacket' which has hindered understanding of the real complexities and ambiguities of Balinese concepts of the supernatural. Far from being polarized into 'good' and 'evil', Lovric found from informants in Sanur that the associations of the directions were far more ambiguous. The sea is not simply dangerous, it is also a source of power, life, and knowledge, and a place of purification. It is, for example, where the purified ashes of the dead are scattered that they may be still further purified, and where sacred masks and ornaments of gods are periodically cleansed. Both sea and mountains, and indeed all parts of the environment, are home to both demons and gods.

Many ritual prescriptions surround the construction of a house and the choice of propitious days for beginning the work or taking up occupation. The elaborateness of this system certainly owes something to Hindu cosmological ideas, as preserved and recorded by the priests. Complicated written texts exist containing the regulations for house building; but most of the time the work is carried out by carpenters who simply retain an oral memory of the general principles. Buildings are always laid out within an enclosed courtyard. Gateways are marked by split gates, often with a screen just inside, so that one turns to the side upon entering. Evil spirits are supposed to be deterred by this layout, since they cannot turn corners easily. In a large aristocratic or princely establishment, which is really an expansion of the courtyard idea into a number of interconnecting yards, all the gateways and entrances are arranged so as to ensure that one takes a winding course throughout the complex. Most of the buildings take the form of open pavilions, and daily life takes place almost entirely in the open air. Apart from granaries, the only enclosed part is the *uma meten* or sleeping quarters of the householder and his wife, which is windowless and dark. Heirlooms are also stored here, sometimes buried in the floor.

The layout of structures within the courtyard conforms to the rules of a ninefold cosmology, consisting of the eight cardinal points and a central point. The centre or 'navel' of the compound is an open yard, scene of many daily activities. The family shrine is always positioned in the holiest, north-east corner. The *uma meten*, probably the next most important building, is to the north. Kitchen and granary are to the south, and open-walled pavilions to east and west (Figure 98). A nobleman may build a *bale gede*, a special square pavilion on a high base, in the east. This is used for various day-to-day purposes such as working, sitting, sleeping, or playing, but is also the site for the performance of certain rites of passage such as birth, a baby's fortieth-day ceremony, tooth-filing in adolescence, and marriage. Dead bodies are also laid in state here before cremation. The entire courtyard is also

compared to a human being, the different buildings having particular associations with a part of the body (Covarrubias 1937: 88).[13]

Village, House, and Cosmos in Sumba

Less formalized than in the Indicized states of Java and Bali, but in their way equally complex, are the world views developed in some other islands of Indonesia. Sumba, which lies east of Sumbawa and south of Flores in the Nusa Tenggara archipelago, was once known to European navigators as the 'Sandalwood Island', but heavy deforestation over the centuries has left it arid and generally infertile. The population lives mainly on maize and raises livestock, especially on the savannah grasslands of the eastern part of the island. Sumba has a flourishing tradition of stone working, and the dragging of funerary stones and erection of carved stone graves are still a source of social prestige for Sumbanese. By far the fullest description of house and village layout in Sumba is to be found in the work of Forth (1981), from which most of the following is

98. Courtyard of a Balinese house at Batuan village, Gianyar, looking north, 1988. In the middle of the photograph may be seen the enclosed *uma meten*, where the householders sleep, with open pavilions to east and west, and the vacant 'navel' or yard in the centre. (Photograph: Garth Sheldon)

drawn.[14] I cannot do justice to his very detailed analysis here but will briefly describe some of the principles of organization involved. Like many 'asymmetric alliance' systems of eastern Indonesia, the Sumbanese make great play of symbolic pairing or opposition of 'male' and 'female' elements, a mode of thought which is reflected in the imagery of ritual verses, as well as in the naming of house parts in 'male' and 'female' pairs.[15] In their conceptions of space, a number of other dualisms are brought into play, though as Forth makes clear, meanings may shift according to context. For example, in ritual the innermost, sacred parts of the house are thought of as masculine, being specially associated with male clan ancestors, but in the context of daily life the house, the running of which is a female concern, is regarded as female by contrast with the outside, which is male (Forth 1981: 40-1).

The typical Rindi village, as described by Forth, is roughly rectangular in plan, sometimes surrounded by a wall or fence (though today these have often fallen into disrepair). An open central plaza (talora) is edged on either side by one or more rows of houses built close together. In the centre of the plaza, and aligned with the rows of houses, are rows of rectangular stone graves. The plaza, according to Rindi ideas, should be kept free of weeds, thereby accentuating the contrast between the ordered, cultural, and 'cool' space of the village and the wild and 'hot' exterior beyond its boundaries; this idea of a 'cool' interior and a 'hot' exterior is also carried over to the house itself. In the centre of the plaza are also situated the yard altar (closely associated with the leading clan house), and 'skull post' or 'skull tree' (andu katiku tau), made out of dead branches, on which in former times the skulls of enemy victims were displayed. As well as providing a potent symbol of the strength and security of the village, the skull tree was thought to ensure fertility and rain, and was the focus of war rituals. The village has two main gates, situated at either end, and called the 'upstream' and 'downstream' gate. In addition, there are also often two other entrances, in the middle of the two long sides, called 'waist gates'. Adams's (1974) plan of a clan capital in Kapunduku domain shows very much the same features, the centre of the village being occupied by a village altar, a crops altar, graves, and a skull tree, while flat stones mark the place where a forked-post altar is erected on ritual occasions.

The Sumbanese have been relatively unenthusiastic converts to Christianity, and the majority of them continue to adhere to their traditional religion, the agama marapu or 'religion of the ancestors'. The marapu are deified founding ancestors of patrilineal clans. The ancestors are closely associated not only with their stone sarcophagi but with the clan house itself, and particularly with its peak where the sacred heirlooms and 'house treasures' are stored. A striking feature of village layout is the intimate mingling of the dead with the living, of tombs and houses, within the same space. In mountain villages of West Sumba, where the terrain sometimes dictates a more crowded disposition of structures within the village, the proximity of houses and graves is even more noticeable than in the east of the island (Figure 99). Another feature is the often triadic division of space within the village, with two opposing ends (called 'head' and 'tail') mediated by a centre.[16] As well as tripartite divisions, which Adams (1980) points out also recur in textile motifs, we find again in Sumba a possible echo of Hindu cosmology in the occurrence of the 4/5 pattern. The four gate altars and the central yard altar together create a pattern of four with a central, uniting fifth element which recurs in conceptions of the spirits associated with the four main house pillars and the centre of the house foundation. Forth (1981: 124, 241) also encountered the idea that the earth itself is supported on four house posts arranged around a central fifth one. According to the people of Rindi, earthquakes are caused when a mouse gnaws this central pillar, or when a cat which guards the pillar chases it away. Like the peak of the ancestral house, which is a sacred but largely empty space at the house's centre, the centre of the village yard is kept empty of graves or other structures and is considered to be the place of a male and female spirit who are superior to those of the various village altars. The central element thus balances and unites the subordinate and surrounding four.[17] The idea of a powerful centre and subordinate periphery is again reflected in some domains at the level of relations between villages, where chiefly villages are built on high ground and surrounded by villages of lower-lying, subsidiary houses (Forth 1981: 48). Village orientations are further influenced by alignments in terms of the path of the sun and of upstream/downstream directions, as well as ideas about 'heads' and 'tails', applied not only to villages but to houses, graves, fields, rivers, and the island of Sumba itself (Forth 1981: 67). Forth meticulously builds up a picture of a set of principles of organization which are applied at many different levels in the

99. Tall-peaked clan houses and stone graves cluster together in the West Sumbanese village of Tarung, Loli district, 1987. Villages here lack the large central plaza typical of the eastern part of the island. (Photograph: Roxana Waterson)

Sumbanese world view, from the house to its geographical surroundings, and, ultimately, the cosmos itself. Most people, he makes clear, do not know (or cannot articulate) all the rules governing spatial arrangements, nor do all settlements necessarily conform to the rules (though those containing ancestral houses do so).

There are two main types of house. Both are built on piles and are structurally similar apart from their roof shapes. Clan houses (*uma mbatangu*) have a tall peak, shaped like a truncated pyramid, rising from the centre of the roof (Plate 9). This peak houses ancestral relics and 'house treasures' of the clan. Such a house is also referred to as 'ancestral house' (*uma marapu*) or 'big house' (*uma bokulu*). The second type of house, with no tower, is called *uma kamudungu*, or 'bald house'. These houses are thought of as 'cool' and are viewed as an extension to the ancestral house, which serves as meeting place and major ritual site for its descendants. The ancestral house, because of its intimate association with the ancestors and the sacred, is by contrast thought of as 'hot'. As in other societies

mentioned thus far, a tripartite image of the cosmos is echoed in the spatial division of the house into an under section (used for stabling of animals and as a place for women to weave), the 'platform' or habitable space, and the roof with its peak, the sacred space associated with the ancestors. Within the house a number of spatial and symbolic oppositions come into play, including upper/lower, right/left, front/back, centre/periphery, and male/female. The pairing of elements as 'male' and 'female' is particularly prominent, as is the choice of auspicious, even numbers, particularly four and eight. The rules governing house layout and the use of space will receive further attention in Chapter 8.

Village and Cosmos in Nias

The island of Nias lies off the west coast of Sumatra. It is mountainous and heavily forested, the land descending in the north toward crocodile-infested mangrove swamps, and fertile plains where rice and coconuts are cultivated, while the south is drier and hillier. Patches of virgin forest remain in the centre of the island, and huge trees furnish the giant house beams and pillars which are such a prominent feature of Nias's finest buildings. Niassans were fierce warriors with a reputation for head-hunting. During the latter half of the nineteenth century the southerners in particular successfully resisted Dutch attempts at a military take-over. Government and missions made little inroad until the early twentieth century. The North, by contrast, was able to offer little concerted resistance and had become heavily Christianized and acculturated by the end of the nineteenth century. Broadly, Nias may be divided into three cultural areas, the North, Centre, and South. The culture of the Central region blends into that of the North. House styles of the North are distinctively different from those of the South, the houses having an oval plan. In the South, a more elaborate social hierarchy, with ranks of nobles, commoners, and slaves, developed. Slaves were sometimes sacrificed as part of rituals or 'feasts of merit'. Well-built and fortified villages were controlled by powerful chiefs, who maintained standing armies, and who in the nineteenth century had gained enormous wealth—and the latest firearms—through the trade of war captives as slaves to the North Sumatran kingdom of Aceh (Feldman 1977: 37). It seems that the slave trade was already a significant factor in the economy by the early seventeenth century, and by 1822 the British reported that 1,500 slaves a year were being exported from South Nias (Feldman 1984: 24). Gold was one of the items sought in exchange; there is no gold on Nias itself, but it could be obtained from Sumatra, and assumed a great importance within the local economy and prestige system—it was used not only to make ornaments for the nobility, but for the payment of bridewealth. Units of gold were (and still are) used to measure the worth of other goods such as pigs. The fullest description of architecture in South Nias is provided by Feldman (1977), from whom much of the following information is derived.[18]

In the Nias language the word for village is banua, which also has the meaning of 'world', as well as 'sky' or 'heavens'. The village thus is a reflection of the cosmos. The nobility are called si'ulu, meaning 'that which is up', and their houses and stone monuments, taller than those of the commoners, occupied the upper, and central, portion of the village. They were traditionally associated in Nias thought with the upper world; with Lowalani, the god of the upper world, and

with the colour golden yellow. Commoners were associated with the lower world and its deity, Lature Danö, and with the colour red (Suzuki 1959: 35, 39). Adult men and women of both these classes were under the obligation to strive to maintain and increase their status by means of the performance of 'feasts of merit'. Individuals during their lifetime tried to work their way through an elaborate series of these feasts, each of which conferred the right to adopt a new ritual title. The right to hold some of these feasts was restricted to the nobility. A man and his wife together had to progress through the sequence, which began with the erection of certain kinds of stone monuments, continued with the smithing of gold ornaments, included the celebration of an elaborate funeral for a parent, and for a chief, ended with the highest and most costly feast of all—that associated with the erection of a 'great house' or omo sebua (Schröder 1917; Suzuki 1973). The building of such a house required among other things the taking of heads, and was so expensive that not every chief could afford it. The massive chief's house of the village of Bawömataluo, today the finest extant building on Nias, provides a magnificent example of the omo sebua. In 1863, after the Dutch beseiged and finally destroyed the village of Orahili, the villagers retreated higher into the mountains and began to build a new village. This was Bawömataluo. The village took several years to complete, and the chief's house here is thought to have been modelled on the huge omo sebua of Orahili, which the Dutch had burned (Feldman 1977: 113).

Houses in South Nias traditionally faced inland, away from the sea. High and deliberately inaccessible places were favoured, and the names of many villages incorporate the words for 'hill' or 'mountain'—such as hili and bawö. Village layouts vary, but the minimal plan is of a flight of stone steps leading to a single street lined with houses (Plate 5). Although the houses in each row are separate, they are all linked together by party walls and by a central corridor (which could be useful as an escape route when the village was under attack). This arrangement resembles somewhat the plan of longhouses, familiar in other parts of the archipelago; the space outside, beneath the overhang of the buildings, might be seen as forming an equivalent of the communal space of the longhouse veranda. Viaro (1980: 20-3), examining a number of village plans, finds a predominance (with due allowance for topographical constraints) of north–south orientations of the village street, but his evidence is not conclusive. If we take the famous village of Bawömataluo as our example, we find that here, considerations of orientation according to the cardinal points or geographical features have been overridden by the concept of the village as microcosm, complete in itself, and organized around its own centre.

The basic plan is of two large streets, crossing each other in the form of a 'T' (Figure 100). The village was under construction for several years. The first stone

laid, at a corner of the intersection of the two streets, is called the *batu banua* or 'village stone'. One of the next stones to be placed was the *füso newali* or 'navel-stone'. Just as *banua* has the double meaning of 'village' and 'sky', so the word *ewali* means both 'sky' and 'street'; thus the stone is the 'navel' both of the village and of the cosmos. Everything within the village, the layout, style, and positioning of the houses, all vividly demonstrate differences in social rank. The first two structures to be built were the chief's house

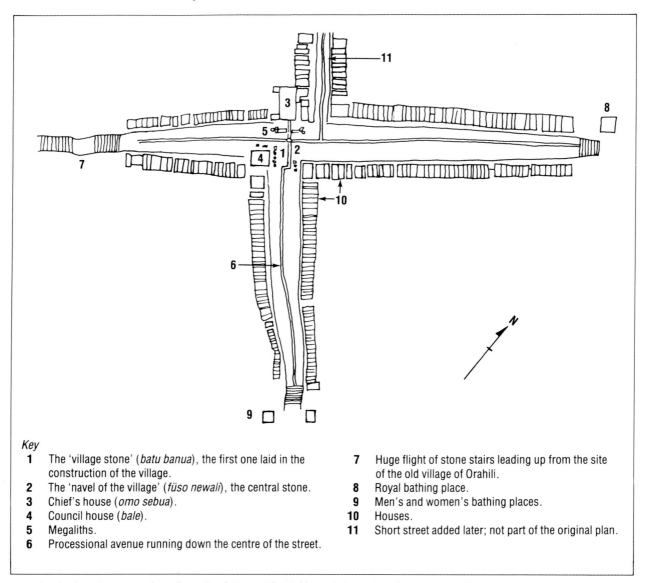

Key

1   The 'village stone' (*batu banua*), the first one laid in the construction of the village.
2   The 'navel of the village' (*füso newali*), the central stone.
3   Chief's house (*omo sebua*).
4   Council house (*bale*).
5   Megaliths.
6   Processional avenue running down the centre of the street.

7   Huge flight of stone stairs leading up from the site of the old village of Orahili.
8   Royal bathing place.
9   Men's and women's bathing places.
10 Houses.
11 Short street added later; not part of the original plan.

100. Sketch plan of Bawömataluo village, South Nias. (After Feldman (1977: 237), from an original by Aileen Matsuyama-Feldman)

(*omo sebua*) and the council house (*bale*). The chief's house is situated in a dominating position at the centre of the intersection, and the first street to be built provides a long view right up to it (Figure 101). Almost opposite, on a corner of the intersection, is the *bale*. The centre of the village is also higher, and here the streets are broader, and the houses (those of the nobility) are larger in scale, with the chief's house being the most massive of all. Lower down the streets are the smaller and less impressive houses of commoners. Stone monuments and menhirs of various kinds are concentrated in the centre of the village, and it was here that most feasts were held (Figures 102 and 103). At the outer ends of the streets, steep flights of stone stairs lead up into the village. The longest and most magnificently proportioned of these leads up from the site of the old village at Orahili, which the Dutch destroyed. These stairs are finely decorated with carved motifs, echoing those found inside the *omo sebua*. They are in two flights, separated by a wide paved terrace set with megaliths, which was used as a meeting place (Schröder 1917, Pl. 89; de Boer 1920, Pl. 2) (Plates 7

and 8). The steps at the entrance opposite to this one lead down to a stone bathing place reserved for the chief, while at the third entrance are bathing places for the rest of the village, one for men and one for women, fed by a system of water channels and pipes. Seven human heads were required to consecrate this village—one being buried at the top and bottom of each stairway and one under the *füso newali*. Heads were also hung in the *bale* and from the roof ridge of the chief's house.

Certain architectural features are common throughout Nias. The huge house piles, both vertical and diagonal, and resting on stones, have already been mentioned. Walls are typically cantilevered outward, the window openings being formed of rows of pierced slats (Plate 6). Inside the house, a bench or shelf built in around the edge of the wall enables those inside to sit and look out through these openings. Flap-like openings in the roof can be propped up from inside with sticks for added light and ventilation. The preference is for heavy and durable woods, making the house very solid. The commonest roofing material

101. Looking down the impressive main street of Bawömataluo from the chief's house, 1986. (Photograph: Roxana Waterson)

103

102. View down a street of Bawömataluo, 1986, showing the stone monuments, commemorating past feasts, which stand before the houses of the nobility. Their curved fronts are a distinctive feature of the architectural style of South Nias. (Photograph: Roxana Waterson)

103. Finely carved detail of a huge horizontal stone 'seat' (*daro daro*), which stands before the chief's house at Bawömataluo. The stone is a funerary monument to Laowo, founder of the village. The raised square represents a treasure-chest; around it twine human figures catching a shark, with a monkey above. (Photograph: Roxana Waterson)

traditionally was sago palm thatch.

In South Nias, an ordinary dwelling always has the width of four upright pillars in the front. The house is much longer than it is broad, the number of pillars in the side depending upon the rank and wealth of the owner. The chief's house has six vertical pillars in the front and eleven along the side. There are no continuous supports from the ground through the roof, so the side walls bear a heavy load. The wall panels are fitted together by means of tongue-and-groove joining, slotting into the huge side beams of the house, called *sicholi*, which are often made from a single tree trunk. Entrance is from the side, by a ladder leading to a trapdoor into the front room. The house is basically divided into a more public front room, and a private rear room. Slaves in Nias society were often debtors (sometimes, according to accounts I was given, tricked by chiefs into a position of dependency). Debtors had to tend the chief's pigs and grow vegetables with which to feed them. The chief might order a debtor to 'go to the pig stalls' for a period of years, upon which he and his family had to move from his own house into a huddle of huts and pigsties behind the chief's house, where they were accommodated in much the same conditions as their charges.

Other types of built form include the *bale* or *osali*, a village meeting place. Early accounts are confusing as to whether these structures also functioned as temples (see Chapter 3). Today the only original *bale* still standing is the one at Bawömataluo (Figure 104). It is rectangular in plan, raised on pillars but open-walled. This was the place where men convened to discuss village affairs and questions of law. Seating arrangements inside reflected the rank of the participants, who engaged in elaborate oratory. Scales for the weighing of gold, and standard measuring devices, were also stored in the *bale*.

The chief's house, or *omo sebua* (Figure 105), is of much the same design as an ordinary dwelling, but of vast and impressive proportions. The house at

104. The *bale* or council house of Bawömataluo, 1986. It was re-roofed in zinc in 1985. Before it stands the jumping-stone, 2 metres high and 70 centimetres wide, over which warriors used to practise leaping in preparation for raids on enemy villages. (Photograph: Roxana Waterson, 1986)

105. The chief's house at Bawömataluo, the most magnificent extant example of South Nias architecture. (From Schröder 1917: Pl. 117)

Bawömataluo is built on giant pillars and reaches a height of 22.7 metres (Feldman 1977: 150). The interior is lined with fine wood panelling, ornamented with motifs carved in relief of animals, plants, and objects representing wealth and status and the powers of the ruler (Figures 106–110). Some of these motifs re-appear on stone monuments and stairways in the village. A treasure-chest, for example, represents the ruler's wealth, while sets of weights and scales for weighing gold stand for his power to control the distribution of wealth, as well as abstract principles of social order. On one of the wall panels is carved a Dutch war ship with cannons, probably very similar to the one sent by the Dutch when they attacked Orahili in 1863. Two ancestral altars, also carved in relief, incorporate chairs or thrones, another element foreign to Nias culture. These elements were absorbed and given their own significance; for example, the ancestor images would

have been seated on a stool on top of the throne, the latter being used as a means of elevating the image rather than as a place to sit down (Feldman 1977: 158). The arrangement of animal and plant motifs reflects the concept of the house itself as micro-cosm. Close to floor level, for example, at the base of the hearths, are found animals such as crocodiles and dogs, while higher on the walls are monkeys, hornbills, and creatures of the air and the tree-tops (Figure 111). Parallels were drawn in Nias thought between the lord of the house, the house and its symbols, society itself, and the cosmos. The house was likened to the ruler, and to the earth; it was called 'the beautiful/virtuous land of fertile plants'. Harvested fruits were hung from the rafters, and if one observed the proper customs, one could pluck them. The complicated structure of the roof forms nine separate levels, comparable to the nine layers of the upper

106. Inside the chief's house, Bawömataluo. (From Schröder 1917: Pl. 144)

107. Carved panel on the left wall of the front room of the chief's house, Bawömataluo, 1986. Depicted are two thrones which formerly held a male and female ancestor figure. (Photograph: Roxana Waterson)

108. A carved ebony wall panel in the front room of the chief's house, Bawömataluo, depicts masculine ornaments, including a single ear-ring, gold torque, and a comb, 1986. (Photograph: Roxana Waterson)

109. Exquisitely carved capital of the central pillar (*chölöchölö*) in the front room of the chief's house, Bawömataluo, 1986. (Photograph: Roxana Waterson)

110. A wall panel on the right of the front room depicts a Dutch steam ship mounted with cannons, surrounded by large fish and a crocodile, 1986. (Photograph: Roxana Waterson)

world in Nias cosmology. The house is also likened to the ruler's body, its beams and pillars like arms and legs. In the ruler's dress—for example, on his jacket and sword—were repeated many of the elements found in house carvings; his head-dress with branching foliate ornaments represented coiled ferns, a design also found on the ridge-pole of the house (Feldman 1977: 172–3) (Figure 112).

111. Carving of a monkey taking fruit, positioned high on the wall of the rear room, 1986. (Photograph: Roxana Waterson)

112. Nias warrior in festive dress, with foliate head-dress. Designs of fern fronds represent fertility and are echoed in house-carving motifs. The rattan ball at his waist held magical substances intended to confer invulnerability. (From Schröder 1917: Pl. 51)

Although I have considered only a handful of examples here, each of them demonstrates how complex are the cosmological ideas informing house and settlement structure in different Indonesian societies. It would be wrong, however, to suppose that these ideas themselves are not subject to change and development over time. Some authors (for example, Fraser 1968) have made the assumption that cosmological schemata must have been passed down unchanging from the ancestors, and are merely reproduced unaltered by each succeeding generation. This strangely ahistorical notion of the supposed conservatism of 'traditional' societies is obviously impossible, however difficult it is to capture the evidence of change in progress. We can point to at least a few examples of such changes. The utilization of Hindu ideas is a case in point. We have seen that the idea of a sacred and powerful centre or 'navel', positioned hierarchically in relation to a subordinate periphery, was most likely an ancient cosmological theme which pre-dated Hindu influence in the archipelago. But Hindu features could conveniently be grafted on to it, so that elements of Hindu cosmology served to strengthen an already existing indigenous idea and, in some cases, lend legitimation to the rulers of newly centralized states.

Bali, Sumba, and Nias all developed rather rigid social hierarchies. In the Sumbanese case, we can see that it is the houses of nobles, and their ancestral origin-villages, in which cosmological rules are most extensively applied. The power of noble ancestors, and the ability of the living nobility to stage impressive and elaborate rituals, must all have helped to reinforce their position of authority. This was ultimately based (at any rate during the last century) on the wealth they gained from their control of horse and cattle rearing for export to other islands, and the production by noblewomen of fine textiles. Bali was the only one of these three societies where centralized kingdoms emerged, and here it is clear that Hindu ideas of purity and status could usefully be incorporated into local ideology to lend justification to a social hierarchy. Hobart (1978), in an interesting examination of this theme, notes that hierarchical relations can achieve far greater stability once they successfully present themselves as 'natural'. He suggests that, for the Balinese, the structure of space becomes most critical as a conveyor of meaning during religious rituals, when the relative position and mobility of participants becomes particularly significant. He gives as an example the towering bier in which a high-caste corpse is placed, which graphically emphasizes its elevation above the low-caste bearers who will carry the bier to the cemetery. Caste purity in Bali is compared with the image of water, which naturally and inevitably flows downhill. Just as water cannot flow upwards, lower castes cannot become higher. By presenting social values as if they were part of an unchanging natural order, the arbitrariness of social inequalities is disguised.

There is no doubt that social changes commonly result in shifts in the perception and control of cosmologies, but to catch this process in action is more difficult. Turton (1978), like Hobart, traces the links between cosmology and politics in northern Thailand, and demonstrates the close interrelation between architectural and political relations in the changes that have taken place in village and locality cults over time. In the first place, he proposes, local communities constructed their own ideas of legitimate relations of appropriation and ownership of nature, but with the passage of time these have become incorporated, first, in wider political units with different ideas of ownership and control, and finally, into the Siamese state with its own concept of the King at the apex of a social hierarchy, recognized as 'owner' of all land and mediator with supernatural powers on behalf of the entire population. The form of rituals performed at all these higher levels of political integration goes on imitating important aspects of ordinary house-building rites, especially the focus on a sacred house post. In this way, architectural symbolism becomes 'not merely a system of classification but ... part of ideology'—that is to say, a system for making statements about social relations. Such statements must be viewed not simply as straightforward 'collective representations' of society, but rather as collective *misrepresentations*, part of the process by which ideology conceals from its adherents the real nature of social relations (Turton 1978: 114).

Nineteenth-century Nias provides us with a particularly graphic example of such changes in progress. Bawömataluo, rather than being the norm, is in several respects an exceptional village. It is the grandest of South Nias villages, and its chief's house is the finest surviving building on Nias; yet it was built just at the moment when the entire social system which produced it was about to undergo rapid, irrevocable change due to Dutch intervention. A succession of powerful and feared leaders had made Orahili an important village, and when this was destroyed by the Dutch it was the ruling chief, Laowo Siduhu, who organized the massive undertaking of building the new village of Bawömataluo. The work was completed by his successor Saonigeho, who like his father refused to concede power to the Dutch, in spite of military confrontations, imprisonment, and the levying of a huge fine on Bawömataluo (Feldman 1977: 117). There were a number of other villages built on a similar plan, with equally large populations, but none has a chief's house still standing to compare with Bawömataluo's.[19] A descendant of the ruling family of Bawömataluo told me a dramatic story of how Saonigeho, determined to ensure the prominence of his own village, sent his aides in secret to sabotage the building of a new chief's house at Hilisimaetano by setting fire to it; as a result, this house was never completed.

After Dutch take-over, the wealth of the ruling nobility declined very rapidly, but Feldman suggests that in the earlier part of the century, these nobles had sought to convert their ever-increasing profits from the slave trade into enhanced prestige by expanding and elaborating on the design of their houses. The founding ancestors of South Nias communities came originally from Central Nias, where houses are of smaller scale and styles are plainer. The oldest surviving houses in South Nias also have a rather flat frontage. Feldman (1984) argues that the present-day style of façade, projecting in several steps, was actually a nineteenth-century development based on the shape of Dutch galleons which at this time were entering Nias waters and were on occasion attacked by the Niassans. This foreign element became a source of inspiration, which was however completely indigenized and integrated into local culture. Whatever its actual origins, it is clear that a development was going on in the style, scale, and elaborateness, not just of the chief's house— symbol of his power—but of the whole village itself and its cosmological arrangement around its own centre— a feature which does not seem to be mentioned in relation to other villages. One may speculate that the closer and closer identification of the ruler's person, and his house, with the cosmos, is part of a process whereby relations with nature begin to pass out of the control of the community in general into that of a ruling group. Cosmology, here, was in process of being appropriated by an élite for purposes of legitimation, and we can catch a glimpse of the process in action. House and settlement lend themselves as a particularly potent vehicle for visual and symbolic messages about social power, and Bawömataluo survives as testimony to the power of Nias chiefs.

1. On the Semang, see Benjamin (1980). On the Punan, see King (1976a) and Hoffman (1981). The Malaysian 'Sea Gypsies' are properly known as Orang Selitar, and are said to number around 300. They live entirely on their small boats and are pure nomads, sailing around the south coast of Johor and the north coast of Singapore and never spending more than one or two days in the same place. The basic social unit is the elementary family, which lives in a single boat. There are three or four main groups of Orang Selitar, whose members move together to fish. They maintain their own religious beliefs, which centre on spirits to do with fishing and the sea (Carey 1976). Another somewhat similar group of sea nomads, called Moken, exists in Thailand (Bernatzik 1958). (The more widespread Orang Laut, or 'Sea People', who are to be found around the coasts of various islands of the archipelago, practise differing degrees of nomadism and often have houses as well as their boats.)

2. Rapoport (1975) provides an excellent brief description of Australian Aborigines' identification with nature and the land. People are 'owned' by the country, rather than vice versa; the entire landscape, which appeared to Europeans so vacant and featureless, is for the Aborigines sacred and charged with mythical associations. The shift in relations with other living species which comes with the abandonment of hunting and gathering life-styles is succinctly expressed by Hugh Brody (1987): animals become servants where before they were relatives.

3. It would be a mistake to assume, all the same, that even apparently simple shelters are devoid of cultural meanings. Rapoport (1975: 41) notes that the *layout* of aboriginal camps, if not the shelters themselves, actually tells a great deal about social relations, for they are generally arranged according to definite rules reflecting phratry, clan, or other kinship group membership. Fires are also important elements of the camp (compare Marshall (1960) on the !Kung Bushmen). Benjamin provides an interesting example from the Semang groups, nearly all of whom practise a range of avoidance relationships with close affines of the opposite sex, such as a spouse's sibling or parent. He observes (1980: 11):

'In traditional forest-dwelling conditions the temporary windscreens which shelter the conjugal-family groups can easily be arranged to prevent the too-close approach of individuals who are in an avoidance relationship. In modern circumstances, however, such as in some Government-built relocation villages with permanent housing, people sometimes complain that a house is "too full" even when there are only three occupants, if an avoidance relationship is included. Some of the Kensiu in Baling district, Kedah, told me that this was one of their major objections to the permanent housing they had been living in for the previous few years.'

4. See Chapter 6 for a full discussion of this subject.

5. These territories could differ widely in size. Some were very small, consisting of a few villages; by contrast, the whole of Bone formed a single *wanua*. Bugis *wanua* can also refer to the 'sheath' of a kris or sword. (Christian Pelras, personal communication.)

6. Prof. I. Jocano (personal communication).

7. Clifford Sather (personal communication).

8. G. Acciaioli (unpublished thesis).

9. Davis (1984: 80) too remarks on the strength of the Muang sense of direction:

'Even at night and in strange surroundings, a Muang is never at a loss to indicate which way lies north.... I once took two people from Landing on an airplane trip to Chiang Mai, where neither of them had ever been before. As soon as we arrived we hired a taxi and rode several miles up a tortuous mountain road to visit a famous temple on a mountain top outside the town. By the time we were inside the temple I had lost all sense of direction, but one of my companions nonchalantly commented on the beauty of the "northern" of two Buddha images in the temple courtyard.'

10. For a fuller discussion of orientations in Toraja, see Waterson (1984a). The significance of house carvings is analysed in Waterson (1988a, b).

11. C. Pelras (personal communication). Crystal (1979: 54) provides another brief account of Tana Towa, which however appears to contain a number of inaccuracies. Pelras disputes Crystal's claim that intermittent contact has been maintained over the centuries between the Badui and the people of Tana Towa.

12. Hanbury-Tenison was also taken to visit a sacred location in outer Tana Towa called Possitana or 'navel of the earth'.

13. Body symbolism in Balinese architecture is discussed in Chapter 6.

14. For recent accounts of Sumba society, see also Adams (1974, 1980), Bonneff and Voisset (1980), Rodgers (1985), and Hoskins (1986, 1987).

15. Asymmetrical alliance systems are those where lineages (groups of people tracing descent from a known common ancestor) ideally exchange marriage partners in a fixed pattern over generations. Most (but not all) of these systems in Indonesia give precedence to the patrilineal tracing of descent (but see Chapter 7). Lineage A gives wives to lineage B, and B in turn provides wives for lineage C, and so on. Every lineage thus stands in a relation of wife-giver to some lineages and wife-receiver to certain other lineages. Wife-givers, who provide another lineage with the means of reproducing itself, are generally regarded as ritually superior to wife-takers, since ultimately they are the source of continued life. Wife-receivers are eternally in debt to their wife-givers, who exercise a beneficent and mystical power over them. Marriages in these systems are accompanied by an elaborate series of gifts and countergifts, in which the types of goods given are themselves often characterized as 'male' and 'female', and are seen to complement each other. Metal jewellery, for example, is often given by the groom's family in exchange for counterprestations of 'female' textiles from the family of the bride.

16. Ideas of the house, the village, and even the island of Sumba itself as a body are examined in Chapter 6.

17. The idea of the *empty* centre recurs in the Balinese court-yard with its vacant 'navel' area, and in Javanese house arrangements, where, according to Gunawan Tjahjono (1988: 8), if a family can afford to build the complete set of structures which constitutes the dwelling, the original 'inner' house (*dalem*) 'would be left empty and thus become a pure spiritual center'.

18. The earliest accounts of Nias society by European observers are to be found in Marsden's *The History of Sumatra* (1811) and the memoirs of Sir Stamford Raffles (1830). The two-volume account of Nias by Schröder, a Dutch administrator (1917), remains to this day the major published work on Nias, his volume of photographs providing much valuable information on architecture, as well as on the appearance of the people themselves before any great social alteration had taken place as a result of colonization and a still very recent conversion to Christianity. A critical review of the early sources is provided by Suzuki (1959). Recent first-hand accounts include Feldman (1977, 1979, 1984, 1985), Viaro (1980, 1984), Danandjaja (1971), Suzuki (1984), and Bambowo Laiya (1980). I also visited Nias for several weeks in 1986.

19. Bawömataluo today has a population of over 5,000, and nearby Hilisimaetano has 6,000; such large populations, it seems, were the result of the practice of waging war against smaller communities and forcing them to become incorporated into the larger and more powerful ones. Vulnerability to slave raids would no doubt have made life in the smaller villages very difficult anyway.

CHAPTER 6
The Living House

THERE is in the indigenous religions of the archipelago a widely shared concept of a vital force which suffuses and animates the universe. This force has been variously labelled in the literature as 'spirit', 'soul-stuff', 'essence', 'vital force', 'cosmic energy', and so on, while in Malay and Indonesian languages it is widely known by the word *semangat* or its cognates. It is this view of the universe which has been called 'animism' by Western writers, some of whom have drawn comparisons between *semangat* and the Polynesian concept of *mana*.[1] There exist local variations in the precise meaning of the cognates of *semangat*, and their place in conceptions of the human 'soul', which is often divided into several distinct aspects or entities—sometimes as many as seven. But underlying these differences is a more broadly shared pattern of ideas about a pervasive life-force, which may attach itself in differing concentrations not only to living things but also to inanimate objects. Everything shares in this vital principle, whether plants, animals, humans, mountains, rocks, heirlooms, textiles—or houses. Much less material entities than these may be included: Benjamin (1979: 13) notes that for the Temiar (an aboriginal people of the Malay Peninsula) the list may include natural phenomena, diseases, dragons, or modes of cooking.

What really is the nature of this animating force? Shelly Errington (1983a), in her discussion of the concept of *sumange'* among the Bugis of Luwu (South Sulawesi) takes as her starting-point the classic paper by Benedict Anderson on the idea of power in Javanese culture. Anderson (1972: 7) writes:

Power is that intangible, mysterious and divine energy which animates the universe.... In Javanese traditional thinking there is no sharp division between organic and inorganic matter, for everything is sustained by the same invisible power. This conception of the entire cosmos being suffused by a formless, constantly creative energy provides the basic link

between the 'animism' of the Javanese villages and the high metaphysical pantheism of the urban centers.

As in Java, the Bugis of Luwu believe that power can become concentrated in people and things, and that people can increase their own potency through tapping the power of the universe, especially by means of techniques of meditation, concentration, and the cultivation of a state of 'awareness' which the Bugis call *paringerreng* (S. Errington 1983a: 561). Power is anchored at the navel (*pusat*, Indonesian or *posik*, Buginese). Not only humans, but also houses, kingdoms, and the cosmos itself are thought of as having a 'navel'. The idea of the navel as vital centre, source of power, or point of origin is a highly important one in the Buginese conceptual framework. As Errington (1983a: 547) notes:

Each person has a navel, and guarding it, and especially the sumange' or life-energy that is attached at it, is a matter of constant concern. Houses, too, have *pinposik* (navel-posts), which run through the house's approximate middle. The house has its own sumange': the spirit that hovers at the navel-post, called the Ampo Banua (roughly, lord of the house). Navels of people, of houses, and of polities all must be guarded and protected from harm.

Another writer on the Buginese, however (Acciaioli, n.d.), raises a query about Errington's abstract conception of *sumange'* as 'formless cosmic energy', for in a community of Buginese migrants in Central Sulawesi he found that it was viewed rather in terms of individualized 'spirits' attaching to objects and living things:

Rather than persons, objects or places being loci of differing amounts of an impersonalized energy, each such entity possesses an individualized *sumange'*. The *sumange'* is likened to an image, but an ethereal one of the objects it animates. The *sumange'* was thus the image of oneself perceived in dreams. Not only the person as a whole, but even the parts of the individual could each have their own *sumange'*.... It is an individualized spirit that can be named or fly off, not a concentration of cosmic energy.

How are we to reconcile these differing definitions? Acciaioli argues that even Errington's own description of the personalized spirit of the house fits with the view of *sumange'* as a more individualized entity, and on the face of it this might appear to accord more closely with descriptions from other Indonesian societies, for example, the Sakuddei concept of *simagere* or 'soul' (Schefold 1976, 1982). One suspects, however, that the two points of view may not be so far apart as they at first appear. Acciaioli notes that his informants were commoners, and that their idea of *sumange'* as individual soul is a radically egalitarian one—everyone has one. By contrast, Errington's informants were almost exclusively members of the nobility, who have a vested interest in the notion of *sumange'* as soul-stuff, which those with the necessary (noble) qualities are able to concentrate in themselves and thus have more of.[2] It seems highly likely, then, that variant characterizations of *semangat* have developed in a way that reflects status distinctions in some societies of the archipelago.

However, Pelras suggests that the differences may be merely contextual, and that both conceptions of *sumange'* may be expressed at different times by the same individual. His informants stated that there was no difference between the house's *sumange'* and its individualized 'spirit warden' (*pangngonroang bola*), who dwells at the navel-post. He found that in certain rituals, *sumange'* is treated as an impersonal force, which can be strengthened, while in others it is addressed as an individual. He concludes: 'The question of what *sumange'* is in the eyes of the Bugis might be difficult to express in abstract terms in our Western languages, but that doesn't mean that it is not clear for the Bugis who speak of it.'[3]

Discussions of Malay animism by Endicott (1970) and Benjamin (1979) offer a further resolution of the apparent contradiction by showing how personal and impersonal characterizations of *semangat* may be articulated. In Endicott's analysis, notes Benjamin, '"essence" may be either incorporeal, in which case it manifests itself as spirit, or corporeal, in which case it forms the "soul" of the body that houses it'. He goes on (1979: 10–11):

The animistic world view posits the division of the cosmos into two dialectically conjoined planes of existence: the plane of things, matter, categories; and the plane of essence, spirit,

soul. Entities on the two planes are readily conceivable as independent autonomous manifestations; but the normal 'resting' state of the cosmos is one in which for each entity on the plane of matter there is an equivalent entity on the plane of essence, and vice versa, in a one-to-one relationship. Any disturbance of this relationship, whereby essence escapes the bounds of matter, will introduce a dynamic imbalance into the system which may come to be regarded as the source of such things as power, danger, pollution, *mana* and so on. . . . In Malayan animism this dialectic works itself out in the following manner: matter (or better, categories) tends to anchor essence progressively such that each category has its corresponding soul; on the other hand, essence tends to break through the categorical boundaries to coalesce and form free spirit (or soul). Tightly bound soul implies health, neutrality, safety, profaneness; free spirit implies unhealth, activity, danger, sacredness.

A feature of this world view is that within it, it is possible for humans to perceive themselves not as alienated from the rest of the cosmos but as participating in existence on much the same terms as everything else. The relationship between persons and things may also be much more intimate since concentrations of vital force may be transferred between them. This idea finds illustration in the frequent use made in ritual of textiles which are able to enhance the vitality and power of those wearing or wrapped in them (Gittinger 1979: 27n ff.; Niessen 1985: 164–5; Mashman 1986: 30). In Sumba, personal possessions of all kinds are thought to share in the 'vitality' (*ndewa*) of their owners, and their loss can cause a diminution of this vital force; the return of a mislaid object, notes Onvlee (1980: 196), 'implies a strengthening of the owner's weakened *ndewa* and the returning of his *mawo* ('spirit')'. In particular, horses and personal slaves may share in a noble's personality; an important individual may be called by the name of his horse, and on certain ceremonial occasions a slave of appropriate sex, heavily costumed in ritual regalia, acts as a substitute for a noble person (Onvlee 1980: 196; Forth 1981: 291).[4]

In just the same way, houses are regarded in many societies of the archipelago as having a vitality of their own, interdependent with the vitality of their occupants.[5] The healthy state of the one may affect the health of the other, a relationship which is particularly vividly demonstrated in Reimar Schefold's account of an incident in his fieldwork among the Sakuddei of Siberut, in the Mentawai archipelago. Shortly after his

113. Mentawai longhouse (*uma*), Bulak Monga, 1965. In common with many peoples of the archipelago, Mentawaians view the house, like everything else in the cosmos, as possessing its own vital force. (Dorothy Pelzer Collection, courtesy of ISEAS, Singapore)

arrival, Schefold spent several days visiting and sketching some of the Sakuddei's longhouses (*uma*), which he admired as being 'among the foremost technical and aesthetic achievements' of their society (Figure 113). His admiration, however, had curious consequences. He writes (1982: 126):

My expedition ended with a violent attack of malaria. People explained this attack as a response to my 'excessive wonderment' (*kissei*). I had admired the houses and touched and measured them to such an extent that I had, in effect, molested them. The houses, on their part, had consequently wondered at me; they had grown annoyed and had concentrated on me with such intensity that they had finally made me fall ill. A healing ceremony was then enacted, to reconcile the offended houses.

Schefold views this incident in the context of the style of relations which the highly egalitarian Sakuddei maintain both with each other and with their en-

vironment, in a world in which there is no appeal to a higher power either on the day-to-day political level or in terms of their religious concepts. He goes on (1982: 128–9):

Man inhabits a world of equal partners, whether these be natural or supernatural. He cannot impose his will on them; he must try to co-exist with them in equilibrium and on good terms. Co-existence is achieved through incessant communication and reciprocation.... The requirement that newcomers should behave inconspicuously in order to allow the souls of house and person to grow accustomed to each other can be understood only if it is seen in the context of the partner-relations which man must maintain with all that surrounds him.

Anger and disturbance are thought of as dangerous heat, and the ritual of reconciliation involved 'cooling down' both the house and the patient with the leaves of sacred, cooling plants. Although the concept of the

117

house as an entity with a soul and powers of its own is given particularly explicit form among the Sakuddei, we shall find that very similar ideas exist in many other societies of island South-East Asia; the indigenous animist religions of mainland South-East Asia also offer close parallels, as, for example, in the personification of house, village, and temple guardian spirits in northern Thailand, whose supernatural actions may be aroused by the acts of the villagers in breaking various taboos, resulting in sickness or other disorders (Tambiah 1970: 263-9; Davis 1984: 59-61).

How exactly does the vitality of the house come into being? Various possible answers to this question present themselves. One has to do with the fact that trees are generally seen as having their own vital force, which must be managed in an appropriate way when they are felled and converted to house timbers. Among the Jörai of the southern Vietnamese highlands, living trees in the forest are considered to have a 'wild' *yang* (vitality, power), which must be converted into the safe, 'domesticated' *yang* of house timbers when they are brought into the village. Otherwise the health of the occupants would be endangered. The cutting of trees, planting of house posts, and entry into the new house are all surrounded by ritual, and on the latter occasion, in particular, invocations are chanted begging the *yang* of the timbers, harmful while in the forest, to be happy and 'cool' in the house, and to become benevolent *yang* now that they have taken a new place in the world of humans (Dournes 1971: 305-6). Among the Minangkabau, so I was told, large old trees are thought to be inhabited by spirits, and to cut them down is dangerous unless a specialist is first called who is able to address the spirit and remove it to another place. When the timber is ceremonially fetched from the forest, it is carried only by members of the kin group which is building the house, while members of other clans assist by playing gongs and drums and the women bring food for the occasion (Navis 1984: 182).

The Sa'dan Toraja, too, traditionally make offerings before felling trees, and the timber for the central 'navel-post' of a noble origin-house must be carried to the site with its upper or 'head' end always held higher than the root end. I have already mentioned how this pile is personified and dressed up before being put in position. A parallel custom is (or was) to be found in Roti, where Wetering describes the dressing of the main house post with textiles to make it 'look like a king'; offerings were made to it when the inaugural ceremony for the house was held. It is the main post which is regarded as the guardian of the house's power. Wetering (1923: 480, 493) records that: 'The new house has a very strong personality, which through its superior strength can kill people.' Hence all participants in the inaugural rite, especially the owner and the carpenters, had to wear new clothes, gold and beads, all of which were considered to protect them from harm.

As for the Malays, they follow a principle of 'one house, one tree' in erecting a dwelling. The nine major house posts must be extracted from a single tree trunk, which is shaped into a large square section and then split three by three into nine equal sections. When the posts are positioned in the structure, they must maintain the same relationship to each other that they had before they were extracted from the tree (Gibbs 1987: 79). In Balinese texts on principles of architecture (the *Hasta Bumi* and *Hasta Kosali Kosala*), it is stated that a tree should be full grown before being felled, and after having been transformed into pillars, a rite must be performed to establish its new life in this form (Soelarto 1973: 44). The frequency with which house posts are personified or become the focus of ritual attention (as I shall discuss below) doubtless reflects the attitude to the trees from which the posts originated in the first place. There is a pervasive idea that the timber continues to be animated, albeit in a new form. Secondly, the process of construction itself must be viewed as contributing to the efficacy of an object. It is this process, after all, which brings the object into being; and, in fact, different sources provide clear confirmation of this idea. According to Malay concepts, the formation of *semangat* occurs in a comparable way in both people and manufactured objects (Figure 114). Endicott (1970: 51) records:

The *semangat* of a person makes its appearance at the moment the umbilical cord is severed. . . . None of the Malays questioned . . . knew if the *semangat* existed before it appeared in the child; they invariably said it 'became of itself' (*jadi sendiri*). The same is said of the boat soul which 'becomes of itself' when all the planks of the boat have been fitted together. Similarly, 'the *semangat rumah*, or "house soul", comes automatically into existence as the various parts of the walls and roof are fitted together'.[6]

Horridge, discussing the relations between canoe owners and builders and their canoes in the Malayo-

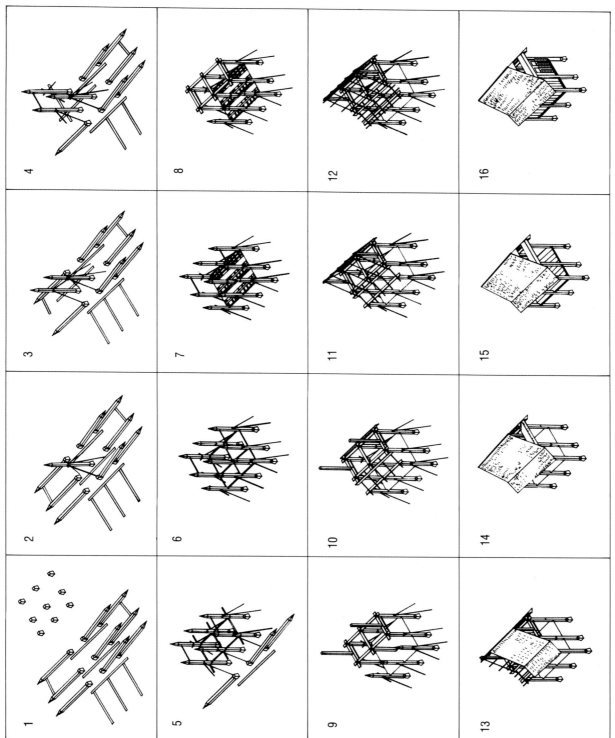

114. Mode of construction of a Malay house. (After Gibbs 1987: 94-5)

Polynesian world, lists a number of objects of human manufacture which are believed to have their own *semangat*, including 'swords, boats, books, ceramics, houses and carvings', and he observes: 'The effort of a craftsman in fashioning an object transfers power into his production, so that it becomes a force to be reckoned with' (Horridge 1986: 3).[7] Moreover, house-carving motifs and decorations, like textile designs, are sometimes regarded as inherently powerful and may serve a protective function for the occupants (Plates 15–17; Figures 115 and 116). Without the addition of these

the construction process may not be complete. Niessen (1985: 210) suggests that this is the case among the Toba Batak, in a comment which also emphasizes the interdependence of the house and its occupants:

The house is a habitation, an altar, and a shrine. Its inhabitants are its soul, and its structure and decorative features serve to protect that soul. The house-decorator is responsible, by medium of his craft, for the inhabitants of the dwelling. Certain of the decorations he inscribes on the walls consist of long flowing lines—of necessity because a broken line may bring misfortune upon the inhabitants.

115. *Bindu matoga* design, representing the eight cardinal points, on the wall of a Toba house. An essential feature of this design are the unbroken lines, maintained by loops at the corners, so that the whole is said to be without beginning or end. (Photograph: Roxana Waterson)

116. Flowing, continuous lines are important in Toba house-painting designs, ensuring unbroken good fortune and the protection of the occupants from harm. The double pair of breasts carved in relief are a common symbol of fertility. (Photograph: Roxana Waterson)

A third, and possibly more significant, source of a house's vitality are the ceremonies performed during its construction. Each society has developed its own set of regulations about the mode of construction and the order in which parts should be erected, as well as the appropriate ritual actions which should accompany the different stages. Thus it is that a house-building expert often combines the roles of carpenter and ritual specialist, like the *acan* of northern Thailand, whom Turton (1978: 114) describes as 'architect, builder and ritual expert, and usually a former monk', or the *sanro bola* of the Bugis, whose role extends from the initial selection of a site and of auspicious days to commence construction, through supervision of the work, to the celebration of annual rituals for several years after the house has been occupied (Pelras 1975: 79).

Not to observe the required rituals, it is believed, would seriously endanger the inhabitants. Kana (1980: 229n.) says of the Savunese house:

For the Savunese, a house is not just a physical structure with a practical value; it has a spiritual significance as well. The series of ceremonies that accompany the building of a house is intended to give the house life. As Savunese say, it is given *hemanga* ('spirit' or 'capacity for life'). A house that has undergone these ceremonies is indeed considered a living being, like a man, animal or plant. As soon as the ceremonies have been completed, *hemanga* enters the house.

Still a further sense in which the house is regarded as animate concerns the way that it is thought of as a body. Frequently house parts are named after parts of the body, and the use of space may also reflect this symbolism. It may be objected that the use of the body as an organizing metaphor, which can be applied to a variety of inanimate structures as well as to living beings, does not necessarily imply that a building is literally regarded as 'alive'. Barnes (1974: 45) makes this point in relation to ancestral villages of the Kédangese, which are divided into sections called 'head', 'feet', 'navel', 'left', and 'right'. His informants tended to laugh when he suggested to them that the village was a human being. Laughter, however, is open to interpretation. Barnes concludes that his question was considered ridiculous; but it is equally likely that the reaction to it, rather than constituting a denial, represents a deliberate reluctance to defuse the power of symbolism by making explicit what it is preferred should remain tacit and implicit.[8] The pervasiveness of body imagery remains suggestive, and in some cases its connection with the 'life' of a building is made quite explicitly—as it is by the Balinese (Howe 1983) or the Tetum of Timor (Hicks 1976, 1984).

Howe's writings on the principles of Balinese architecture are of particular interest, since they make clear that the idea of buildings as animate structures (which has been largely overlooked by previous writers on Bali) rests upon a combination of factors such as we have been considering here. Howe (1983: 139) writes:

The first fact to report, and one whose omission from the literature is quite remarkable, is that all buildings are considered to be 'alive'. All temples, houses, meeting places, shops, offices, factories and indeed all important constructions, whether permanent or temporary, are 'brought to life'. It is not, however, a simple matter to describe what is entailed in 'bringing to life' a building. It is obviously of a different phenomenological order to human life as the Balinese readily admit but just what the difference amounts to is not easy to discover. The Balinese themselves cannot say what it means; their explanation takes the form of a description of the procedures whereby actual buildings are in fact animated.... [These include the following rules:] a) (i) the buildings within the compound are set out in accordance with a cosmological scheme, the *nawa sangan*, (ii) the house, as a unit, is constituted of parts each of which is analogically related to a part of the human body; b) the limbs of the owner's body are used to derive the standard measurements employed in determining the dimensions of the parts of the buildings; c) when the size of any particular part has been so determined a small, additional length known as the *jiwa ukuran* ('the soul of the measure') or the *pangurip* ('life') is tacked onto the end; d) a series of ceremonies to cleanse, sanctify and animate the construction is performed at various points throughout the building process.

Here, then, we find the superimposition of cognitive systems—one cosmological, the other based on the organization of the body—which together give the house compound its special form and, coupled with the rules and rites observed during construction, ensure that the structures will have 'life' (*urip*). The two aspects of house-building ritual, and of body symbolism, will repay some further investigation, and I shall now look more closely at each of them.

Rituals of House Construction

One of the first things that must be done in building a house is to ensure that a favourable site is selected. Since the land may already be occupied by a spirit of the locality, its permission must be sought, and there are a number of ways of doing this. The Sa'dan Toraja traditionally stick two stems of particular plants into the ground with a section of bamboo filled with water propped up against them. If after three days and three nights the water in the bamboo is still full to the brim, the spirit of the locality is considered to have given permission. Then a chicken is killed and offerings made on a small offering platform woven from grasses, and a piece of iron from an old frying-pan and a bead—representing longevity and nobility, respectively—are buried at the spot. If this is not done, the spirit may disturb the occupants and cause misfortune. One house which stands above the road half-way between Ulusalu and Ma'kale was said to be haunted in this way, and the frequency of accidents on that particular

bend of the road was attributed to the anger of the local spirit. (Nowadays, only the more traditionalist Torajans would be likely to observe the ritual, but its omission may still provide convincing explanation of misfortune after the event.) Rather similar tests are carried out by some other peoples of the region. When the Iban are building a longhouse, they go to great lengths to take auguries, observe omen-birds, and ritually cleanse the site of any evil influences. Various items are placed into the hole of the first post to be erected—an offering, together with a river stone to make the house 'cool', the blood of a sacrificial cock, and fluid in which the ritual leader's charms have been rinsed (Freeman 1970: 121). The Malays likewise perform divination to ensure that the spirits of a locality are amenable to a house being built there, and place various offerings into the hole for the centre post: hardwoods, candlenuts, iron or copper objects, and the blood of a sacrificed chicken, goat, or buffalo. The latter represents an offering to the earth demon (Skeat 1900: 144), while the candlenuts may be intended to propitiate termites and prevent them eating the post—a similar custom being followed by the Kédangese (Barnes 1974: 71). The centre post (*tiang seri*) of the Malay house is traditionally regarded as the guardian or 'strength' of the house, anchoring its *semangat*.[9] In northern Thailand, a ritual of 'exorcising the earth' is performed before planting the house posts to ensure that no evil influence will be present (Figure 117). Some earth is removed from each of the extreme corner post holes, placed in an offering tray, and disposed of outside the house site in order to 'remove spirits', and precautions are also taken to ensure that the spirit residing in timbers taken from the forest is appeased. Davis's (1984: 143–4) description of the Northern Thai concept of *khwan* or 'energy elements' present in humans, some animals, and 'wooden objects which are inhabited by wood-nymphs' (including the main posts of new houses) makes it sound very much like a variant of the *semangat* beliefs which we have been examining—as he himself suggests. Thai house compounds generally include a small 'spirit house' near the entrance, a miniature structure of bamboo raised on posts, with a thatched roof and often a miniature ladder. This serves as a shrine for the locational spirit who may have been disturbed by the clearing of the site (Krug and Duboff 1982: 92).

Ritual attention often focuses on the main structural members, particularly house posts. We have

122

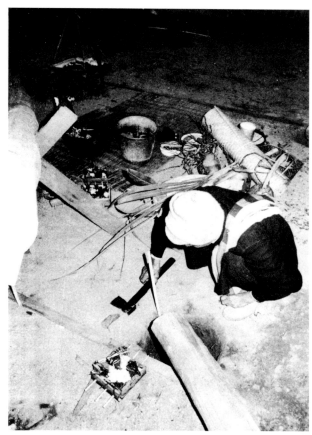

117. Northern Thai house-building expert 'exorcising the earth' in a ritual performed prior to the 'planting of the house posts'. Behind the expert are offerings to his 'spirit teacher' (a rolled mat, rice alcohol, etc.) and to the *sao phaya* or senior of the two principle house posts (coconuts, sugar-cane, and large offering tray at top left). (From Turton 1978: 114)

and then dropped the pile down onto him, smashing him to pieces. His soul became a spirit. When the house was finally completed and was to be consecrated, he brought about an earthquake which cost many lives. The house collapsed but all other houses constructed since then were originally made possible by him.

All Sakuddei longhouses maintain a friendly relationship with this spirit and make offerings to him during their rituals. This mythical killing is of some interest, for among the many formerly head-hunting peoples of the archipelago, more than one instance can be found where the erection of a house demanded a literal sacrifice in the form of a head. Avé and King (1986: 61) note that in Borneo's more stratified societies, a slave sometimes used to be killed before the placement of the chief's first apartment support post, and the body thrown into the post hole. These posts might also have human images carved on them, and in head-hunting days, human skulls were suspended in the rafters very near the support posts. They add: 'Even today some Borneo communities occasionally present offerings to house posts which are thought to be inhabited by guardian spirits, which look after the well-being of the house and its inhabitants.' In South Nias, with its hierarchical social system, the 'great house' of a chief and also the village council house both required the taking of a head, and to consecrate the village of Bawömataluo, a total of seven heads were used, one being buried at the top and bottom of each of the three great entrance stairways and one beneath the village 'navel-stone' (Feldman 1977: 122). The people of East Flores used to kill an enemy man and bury his head under one of the posts when rebuilding a village temple (Arndt 1951: 79). Ellen (1986: 10), too, records that construction of a house among the Nuaulu of Seram formerly required the taking of a head, which was buried beneath the most sacred main post, situated in the north-east corner. One finds little discussion of the precise motives for this custom, but there may have been some idea that the vitality and potency represented by the head could be transferred to the building, and have a beneficial effect on the occupants. In Burma, human sacrifice was practised apparently with the idea that spirits of the dead would perform a protective function. Shway Yoe (1882: 481) records that at the construction of the walled city of Mandalay in 1858, fifty-two people were buried alive under the walls, at other boundaries such as the palace gates, and under the king's throne. Their spirits were

already come across some examples of this. The main house post may, as among the Bugis, be thought of as anchoring the vital force of the house, and/or it may be described as the residence of a personified spirit. The Sakuddei believe that the spirit of a culture hero dwells beneath the main post of the longhouse. This spirit is called 'the shaker' and is thought to cause earthquakes. Schefold (1980: 92) records:

In a myth, it is told that he was originally a human being, an orphan who, early in life, displayed supernatural abilities and taught men how to build houses and perform the associated ceremonies. His relatives killed him out of envy: during the construction of the house, they bade him climb down into the hole that had been dug out for the main pile

thought to haunt the place and attack any enemies approaching.[10]

House posts may also be closely associated with house ancestors.[11] The frequently encountered belief that ancestral spirits are present in the house should perhaps be regarded as a factor contributing to the vital force of the house, especially since ancestors are associated with fertility. Barnes (1974: 74), for example, observes that, whether or not the Kédang house is literally alive in the sense of animals or humans, it is inhabited by an ancestral spirit. The house posts, especially the main one, are 'the means by which the spirit has access to the building'. The Atoni of Timor also make offerings to ancestors at the front left house post, which is called the 'head mother post' (Cunningham 1964: 42). The Yami of Lanyü Island depict the ancestral culture hero Magamaog on highly valued central house posts (Figure 118). So important are these posts that malicious damage incurred to them provides sufficient reason for violent retaliation (Beauclair 1958: 88), a fact which Cameron and Sumnik-Dekovich (1985: 174) suggest might be due to the scarcity and consequent high value of wood, as well as to the importance of the ancestral motifs carved on the posts. It is far more likely, however, that such damage would not only be construed as an insulting attack on the 'house' as a group of kin, but would also be seen to threaten the 'vitality' of the house and consequently the well-being of the occupants.

An apparently universal rule in South-East Asian societies is that house posts must always be 'planted' (literally the term used in most instances) with their root or 'base' end down, the same way as the tree originally grew. Symbolism of 'base' and 'tip' is highly elaborated in some Indonesian societies, and rules may even extend to the placing of horizontal members. In the Toraja house, beams on the long sides must be oriented with their base ends to the south. Volkman (1985: 47) notes that in the Sesean region of Toraja, the southernmost room of the house is consequently known as the 'root' of the house, and sacred heirloom cloths and swords are sometimes stored here. For, as a priest explained, 'The roots must be fertilized, so that the "branches and the leaves" (the heavily-decorated façade of the house) will be beautiful.' Even humble pieces of fire-wood must follow the rule, the 'trunk' end being placed in the fire first; the same is true for the Sumbanese, who believe that, if this is not done

118. Yami house post. The horned figure represents the ancestral culture hero Magamaog. (From Feldman 1985: 173, courtesy of UCLA Museum of Natural History)

when a woman of the house is pregnant, a breech birth will result (Forth 1981: 32). Other parts of the tree besides the wood also have their 'bases' and 'tips'; for example, the betel leaves and pieces of areca nut used in Toraja offerings, which are arranged in particular patterns, depending to whom the offering is being made. The pervasiveness of this symbolism is indicative of the importance of the theme of growth in the ideas of Indonesian societies. It appears that we are dealing here with a distinctively *Austronesian* theme, since not only are the ideas extremely widely distributed, but a variety of words for 'trunk' and 'tip' occur in Proto-Austronesian reconstructions, showing similar clusters of meanings (Wurm and Wilson 1975: 13, 187, 225).

The same metaphors of 'trunk' and 'tip' are used by the Buginese. Acciaioli (n.d.) notes that the Bugis term *pong* encompasses a range of meanings from 'tree', 'trunk', 'financial capital', to 'origin, source, spring, beginning, base, ground, essence', and that it forms the central term in the Buginese language of 'those dualities found throughout the languages of the archipelagic region that contrast trunk and tip, centre and periphery'. In Kédang, writes Barnes (1974: 68):

The major parts of the house must be placed in a prescribed way; to fail to follow the rule would cause disaster.... The first rule is that the house posts must stand in the ground in the same position as that in which the trees grew from which they are made. One of the phrases for incest, *huneq-koloq*, which means 'to turn upside down', is also applied to putting a house post in the ground in the reverse position from that in which it grew. Another part of this rule is that all major vertical beams and rafters in the building must also preserve the natural orientation of the piece from which they are made; and major parts lying horizontally must be put in place according to the imperative *wana pan*, 'travel to the right'. By this last phrase is meant that the tips of the boards and poles must all point counter-clockwise around the rectangle of the building.

He goes on to note how widespread is this rule (with minor variations regarding the placing of horizontal members) in eastern Indonesia. The whaling boats of Lembata even follow a version of it, having all the 'base' ends of timbers pointing to the prow of the boat, and the masts planted base down.

Of Bali, Covarrubias (1937: 94) notes: 'The house must stand "upright"; that is, the bottom of the posts should be the end nearest to where the roots were in the tree.' In Sumba, according to Forth, distinctions between 'trunk' and 'tip' (*pingi* and *kapuka*) are fundamental to notions of order:

Pingi has been glossed as 'trunk', 'source', and 'origin'; it might also be translated as 'basis', 'fundament' or 'principal part'. The complementary term, *kapuka*, thus refers to the tip,

top, or uppermost part of something, and has the further senses of 'derivative', 'superficial', and 'recent'.... In respect of the house, it is the basis of the rule that all vertical parts—the posts, spars, and wall supports—must be placed so that the *pingi* end of the wood points downwards. To erect a house is *pamula*, 'to plant'.... If the order were reversed, the Rindi say, the building would not be durable: the posts would then rot in the ground. Moreover, the wellbeing of the inhabitants would be threatened; thus the improper inversion of a house post, before it was corrected, was once divined to be the cause of illness and a number of deaths in a house.

As for horizontal members, the rule is that the trunk end of one piece must meet the tip end of the next, following a principle identical to the Kédangese of 'movement to the right', in an anticlockwise fashion around the building.[12]

The metaphor of 'planting', and its implications for the 'life' of the building, are addressed by Ellen in the case of the Nuaulu of Seram. Noting the degree of ritual which surrounds every detail of house construction, Ellen (1986: 26) observes:

[The house] is at once both natural and cultural. Its organic connections with the natural universe are evident in the ritual continuity expressed between the living trees destined to become house timbers and the house timbers themselves. The major timbers are subject to ritual from the very moment they are singled out to be cut; they are temporarily placed on racks to prevent them touching the ground inauspiciously, that is, length-wise or top-down. They must be carried to the village foot first, they are stored on trestles in timber stores which are themselves sacred. When it comes to their emplacement, they are quite literally 'planted' (*irahu*, to plant, as in *irahu sikewe*, 'planting yams'), and always according to their natural orientation, that is, root end first.... In this respect it is instructive to compare rituals in which sacred shrubs are planted with the 'planting' of [house posts]. The similarities are detailed and astonishing. The house is thus considered to be, in a very real sense, 'living'. This aliveness is often expressed in anthropomorphic terms.

Barnes (1974: 69), in his description of Kédang 'planting' of house posts, notes that not all Kédangese idiom supports the idea of the posts as 'alive'. But he adds the thought-provoking observation that the Indonesian word 'to plant' (*tanam*) and its cognates also have the sense of 'to bury'. 'Comparatively, planting and death may not prove such distinct ideas. Many Indonesian stories of the origin of rice or other grains turn upon the equation.'

The imagery of 'trunk' and 'tip' may be extended to descriptions of social relations. The Mambai of East

Timor, for example, utilize this botanical metaphor to express the hierarchical relationships between houses. New 'tip' houses branch off from older, ancestral 'trunk' houses, as in myth the ancestors 'cut a slip' from the central pillar of the first house and spread out to found new settlements, 'planting' their cuttings on the sites where they chose to build new houses (Traube 1986: 168). A final example may be taken from the Karo Batak, where the arrangement of 'bases' and 'tips' has a substantial impact on the designation of interior space. Here, the bases of all beams are oriented to the north-west corner of the house, and the apartment in this corner is called *benakayu*, 'base of the tree'. It is occupied by the chief of the house (*pengulu rumah*). His deputy, who is one of his wife-taking kin, occupies the opposite, south-easterly apartment which is called *ujungkayu*, 'top of the tree'. In a standard arrangement of eight apartments (none of which are actually partitioned off from each other, the interior of the house being completely open), the remaining apartments are all given names which relate them to these two points of reference. They are called 'opposite the base of the tree', 'opposite the top of the tree', 'sharing a kitchen with the base of the tree', 'sharing a kitchen with the top of the tree', 'sharing a kitchen opposite the base of the tree', and 'sharing a kitchen opposite the top of the tree' (Singarimbun 1975: 58, 60).

In the houses of both the Northern Thai and the Acehnese of North Sumatra, we find some remarkable parallels in the categorizing of a pair of main pillars as 'male' and 'female', as well as in the rites performed for their erection. Among the Northern Thai, the first pillar to be put in place is called the *sao mongkhon* or 'Auspicious Pillar', and is conceived of as male. It forms a pair with the *sao nang* or 'Lady Pillar', within the inner room of the house. They may also be referred to as the 'king' and 'queen' posts. The king post stands to the right of the Ancestor Shelf (where offerings are made) in the finished house, with the queen post opposite, on the right-hand side of the foot of the bed. People sleep with their heads pointing towards the shelf and their feet toward the posts. In the holes dug for the posts, gold leaf, silver coins, or ornaments will be buried, together with various food offerings, red and white cloth, and leaves with auspicious-sounding names (having such meanings as 'gold', 'jewels', 'to support', etc.). The food offerings are for the *naga* or spirits of the earth (Turton 1978: 116; Krug and Duboff 1982: 52). The posts themselves are cut in a special

way and carried to the site by people with auspicious-sounding names. They are decorated with young coconuts, a bunch of bananas, and a sugar-cane top, tied on with sacred homespun cotton thread. On the king post is tied a shirt belonging to the male householder, and on the queen post a blouse of his wife. The tops of the posts may be dressed with white and red cloth, zinc or silver, designed to ensure good fortune. The cloths may have cabbalistic diagrams inscribed in the Northern Thai alphabet (Charernsupkul and Temiyabandha 1979: 60). A ritual is performed at this time of 'tying the soul (*khwan*)' of the two posts (Turton 1978: 117). Further offerings must be made as the beams at the four corners of the house are put in place, in order to propitiate the guardian spirits of the four quarters.

In Aceh, as described by Snouck Hurgronje (1906) and Dall (1982), the main frame of the house is erected with the aid of communal labour, supervised by the village elders, religious leaders, and a master builder. To begin with, the site must be prepared and blessed and a favourable time appointed. First to be erected, again, are the two main house posts with their cross-beams, while prayers are recited from the Koran. These two posts are called the *raja* and *putröë*, or 'prince' and 'princess'. In the finished house, these posts stand in the main bedroom, regarded as the most important room in the house. During a wedding ceremony, they symbolize the bride and groom, who sit next to their appropriate pillars in this room.[13] These posts (as well as some others) are further personified in having red, white, and black cloth tied around their tops like a turban.[14] Between each layer of cloth is placed a written verse from the Koran. Evil spirits, notes Dall, are thought most likely to enter the building through openings, especially near the roof, and this clothing of the tops of the posts is designed to protect the inmates of the house from harm. Koranic verses are also commonly placed above door and window openings (Snouck Hurgronje 1906: 43; Dall 1982: 50–1). The striking parallels with both Thai and Malay custom suggest that we are dealing with an ancient and widespread tradition, to which elements such as written formulae have been added as later accretions. What is most noteworthy is the personification of the main posts and their identification with the husband and wife who occupy the house. This identification is further strengthened in the Thai case by the rule that the two posts may only be re-used in the same function and for the same household (Turton 1978: 117). In north-west Malaysia, the *tiang seri* itself is designated 'female' (*tiang seri betina*), while the middle post in between the main body of the house and the veranda is called the 'male' post (*tiang seri jantan*). According to Gibbs (1987: 91), at the ceremonial planting of the *tiang seri*, the woman of the house places her hands upon the post: 'This is a sign that the house belongs to her and will be under her care when it is completed. It is also an admission from the woman that it will be her responsibility to look after the house when it is completed.'

Roofing a house is often an occasion for communal assistance, all the members of a community lending a hand. Completion of the roof is another moment in the construction process which is likely to be accompanied by ritual. The Toraja hold a dramatic rite called *ma'bubung* (*bubung* means 'roof ridge') to complete the inauguration ceremony of an aristocratic origin-house (Figure 119). Formerly a particular house slave had the special task of mounting the ridge to make an offering of pig's fat which is burned with a torch so that the fat melts and runs over a pile of rice placed in a winnowing basket. Water is sprayed out from a bamboo tube over the people gathered below. This is considered to be 'cooling' and to represent a wish for the houseowners to enjoy health and good fortune. It is also referred to as 'children's urine' (*tene pia*), that is, it represents the hope for many offspring. In some areas, the person who mounts the ridge is supposed to carry a huge bamboo torch, with which he treads up and down the length of the ridge three times, dancing and shouting. The flaring up of the torch represents the hope that the houseowners' fortunes too will 'flare up'; should it go out in the process, this would be highly inauspicious. However, the only time I witnessed the performance of this rite the torch was not actually lit, since the participants were too afraid of the risk of starting a fire! Ending at the north (front) end of the ridge, the officiant must then throw down the torch so as to strike a wooden bowl which has been placed on a mat in front of the house and filled with water containing various items: a bead (representing nobility), a piece of iron (longevity), a gold bead (health and life), and certain leaves thought to have 'cooling' and health-giving properties.

The house while under construction is in a sort of liminal state, during which it is under the responsibility of the head carpenter, who as we have seen is himself often a ritual expert. It has been his duty to ensure that everything has been done in the proper way, so that the occupants will enjoy health and prosperity. The latter, meanwhile, have been supplying the wants of the carpenters, often including all their food, drink and cigarettes. Among the Mambai of Timor, the carpenters while at work have to observe prohibitions on bathing, hair cutting, and sexual intercourse (Traube 1986: 83). The inauguration of a house brings to an end this marginal period, and is not infrequently marked by a rather elaborate rite of handing over charge from the carpenter or ritual expert to the houseowners themselves, whose first entry into the finished building is a solemn moment. An elaborate rite is performed not only by the Toraja, but also by the Northern Thai, the Karo, and others. In the Karo case, the emphasis is on chasing out any evil influences which might still be lurking about, with the help of a priest, a solemn procession, and a traditional orchestra. As the occupants enter the house, the priest anoints their foreheads and cheeks with 'cooling' rice flour paste (Singarimbun 1975: 68).[15] Among the Northern Thai, as Turton (1978: 119) describes, the houseowners must pass through several stages in the assumption of ownership:

First, there are gun-shots fired before the householders across the lower threshold, where a bamboo slat is placed across the threshold. There the new householders are interrogated as to who they are, what their intentions are, and why they want to enter. This is followed by further gun-shots marking each transition. There is another barrier at the top of the stairs; in the case I observed this was a woman's silver belt. Here the expert, who is still in charge of the house, challenges the householder and a symbolic sale is conducted with a kind of inverted bargaining. The householder asks to buy the house say for 1,000 *baht*, the expert says: 'Won't you buy it for 500 *baht*?' and the householder says: 'No, 2,000', and so on, and with much joking they are allowed to pass. There are more gun-shots. Auspicious objects are brought into the house. And then the expert cedes the house to the householders....

The climax of this ritual is the offering of food to a group of male elders, who bless the householders and invoke 'happiness, fertility, wealth, safety, health and long life'. Then the other guests are fed. The whole is accompanied by much eating, drinking, and singing, with moments of licence, horse-play, and water throwing such as take place at New Year ceremonies.

In the Toraja rites, a number of stages can also be

119. The renowned Toraja *tongkonan* (origin-house) of Nonongan, hung with precious heirlooms on the occasion of the ceremony held to celebrate completion of its rebuilding, in January 1983. (Photograph: Roxana Waterson)

discerned. On the day of the inauguration, an exchange takes place between the houseowner and the head carpenter, who sit on a mat with a basket of rice between them. The carpenter has his tools beside him. The owner recites a verse calling down blessings on the carpenter and expressing hopes that he may excel in his craft, and the carpenter reciprocates by wishing him wealth, fortune, and fertility, as well as long life for both of them. In another stage of the proceedings, the dreams of all the house descendants are interpreted by a traditional priest (the *to minaa*), who attributes to all of them favourable meanings. The priest prepares to spend the night in the as yet unoccupied house, when the houseowner comes and knocks at the door. The priest questions him, saying, 'Who is it?' and 'What have you brought?'. The houseowner carries a basket full of pieces of wood and stone, which he says are valuables such as gold daggers and ornaments, necklaces, rice, buffaloes, and pigs. Finally, the basket is taken up into the house and they both sleep there. On the following day the roof-ridge ceremony is held, completing the rites.

House construction, then, is in most cases as much a ritual as a technological process. Through the following of the proper rituals, the house and its vital power are constituted and the well-being of the inhabitants is assured.

The House as Body

The idea of the house as a 'living' thing is often reinforced by the use of anthropomorphic imagery. We have already considered the possibility that this is nothing more than a convenient means of classifying and ordering space—and yet, so many examples of body imagery are coupled with definite statements about the 'vitality' of the house that the link between the two can hardly be overlooked.

House parts may be named after body parts in quite an elaborate way: for example, in Savu, as well as being compared to a boat with a bow and a stern, 'a house has a head, a tail, a neck, cheeks, a space through which it breathes, a chest, and ribs' (Kana 1980: 228). For the Tetum of Timor, 'the house is credited with a backbone, eyes, legs, body, anus, face, head, and bones, as well as a womb and vagina', which, together with the buffalo horn gable finial, suggests that the body symbolized is simultaneously that of a woman and a buffalo cow (Hicks 1976: 56ff.). A link with the owners of the house is further reinforced by the fact that measurements for house parts are frequently based on their own body measurements. In the Balinese case, the male householder provides the proportions, while the Sasak choose those of the wife, since it is she who is most often in the house and has to work in it (Howe 1983: 139; Gunawan Alif 1985: 61). Measurements based on the human body (usually the hands and arms of the carpenters, but on some occasions of the woman of the house) are used also by the Malays (Wardi 1981: 63; Gibbs 1987: 75), and by the Bima and Donggo of Sumbawa (Hitchcock 1983: 214; Just 1984: 41).[16] In Bali, as already mentioned, the adding on of an increment to all measures is essential to ensure that a building has life. Howe (1983: 149) notes:

According to the villagers the main measure is like the body of a person (which, since the units are taken from the human body, is exactly what it is) and that this can only come to life by the infusion of a soul, which in this case is the *jiwa ukuran* ('the soul of the measure').

Adding bits on, like the use of uneven numbers, symbolizes life, which itself is a continuing, never-completed process.[17] With regard to the latter, Howe (1983: 144–5) explains:

If there has been a mistake in measuring the walls such that their lengths total an even number or that the difference between them is an even number then the compound is said to be *embet* ('closed up', 'blocked up'), *mati* (dead) and 'not to have any doors'.... It is also said to be like a body without a soul.... Conversely a properly measured compound is said to be 'alive' (*idup/urip*). A compound which is *embet*, which 'has no doors', cannot be brought to life because, conceptually speaking, the gods cannot enter and the evil spirits cannot be expelled. Such a compound cannot support life within it since it is, itself, dead. It is therefore worth noting that in previous times, just before a cremation, the corpse was not allowed to be taken out through the doors but instead had to be carried over the wall or through a hole smashed in the wall (Covarrubias 1937: 373, 378). This seems entirely reasonable since a death in the compound entails that something may have gone wrong during its construction resulting in the consideration that 'there are no doors'.

Once again we see the interdependence of the 'life' of the compound and its buildings and that of its inhabitants. Like the Acehnese and Buginese, the Balinese regard mystical influences as entering a structure through the corners. The corners are associated with odd numbers, with transitional nodes of time (such as dusk) and space (sea-shore, bridges, crossroads), and the joints and orifices of the body. Illness is caused by a disruption of the flow of substances, including spiritual essence, in and out of the body and the dead body is also described as 'blocked' (embet) (Howe 1983: 146-7). Like the cosmos itself, the body is also conceptually divided into three: head, trunk, and legs. Villages are spatially divided into temple, habitation, and cemetery areas corresponding to these bodily divisions (Soelarto 1973: 45). Within a house courtyard, space is similarly conceived. According to Covarrubias (1937: 88):

The Balinese say that a house, like a human being, has a head—the family shrine; arms—the sleeping quarters and the social parlour; a navel—the courtyard; sexual organs—the gate; legs and feet—the kitchen and the granary; and anus—the pit in the backyard where the refuse is disposed of.

We can see, therefore, as Howe in particular makes clear, that the principles governing house construction are precisely in accord with those which shape many other domains of Balinese cultural life.

In Sumba, body imagery is applied to houses, graves, villages, fields, rivers, even the island itself, all of which are conceived as having a 'head' and 'tail' (Forth 1981: 67).[18] The gates in the centre of the two long sides are called the 'waist gates', and the centre of the village is referred to as 'abdomen' (padua), or 'navel', or 'heart' (puhu). In parts of East Sumba, these sections of the village used to be separated by stone walls. The 'head' is regarded as superior to the 'tail', but both of these in turn are subordinate to the centre. In the village of Parai Yawungu, the oldest ancestral house of the noble clan is situated in the centre of the village, with the 'cool' (that is, less sacred) houses of the higher ranking nobles in the 'head' section and of lower nobles in the 'tail' (Forth 1981: 54). In Paraingu Umalulu, the capital of Melolo district, the opposite ends are occupied by two opposing warrior clans, each with a ruler of equal status, while in the centre dwell mediating priestly clans which serve both sides and adopt a neutral role in disputes. Adams (1980: 212-14) notes that this triadic relationship is echoed in the relations formed between a clan and its wife-giving and wife-taking clans, in the arrangements made for various kinds of negotiations and trade exchanges, and in women's designs for textiles, where the two outer sections mirror each other and are joined by a

central section filled with abstract geometric designs. This section is regarded as 'noble' and superior to the others. Again, we find spatial divisions echoed in social arrangements, though superiority is here granted to the navel rather than the head.

That the house is conceived of as a body is reflected in several usages, referring to both the horizontal and vertical planes. The front of the house is said to be like a man's head and the back his 'tail'. One term for the front of the house is mata yaba, yaba having the sense of 'mouth', 'opening', or 'forward part'. The front faces inward toward the village square, while the rear, called hambeli ('back' or 'outside'), faces the outside of the village where people go to defecate. The peak of the house is sometimes referred to as the 'body' of the house or its 'hair-knot'. This, according to Rindi ideas, reflects the fact that the peak is seen as the most important part of the house, with the rest of it, the inhabited part, as its extension or 'limbs', in the same way that the 'cool' houses of the clan are seen as extensions of the ancestral clan house which is the clan's ritual centre (Forth 1981: 29).

The symbolism of the house among the matrilineal Tetum of Timor is of particular interest. The house is both secular dwelling and sacred abode of the ancestors. It combines the complementary symbolism of male and female, and yet is distinctively feminine in its associations. 'In the home, wives are definitely the masters' (Hicks 1976: 30-2, 56-66). The Tetum house is a long, gabled structure on fairly low piles, erected, somewhat unusually, with no house-building rites. The front is called its 'face', and the front door (which is masculine, used only by men and boys who have reached puberty) is called 'the eye of the house'. The rear, feminine door is called the 'house vagina'. The side walls are 'legs', the ridge the 'backbone', the rear wall the 'anus'. The house has three rooms. By far the largest and most important—both ritually and domestically—is the rear room, called 'the womb of the house' (uma lolon). This room is the female half of the house. It contains the hearth and the ritual pillar, extending from floor to roof. This pillar has a shelf on which are kept the household's sacred water pitcher, plate, and cloth, and the pouch of the ancestral ghosts, in which they may rest, sleep, eat the food, and chew the betel-nut placed inside it. Every living member of the household owns a sacred pitcher, called the 'little womb'. A pregnant mother purchases a pitcher for her child some time before giving birth, and shortly after it is born she fills the pitcher with cool water. If a child of the household leaves the village for more than a month, his mother replenishes the pitcher and keeps water in it till he returns. At marriage, a person takes his or her pitcher and places it on the ritual shelf of their new home. At death, the pitcher is destroyed along with some other possessions.

The close association of women with the sacred, and of the house with women and birth, is a continuous thread running through Tetum religion. The earth itself is a sacred womb, from which the first humans emerged through limestone craters which the Tetum call 'vaginas'. The word *lolon*, in fact, applies to rooms, wombs, and tombs. Birth ritual begins in the house, where a woman gives birth on a mat in between the ritual pillar and the hearth. The child's first entry into the world outside the 'house womb' takes place four days after the cord drops off for a girl, or five days for a boy, when the father carries it out through the house vagina and places it on a mat in the village plaza. The emergence from the house thus forms a kind of second, ritual 'birth'. In the ensuing ritual, both the father's and mother's clansfolk participate, publicly affirming the creative bond of affinity which unites them.

Representations of the house as buffalo's body, hinted at in the Tetum case, are much more explicit in some other instances, notably among the Karo, Toba, and Simalungun Batak of Sumatra, and the Northern Thai. The gables of Karo buildings are decorated with modelled heads of buffalo, said to protect the occupants from harm. The buffalo head on the front gable of the old chief's house in the village of Lingga, which I visited in 1986, has a small pot hanging around its neck. The pot, I was told, when put in position, is filled with water and lemon juice. It is intended for the buffalo to drink, since if it became thirsty it would suck the blood of the house's inhabitants instead of protecting them. The great raja's house of the Simalungun at Pematang Purba has a buffalo head at the front and a tail of *ijuk* (sugar palm) fibre hanging down from the rear gable-end. In traditional Toba Batak conceptions, the world itself, as well as the body of participants in the important regenerative rite called *bius*, is identified with the body of a buffalo. In addition, Niessen (1985: 221) draws together a variety of sources on the Toba concerning the conception of house and rice barn as buffalo body. Van der Tuuk (1864–7), for example, recorded a number of 'buffalo' features in the structure

of these buildings:

The upper third of the structure is called the pinarhorbo = buffalo representation. The front gable is decorated with an ulu horbo = buffalo head, and the roof gently curves back to end, in some cases, to a tail at the back gable. The painted decorative board pointing downwards from the roof is the dila paung = buffalo tongue, and 'the piece of cotton or linen hanging out of the mouth of the buffalo head' doesn't have a specific name, but is called by the general term gagaton, 'that which is eaten by grazing animals'. The lengthwise roof spars are called pamoltoki, from boltok meaning stomach, or belly. This is where the rice is stored. Van der Tuuk does not mention the tiang (house-posts), but it is a defensible hypothesis, given the meat shares of the raja na opat [four officiants in the *bius* ceremony] and their association with the posts of the offer-house, that they are the legs of the buffalo. The doorway of the house is colloquially called baba or 'animal mouth' (Sherman 1982: 358). The window in the back of the house opposite the door is the hosa-hosa meaning breath or wind, and is perhaps comparable to the posterior of a female buffalo as it is through this opening that the placenta is disposed [of] after the birth of a child (de Boer 1946: 385).

The Northern Thai house with its carved crossed gable-finials is said to resemble a huge male buffalo, the finials being its horns.[19] There is also an elaborately carved teak lintel above the door into the sleeping room, which is known as *ham yon* (literally 'magic testicles'), and which is supposed to represent the buffalo's genitalia. Its size is determined in relation to that of the householder's feet. The lintel symbolizes power over evil, and protects the fertility of the houseowners, man and wife, and the strength and well-being of the family. It becomes more powerful the longer they live in the house, and is used for only one generation before being changed. If the house has a new owner, he must change the lintel and dispel its accumulated power by beating it with a stick (Kraisri Nimmanahaeminda 1979). Noticeable again in this custom is the remarkable concentration of vitality in the house part, and its intimate association with the lives and fortunes of the residents. Such lintels are apparently no longer made, and probably have not been for the last sixty years or so (Krug and Duboff 1982: 48).

Why exactly the house should be thought of as a buffalo is not made explicit by any of these authors, but it must reflect the ancient symbolic and ceremonial importance of this particular animal in South-East Asian societies. The power of the buffalo to protect has already been met with in Chapter 1, where we encountered the suggestion that house horns have a protective function. In more general terms, it would appear, the house body forms a protective outer skin outside the actual bodies of its inhabitants. The house is a secure and well-defined space where people may feel at ease. For the Bugis, as Shelly Errington makes clear (1979; 1983a: 562), threat is visualized very much in terms of *penetration* from outside. The individual, through concentration and awareness, can deflect such threats to his person, because he will develop a powerful *sumange'*. The house 'body' offers extra protection not because it is an impenetrable envelope—on the contrary, just like a human body it is liable to penetration through joints and apertures—but through the concentration of its own *sumange'*, attached at the navel-post just as human vital energy is attached at the navel. House *sumange'* encompasses that of the occupants, leaving them free to relax their attention, to eat, sleep, and express their emotions freely. Even so, one is vulnerable when eating (which involves the opening of a bodily orifice), and so people take care to protect themselves by closing all the outer doors and windows of the house at meal times. Those with high rank are thought capable of attaining higher concentrations of *sumange'*, so that a respected, high-status elder of one's kin group can also provide the sense of security that comes from being near a navel-centre: 'People say that they feel cool and calm within their Opu's (a titled noble's) presence.' At the level of the state, it is the ruler at the navel-centre of the kingdom who ensures the protection of the realm.

We can see clear parallels here with Howe's analysis of Balinese concepts of the body and health. We find the same liability of the body to penetration through joints and apertures, and the potential danger of 'transitional' times and spaces—in the Buginese case, the moments of entering and leaving the house, for example, or of dawn and dusk. The anthropologist earned reproach for her foolhardy behaviour in standing by windows to watch the sunset (S. Errington 1979: 10–11). There is an equally strong similarity in the concepts of the Acehnese. The dressing of the house posts with coloured cloths and the concern with doors and windows which we have already described, all indicate the attention paid to boundaries, apertures, and joints as points of entry by outside influences. In Acehnese thought, writes Dall (1982: 50), 'the house is not seen as a shelter from the sun and rain. It is regarded as a refuge from evil forces and influences.'

The protective function of the house among the Toba Batak has been well analysed by Niessen. She notes the strong similarities in form between house walls—'massive canoe-shaped slabs of wood originating from gigantic carved heads protruding from the front wall'—and the side planks of wooden beds (and coffins) (Figure 120). The stout earth walls topped with spiny bamboos which formerly protected most Batak villages provide an added outer ring of protection for the villagers (Figure 121). Poetic names for house walls compare them to twining snakes and vines. Bed within house within village together form a concentric image of protection. 'The same "walls" are found in each habitation of the soul in living or spirit form, including coffins, sarcophagi, and certain altars to the ancestor spirits. Although the village walls do not have the same form as the house walls, they are clearly perceived as analagous to them' (Niessen 1985: 212–14). A different, but charming image of protection was evoked to me by a Toba acquaintance who remarked that houses where the entrance is underneath the house, by way of a trapdoor in the floor, are thought of as being like the hen that gathers its chicks (the inhabitants) under its wings (Figure 122). At one time, the positioning of the door served a very practical defensive function, as well as a psychological one, for the house members.

In all these instances the recurrent use of 'body' metaphors powerfully expresses the idea of the house as a living extension of the group of its inhabitants.

The 'Death' of a House

If the house may be 'brought to life' through the process of construction, through ritual, or even through being inhabited, what happens to its 'vital force' should its material form be destroyed? There is, as several examples above have shown, a close relationship between the 'health' of a house and that of its occupants. In most cases, health is conceived of in terms of 'coolness', while any imbalance of forces caused by illness or attack by evil influences generates dangerous 'heat'. Snouck Hurgronje (1906: 305) commented at some length on the recurrence of this set of ideas throughout the archipelago, as have numerous later ethnographers. The Iban provide a particularly vivid example, as Freeman (1970: 123) describes:

When the Iban speak of the ritual condition of a long-house they liken it to the temper of a human organism. When in

120. Toba clan origin-house at Simanindo, Samosir Island, Lake Toba, Sumatra, 1986. (Photograph: Roxana Waterson)

133

121. Stone gateway in the high earth wall surrounding Simanindo village, Samosir Island, Lake Toba, 1986. Formerly such walls, topped by spiny bamboos, were a common defensive feature of Toba Batak villages. (Photograph: Roxana Waterson)

with a medley of abandoned possessions, the house stands aloof, silent and deserted, as though its owners had indeed been suddenly spirited away.

A great danger to all timber buildings is that of fire, and the possibility of the 'death' of a house was suddenly brought home to me when, after a long drought in 1982, the Toraja village in which I had lived four years previously during my first period of fieldwork suffered a fire. Started by a spilled oil-lamp, the fire swept through the village and destroyed fourteen out of twenty-four houses, including two old noble origin-houses (*tongkonan*) and numerous granaries with their stocks of rice. This disaster happened just a few days before I returned to the field for follow-up research, and I reached the village to find the ashes still smoking and the local *to minaa*, or traditional priest, presiding over a ceremony for the oldest of the two burnt *tongkonan*—and by extension, all the other houses which had been destroyed (Figure 123). The small buffalo calf sacrificed on this occasion was described by one person as a funeral offering for the house, which like humans, had a *bombo* or spirit which exactly resembled it, and which would require food, like humans, on its journey to the afterlife. People were in mourning, he observed, for three nights, during which they abstained from eating rice (in this case, the prohibition was observed only by the woman in whose house the fire had started). Others laid emphasis on the rite as symbolizing continuity, rather than death; an origin-house should never be allowed to disappear, and if the family could afford it, it would eventually be rebuilt. The names of origin-houses which have not been standing for decades, or even centuries, are always remembered, and there always remains at least the theoretical possibility that their descendants might, some day, give them material form once again.[20]

Rites performed following the tragic fire in the Kraton or Sultan's palace of Solo (Central Java) in February 1985 again reveal an emphasis on continuity. The palace is considered to be *keramat*, that is, to have a particularly strong concentration of vital energy, and its destruction (still more of the valuable library and antique treasures it contained) was a sad loss. Newspaper reports of the event and its aftermath described how the ashes of the burnt building were carefully gathered up into bags, some to be reburied beneath the new Kraton, when it should be rebuilt, and some thrown out to sea as an offering of appeasement to the Goddess of the Southern Ocean, Nyi Roro

122. Toba chief's house in the village of Lumban na Bolon, on the east shore of Lake Toba, 1986. Entrance is beneath the house by means of a trapdoor in the floor; Toba compare houses of this style to a hen gathering its chicks under its wings. (Photograph: Roxana Waterson)

sound and normal health, a man's body is said to be *chelap*, or cool, and when it is afflicted by disease or disorder, *angat*, or feverish. These same terms are applied to the long-house. Ritually, it may be in a 'cool' and benign state (*rumah chelap*), or, what is greatly feared, it may become 'heated' (*rumah angat*), charged with a kind of evil and contagious essence that threatens all of its inhabitants.... This dangerous state of affairs is liable to be brought about by any serious transgression of a ritual prohibition.... A long-house may also become *angat* from an invasion of malevolent spirits. This is made known in dreams, and should there have been a series of unwarranted deaths, a community will often flee their long-house, and stay away for months, while waiting for it to become 'cool' again. One of the strangest sights which the hinterland of Sarawak has to offer is an Iban long-house, whose inhabitants have fled in terror of 'unseen monsters'. Hung about with esoteric emblems and charms—an unavailing barricade of protective magic these—and strewn

123. Toraja priests gather to make offerings for an origin-house accidentally destroyed by fire in the village of Buttang, Malimbong district, Tana Toraja, 1982. Some villagers compared the occasion to a funeral for the lost house, while for others the rite served to symbolize its undying existence until such time as it can be physically rebuilt. (Photograph: Roxana Waterson)

Kidul. The beginning of 'restoration' started only a few months later, with a rite in which a deer's head and other offerings were buried in a casket beneath the fire-damaged part of the palace (*Tempo* 16 February 1985; *Straits Times* 26 June 1985). Just as ritual helps to constitute a building in the first place, then, it can also help to tide over the period after the physical loss of a house, whose identity must be preserved until rebuilding can be undertaken.[21]

*   *   *

All the evidence presented here serves to show how widespread are South-East Asian ideas of the house as an animate entity. It is clear that concepts of *semangat* as applied to the house are multi-faceted; the vitality of the house is seen to derive from a number of sources, including the life-force present in the trees used for timbers, the process of construction itself with its attendant rituals, and the association of house and body (either human or animal) by which the building becomes a sort of extension of the bodies of its inhabitants. There remains one, perhaps most obvious and most important, way in which a house becomes animated, and that is through having people living in it. Niessen, for example, in a passage quoted above, states of the Batak house that 'its inhabitants are its soul'. Westerners themselves may refer metaphorically to a house as seeming 'alive' or 'dead', a feeling which is derived from the quantity and quality of life being lived in it. But that this idea has much deeper resonances in South-East Asia will be seen when we turn, in the next chapter, to the association of houses with kin groups in the South-East Asian world.

1. For recent definitions of animism, and analyses of *semangat* and related concepts, see Endicott (1970), Benjamin (1979), and S. Errington (1983a). For comparisons with the Polynesian concept of *mana*, see Fischer (1931) and Kooijman (1942).

2. G. Acciaioli (personal communication).

3. C. Pelras (personal communication).

4. In Sumba, a certain class of slave was very intimately integrated into the families of their aristocratic masters; this close association is, in many cases, maintained today, in spite of the official abolition of slavery.

5. As we might expect, there is some evidence of these ideas extending into Oceania. On the 'thou-ness' of Maori architecture, and the possibilities of *speaking to* a Maori building rather than simply *talking about* it, see Linzey (1988).

6. Indeed, this sense of a house's 'presence' coming into being can be vivid, given the rapidity with which prefabricated wall or roof panels can often be raised into position to clothe the 'skeleton' of the framing members.

7. Horridge draws attention to the similarities both in boat-building techniques and associated rituals throughout both Indonesia and Polynesia, pointing to the existence of a shared and ancient (Austronesian) tradition.

8. I am grateful for this observation to Geoffrey Benjamin, who draws a comparison with the attitudes not only of his own Orang Asli informants, but to those, for example, of a Catholic priest who insists on a literal rather than symbolic understanding of transubstantiation in the Mass. Explicating symbolism *as symbolism* may be seen to threaten its potency.

9. *Seri* means 'radiating beauty'; the word is also used as an honorific title for royalty.

10. Woolard (1988: 10) notes that in former times, Fijian temple building also involved human sacrifice: 'The posts were cantilevered from holes in the ground where warriors stood holding the post vertical. They were sacrificed as the holes were filled with their arms encircling the post.'

11. The association of ancestors with the house is explored in Chapter 9.

12. Movement 'to the right' is, in Rindi, the way of the living; the dead, by contrast, wind on their clothes 'to the left' and erect their house posts in reverse order to the living (Forth 1981: 172, 200).

13. See Chapter 8 for a fuller analysis of gender symbolism in the Acehnese house.

14. The same practice is observed by the Malays (Lim 1987: 100; Gibbs 1987: 85–8). Lim states that of the three layers of cloth, the black represents mysterious powers, the red, life and courage, and the white, purity; while according to Gibbs, their placement on the house posts is a means by which *semangat* may be induced into the house. At the *tiang seri*, three strips of cloth are also tied round the middle, together with a coconut and a double-ended phallus carved out of wood.

15. In the Acehnese rite, the same kind of paste is applied to all the house posts (Snouck Hurgronje 1906: 43).

16. Bimanese women weavers use the same system for measuring cloth (Hitchcock 1983: 157).

17. This open-endedness is reflected also in Kis-Jovak's (1982: 24) statement that the Mentawai house is 'alive' and is never really finished, since the inhabitants are always adding on parts or details as required. A number of societies, including Aceh, also have a rule that the number of steps in the house stairs must be uneven, or misfortune will result. The image of 'adding on' is vividly employed in a Bugis custom of divination at a new house site:

'When determining where the navel post of a new house should be placed, the *sanro bola* (house building expert) must place a small piece of wood or bamboo in the ground three times. If after such placement, the piece is found to have extended its length, the householder is sure to receive good fortune if his house is centred on that spot. But the wood must not be extended to too great a length, for what is desired is obtaining good fortune, but not too quickly' (Acciaioli, n.d.).

A similar method of testing the site is used by the Malays (Gibbs 1987: 82; Lim 1987: 98). By contrast, some other Indonesian societies (for example, the Toraja and Sumbanese) do show a preference for even numbers, especially eight, as symbolizing completeness—without making any negative association between completion and death.

18. The Savunese, too, picture their island as a living being with a 'head' and 'tail' (Kana 1980: 222).

19. The finials are actualy called 'glancing crows' or 'glancing pigeons' by the Northern Thai, though the reasons for this are obscure (Krug and Duboff 1982).

20. Several of the villagers kept lumps of charcoal from the ashes, to grind up and use as medicine, although an informant from another district of Toraja said that there, the ashes were gathered and thrown far away, since some sin of the villagers must have caused such an unfortunate event.

21. A case of deliberate dissolution of a house's identity has been brought to my attention by Vivienne Wee (personal communication). In 1911 the Dutch forced the Sultan of Riau to abdicate and drove him into exile. Before abandoning the court, he and his noble followers deliberately destroyed all their palaces, since it was considered impossible for anybody but their original owners to inhabit them. Destruction of the buildings, then, paralleled the Sultan's own political demise. Where buildings are so closely associated with their occupants, suggests Wee, an unoccupied house is an anomaly; it is entirely possible that where such a house is regarded as 'haunted', it is the house itself that is doing the haunting.

137

CHAPTER 7
Kinship and 'House Societies'

THE identification between houses and people provides us, ultimately, with the real key to the understanding of the house in South-East Asia. Conversely, certain problems in the analysis of kinship systems can, I believe, be clarified by looking at them as house-based systems. How then does the house function to give shape and identity to kinship groupings?[1]

Indonesia is my focus in this chapter. Patterns of Indonesian kinship organization include a wide variety of types which, however, rarely fit comfortably within the framework of more traditional anthropological ideas about descent; labels such as 'patrilineal', 'matrilineal', or 'double descent' have a disquieting tendency to come unstuck. The cognatic systems typical of western Indonesia have in the past puzzled anthropologists because of their apparent amorphousness and lack of clearly bounded groups. Difficulties in the analysis of eastern Indonesian systems, on the other hand, have necessitated the development of a more sophisticated understanding of indigenous concepts of descent as a non-unilineal process. The actual composition of 'descent groups' is typically highly irregular, and there is great flexibility in the choice of alliances.[2] Fox (1980: 12) concludes that 'House' is 'a fundamental cultural category used in eastern Indonesia to designate a particular kind of social unit', though it is 'remarkably flexible in its range of applications'. He speaks of the house in eastern Indonesia as serving as a *metaphor* for the descent group, or as the *localization* of a descent group. Indeed, the idea of localization or origin is implied by its nature as a physical structure. Some societies, such as the Atoni, do apparently talk much about (non-unilineal) descent as an organizing principle. Nevertheless, there are a number of other cases where an alternative explanation presents itself; we can make more sense of the apparent irregularities of these systems only if we reverse matters and treat the *house* itself as the determining feature of the system.

The idea that there are certain forms of organization which can best be described as 'house societies' has been put forward by Claude Lévi-Strauss (1983) in his important analysis of the kinship systems of the North-West Coast of North America. The application of this idea to Indonesian societies promises to be highly rewarding, and makes sense of data which have persistently resisted analysis in terms of more conventional categories. I shall argue that the kinship systems of the archipelago, in all their variety, can best be understood only when the house is taken as their main organizing principle.

Lévi-Strauss and 'House Societies'

In a recent work, *The Way of the Masks*, Lévi-Strauss devotes a chapter to 'The Social Organisation of the Kwakiutl'. He points out the difficulties experienced by Boas and Kroeber in defining the kinship systems of the Kwakiutl and Yurok of the North-West Coast of North America. They found it virtually impossible to decide whether these societies were really patrilineal, matrilineal, or bilateral, since they seemed to be putting into operation simultaneously a number of principles which anthropologists have generally considered to be incompatible. They tended, in their efforts to decide the question, to concentrate on negative aspects of the system: they were not this, nor yet quite the other.

In Lévi-Strauss's view, the positive feature uniting these societies is the manner in which houses function as foci of kin organization. 'House societies', he suggests, may be identified over a wide historical and geographical span, including, for example, both feudal Europe and Japan, and the societies of the Philippines, Indonesia, Melanesia, and Polynesia, as well as the North-West Coast (Lévi-Strauss 1983: 176). Concern with questions of inheritance—in some cases of land or kingship, in others of titles and names—means that

138

kin and marriage ties are frequently activated in strategic ways. Houses in this sort of society, suggests Lévi-Strauss, generally share a number of features: they have a name, which may be inspired by the location or some other feature; they are perpetuated over time and not allowed to disappear, at least from memory; they may be elaborately decorated, especially on the façade; and they are the sites for the performance of ceremonies. House societies are characteristically divided into groups putatively tracing their descent from ancestors who founded the houses. Additional features may include an alternation of generations, with a belief in the reincarnation of grandparents in their grandchildren— a feature of Tsimshian society, as well as of some Indonesian ones. He also notes (1983: 176) the difficulty of distinguishing whether a society of this type has 'Hawaiian' or 'Eskimo' terminology, since one's judgement on this will be affected by which usages and contexts one chooses to dwell on.[3] What, however, *will* be noticeable is the recurrent use of 'house' imagery to express aspects of kinship and marriage relations. Where rank and inheritance are prime concerns, the tactical aspect of marriage will be seen in the occurrence, typically, of both very close marriages, in various classic patterns of cousin marriage, and of very distant marriages, uniting kingdoms, or laying claim to new titles and lands. Lévi-Strauss (1983: 166, 177) compares the opportunistic tracing of genealogical ties in the royal houses of medieval Europe (which frequently exploited links through women or by adoption, in spite of a patrilineal law of succession) with the practice in Kwakiutl noble families of allowing succession through marriage, from the wife's father to the son-in-law. So important was this potential mode of succession that 'an individual desirous of "entering a house" where there was no marriageable daughter, would symbolically marry a son, or failing a son, a part of the body (arm or leg) of the house chief, or even a piece of furniture'.

The fundamental feature of Lévi-Strauss's analysis is that it groups together as 'house societies' a range of North-West Coast societies with ostensibly very different kinship systems: in as much as the labels can be applied at all, the Kwakiutl, Nootka, and Bella-Bella systems are cognatic, the Tsimshian, Haida, and Tlingit are 'frankly matrilineal', while the Yurok of northern California were described (with reservations) by Kroeber as patrilineal. Kroeber considered the houses of the Yurok only in a chapter on material culture, from the point of view of techniques of construction and utilitarian function, and ignored them when he spoke of social organization. Yet, his own data demonstrate quite clearly that houses were enduring units of social organization, with important jural and ceremonial functions, and that their owners even took their names from the house itself. At the same time, finding that available analytical categories, such as 'tribe', 'clan', or 'village community', failed to fit the Yurok case, Kroeber was reduced to the conclusion that they simply had 'no society as such ... no social organization ... no authority...'. Contemporary ethnology did not supply him with the concept of 'house' which might have helped to make sense of such apparent formlessness (Kroeber 1925; Lévi-Strauss 1983: 171–3).

Lévi-Strauss's approach to these kinship systems as 'variations on a theme' parallels his treatment of myths as variant sets. Within island South-East Asia we find a similar range of apparently very different kinship systems which have given anthropologists just as much trouble as those of the North-West Coast, but which, if treated as 'house societies', suddenly come into sharper focus. It has always been something of a puzzle for anthropologists to explain the concentration of cognatic kinship systems in western Indonesia and of unilineal, 'prescriptive alliance' systems in eastern Indonesia (as well as parts of Sumatra). Adopting a Lévi-Straussian approach, we may begin to see all these systems as possible variants, whose common feature is the importance of the house as a focus of social organization. A good starting-point for such a generative approach may be found in a paper by James Fox (1985) on the possible reconstructions of early Austronesian kinship organization. He suggests how a whole range of regional developments might have taken place, accompanied by fairly minor modifications to a basic set of original Proto-Austronesian kin terms.[4] At the same time, new and detailed research in the archipelago allows us to bring to bear the concept of 'house societies' on problems of present-day Indonesian kinship organization.

Kinship and Rank

Clearly, the construction of buildings on the scale of a Borneo longhouse, a Nias chief's house, or a Toraja *tongkonan*, demands either the co-operation of a large group of people, or else a concentration of wealth on the part of the owners, and the ability to mobilize a large labour force. The same, indeed, may apply to other projects, such as the dragging of huge stones for tombs or monuments—in Nias, Sumba, or Toraja, for example—or the building of temporary ritual structures—as in Toraja, where thousands of guests may be accommodated for a large ceremony.[5] But often enough we find a combination of these factors—both the co-operation of a large group associated with the house, and the existence of a social ranking system within which members of an aristocracy enjoy the wealth and power which enable them to undertake impressive construction projects. In such cases, the house is designed, by its impressive size, distinctive shape, and fine ornamentation, to give visible substance to a family's claims to superior status, and to serve as an enduring sign of their prestige. Its construction involves expensive ceremonies, and when finished it becomes the site of rituals, as has been discussed in Chapter 3. Each of these adds to its glory and may be commemorated by the addition of specific ornamental elements to the house—gable horns for the Naga, or among the Toraja the carved head of a buffalo for those who have held the highest level of funeral ceremony. The horns of sacrificed buffaloes fastened to the house posts, in Toraja (Figure 124), Sumba, Flores, and elsewhere, likewise bear witness to past ceremonies. The aristocracy may, as among the Toraja, reserve to itself the right to construct a certain type of house, erect a particular kind of stone monument, or hold a particular ritual. But they depend upon the co-operation of the rest of the community to help them execute these projects, a fact which is generally acknowledged in the distribution of meat from sacrificed animals in order to feed all those who have assisted.

In what follows, I shall deal with a range of examples, in which we may see the house functioning (as far as rank and ritual systems are concerned) in a number of slightly different ways. One special category is formed by longhouse communities, in which the house itself constitutes both the social and the ritual universe: it shelters an entire community, and serves as the largest ritual unit. Longhouse societies may be highly egalitarian like the Iban or the Sakuddei, or hierarchical like the Maloh, Kenyah, or Kayan; but, as we shall see, the phenomenon of multi-family dwelling arrangements is also extremely common in South-East Asia. Then there are societies within whose village communities some houses enjoy higher status than others, but which have no overall ranking system cutting right through the society—no hereditary classes of nobles, commoners, or slaves, for example—only a ranking of houses within a particular village community in terms of seniority or closeness to a founder. An example is Tanimbar, where rank is fluid rather than fixed and may be lost over time as branch houses become further removed from core origin-houses, or through debt and clientage. Conversely, a debtor reduced to slavery could in time, if he had enough children to help him, work himself out of penury and back up to commoner status (McKinnon 1983: 276–80). The Toba Batak provide another example, for traditionally each Toba clan or lineage dominated others within the villages which its own members had founded, while occupying a subordinate role in other villages where they were not the founders—for example, where members resided with their wife-givers. Thirdly, there are distinctly hierarchical societies like the Toraja, Tetum, Savunese, or Sumbanese with their hereditary ranks of nobles, commoners, and (formerly) slaves. Here, aristocrats often presided (both politically and ritually) over a much larger district community or domain. Their houses were the political focus of their communities and were especially impressive structures, built to last. Identification between ruling nobles and their houses was a very close one. In Roti, indeed, the rulers of domains are called by the name of the house from which they are descended.[6] In this type of society it is sometimes the case that 'house' ideology is largely monopolized by the aristocracy—ordinary people have only a shallow genealogical memory and less attachment to houses. Fox suggests this is the case for the Atoni, except in the Insana princedom studied by Schulte Nordholt and Cunningham—an area which has been influenced by their strongly house-oriented neighbours, the Tetum. In a case like the Toraja, by contrast, nobles monopolized the right to build fine carved wood houses, yet the organization of kinship ideology around the house is, as we shall see, a principle which applies throughout the society.

At the end of this continuum we find centralized state systems, organized around a court where hierarchy and the etiquette of rank assumed still greater social importance. In a number of petty states, an ideology of kingship (often including a strong ritual component) was grafted on to ideas about the house—as for the Atoni or the Bugis with their concept of the ruler as ideally remaining in his/her palace (basically an extra large house of traditional style), representing

124. Buffalo horns attached to the front posts of this old origin-house on Mount Sesean, Tana Toraja, provide prestigious evidence of past sacrifices, 1983. (Photograph: Roxana Waterson)

the powerful navel or 'still centre' of the kingdom. Similarly, the Minangkabau *raja* dwelt inland in the heart of Minangkabau territory, occupying the large timber palace at Pagarruyung. The *raja* had almost no political power and principally fulfilled a sacred, symbolic role, representing the unity of the Minangkabau world (P. E. de Josselin de Jong 1951: 108). We can see, then, how closely kinship and ranking systems are intertwined within the house; the above framework should help to clarify the examples which follow.

'House Societies' in South-East Asia

Wherever we look in the archipelago, we find societies in which the word 'house' designates not only a physical structure, but the group of kin who are living in it or who claim membership in it. *Rumah* among the Karo Batak or the Minangkabau, *uma* among the Sakuddei of Siberut, *amu* in Savu, *uma* again in Roti or among the Tetum and Ema, *fada* for the Mambai, *rahan* in Tanebar-Evav, *tongkonan* in Toraja, are all examples of such words. Even on the northern fringe of the Austronesian world, among the aboriginal peoples of Taiwan, the same centrality of the house can be seen in kinship organization. Shih Lei (1964: 110), writing of the Austronesian-speaking Paiwan, states:

The family as institution is recognized by three aspects: the house, the name attached to it, and the people living in it. Even a single man or woman when provided with a house along with its traditional name may be considered as a family. A house-name represents not only a house but also the members of a family living in the house.

In Sumatra, among the patrilineal Karo, each house has its own name and lands, while among the matrilineal Minangkabau, the most important unit is the *saparuik* (sublineage), or 'people of one womb', usually associated with a group of people living in one *rumah adat* ('traditional' house, or one where rituals are observed) or *rumah gadang* (great house). A great house ideally may accommodate three generations of people related through women; the *saparuik* has been described as 'the most important functional unit' of Minangkabau society (P. E. de Josselin de Jong 1951: 11; Kato 1982: 44).

For the Sakuddei, *uma* refers both to the longhouse itself and to the patrilineal descent group which lives in it. As we saw in Chapter 3, the *uma* represents an ideal unity, reflected in communal participation in rituals, for which the house provides the setting. At the same time, these rituals are designed to diffuse and overcome the conflicts inherent in this style of group living, which demands intensive interaction between its members. In the case of a conflict between two *uma*, a third longhouse may intervene to act as a neutral negotiator (Schefold 1982: 126-7). In Savu, both the house and the group tracing descent from its founding ancestor are called *amu*. The 'house' has controlling interests in land, livestock, and the marriages of its members. The Savunese compare their houses and villages metaphorically to boats. 'Like the members of a village,' writes Kana (1980: 228), 'the members of a house form a group of passengers on a perahu [boat].'[7]

The identification of house and kin group is explicit also in West Sumba. Van Wouden (1956: 192) states that here, the word *uma* means both the house and the patrilineal descent group associated with it. Building a new house makes a person the founder of a lineage, conferring undying prestige and ensuring that he will be worshipped as an ancestor (*marapu*) by his descendants. Even if the house should disappear, it will still be remembered and the group of its members retains the possibility of rebuilding it, most particularly in the context of a feast or ceremony. A house maintains ceremonial links with other houses from which it has branched off; thus some rituals of the oldest house in a community may embrace the whole village (van Wouden 1956: 193).

Among the Ema of Timor, Clamagirand (1975: 44) notes that kin groups (or groups of wife-givers and wife-takers) are also thought of as 'houses' (*uma*). Some houses are rendered sacred by the presence of heirloom valuables (gold and silver discs which constitute the house's insignia). A house of this kind plays a central part in the lives of the group of brothers who are linked to it (though not necessarily resident in it). Certain rituals essential to the life of the group can only take place here. Clamagirand calls a house of this kind a 'core house' (Figure 125). It always has a round roof and is built on land which is subject to ritual prohibitions, whereas ordinary houses, dependent on their core house, may have a ridged roof and can be built on open land. Clamagirand (1980: 136) stresses, however, that the 'house' group, consisting of a group of elder and younger brothers resident in the core house and its dependent houses, cannot be equated with a lineage:

Although all members of a group recognize a common ancestor, genealogical ties are not memorized. Rather, a group

142

125. A 'core-house' or origin-house of a kin group in the Ema village of Atu Aben, Central Timor, with its characteristic domed roof. In the foreground is a rice granary (*lako*), with an open platform beneath the storage area. (Photograph: Brigitte Clamagirand)

consists of a collection of lines, whose members live in separate conjugal family dwellings, since, according to the rule of residence, a man and his married sons or married brothers generally do not live together and married daughters live in their husbands' houses.

Although there is an expressed preference for marriage with the mother's brother's daughter, Clamagirand (1980: 141) goes on to say:

... the members of a core house may choose spouses from any of the group of core houses with whom their core house has permanent matrimonial ties. These houses are classified as either wife-givers (uma mane: 'masculine houses', that is, core houses from which brothers may choose their wives) or wife-takers (mane heu: 'new men', that is, core houses into which sisters may marry).

A group of core houses may share the same name, and all acknowledge descent from a common ancestor, the founder of a 'mother' core house from which they all derive; actual genealogical links between them, however, are forgotten. So dominant is the house in Ema thinking about social organization that other units, such as the 'village', can hardly be said to exist; indeed there is no word for 'village' (Clamagirand 1980: 140).

All these examples show the explicit identification of kinship groupings with the house, confirming that they must truly be viewed as 'house societies'. I turn next to a brief discussion of longhouse and multi-family dwellings, before going on to look at three specific applications of the concept of the house society to Indonesian kinship systems, which I hope will provide more vivid demonstration of the utility of the concept to kinship analysis.

The Longhouse and Other 'Multi-family' Dwellings

Longhouses perhaps most dramatically exemplify the potentials of co-operative construction in the South-East Asian world. This form of dwelling is not only widespread in Borneo, but also in Mentawai and in the highlands of Vietnam. It is to be found in both egalitarian societies such as the Iban and the Sakuddei, and in more hierarchical ones such as the Kenyah and Kayan (Figures 126 and 127). Houses which may not be literally 'long', but are designed to accommodate several nuclear families, are even more common. Multi-family living arrangements were to be found (though they have become increasingly less common) among the Toba, Karo, Simalungun, Gayo, and

Minangkabau peoples of Sumatra, in some Sumba clan houses, in Manggarai (West Flores), in the Kai Islands, and in Minahasa (North Sulawesi) in pre-Dutch times (Padtbrugge 1679). In the southern Philippines, the houses of Maranao nobles (Figures 128 and 129) also accommodated several families, who might be directly or indirectly related to each other; their presence in the house added to the owner's prestige (Saber and Madale 1975). On the South-East Asian mainland, longhouses occur among the Kachin, and for a while during the nineteenth century were also to be found among the Sgaw Karen of Burma, who appear to have resorted to the construction of such houses at this period as a defensive measure in reaction to raids by their neighbours, the Kayah Karen.[8] Villages of longhouses and of separate houses thus coexisted for a while among the Sgaw, who no longer build longhouses today. In the highlands of South Vietnam, multi-family houses (which are often literally very long, and referred to as 'longhouses' in the literature) are built by a number of peoples, both Austronesian- and Austroasiatic-speaking, including the Jörai, Eddé (or Rhade), Böhnar, Halang, Ködu, Sré, Ma, Nop, and Mnong (Dournes 1971; Condominas 1957). The actual composition of families sharing these multi-family arrangements may differ quite widely. In Borneo societies, the classic longhouse consists of a number of separate apartments joined by a long gallery and sometimes also an open veranda. Each apartment houses a single household or nuclear family.[9] Those who reside in a longhouse apartment share certain rights over heirloom property or access to land for cultivation. If one goes to reside in another longhouse—for example, at marriage—one temporarily abandons rights in one's longhouse of birth in order to take them up in the longhouse of one's spouse (Freeman 1970: 26). An entire village community lives in the longhouse, although its members at the busiest times of the agricultural year are more likely to be found out in their field huts guarding and tending their crops. Some Borneo peoples build villages consisting of more than one longhouse.

Leach (1950: 61) long ago drew attention to the importance, in both hierarchical and egalitarian Borneo societies, of 'a politically influential "house-owning group"', which he defined as 'a small group of closely related families the members of which had a more direct descent linkage with the ancestral founders of the house (or village) than other members of the

126. Iban longhouse at Segu Bumuk, Sarawak, 1968. An open veranda runs the full length of the front of the building; beneath the roofed section runs an enclosed gallery giving on to the individual family apartments. (Dorothy Pelzer Collection, courtesy of ISEAS, Singapore)

127. Interior of an Iban longhouse, showing the gallery (*ruai*), scene of much daily and ceremonial activity. Nanga Baran, Rejang River, Sarawak, 1968. (Dorothy Pelzer Collection, courtesy of ISEAS, Singapore)

128. *Torogan* or house of a Maranao noble family at Masiu, Mindanao, southern Philippines, 1968. (Dorothy Pelzer Collection, courtesy of ISEAS, Singapore/Smithsonian Institution, Washington)

129. Detail of the magnificently carved flared beam-ends (*panolong*) of the Maranao house. Note the dragon motif, here called *niaga*; another common design represents coiled fern shoots (*piako*), 1968. (Dorothy Pelzer Collection, courtesy of ISEAS, Singapore/Smithsonian Institution, Washington)

community.' In the more stratified societies, such as the Kayan, Kenyah, Melanau, or Maloh, this group has formal recognition as the hereditary aristocratic élite from which political leaders are drawn (Figures 130 and 131). They may maintain a joint estate consisting of land rights and the prestige derived from their descent from a noble ancestor, and they may exercise considerable economic and ritual, as well as political, power. Anthropologists have argued over whether these groups constitute genuine corporate descent groups or not, since in certain cases no permanent use rights in land are recognized (King 1978: 21–2). However this may be, the fact of longhouse residence and the existence of a 'house-owning group' within the longhouse demonstrate both the centrality of the house as an organizing principle, and the potential for ranking and kinship systems to be brought together within it. In the Kenyah case, the chief's apartment in the longhouse is even designed to stand

out from the rest, being larger in size and with a taller roof, and situated in the middle of the longhouse (Figure 132). Chiefs could also have their apartment walls and support posts carved and painted with designs exclusive to their rank (Avé and King 1986: 64) (Figures 133–136).

Longhouse domicile appears to be an especially deeply rooted element of most Borneo cultures, but extremely large houses were formerly common throughout the archipelago. 'Multi-family' is the word sometimes used to refer to arrangements where a group of close kin live together—for example, a couple and several of their married children. But this is just one possible type of multi-family arrangement. Both village and household among the Karo Batak, for example, ideally included three groups: a founder lineage, together with members of both its wife-giving and wife-taking lineages. The composition of these units thus reflects the great importance of affinal ties in shaping social and

130. This splendid building was erected by the villagers of Long Nawang in the Apo-Kayan region of Central Borneo as a lodging house for the members of the Nieuwenhuis expedition of 1900. It was erected by 700 men in the space of only seven days. Behind it may be seen the house of the village chief, Pingan Sorang. Tillema, who visited the region in the 1930s, commented: 'Thus did the simple "savages" pay a royal honour to the intrepid explorers!' (Photograph: Jean Demmeni, courtesy of Times Editions, Singapore)

147

131. Longhouse of the Kayan chief Kwing Irang under construction, photographed by Jean Demmeni, official photographer of the
Nieuwenhuis expedition, in 1900. A sense of scale is provided by the
man standing at the top of the scaffolding; the structure is about
50 feet high. Such longhouses might be as much as 150 yards long.
(Photograph: Jean Demmeni, courtesy of Times Editions, Singapore)

132. Model of a Kenyah longhouse, showing the raised central portion where the chief's apartment would be located. (VIDOC, Koninklijk Instituut voor de Tropen, Amsterdam)

133. Section of the front wall of a chief's apartment in a Kayan longhouse, photographed by Tillema on his expedition to the Apo-Kayan in 1932. The design, a predominant motif in Kayan art, is called *aso* (literally, 'dog', but resembling more closely the dragon or *naga*; compare the carved ridge decoration in Figure 130. (From Tillema 1938: 69, courtesy of Rijksmuseum voor Volkenkunde, Leiden)

134. The carving of these beams in the gallery before the chief's apartment in a Kayan longhouse testify not only to the exuberant artistic sense of the Kayan but to the privileged status accorded to their leaders. Photographed by Tillema at Nahakramo in the Apo-Kayan region of Central Borneo, on his expedition of 1932. (From Tillema 1938: 163, courtesy of Rijksmuseum voor Volkenkunde, Leiden)

135. Door to Kayan or Kenyah chief's quarters. (From Nieuwenhuis 1904–7, Vol. I: Pl. 13)

136. Equally fine woodcarving, as well as the use of *naga* or dragon motifs, may also be seen in this entrance to a cult house in the Ngada region of West Central Flores, *c*.1927. (VIDOC, Koninklijk Instituut voor de Tropen, Amsterdam)

political relations in Karo society. Even a chief, in such an arrangement, could not afford to behave too arrogantly, for he had to reside with his ritually superior wife-takers, to whom he owed deference and for whom he was supposed to work on ceremonial occasions. The arrangement thus acted as a check on personal power, and provides us with a graphic example of how the division of inhabited space has a shaping impact upon social relationships (Figures 137–139).

Sometimes a multi-family arrangement can be found, not in a single building, but in a compound of related houses. This pattern has become increasingly common among the matrilineal Minangkabau, for example, where a compound may contain several houses built at different times and occupied by married sisters and sisters' daughters. But in earlier times, such a group commonly all lived in a single house. In the past, Minangkabau 'great houses' lived up to their name in being able to accommodate huge numbers of

people (Figure 140). A Dutch official in 1871 found over a hundred people residing in a single house in Alahan Panjang, and between sixty and eighty resident in another (Kato 1982: 45). I visited one such house still surviving in 1986 in the village of Sulit Air. It is 64 metres long and has twenty apartments, though today the house is occupied by only seven nuclear families. The compound occupied by a cluster of female relatives is typical, too, of Aceh in northern Sumatra. Aceh provides an interesting example of a system which has at various times been described as 'patrilineal' with 'matrilineal features' (P. E. Josselin de Jong 1975: 17) and as 'bilateral' or even 'bilineal' (Siegel 1969; Wessing 1984: 6). Here, women inherit houses from their parents, and as in Minangkabau, take charge of subsistence agriculture while their husbands are often absent, earning a living by trade or other occupations outside their homeland.[10] Ideally, parents aim to build a house for each daughter as she

137.   Karo Batak house in the village of Lingga, 1986. These buildings traditionally housed as many as eight or more related nuclear
families. (Photograph: Roxana Waterson)

138. Detail of carving on the ring beam of the Karo house shown
in Figure 137. (Photograph: Roxana Waterson)

139. Interior of the same Karo house at Lingga, 1986, showing its four hearths, each for a separate family unit, with large hanging racks above, and a gulley down the centre for disposal of waste. (Photograph: Roxana Waterson)

140. One of the oldest surviving 'great houses' (*rumah gadang*) in the Minangkabau highlands, at Balimbing, not far from Bukittinggi, 1986. It is said to be over 250 years old and would formerly have housed a group of matrilineally related women and their families. Its compound contains a number of smaller new dwellings built by female descendants of the original house. (Photograph: Roxana Waterson)

154

marries, and 'may end their lives living in a shack surrounded by the houses of their married daughters' (Siegel 1969: 52). Many couples cannot afford this ideal, in which case they move into the kitchen and abandon the house itself to a married daughter.[11]

Longhouse domicile has proved remarkably enduring in Borneo, though not every Borneo society traditionally built longhouses—the Ma'anyan, for example, did not—and the Ngaju, rather than longhouses, built large extended family dwellings called 'great houses' (umah hai) (Figure 141). These were solidly built, with access by a stairway which was usually divided by a platform on which stood carved wooden figures or hampatong (Avé and King 1986: 52). There is some debate as to whether they ever built longhouses, although Miles (1964, 1976), who studied the community of Tumbang Gagu, describes in some

detail the longhouse there, which was built in 1908 by a man called Idang and his nephew, Antang, who had both amassed unusually large fortunes from trading expeditions to Singapore (Miles 1964: 55). According to Miles's account, the construction of a Ngaju longhouse is not a purely communal effort but requires the sponsorship of some wealthy person. It represents such a great investment of capital that it is only rarely, in the relatively egalitarian society of the Ngaju, that individuals emerge who are capable of sponsoring such a project. This would account for the relative rarity of longhouses among the Ngaju and their coexistence with villages of single houses. It would explain, too, why the occupants of a longhouse are loath to abandon it even after it has come to be inconveniently remote from their shifting swidden fields. Miles, then, concluded that for the Ngaju, longhouse

141. Ngaju 'great house' (umah hai), occupied by an extended family group, with a platform on the stairway and wooden statues (hampatong) in front. Photograph taken at Batu Njiwoeh in 1937, at which time the house was already about 100 years old. (Photograph: Karl Helbig, courtesy of Rijksmuseum voor Volkenkunde, Leiden)

building may follow a cyclical pattern, the longhouse representing only one possible mode of residence, although a very enduring one. Today, the house at Tumbang Gagu is the only extant Ngaju longhouse, and Avé offers a different explanation for its existence. According to him, Antang believed when he built the house that he was re-establishing an old Ngaju tradition; but he finds it significant that no description of longhouses is known from old folk-tales and legends (Avé and King 1986: 53). The houses which feature in many traditional Ngaju paintings, as illustrated by Schärer (1963), are not longhouses either. Miles cites the accounts of several nineteenth-century sources which mention 'longhouses' in Ngaju areas, including a Dutch colonial officer who in 1880 reported seeing a very few on the Upper Mentaya River. He also mentions that, besides Tumbang Gagu, two longhouses on the Seruyan River had recently ceased to be occupied at the time of his fieldwork (Miles 1964: 46). It seems most likely that what these examples refer to were in fact 'great houses'; even the Tumbang Gagu house, though very massively built on extraordinarily large piles, contains only eight apartments—not very many by, for example, Iban standards—and may perhaps best be viewed as an outstanding example of the 'great house'.

Some early authors viewed the longhouse as an adaptation for defensive needs, and speculated that it would disappear in the more peaceful conditions established, for example, in Sarawak under British rule. Leach (1950: 68), on the other hand, saw that the longhouse had proved itself a highly resilient institution in Bornean societies, and stated that 'longhouse domicile is not abandoned until the traditional social system has suffered irreparable damage'. As examples he noted that some groups who had contact with coastal Malays in Sarawak had undergone a process of Malayanization, to the point where they had split up their longhouses into separate dwellings. Nowadays, it is quite common in many parts of Borneo to see small individual family dwellings erected in the vicinity of longhouses.

How is a longhouse constructed? Most ethnographers stress the fact that it is really a series of individually owned family apartments. Heirlooms, too, belong to each apartment unit, not to the longhouse as a whole. Each individual family of the longhouse has responsibility for its own section of the building—its own private apartment, together with its adjoining section of public space, the gallery and veranda outside it. Thus it may come about that certain sections of the longhouse are maintained in much better condition than others: some have stout boards for the gallery floor and ironwood shingles for the roof, while an adjoining part may have only *atap* thatch and prove treacherous going underfoot (Geddes 1957: 29; Freeman 1970: 7). In the Ngaju longhouse at Tumbang Gagu, unusually, there are also some communal areas of the house which are a matter of shared responsibility; these may be less well maintained than individual sections (Miles 1964: 50). Although each household, then, contributes to construction and maintenance, the initial effort of building the longhouse may none the less require an extra degree of energy and organization. Miles (1976: 66–8) provides us with a very interesting account of the construction of the Tumbang Gagu longhouse. He notes that its pillars consist of single trunks of ironwood 35 feet in length and with a diameter of 5–7 feet, whose average weight he estimated at 3 tons. To fell these great trunks in virgin forest, move them to the site, and raise them is the most difficult part of the whole enterprise, demanding the recruitment of a large work-force. In this case, it was done by means of a system called *hindjam*, whereby individual sponsors hold a large feast and slaughter animals with which to feed the assembled workers. The sponsors were Antang Kalang and his nephew, who were remembered as the longhouse founders. The total cost to each of them was thirty cows, one having been slaughtered for each pillar of the longhouse. The longhouse thus represented a considerable capital investment. The current members of the longhouse community at Tumbang Gagu all traced their descent from one or other of the two founders, forming two corporate descent groups (which Miles terms ramages), each holding rights in their section of the longhouse, which at that time was already seventy years old.

These multi-family arrangements are likely to be always throwing out or pulling in new members, expanding and contracting either in the course of a single agricultural cycle—when people temporarily disperse to their field houses and then return—or in a longer-term pattern, reflecting the development of families or of kin-based political groupings. The fact that at the present time this form of abode appears to be becoming less and less common may be attributed to a number of factors. It is generally recognized that the intense interactions which characterize this style of arrangement may produce their own tensions between co-residents. Hence, for example, the emphasis in Sakuddei ritual on mutual participation aimed at dispelling such conflicts. Where multi-family arrangements are maintained, therefore, we may surmise that particular pressures encourage this mode of living, or else, as Leach suggests in the Borneo case, that there is a distinct and conscious commitment to longhouse life. In other areas where the commitment is less strong, other factors such as the decline of the need for a defensive advantage, or simply the loss due to deforestation of suitable large trees to supply the massive timbers required (as seems to be the case among the Minangkabau) may all contribute to the development of smaller households. It can happen, too, that given the opportunity, married couples willingly opt for the greater privacy that an independent household affords, without necessarily ceasing to interact a great deal with other relatives. In the Minangkabau case, for example, the cohesion of groups of female kin sharing a compound remains strong. Nowadays, those who are economically successful hope to be able to demonstrate their success by building a new house, which may or may not be in traditional style (see Chapter 10).

In spite of these modern trends, however, it is clear that in the past, longhouse and multi-family living arrangements were a widespread feature of South-East Asian kinship systems, just as they were in the 'house societies' of the North-West Coast. This is one especially obvious way in which the house forms a dominant element in indigenous patterns of kinship organization. But to explore further the meaning of the house within these systems, I now turn to examine the role of houses in three selected societies: the Atoni of western Timor, the Tanimbarese of the southern Moluccas, and the Sa'dan Toraja of Sulawesi. These examples have been chosen partly because of the availability of recent information about them, and partly because they exemplify particular variations in kinship systems which, nevertheless, can all be described as 'house societies'.

The Atoni of Timor: An Ambiguous Case

I select the Atoni for special consideration here because, on the one hand, two well-known authors describe them as a quite obviously house-based society, while on the other, a third expresses some reservations about this analysis. This instance, then, may serve to illumi-

nate the extent of variation in application of principles of 'house' organization in eastern Indonesia.

The identification between houses and people, and of both with the idea of 'vital force', is given startlingly explicit expression in the writings of Schulte Nordholt on the Atoni. From his account, one would certainly conclude that the Atoni are as classic a 'house society' as one could find. For the Atoni, according to this author, the most important unit of social organization is the *ume*, or house. The house is a repository and source of life force; it functions as a strictly exogamic unit, so that marriages between houses become the mechanism by which this life force may be controlled and reproduced. Schulte Nordholt's (1971: 137–8) account weaves a set of linkages between the nature of relations between houses, the functions of bride-wealth, and indeed of Atoni ideas about life itself:

The *ume* contains a number of people, living souls (*smanaf*—the word is also translatable with 'vital force'). Now, when a woman capable of reproducing life is married into another *ume* her own *ume* loses not only one *smanaf*, but future lives as well. It therefore exacts life in return: in the first place in the form of bridewealth, which is paid in instalments, each instalment being regarded as compensation for a part of the body of the woman in question. For example, one part of the bridewealth is given in return for her head, another for her hands and feet, and so on. The number of payments and their names vary from case to case, but they are always named after parts of the body. Originally the bridewealth consisted mainly of cattle, while later on silver was introduced, and later still silver in the form of coins. These latter are not actually money in the economic sense of currency but as objects with an intrinsic, fixed value, which may be used as ornaments and thus permanently retain their value in the exchange of life (*smanaf*). In the second place the *ume* exacts bride services. Through his labour the husband produces rice and corn, which are also *smanaf*, for his wife's *ume*. He works the soil, which brings forth life. Hence the husband's *ume* pays for what it will receive, namely *smanaf*, by means of bride services.... In areas in which the husband is integrated into the wife's *ume* and remains there permanently there is of course no bridewealth, as in that case the husband's *ume* itself is giving a *smanaf*, which it has returned to it in the form of one or more children.

The method by which the balance between two *ume* is achieved and the principle of reciprocity is expressed may vary a great deal. It may vary from a substantial bridewealth and a short period of bride service, as in Ambenu, to an insignificant bridewealth, or none at all, and a long period of bride service, or the definite obligation to return a 'soul' brought forth by the wife to her *ume*.

Here we find eloquently expressed the central importance of the concept of vital force (*smanaf* is a cognate of *semangat*), and the necessity of maintaining balance and reciprocity of *smanaf* between houses. Human beings contribute to the sum of a house's life force, which must not be allowed to diminish; the house *is*, in this sense, identical with the group of its members, without whom it would cease to exist. Furthermore, although some writers have described the Atoni as patrilineal, it immediately becomes clear that more than one type of marriage exists, depending on the type of bridewealth paid and the residence of the couple after marriage. This affects the filiation of the children, who may thus belong either to the husband's group or to the wife's. Virilocal marriages predominate in some areas, making the house group appear to be patrilineal, but Schulte Nordholt (1971: 435) found that in the area where Atoni territory borders on that of the Belu, matrilocal marriages without bridewealth frequently took place over generations, creating lines of matrilineal descent. The 'house' idiom recurs in

Atoni descriptions of social relations: the village community is described as 'one house, one *lopo*' (*lopo* is the name for the circular, open-walled community house). This expression symbolizes both genealogical unity (the house) and geographical unity (the community house) (Schulte Nordholt 1971: 96, 432) (Figures 142–145). Marriages are said to create 'paths' (*lalan*) between houses. The preference for cross-cousin marriages (which repeat an already established link between houses) is expressed in the idiom by which the mother's brother's daughter is called 'the woman of the path', and the father's sister's son 'the man (or husband) of the path'. Such unions are also termed 'marriage within the house' (Schulte Nordholt 1980: 235).

Cunningham's writings on the Atoni present a very similar picture, but this is where some qualification is required. Schulte Nordholt and Cunningham both worked in one particular district of Atoni country, Insana, which borders on the lands of the Belu (or Tetum). The latter appear to be much more strongly

142. Atoni house near Kefamenano, West Timor, 1965. (Dorothy Pelzer Collection, courtesy of ISEAS, Singapore/Smithsonian Institution, Washington)

house oriented than the Atoni generally are, and they have had a marked influence on Insana. Insana is much more hierarchical than all the other Atoni regions (which extend over most of western Timor) and it has an extremely articulate *raja* who has been a major informant to both Schulte Nordholt and Cunningham.[12] Fox found in other Atoni areas that ideas about *smanaf* were often talked about, but not in relation to houses so much as to descent groups (*nono*) and their rituals. It appears also that 'house ideology' is chiefly a matter for the aristocracy, who can afford to contract bridewealth marriages; some 70–80 per cent of Atoni do not pay bridewealth, but return a child to the husband's family (if residing uxorilocally) or the wife's family (if residing virilocally), both patterns of residence being very common. Thus many people have dual allegiances to houses of the mother's and the father's side.[13]

Genealogical reckoning rarely extends back beyond four generations even among the aristocracy, but rather than using houses as a substitute device for recalling origins, as the Toraja do, Atoni describe the development of a *nono*, or descent group, by reference to geographical locations. Oral traditions include elaborate histories, recounted in the first person, of the movements of a descent group founder from place to place. Only this individual is described as moving, though what is really being recounted is the spreading of his descendants as they established new settlements. In fact, given that the Atoni practise shifting cultivation, and consequently move their settlements every two generations or so, few houses are built in a sufficiently permanent way to last very long as origin-places. The sense of place (which is clearly profound) is thus attached rather to geographical landscapes than to built structures.

Schulte Nordholt's description of the *ume* must therefore be regarded as a somewhat idealized abstraction; as a physical structure, it differs from the much more permanent cult houses of the Ema and Mambai, or the origin-houses of highly hierarchical societies like the Sumbanese or Toraja, which may

143. Atoni community house (*lopo*) near Kefamenano, West Timor, 1965. (Dorothy Pelzer Collection, courtesy of ISEAS, Singapore)

144. Atoni house in the hill region of Soa'e, West Timor, 1987. Nowadays, the local administration, finding the old beehive style of house to be unhygienic, encourages people to build these structures on a smaller scale and use them only as kitchens. A separate, rectangular house is then often built in front. (Photograph: Garth Sheldon)

145. Framework of an Atoni house, Soa'e, West Timor, 1987. The beehive structure of tall saplings encloses the four more solid main posts, notched to carry beams which support the attic floor. (Photograph: Garth Sheldon)

last up to 200 years or are constantly renewed on the same spot. But even Fox concurs that in theory, every Atoni *nono* should have a house in which to store heirlooms—though not all do. It appears, then, that Schulte Nordholt's and Cunningham's versions of Atoni kinship structure are not so much wrong as applicable in their entirety only to one, somewhat untypical, Atoni area, or to the aristocracies of other regions.

Houses in Tanimbar

The variety of possible marriage patterns in the Tanimbar Islands shows considerable similarities with Timorese systems. The data on eastern Indonesian alliance systems has always appeared confusing, for among them may be found a variety of both matrilineal and patrilineal systems, patterns of marriage with the matrilateral and the patrilateral cross cousins, sister exchanges, and a number of other variations. In her thesis, entitled 'Hierarchy, Alliance and Exchange in the Tanimbar Islands', McKinnon begins by examining this confusion. She discusses the role of the Dutch scholar van Wouden who, in his 'Types of Social Structure in Eastern Indonesia' (1935), made the first attempt to create order out of the chaos. His solution was to posit an original 'ideal' type of double descent, with societies divided into opposing moities and marriage classes. This type, he hypothesized, must have disintegrated to the point where it was no longer to be found in its 'pure' form.

In fact, McKinnon points out, it is evident that different forms of marriage and descent may here exist *within* a single society, particular types of marriage being related to schedules of bridewealth exchanges, which also determine patterns of residence and affiliation. Throughout eastern Indonesia, in early stages of marriage men may dwell uxorilocally and their children affiliate with the mother. Later, with the completion of second or subsequent bridewealth transactions, the couple may shift their residence to the husband's village and the children will now affiliate patrilaterally. There is no need to postulate a system of double descent to explain this system, which McKinnon (1983: 5) suggests would be better characterized as one of 'alternate structural possibilities in a single system regulated by the principle of exchange'. Marriages create and maintain links between houses, and it is often the case that prescribed forms of alliance (such as cousin

marriage) are the duty in particular of members of a senior line, or of the eldest brother in a group of siblings. Their marriages serve to perpetuate particular long-established ties with other houses, while members of junior lines are free to marry within a wider circle and to initiate new alliances. With such variable rules of residence, it is clear that the membership of the 'house' as an exchanging unit in marriage alliances must be of mixed composition. Rather than retaining the term 'descent group' for such units, as Fox does, McKinnon prefers to view the house itself as the essential (and complex) unit of organization. She suggests that Lévi-Strauss's concept of 'house societies' is the one that makes most sense of Tanimbar organization. It is the house which constitutes a corporate body, perpetuating itself, in Lévi-Strauss's words, 'through the transmission of its name, its goods and its titles down a real or imaginary line, considered legitimate as long as this continuity can express itself in the language of kinship or of affinity and, most often, of both' (McKinnon 1983: 7; Lévi-Strauss 1983: 174) (Figures 146 and 147).

In Tanimbar, blood is said to come from the mother, and female blood is said to create exchange 'pathways' between houses. But eventually, specific women on a 'blood line' may be forgotten, and the relations remembered in terms of a 'row of houses' or *lolat*. The *lolat* is 'a row of wife-taking houses that stand, ranged one after the other, along the female line that descends from a woman of the house given out in marriage three or more generations previously' (McKinnon 1983: 68). Only important, named houses belong to *lolat* rows. A row may have between six and twelve houses, though some lines feed into each other, creating longer rows, while a few form closed cycles, such as the so-called 'Great Row' (*Lolat Ila'a*) consisting of four noble houses of equal rank on each of the two islands Sera and Fordata. These houses also have many minor 'rows' feeding into them (McKinnon 1983: 70). Valuables exchanged in marriage transactions make their way along the rows, and are said to 'search for their spouses', to 'rest' in houses in between transactions, and to 'marry each other'. These valuables consist of symbolically 'female' gifts from 'male' wife-givers—*ikat* sarongs, gold ear-rings, bead and gold necklaces, and pairs of conus shell arm-bands, as well as garden produce, particularly rice, both raw and cooked; and 'male' gifts from 'female' wife-takers—large, imported gold disk pendants worn by men (and by women, in ceremonial dances), elephant tusks (imported by Bugis

146. Tanimbar village of Sangliat Dol. Before the houses stands a boat-shaped stone ritual and dancing place (*natar sori*). These were formerly a central feature of Tanimbar villages, but since the coming of Christianity they have been destroyed. (From Drabbe 1940: Pl. 19, courtesy of SOAS, London)

traders from Singapore and Sumatra), pairs of men's ear-rings, antique swords, palm brandy, and the flesh of pigs and fish hunted by men, either raw or cooked.[14] We can see that an elaborate series of symbolic oppositions is built up around the division between wife-givers and wife-receivers in Tanimbar society, and that material objects (houses and exchange valuables) are essential in giving tangible expression to social relations. 'The history of an alliance is remembered, in great part, through the named valuables which have travelled between the houses concerned' (McKinnon 1983: 88). Actual genealogical links through individuals in a family tree may be forgotten, but the histories of houses and valuables are not. Big men know the names and histories of all the most important valuables, their location in particular houses, and the possible ways they might move in future alliances. Clearly, the whole system has particular importance for noble houses, who maintain their status over generations by ensuring that the eldest sons and daughters of a senior line repeat prescribed patterns of marriages with other high-ranking houses. As we might expect

of a 'house society', a certain degree of manipulation is admissible, however. For example, a commoner woman who is to marry a noble man can first be unofficially adopted into a noble house, and 'weighed down' with valuables to make her 'noble' too (McKinnon 1983: 266).

The arrangement of houses fits, too, into a system of beliefs concerning the ancestors (intimately associated with particular houses) and the supreme deity, Ubila'a—an all-encompassing, bisexual being whose name has the sense of 'Great Ancestor'. As in other prescriptive alliance systems in Indonesia, wife-givers are the ritually superior source of women (and thus of continued life and fertility) for their wife-takers. Ultimately, the 'rows' of houses are conceived as stretching back to the ancestors and the heavens, both regarded as sources of life. Status is thought of in terms of the closeness of a house to the 'Great Row', for these houses are regarded as closest to the ancestors and the heavens.

Tanimbar society, then, has developed an ideology of kinship in which the house consistently emerges as the major focus of concern, so much so that the re-

162

147. An impressive flight of stone steps leading to the village of Sangliat Dol, Tanimbar Islands. (From Drabbe 1940: Pl. 18, courtesy of SOAS, London)

membering of alliances between houses takes precedence over a recall of the actual genealogical links behind them. McKinnon's analysis demonstrates that Tanimbar kinship and ranking systems cannot properly be understood until the 'house' is treated as the main unit of organization in its own right. Conventional labels such as 'patrilineal' cannot adequately describe such a system and are actively misleading. To conclude, I now turn to examine a markedly contrasting system, that of the Sa'dan Toraja, in order to show how this, too, is organized around houses. The functioning of the Toraja system appears vague and confusing until full consideration is given to the role of houses within it.

Houses among the Sa'dan Toraja

The Sa'dan Toraja live in the mountainous northern highlands of South Sulawesi. Like most of the peoples of western Indonesia, they have a cognatic kinship system, in which descent is traced equally from both mother and father, and all children of both sexes have equal rights of inheritance. Toraja ideas about conception reflect this bilateral organization. Toraja often talk about kinship in terms of 'blood and bone' (*rara buku*). Unlike the Tanimbarese, however, who regard blood as the 'female' contribution to conception while bone is a 'male' element said to derive from semen, for the Toraja 'blood and bone' are indivisible, being inherited equally and in an undifferentiated manner from both mother and father.[15] To say that Toraja society is cognatic, however, tells us little about the actual functioning of kinship relations and ideas in everyday life. To understand this, we must look at the part played by houses in Toraja society.

Every Toraja traces descent from a number of different origin-houses or *tongkonan*, the birthplaces of their parents, grandparents, and more distant ances-

163

tors (Plates 10 and 11; Figure 148). The founding ancestors of a *tongkonan* are always a married couple, though in certain circumstances either the woman or the man may be more often remembered and named as the founder. Theoretically, any one person may belong to hundreds of different houses, but in practice most people only maintain ties with those of their parents and grandparents, and of their spouse's parents and grandparents. Most men move to live with their wives at marriage, and women often have controlling rights in houses. An individual's ties with his or her houses of origin are in no sense weakened by marriage, for a couple are expected to contribute equally to the ceremonies of both sides. Allegiance to several houses is possible because links are only demonstrated at intervals, in the context of ritual or of the rebuilding of a house, to which all members should contribute. The expense of participating in ceremonies is the most obvious factor which curtails involvement in too many houses; residence is not a limiting factor. Indeed, it can happen, as we saw already in Chapter 3, that a house is left empty and not inhabited at all, and yet is still regarded as the point of origin of its descendants and as the appropriate place for the holding of ceremonies.

Expressions to do with kinship are often couched in a 'house' idiom. There is a preference for marriage with 'distant' cousins, defined as those more distantly related than third cousins. The actual ancestors linking them are more often than not forgotten, but people invariably are able to state through which *house* they are related. They call themselves 'siblings within the *tongkonan*' (*siunu' lan tongkonan*) or say that 'their *tongkonan*s join' (*sikande tongkonan*). To marry a cousin is called 'to return to the house' (*sule langan banua*). Links with a spouse's *tongkonan*, at first tenuous, become stronger once children are born.

Descendants of a *tongkonan* generally elect one family from among their number to reside in the house as its guardians. The resident of a ruling noble *tongkonan* in the past also exercised political power over the community of which the house formed the conspicuous centre. Although the principles of member-

ship in houses are the same for everyone, regardless of rank, in some parts of Toraja only the houses of the nobility are actually called '*tongkonan*'. The nobility reserved for themselves the right to build the great carved and painted houses with their huge saddle roofs and extended eaves which are such a feature of the Torajan landscape. These houses are the sites of some of the most important rituals, which only the nobility may hold or sponsor. Noble houses often have particular ritual offices attached to them. If, for example, a house is destroyed, the office will be transferred to another related house, but it will still be remembered to which house it formerly belonged, and if rebuilt it will return there. Noble houses also gain prestige from myths about their founding ancestors, and from the sacred power of the heirloom valuables stored within them (gold and silver ornaments, swords, krises, old Chinese porcelain, textiles, and beadwork). Some houses themselves are claimed to possess supernatural powers, which may on occasion have saved their villages from disaster. Volkman (1985: 118), for example, describes a village in the Sesean region whose old *tongkonan* was said to be protected by two snakes which curled around it. When the area was attacked around the turn of the century by an expansionist neighbouring big man, all the houses burnt except for this one and its granaries. Water miraculously came out of the house walls and extinguished the blaze. In present-day Toraja society, the continued importance attached to the ceremonial rebuilding of origin-houses testifies to the continuing centrality of houses in Toraja concepts of kinship, individual and ethnic identity, and social prestige.

In an earlier article on Toraja kinship, I aimed to show how uses of kin terms tend to be shifting and context-bound (Waterson 1986). There are no clearly bounded groups of kin, and it is almost impossible to trace the limits of an individual's allegiances to kin, since the tendency is to use terms in a highly 'inclusive' way whenever possible. Thus, even distant relatives are often referred to as 'siblings', and so on. Looking at Toraja in the light of Lévi-Strauss's concept of 'house societies', however, we find that it fulfils virtually every one of his defining criteria. It is easy then to see the importance of houses in shaping kinship relations in Toraja. Not that houses need function to produce neatly bounded groups of kin; if boundaries are porous and groups continually being redefined according to the context of the moment, this is, I have argued, exact-

◄ 148. Toraja origin-house (*tongkonan*), Ulusalu district, Tana Toraja, 1977. The elaborately carved façade indicates that the house belongs to an aristocratic family; even ordinary people, however, trace their descent through houses where their parents or more distant ancestors were born. (Photograph: Roxana Waterson)

ly what we should expect, for most cognatic systems of this region share a highly flexible and strategic approach to kin relations.

* * *

In dwelling on the examples of Tanimbar and Toraja, I have aimed to show how useful the concept of 'house societies' can be in making sense of South-East Asian kinship data. This way of looking at kinship cuts right across the more familiar categories which anthropologists have based on modes of descent and an over-emphasis on unilineality. My examples show just how far two 'house societies' may differ in the actual details of their systems of kinship and alliance; yet in both instances, the approach helps to make sense of apparently vague or contradictory data. It simultaneously removes the temptation to squeeze the evidence into the strait-jacket of descent categories which by themselves can neither fully contain nor explain these systems.

1. I am particularly grateful to James Fox for his comments on an earlier draft of this chapter, and especially for his enlightening discussion of points relating to the Atoni and other eastern Indonesian systems.

2. With reference to cognatic systems, see Waterson (1986). For an introduction to recent work on eastern Indonesian kinship systems, see Fox (1980).

3. 'Hawaiian' kinship terminology is basically generational, extending immediate family kin terms to all those of the same generation. No distinction is made between lineal and collateral relatives, and all cousins are referred to by sibling terms. 'Eskimo' terminology does have a distinctive term for cousins, though it also makes no distinction between cross and parallel cousins. The problem of definition arises in a case like the Toraja, who do have a word for 'cousin', as well as terms by which first, second, third, etc. cousins may be distinguished, but in practice make a point of avoiding their use, preferring to class all cousins as 'siblings'.

4. Fox's paper provides a critique of the very different approach taken by Robert Blust (1976). Blust's formulation of a choice between two radically different models for early Austronesian kinship organization, only one of which can be 'right', shows unnecessarily rigid adherence to ideal types and is unlikely to yield profitable results, however high his standards as a linguist.

5. See Hoskins (1986) on the politics of stone dragging in Sumba, and Zerner (1983) for a discussion of ritual architecture among the Toraja.

6. James Fox (personal communication).

7. Kana does not specify whether this is the statement of his informants, or his own inference, but Fox (personal communication) confirms that the Savunese do make explicit use of the ship as an organizing metaphor in speaking of houses and villages.

8. Iijima (1979: 101–3); Anthony Walker and Ananda Rajah (personal communication).

9. The word for the apartment, and the household, is *bilek* among the Iban. Variants of the term appear in a number of other Austronesian languages, for example, Minangkabau *bilik*; Wurm and Wilson (1975: 174) give Proto-Austronesian *bilik* = 'room'.

10. This pattern of voluntary migration is called *merantau* in Indonesian, and is discussed in Chapter 10.

11. R. Wessing (personal communication).

12. James Fox (personal communication).

13. When a child is returned to the wife's line, his status is somewhat ambiguous; he is now affiliating with the superior, wife-giving line but is attached to an inferior, 'female' line within the dominant 'male' descent group. However, it can happen that the dominant position of the 'male' line becomes eroded to the point where the 'female' line may reverse its position by marrying into the 'male' line and making itself a wife-giver in its turn, reversing the flow of women; or alternatively, branch out and establish its own new alliances. The fact that such reversals in the direction of exchanges are possible indicates that the Atoni system of alliance is, in fact, not purely asymmetrical, but only partially so.

14. Wife-givers are viewed as symbolically 'male' because of their association with the brothers of a house, who 'sit' or stay put in it. Wife-takers are 'female' because they are associated with the sisters who are given as wives and move to other houses. There is also perhaps the fact that ritual superiority is accorded to the wife-givers, while the wife-takers, who should be submissive and respectful, are in this respect also symbolically viewed as 'female' in relation to them.

15. An ideology of 'bones' and 'flesh' as distinctively male and female contributions to conception is widespread in India, Tibet, Assam, Siberia, and China, as well as in New Guinea. Lévi-Strauss (1969: 393–405) hypothesizes that the presence of such ideas is always related to the existence of systems of 'generalized exchange', where society is divided into lineages or groups relating to each other as wife-givers and wife-takers. These relationships are exclusive, each group supplying only 'bones' or 'flesh' to any one particular partner group. The differences in ideas about 'bones' and 'flesh' which exist between Tanimbar, a prescriptive alliance system of the above-mentioned type, and Toraja, a cognatic system where no such wife-giving or -taking groups exist, are clearly consistent with this hypothesis.

CHAPTER 8
Space and the Shaping of Social Relations

How do people order their daily activities and interactions within the built forms that they have created? This chapter aims to examine how the everyday uses of space within the house may serve to shape the relations of those who inhabit it. Rules about the uses of space provide one of the most important ways by which the built environment can be imbued with meaning; reflexively, that environment itself helps to mould and reproduce a particular pattern of social relationships. This production of meaning may take place, firstly, through the positioning and manipulation of objects in space, and secondly, through the human body itself—its placement in, movement through, or exclusion from a particular space, or in people's spatial interactions with each other.

Through rules about how space is to be used, people are obliged to *act out* their relations to each other in a particularly personal and immediate way. Bourdieu, in his analysis of the Berber house (1973), contends that the child growing up in a Berber house will automatically absorb Berber notions and values about human relationships, in particular the relation between genders. The 'inward' orientation of women and the 'outward' one of men is reflected in contrasts within the house between interior and exterior, dark and light, low and high, back and front, night and day, nature and culture. Learning how to move and act within the organized space of the house, an individual insensibly undergoes a cultural 'apprenticeship'. This unverbalized form of socialization ultimately extends beyond the division of space in the house itself, outward to encompass the rest of the world (the house as a whole is opposed as 'female' to the public world of men, which includes the place of assembly, the mosque, the café, the fields, and the market) and inward to the individual's own bodily postures, style of walking, con-

struction of sexuality, and sense of self. It is precisely the unverbalized nature of this process of 'em-bodying of the structures of the world' which makes it a powerful tool for the reproduction of culture, for as Bourdieu (1977: 94) notes, the principles thus transmitted in condensed, symbolic form are simultaneously placed beyond the grasp of consciousness. The symbolic *is* essentially the non-articulated (Benjamin 1987: 10), and it derives its efficacy from the fact that, whether it is being 'em-bodied' in movement through space, in interactional patterns, in language, ritual, or whatever else, that which is inarticulable is not open to challenge.[1] It is for this reason that rules about the uses of space provide, in all cultures, a potentially powerful means of encoding aspects of social relationships, and causing them to be 'lived' at a tacit or subconscious level by the actors themselves.

An unusually graphic example of this process may be found in Caroline Humphrey's (1974) analysis of the Mongolian tent, and the rigid rules which exist for the placement of objects within it. Set down upon the vast expanses of the steppes, the tent becomes a tightly ordered microcosm of the social world, a world in which the placement of people and objects in space serves to define social positions. Categories of age, sex, genealogical seniority, wealth, and religious status were all maintained in the traditional Mongol tent by means of explicit rules about where one sat, ate, or slept, and what objects one was permitted to touch within the tent. Spatial divisions (front and back halves of the tent, and left and right halves) cut across each other and were used to place people according to seniority on the one hand, and gender on the other. The 'male' half of the tent, to the left of the door as one entered, was the ritually pure half, the 'female' the impure half. Rules about the appropriate placement of objects in the two halves were rigid, as Humphrey (1974: 273) describes:

It was considered a sin to move any utensil from its right place into another part of the tent. A woman's object was considered to pollute the men's area and a special ceremony might have to be performed to erase this. Men were not allowed to touch cooking and other 'female' things, while women were forbidden even to step over a whole range of men's goods. There was even a difference in the vertical heights at which objects could be placed: some things had to be wedged behind the roof-poles, some hung from pegs in the wall-lattices, and yet others were placed on the ground.

This system is related to a rigid division of labour in the world outside the tent, as well as to hierarchical patterns within the kinship system, for example, the dominance of a father over his sons, and the subordination of the in-marrying daughter-in-law, who also had to 'live' her role through the observation of a range of verbal taboos, which enforced upon her a continual linguistic vigilance (Humphrey 1978). Social changes in modern socialist Mongolian society are mirrored in changes in the placement of objects, as well as the objects themselves, but the principle of categorizing social relationships by this means remains. Whereas in the West, Humphrey suggests (1974: 275), the presence and distribution of objects is often used to indicate class differences, in Mongolia they now show that a family is more or less 'progressive'.

Here we find already outlined some of the main dimensions of social relations which spatial position, movement, or avoidance may be expected to convey. Certain spatial oppositions will always present themselves as potential means of encoding opposed social categories: front/back, right/left, high/low, inner/outer are contrasts which can be made to apply to virtually any kind of architectural form or socially constructed space. Certain kinds of social contrast will also be of varying relevance in any society: male/female, married/unmarried, senior/junior, close/distant kin, kin/stranger, and so on. These categories can be given visual expression by mapping them on to spatial contrasts; but we must be aware that such oppositions need not occur in a fixed 'list', for they may cross-cut each other, or shift according to particular contexts. Intermediate categories may also occur, for example, where degrees of social status or ritual purity are concerned. In a rank-conscious society, such finer distinctions will often be revealed in rules about the seating of guests within a structure or space. Further-

more, one may look to see whether there is any association of particular people or groups with specific structures, and their place within the overall settlement pattern. (This topic was touched upon in Chapter 3, but I shall return to it again.) Thus far, the argument may be applied to any society whatever; my task in this chapter is to try to develop a picture of what, if anything, may be deemed particularly characteristic about patterns of spatial use in South-East Asian societies.

It is no accident that, among several of the most detailed anthropological studies so far produced on the uses of space, the symbolism of gender should occupy such a prominent place. The studies discussed above provide two rather extreme examples, but other work such as that of C. Hugh-Jones (1978, 1979) and S. Hugh-Jones (1979, 1985) on the Barasana of Columbia similarly reflects the prominence of gender as an organizing theme in house layout and uses of space. This, one may claim, is hardly surprising given that almost any household, however constituted, is liable to contain members of both sexes; but it is also indicative of the extent to which, in many societies, gender symbolism dominates in the organization of social categories. Given the subordinate role of women in many of these societies, it is no surprise to find women persistently relegated to 'inferior' spaces such as the back of buildings, excluded from (or at best barely tolerated in) public or ritually important areas, or trapped and imprisoned within a tightly circumscribed domestic sphere which is intended to be restrictive both physically and mentally. Thus we find Indian Muslim women in purdah describing themselves as 'frogs in a well', prevented from knowing the outside world (Jeffery 1979), while Berber proverbs say of the woman 'Your house is your tomb', or 'Woman has only two dwellings, the house and the tomb' (Bourdieu 1973: 104).[2] These oppressive images convey the sort of over-association with the house through which, in these societies, a woman's isolation from and powerlessness over the rest of the world is enforced. There are, of course, two sides to this question, since where segregation of the sexes is so radical, men find themselves excluded, too, from the cosy intimacy of the women's domain. Berber men are expected to leave the house at daybreak and spend the day in public places under the gaze of others; Bourdieu (1973: 103) remarks that 'one is not justified in saying that the woman is locked up in the house unless one also observes that the man is kept out of it, at least during the day'. Nevertheless, there is no question about which sphere is dominant: 'The orientation of the house is fundamentally defined from the outside, from the point of view of men, and, if one may say so, by men and for men, as the place from which men come out' (Bourdieu 1973: 110).

The division between 'public' and 'domestic' spheres, and the attempt to relegate women to the latter, has frequently been identified as a prominent feature of Western industrial societies. It reached an extreme among the nineteenth-century bourgeoisie, as a by-product of the development of a capitalist industrial economy. Within this economy, production and paid labour take place outside the household, which becomes the locus merely of consumption and the unpaid labour of women in reproducing the work-force. Both political and economic power, not to mention religious authority, reside outside of the domestic domain, so that the latter becomes identified almost by definition as the place where power is not.[3] Within this social system, those confined to the domestic domain risk finding themselves in a marginalized and dependent status both economically and politically, indeed cut off from 'cultural' activity in general. The domestic sphere, by contrast, is closely associated with the function of reproduction, which is deemed to be 'natural' to women. Ortner (1974) and others have argued that this structure of ideas can be used much more universally to explain the subordination of women cross-culturally. Concepts of personhood are built around the paradigmatic opposition between nature and culture; women, through their symbolic association with nature and the domestic sphere, risk being thought of as less than complete persons. Entry into the public sphere enables women to claim greater status and autonomy.

Since these constructs really derive from a Western framework of ideas, however, we cannot uncritically assume that they will apply in other cultures too, however temptingly universal their themes may sound. In response to Ortner's work, a number of anthropologists have been prompted to develop much closer analyses of the variable symbolic patterns linking male and female, nature and culture, and the public and domestic spheres in different societies. Notably, MacCormack and Strathern (1980) and Strathern (1984) have demonstrated how far patterns of symbolic opposition, the content of ideas like 'na-

ture', or notions of personhood, in other societies may fail to coincide with our own. Strathern (1984: 26) notes that the particular set of ideas associated with the 'denigration of domesticity' in the West may be absent in other societies; even where domesticity is disvalued, as in Hagen (Papua New Guinea), it may be through a different set of associations, and only in relation to certain things; the consequences for views of women as persons are also different. Tiffany (1978) exposes the weaknesses of assuming that the 'domestic' is by definition also the 'non-political'; she points out the lack of consensus in anthropology over what constitutes 'politics' (in particular the tendency to dismiss or overlook informal processes) and argues that the 'domestic' and what it encompasses is a culturally relative concept. La Fontaine likewise argues that the domestic group, far from being the irreducible 'building block' of society, is itself a product of wider social relations; its isolation is only apparent, for its very existence in fact implies its relations with other similar units, and the main demands upon it generally involve production for wider ends than mere subsistence: bridewealth, tribute, feasting, or prestations of different kinds. She concludes (1981: 346) that 'The division into domestic and public which is made in some, but not all societies, is not a description of structural cleavages but a symbolic statement whose meaning we must interpret in each instance where we find it.' Weiner, writing on Trobriand society, shows how even the idea of women's reproductive powers as 'natural' is culturally relative; in matrilineal Trobriand society, she argues, reproduction is viewed as a *cultural* achievement. Through childbirth, but also through their roles in ceremonies and wealth exchanges, women replenish the matrilineal kin group or *dala*, and thus perpetuate *social* groups and identities (Weiner 1978: 175, cited in Strathern 1984: 19). The idea of women as isolated within the 'domestic' domain as a result of their 'natural' reproductive functions makes little sense of Trobriand social reality.

It is clear that 'domestic' and 'public' spheres, where these concepts do exist, may be demarcated along a number of dimensions. Where they are contrasted, this may be in terms of political, economic, or religious/ritual arrangements. All of these may coincide to make the public realm appear as the 'real world' in which people act—as would appear to be the case in Western societies, or in the Berber example. As we have seen, action in the public world may then come to define personhood and power. The Berbers with their symbolic themes of the house as womb, its innermost parts dirty and dark, its opening 'inevitably soiled' in Bourdieu's words, would seem to fit within Ortner's pattern. The reproductive powers of women are located firmly within the domestic sphere, and viewed as 'natural' in opposition to the cultural, spiritual, and political world of men which lies beyond the household. Finally, the demarcation of spheres is most vividly embodied in the definition of space itself, and movement of bodies through it. Where the appropriation of public power by men has reached the extreme which it has in most Arab societies, the very presence of a woman in a public space may come to be viewed as a provocation (Mernissi 1975: 85). Hence the emphasis on stooping bodily posture, downcast eyes, etc., described by Bourdieu, by which a woman must signal her awareness that she has, in fact, no right to be there.

Having defined the dimensions along which the public/domestic contrast may be organized, it should be much easier to see whether these same contrasts apply elsewhere. For there is clearly no reason to assume that the dimensions will always align themselves in the same manner, for example, that 'ritual' or 'politics' will always take place outside the household, or that the 'public' sphere will always be associated with the male. I shall argue that in the South-East Asian world, the meanings associated with the house and its space are significantly different. Where the economy itself is organized around the household as the basic unit of consumption and production, the distinction between a public world of production and a domestic sphere in which consumption and unpaid labour takes place, clearly does not apply. Where the house is such a prominent and central feature of kinship and ritual systems as it is in South-East Asia, it cannot be assumed that association with it will carry implications of inferior status. Given the importance of house units in traditional political processes, too, it would be unwise to regard the house as being 'outside' the sphere of politics. Moreover, the idea that 'a woman's place is in the home' may have very different connotations where she is actually the house owner, as is likely to be the case, for example, among the Northern Thai, Acehnese, Minangkabau, or Toraja. Here, rather than woman belonging to the house, it is the house which belongs to her. Toraja women may (and do) claim a special association with the kitchen and the hearth, but where was the hearth in the tradi

tional Toraja house? In the very centre of the house, set on the most auspicious eastern side, the side associated with life and fertility. We must therefore avoid any preformed conclusions about the hierarchical implications of associations between gender and the uses of space. Even where we may encounter a contrast between male mobility and female immobility, I shall argue that interpretative caution is required. Though it is tempting to equate mobility with independence, freedom, and power and its reverse with dependence and confinement, we shall find that this theme in particular demands a very careful evaluation in the South-East Asian world, for in ritual contexts immobility is frequently used to signal high status and concentration of power. Moreover, whether the 'still centre' is identified as male or female will be found to vary according to context.

South-East Asia is one key area in which anthropologists are currently trying to work towards a fuller understanding of the interplay between gender and other culturally constituted categories, such as rank. In this discussion of spatial organization, I shall therefore be paying particular attention to gender, but I shall argue that in the South-East Asian context, gender distinctions and ideas of gender hierarchy do not provide the dominant mode of organization. Though I shall present some evidence of a specific association between houses and the female, the joining of male and female elements within the house will also become apparent. In order to develop this picture, I have found it necessary to present in some detail a number of studies, the subtleties of whose arguments are difficult to summarize; I therefore ask the reader to bear with me where I have quoted the authors at some length.

Working towards a more comprehensive view of the construction of gender in South-East Asia, Shelly Errington (1984: 2) has also pin-pointed some of these areas of concern. She suggests that in some societies gender difference is used as the fundamental image of differences between humans, and other aspects of the world are modelled upon it. But in South-East Asia, other preoccupations dominate:

The system of gender there may include notions of a difference, but, one suspects, it is *not the difference that makes a difference*, the fundamental difference on which other differences are predicated. Sexual difference becomes, there, less a concept that organises other concepts, than something that is organised by other concepts (emphasis added).

Rank, merit acquired through ritual performance, notions of life potency (namely, the *semangat* ideas already discussed in Chapter 6) may assume more importance. There are numerous contexts in which high-ranking women outrank low-ranking men; rank can entitle a woman to ritual offices, titles, or even the rule of a kingdom.

Certain important themes may be detected in the way these ideas are organized. Errington relates these to differences in political organization, though in my view they would seem to have more to do with variations in kinship ideology. Ideas about the relative contribution of the sexes to conception, for example, tend, as we have seen (Chapter 7, n. 10) to show a strong correlation with types of descent system. In the bilateral systems typical of western Indonesia and parts of mainland South-East Asia, people consider the substance contributed by each parent to their offspring to be equal in kind and quantity. Furthermore, there is a general underplaying of themes of biological difference, an absence of ideas about female pollution, and an assumption that men and women are basically similar beings. Gender categories themselves are not necessarily immutable, as evidenced by the widespread importance attached to transvestism in ritual contexts. In eastern Indonesia, systems of asymmetrical alliance demonstrate an almost obsessive emphasis on dualism and the identifying of *paired* oppositions between male and female. This, we shall see presently, is reflected in the naming of house parts and division of space in such eastern Indonesian societies as Sumba and Savu. But the stress here is on the complementarity or creative fusion of the male/female pairs, not on fixed and immutable oppositions. Thirdly, there is the theme of concentric dualism, and a hierarchical opposition between centre and periphery which, as we saw in Chapter 5, is especially elaborated in (though not exclusive to) the more centralized state societies. In these societies, suggests Errington (1984: 5), rank is an essential organizing principle, while gender is frequently construed as changeable or ambiguous. She notes that here, too, transvestism is a common feature in the ritual, drama, and dance of both court and folk traditions. It will help us to bear these themes in mind as we turn to the examples which follow.

The Atoni House

One of the best known of all anthropological analyses of house symbolism and uses of space is Cunning-ham's 1964 study of the Atoni, to which reference has already been made in earlier chapters. Atoni houses are unusual in the archipelago in being built on the ground, with a beehive roof reaching almost to the ground and resting on a low wall constructed from many short posts in the same manner as the Atoni make fences. The roof and attic floor (which is essentially a platform construction) are supported on four main posts, and smaller raised platforms provide the main items of furniture in the interior (see Plate 13; Figures 149–150).

Cunningham provides a very detailed analysis of the interplay between spatial contrasts (high/low, inner/outer, right/left) and social categories (male/female, senior/junior, kin/affines, children/marriageable youths, high/low rank, and ritual superiority/inferiority). For example, when guests are entertained, the inner section of the house is reserved for agnates of the householder, while affines or other guests will normally be entertained in the outer section at the front. If there are many guests, high-ranking ones will be seated on a platform on the right side of this section, the lower-ranking on the left. If food is served, men will eat in the outer section and women in the inner one. Here, already, we see basic spatial divisions being used to signal multiple messages about sex, rank, or kinship relation. Broadly speaking, women are associated with the inner part of the house and the left side, men with the outer part and the right side. However, these associations are not immutable: in another sense, men as members of patrilineal descent groups are more closely associated with the centre of the house and the attic, which is a supernaturally important part of the house. A wife, as an in-marrying affine, has access to the inner section of her husband's parents' house only after initiation into his descent group ritual (Cunningham 1964: 39). This temporary restriction thus marks the process of her acceptance by the husband's kin group (though in practice a fairly large proportion of Atoni marriages are uxorilocal, the husband moving to live with the wife's group).

Internal space is ordered around certain fixed points such as the door, water jar, hearth, and the platforms which form the main items of furniture. The platforms are used for a variety of purposes from sitting, eating, and sleeping to storage of utensils, foodstuffs, and other goods. The largest of these is called the 'great platform' and is always situated on the right-hand side as one faces the door. Women and affines

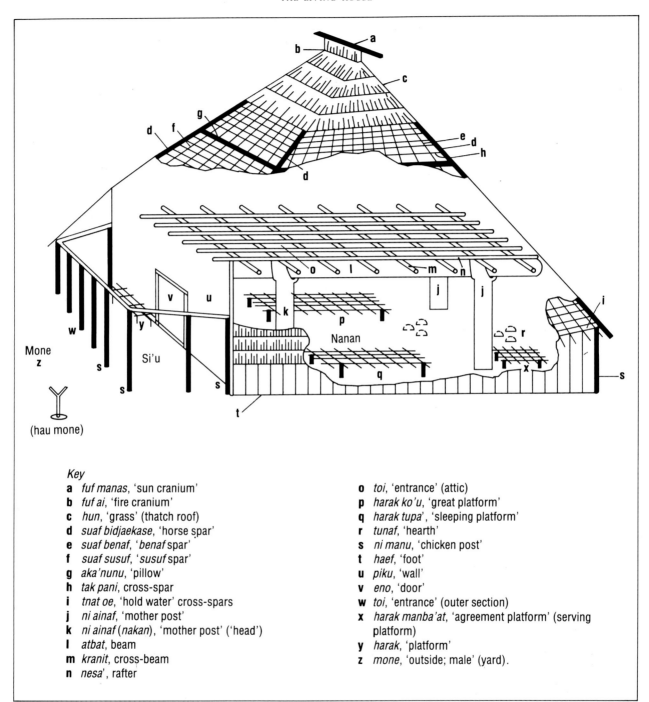

Key

a *fuf manas*, 'sun cranium'
b *fuf ai*, 'fire cranium'
c *hun*, 'grass' (thatch roof)
d *suaf bidjaekase*, 'horse spar'
e *suaf benaf*, '*benaf* spar'
f *suaf susuf*, '*susuf* spar'
g *aka'nunu*, 'pillow'
h *tak pani*, cross-spar
i *tnat oe*, 'hold water' cross-spars
j *ni ainaf*, 'mother post'
k *ni ainaf* (*nakan*), 'mother post' ('head')
l *atbat*, beam
m *kranit*, cross-beam
n *nesa'*, rafter

o *toi*, 'entrance' (attic)
p *harak ko'u*, 'great platform'
q *harak tupa'*, 'sleeping platform'
r *tunaf*, 'hearth'
s *ni manu*, 'chicken post'
t *haef*, 'foot'
u *piku*, 'wall'
v *eno*, 'door'
w *toi*, 'entrance' (outer section)
x *harak manba'at*, 'agreement platform' (serving platform)
y *harak*, 'platform'
z *mone*, 'outside; male' (yard).

149. Diagram of an Atoni house. (From Cunningham 1964: 37)

172

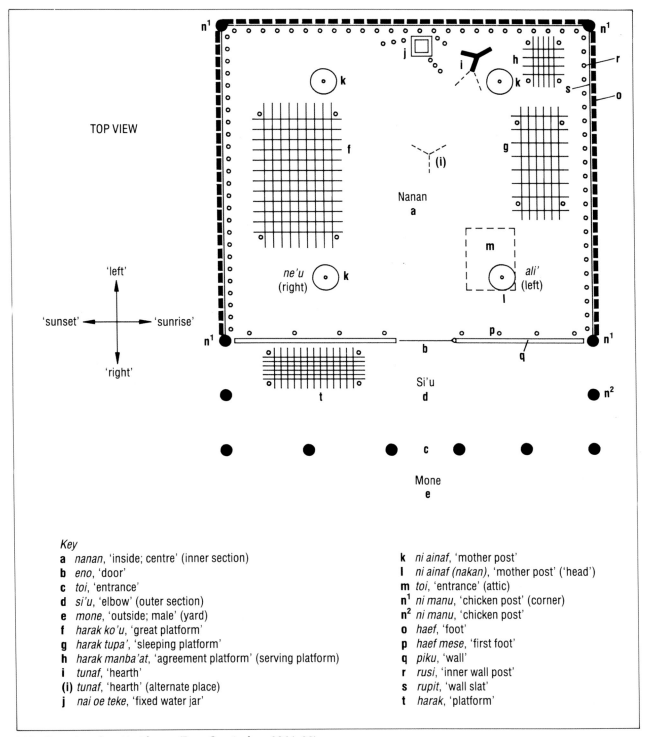

Key

a *nanan*, 'inside; centre' (inner section)
b *eno*, 'door'
c *toi*, 'entrance'
d *si'u*, 'elbow' (outer section)
e *mone*, 'outside; male' (yard)
f *harak ko'u*, 'great platform'
g *harak tupa'*, 'sleeping platform'
h *harak manba'at*, 'agreement platform' (serving platform)
i *tunaf*, 'hearth'
(i) *tunaf*, 'hearth' (alternate place)
j *nai oe teke*, 'fixed water jar'

k *ni ainaf*, 'mother post'
l *ni ainaf (nakan)*, 'mother post' ('head')
m *toi*, 'entrance' (attic)
n¹ *ni manu*, 'chicken post' (corner)
n² *ni manu*, 'chicken post'
o *haef*, 'foot'
p *haef mese*, 'first foot'
q *piku*, 'wall'
r *rusi*, 'inner wall post'
s *rupit*, 'wall slat'
t *harak*, 'platform'

150. Floor plan of an Atoni house. (From Cunningham 1964: 38)

are not allowed to sleep on the 'great platform', though on some occasions wife-giving affines are honoured by being seated here (Cunningham 1964: 40, 59) A smaller, lower platform on the left is called the 'sleeping platform', and is used by the elder male and female of the household. They should always sleep on a platform, whereas children sleep on mats on the ground. Near the hearth on the left may be a third platform, the so-called 'agreement platform', from which cooked food is served, and where women may give birth. At the conclusion of all rituals (in which women occupy a pivotal position between wife-taking and wife-giving lineages), the idea of 'agreement' or 'putting things in order' is symbolized by the woman's serving food to the guests from this platform.

Cunningham illustrates the interweaving in Atoni concepts of order of both lateral (right/left) and concentric (centre/periphery) principles. Contrasts between male and female are an important part of the arrangement, but the question of superordination or subordination is a complex one. Male activities and symbolism are associated with the more honoured right side of the house, with the outer section, and with the attic. The attic is used for storing heirlooms as well as maize and rice, and an altar stone used in agricultural ritual is also kept here. Cunningham (1964: 45) states that 'Entrance to the attic is forbidden to anyone who is not an agnate of the householder. Atoni say that the presence of another person in the attic "makes the soul of the rice and maize flee".' But he goes on to say that 'the elder male and female in the household usually manage it, sometimes with the help of a son, but daughters rarely go there.' Is this 'elder female' the householder's wife? In this case, one must assume that initiation into the husband's descent group ritual, or else her seniority, eventually overrides the fact that she is not an agnate. Or are there always older women of the householder's own clan living in the house? Cunningham (1964: 58) is not clear on this point, though he notes that [as a result of uxori-local marriages] many people trace their lineage affiliation through the mother; most lineages are said to have a 'male house' and a 'female house', that is, people who gain affiliation through the father or the mother.

Cunningham describes the use of the inner (or back) section of the house principally by women and the outer (or front) by men as being co-ordinate with Atoni ideas of subordination and superordination re-

spectively. But he goes on to draw a comparison with traditional political arrangements, and it is precisely at this point that we encounter Atoni ideas of sacredness and the 'still centre' of the kingdom, a palace where a sacral ruler, actually a man but characterized as 'female' (feto), ideally should remain motionless. The rest of the kingdom was divided at the cardinal points into four 'great quarters', each headed by a secular lord called monef-atonif ('male-man'). (Note the symbolic relativity of gender here.) The secular lords exercised more immediate political power in their control of warfare, adjudication, and tribute to the sacral lord. They guarded the princedom against intruders. Cunningham notes (1964: 54):

In village wars, men went outside the hamlets, whereas women remained behind to play drums and gongs and conduct ritual. In wars of the princedom as a whole, the symbolically 'female' sacral lord remained at the center to conduct ceremonies. It should be noted that the secular lords (the 'male-men') are on the periphery but within the circle of the princedom. Similarly, the symbolically male area in a house is outer, but within the circle of the 'chicken posts' [tightly packed small posts which form the low outer wall of the house] and under the roof. In neither case are the males 'outside' (kotin), which is another sphere entirely....

Within the Atoni princedom, the sacral lord called atupas (sleeping one), who was considered 'female' and who occupied the 'inside' or 'center' (nanan) position in a palace area called the 'root,' is a symbolic correlate of the woman and her position in the house, on whose side (the left) is located the hearth and 'sleeping platform.' Informants said of the sacral lord, 'He only knows how to sleep and eat,' and these are the two secular activities of the left side or back of any Atoni house. The door (eno) is opposed to these points, at the front in the male section. Appropriately, in the princedom the secular lords (the 'male-men') were responsible for guarding the 'door' (or gateway) to the princedom.

It becomes a nice point whether it is the periphery or the centre which should be considered superior. In some contexts, the 'inner', left or 'female' section is treated as if it were subordinate. Yet it is the left which, in fact, is most closely associated with ritual, in which the 'female', and women themselves, play a pivotal role. It is women, after all, who form the mediating category between wife-givers and wife-takers. The wife-takers depend on their wife-givers, not only for the perpetuation of the lineage, but for their co-operation in most major rituals. Cunningham furthermore notes that the four main house posts are called 'mother posts' (ni ainaf); the most important, called the 'head mother post', is located on the inner left. The 'inner' section is the ritual centre. Does this mean that ritual is being associated with a subordinate sphere? In the princedom, too, the secular lords predominated in daily affairs, and even had the right to beat the sacral lord and his guardians if they left the palace area without their permission and an escort. But, Cunningham continues (1964: 60):

The association of ritual or supernatural concerns with a subordinate sphere is not, however, the case; spiritual matters are considered superior to secular ones. When spiritual matters are at hand, the idea of *nanan* as 'center' is expressed, and the symbolically 'female' becomes pivotal in the relation of Man to Divinity. The presence of the 'head mother post' on the left illustrates this fact within the house. As 'head' it is foremost: the route to the attic (which has symbolic superordination) and to the supernatural, being the place for prayer and certain sacred heirlooms. . . . It is the left side of the house which is the way to the supernatural for Atoni men who would pray to Divinity or their agnatic ancestors. The same was true for the secular lords, the 'male-men' in a princedom, who would pray for fertility or rain for their land crops. They had to do so through the sacral lord, the symbolically female 'sleeping one' at the center of the territory.

Thus we find a mixture of jural subordination, on the one hand, and ritual centrality, on the other, both in the relations of women to men, and of the sacral, 'female' ruler to secular 'male' ones. According to Cunningham (1964: 61), the idea of the female as the 'pivotal' centre is elaborated in very general attitudes about the sexes: '*Atoni consider women to be more fixed generally than men*, more trustworthy and more stable in personality. Women control the purse-strings, and children in a home . . . gravitate towards the mother' (emphasis added).

Symbolic Duality in Other Eastern Indonesian House Forms

In Cunningham's analysis we may discern a number of general principles of spatial organization, as well as more specific themes which can be seen to recur in other societies of the archipelago. Let us first consider some neighbouring societies in which the concern with male/female dualities is equally evident, and where the idea of exclusion from certain areas of the house is similarly used to emphasize the status of in-marrying women. Among another Timorese society, the Ema,

for example, kinship ideology is also patrilineal and marriages usually virilocal. As among the Atoni, relations between wife-giving and wife-taking clans are very important. Like the Atoni's, the Ema house has a conical thatch roof reaching almost to the ground, but it differs in being pile-built. The floor is thus formed from a single large platform enclosed by the roof, rather than the Atoni earth floor with smaller separate platforms erected as furniture. The Ema floor, however, is divided by a raised beam into two unequal parts, a 'male' and a 'female' side, referred to as the 'great' and 'small' platforms. Two posts, called the 'male' and 'female' posts (*ri ulun mane/ri ulun ine*), support the transverse beam on which rests the king post of the roof. Additional support for the roof is given by a structure of cross-beams and posts within the dome (Figures 151 and 152).

The great platform is used for the performance of rituals, and here are stored most of the ancestral heirlooms, house treasures, and sacred objects which are the essential possessions of a lineage's original 'core' house and its members. These items include, most importantly, gold and silver discs which are like the 'insignia' of the house. They are worn on the chest on ceremonial occasions, and are used in traditional marriage exchanges. There are also ancestral stones, calabashes and other objects used in rituals, spears, and old swords. Most of the ritual objects are hung on the east wall, on either side of the 'male' post, while heirloom discs will be stored at the base of the post itself. The presence of all these objects renders this part of the house especially sacred, and in rituals, preliminary offerings are always made here. Textiles, cotton, clothes, and grains (items of more 'feminine' associations) are stored in their various baskets on the small platform, or at the edges of the great platform furthest from the place where the sacred items are kept (Clamagirand 1975: 42; 1980: 136).

Clamagirand's informants related that, in earlier times, it was the rule that an in-marrying woman for whom bridewealth payments and counter-exchanges had not been completed was not allowed to set foot on the 'great platform', since until her link with her own house of origin had thus been symbolically broken, she 'remained a stranger to that which symbolized the specificity of the house into which she was entering' (Clamagirand 1975: 42). Here again, then, spatial restriction on an in-marrying spouse was used to accentuate the period of her still incomplete bonding with

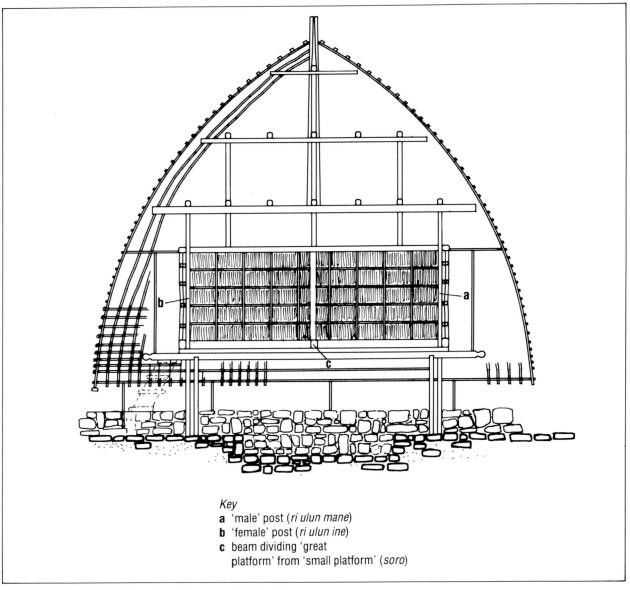

Key
a 'male' post (*ri ulun mane*)
b 'female' post (*ri ulun ine*)
c beam dividing 'great
   platform' from 'small platform' (*soro*)

151. Section of an Ema house. (From Clamagirand 1975: 38)

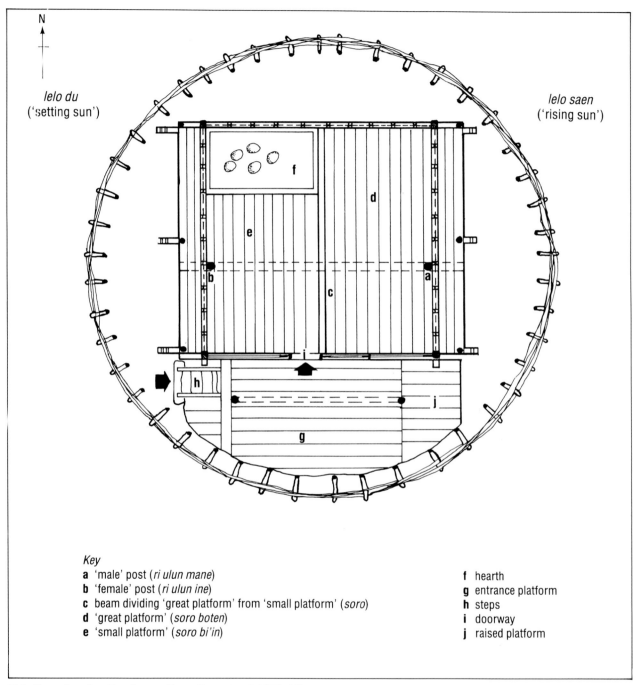

152. Floor plan of an Ema house. (From Clamagirand 1975: 40)

Key
a 'male' post (*ri ulun mane*)
b 'female' post (*ri ulun ine*)
c beam dividing 'great platform' from 'small platform' (*soro*)
d 'great platform' (*soro boten*)
e 'small platform' (*soro bi'in*)

f hearth
g entrance platform
h steps
i doorway
j raised platform

the 'house' (that is, kin group) of her husband. (Clamagirand (1975: 44) specifically mentions that Ema wife-giving and wife-taking groups think of themselves as 'houses'.)

A third example from eastern Indonesia is provided by Forth's study of the east Sumbanese domain of Rindi. The pairing of 'male' and 'female' building elements in the structure of the Rindi house is very marked, as is the symbolic opposition of certain areas of the house in terms of gender. In fact, Forth (1981: 37) goes so far as to state that 'The distinction of symbolic gender governs all dimensions of the house in Rindi.' An obsession with even numbers of house parts reflects the emphasis on pairing. Again, there is some shifting of symbolic significance according to context. In daily life, the house is particularly the domain of women, who are responsible for running it and are not supposed to wander too far from it without good reason; in this sense, there is an alignment of inner/outer and female/male categories. However, in ritual terms, men are most closely associated with the patrilineal clan ancestors and rituals, and in this context the 'inner' is thought of as 'male'. Women of the house, who either derive from other clans or will leave their clan at marriage, are in this context peripheral (Forth 1981: 40–1).

The Sumba house is formed chiefly of roof, enclosing an interior platform which is symbolically divided into a right-hand, 'male' section and a left-hand, 'female' one. The four main central posts, which extend to the base of the house peak, are also categorized as 'male' or 'female', and must be erected in a specific order. The first to be placed is that at the right front corner. Its name means 'to divine', 'to perform religious service', and it is here that offerings are made and the clan ancestor and other spiritual beings are addressed. During a rite, the priest sits beside this post. Second to be erected is the post at the right back corner, called 'the post which divides', since this is the place where men butcher the carcasses of sacrificial animals. The third, at the left back corner, is called the 'post that feeds the pigs and chickens', since this part of the house is chiefly used by women, who look after these animals. The pig trough and hatching baskets are usually kept beneath this part of the building. Finally, the post in the left front corner is called the 'post which scoops (the rice)', since this is where women cook and serve the offering rice, which is passed over to the priest who sits by the front right pillar. The same division of space

into four quarters is observed for ritual purposes even in simpler houses lacking the four main posts (Forth 1981: 27).

Here we see how fundamentally the use of space is defined by reference to the house structure, and how important are ritual functions in shaping this space. It is the right side, and particularly the front, which has the strongest association with ritual (though we may note that the front left post is associated with a *female* ritual function). The floor on the right is called the 'big floor' (*kaheli bokulu*), while that on the left is called the 'cool floor' (*kaheli maringu*) (heat being associated with ritual potency). Forth provides a detailed account of the gender associations of the two halves. The two central posts to the right of the hearth are called 'male posts' and those on the left, 'female posts'. The hearthstones on the left side of the hearth are called the 'female hearthstones', and are the only ones used in the daily preparation of food, while those on the right, called the 'male hearthstones', are only used on ritual occasions, to burn off the feathers of fowls prior to using their entrails for augury, and to cook the meat of sacrificial animals. (At rites, rice for the ancestor is cooked by women on the female hearthstones, but we may still note the closer association of 'male' and 'ritual' categories, symbolically opposed to that which is 'female'.) Again, of the two water jars kept in an ancestral house, one is designated 'female' and contains water for daily consumption, while the other, which holds water used in rites of offering, is called the 'ancestral jar'. Forth goes on to observe (1981: 38):

Also consistent with the symbolic masculinity of the right side of the the lower part of the house is the prohibition of wives for whom bridewealth has not been fully discharged from entering this section of an ancestral house.... This further accords with the possible characterization of this area as one of the symbolically inner parts of the house.

Here again, there is a part of the house which is characterized as more intimately associated with the kin group which owns it. Rules about access to this core space may then be used to emphasize to those concerned (most obviously to the individual who is required not to enter it) her status as a new arrival in the household, and as someone who is still closely bound to her natal kin group. Not that the eventual full payment of bridewealth will represent severance of her ties with her own kin, since this is not characteristic of affinal transactions in Indonesian systems of asymmetrical alliance; the continuing payment and counter-payment, rather than effecting a total transfer of a woman into her husband's kin group, serve continually to reaffirm the bond created between wife-givers and wife-takers.

In all these cases, it is apparent that the restriction applies to *sacred* space or to parts of the house most associated with kin group ritual; in the Atoni case, it is induction into the rituals of the husband's descent group which serves to lift the prohibition on the wife. In Rindi, there is a further restriction on entering the tower or peak of an ancestral house, where heirlooms are stored; only mature and older men of the lineal group which owns the house may do so. In some parts of Sumba, there are ritual clan houses, normally uninhabited, the upper parts of which may only be entered by special ritual functionaries, the *ratu*.[4] Note also that in all these three examples, kinship ideology tends toward the patrilineal; thus, where the restricted space is conceptualized as 'male' this is not necessarily in any absolute sense, but rather because of its association with male clan ancestors and rituals of the patrilineal kin group. Unfortunately, there is no information about whether any such restriction operates for men where they are married uxorilocally, as in Timor frequently is the case in practice—but marriages of this type do not involve bridewealth payments either, and given the patrilineal bias, emphasis on incorporation of the man into the wife's group is unlikely.

One final example of this pattern comes from the southern Moluccan islands of Tanimbar. Here, high-ranking 'houses' aim to repeat marriages with each other over generations. When a high-ranking woman is married in such a repeated alliance, she cannot return to her village at just any time, but must wait until her husband and the wife-taking group of his house are ready to make another major prestation to their wife-givers. Her return with the wife-taking party (often by boat from another island) is called 'she sets foot in the village'; as their boat reaches the shore, representatives of the husband's house must 'throw out an elephant's tusk bridge' (a 'male' valuable) into the waves on the beach for the 'house masters' (wife-givers) waiting on shore, who reciprocate with a 'small sarong' (any type of 'female' valuable). Further exchanges then take place which are called 'tying the paddles and punting poles', and for each log roller used to haul the boat ashore. They will stay for some days or weeks in the wife's village, negotiating a further

prestation called the 'sail' or 'rudder' (parts of the bridewealth being customarily given the names of parts of a ship) (McKinnon 1983: 250). Once again, the restriction is related to the progress of bridewealth payments; only here, it is the home village rather than a part of the spouse's house which becomes temporarily off limits to the bride.[5]

It is clear that in all of the above examples, we are dealing with asymmetrical alliance systems, which conceptualize marriage in terms of the transfer of women between houses. In all four, kinship ideology tends toward the patrilineal (even though, among the Atoni at least, only a proportion of marriages actually involve bridewealth payments and virilocal residence).[6] We might surmise that this kind of spatial rule will be less likely to occur in societies with bilateral kinship systems, such as the Toraja—where house membership for the individual is much less exclusive, and the apparent contradiction posed by the arrival of a new member will therefore present less of a conceptual problem—and this is, in fact, the case. Might such rules however occur in inverse form in matrilineal/matrilocal systems, where it is men who are the newcomers in their wives' houses? What of peoples like the Acehnese and Northern Thai, whose kinship systems are bilateral but with a distinct matrilineal bias and rules of uxorilocal residence? Below I present one or two examples where spatial restrictions are placed upon the incoming husband instead of the wife.

Matriliny, Uxorilocality, and the Uses of Space

In his well-known article on the classification of animals in northern Thailand, Tambiah (1973) demonstrates a parallelism, in Thai cognitive categories, between three distinct schemes of classification, all of which serve to define scales of social distance: marriage and sex regulations, the categorizing of space within the house, and rules about the eating of domestic and forest animals, which constitute a scale of 'edibility distance'. Here I shall mention only a few points relating to the interlinking of the first two of these; the interested reader is, however, recommended to the original article in its entirety.

Within a Thai village, houses are spread apart, each house or group of related family houses surrounded by its own fenced compound. Given the generally uxorilocal pattern of marriage, extra houses in a compound are usually those of married daughters. A compound may also include a granary, a shed with a rice-pounder, and a well. The house is called *baan*, a word which may also refer to the house site itself or the village settlement. A house should always have an odd number of rooms, since even numbers are regarded as unlucky. The poorest house has a minimum of kitchen, sleeping space, and veranda, while bigger houses may have several bedrooms and an open space for the reception of guests. The house is built on piles and the underfloor space is used for storage and the keeping of domestic animals (Figure 153).

A notable feature of house architecture is that the floors of the different portions of the house are all on different levels (see Figure 154). Floor levels are important indicators of the relative importance or sacredness of the different sections. Lowest in level is the washing place, on which pots of water are kept; next the entrance platform and kitchen, both on the same level. The guest room is higher than these, and highest of all is the sleeping room or 'large house' (*huean yaai*). Ideally, the house should face south. There is an as-

sociation of men (who are more sacred according to Buddhist doctrine) with the east and the right-hand side, and women with the west and the left. The position of the kitchen fits with the fact that cooking is chiefly the work of women. If the house faces south, east and right coincide as one enters the house. Sleeping arrangements further echo the concern with orientation. One sleeps in a north–south direction in order to avoid facing to the west; the husband is supposed to sleep on the right of his wife, though the status of an incoming son-in-law is reflected in the fact that he should sleep to the west and on his wife's left. The sleeping room is the most sacred in the house and is divided in two by an invisible partition, the householder and his wife always sleeping in the eastern part (*haung phoeng*) with their heads below a shelf dedicated to the ancestors, while a married daughter and son-in-law occupy the western part (*haung suam*). A raised threshold, intended to deter the entrance of evil spirits, separates the sleeping room from the guest room, and

153. The Kamthieng house, a fine example of a North Thai house, built in Chiang Mai in the mid-nineteenth century and now re-erected as a museum in the grounds of the Siam Society, Bangkok. (Dorothy Pelzer Collection, courtesy of ISEAS, Singapore)

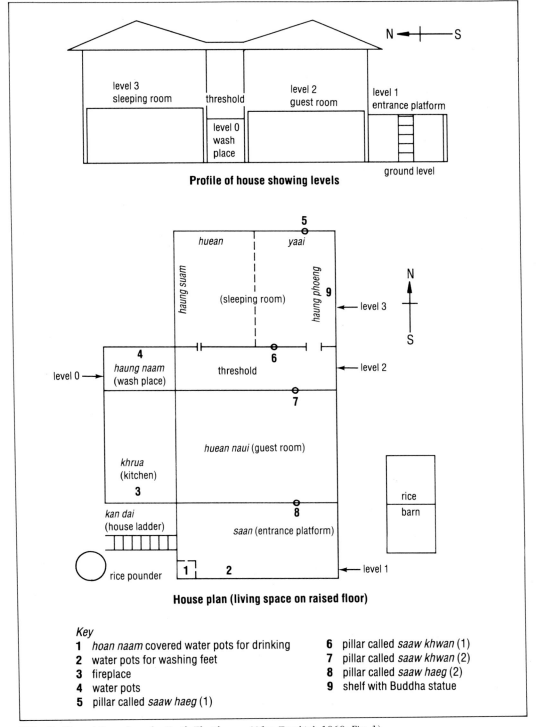

Profile of house showing levels

House plan (living space on raised floor)

Key
1 *hoan naam* covered water pots for drinking
2 water pots for washing feet
3 fireplace
4 water pots
5 pillar called *saaw haeg* (1)

6 pillar called *saaw khwan* (1)
7 pillar called *saaw khwan* (2)
8 pillar called *saaw haeg* (2)
9 shelf with Buddha statue

154. Profile and floor plan of a North Thai house. (After Tambiah 1969: Fig. 1)

there is a separate entrance into each half. Tambiah (1973: 135) notes:

The most conspicuous social feature of the division in the sleeping quarters is that a son-in-law must not enter the sleeping quarters through the doorway of the parents-in-law; furthermore, once inside the room he must never cross over into their 'room'. This taboo does not bear on children of either sex, including the married daughter. There is only one occasion on which the son-in-law ever enters through the doorway of his wife's parents. At his wedding ceremony, he is ceremonially led through that door by the ritual elders (*thaaw*) for the ritual of *sukhwan* (binding the soul essence to the body). This symbolizes that he is accepted into the house by the bride's parents and that he is legitimately allowed into the sleeping quarters as a son-in-law.

Here we see the deference of the incoming son-in-law to his wife's parents clearly marked by the restrictive rule on his entering the most sacred part of the house. Yet, in the marriage rite, his low status as a newcomer is denied by means of a reversal of this rule—for he also has to be accepted in the house if the marriage is to be a success. In this rite, he is presented to the ancestors at their shelf in the eastern corner. The ancestors are very particular, and no couple may sleep together in the house without first being presented to them. Rules about sleeping positions for the whole family reflect a concern with incest taboos and the requirement to separate unmarried sons and daughters, and junior and senior generations. Other rules define the areas open to guests, who are normally neighbours and relatives—they are received in the guest room, but are forbidden to enter the sleeping quarters unless they marry a member of the household. One must be invited before mounting the house ladder to the entrance platform. The compound fence marks the boundary of private property, and outsiders are not expected to enter it. Tambiah relates these spatial rules to incest prohibitions and degrees of marriageability: within the sleeping quarters, arrangements reflect incest taboos, while guests (who normally come within the category of those with whom marriage is specially desirable) are freely entertained in the guest room, and outsiders (not coming within the recommended marriage category) remain outside the boundary of the compound. In a parallel way, degrees of proximity determine rules about the edibility of animals. As with marriage categories, both those that are very close and very far away are subject to taboo: dogs and cats—domestic animals which live inside the house (as opposed to those like the buffalo and pig which live under it)—and certain powerful animals of the forest, such as elephant and tiger. Tambiah's analysis remains one of the most comprehensive attempts in anthropology to analyse the meanings of spatial categories within the house and relate them to other patterns of social relationship.

Davis's work on the Northern Thai sheds further interesting light on the matrilineal bias in kinship structure. He indicates that inheritance patterns, although nominally bilateral, have traditionally tended to favour women, while spirit cults are matrilineally organized; matriliny and uxorilocal residence tend to operate as mutually reinforcing principles (Davis 1984: 52ff.). Of particular interest is his observation that the ancestral house spirits residing in the sleeping room are but one particular form of a more general association between women and domestic spirits. Reference to these spirits is made to explain the avoidance of virilocal marriage. Every woman possesses a mystic essence derived from her clan spirit; when two women of different clans reside in the same house, this is thought to create a potentially dangerous situation since their spirits, deriving from different clans, are regarded as incompatible and will be in conflict with each other. In the exceptional instances where the rule of uxorilocality is not followed, special sleeping positions within the house must be followed (Davis 1984: 61):

In case of virilocal residence, if the resident daughter-in-law is of a different clan from that of her husband's mother, she and her husband are not allowed to sleep in the *huean* if the husband's mother or sister is living in the house. This formalized resolution of potential conflict between female affines encourages a married woman either to live with her own parents or to set up an independent household.... In Landing, people ... relegate this potential conflict to the spiritual realm, saying, 'People may be friendly, yet their spirits are hostile.'

Potential human conflict is thus defused by being projected into the spirit world, at the same time as it is symbolized through the placement of individuals within the house.

Among the Northern Thai, it is clear that there is a particularly close association of women with the house, brought about by norms of uxorilocality, female ultimogeniture, and the matrilineal organization of ancestor spirits. Davis (1984: 68) speaks of a 'social structural dominance of females', which complements an official ideology of male dominance. Association of women with the house is mirrored in ideas of men as mobile, women as fixed elements of society: men are expected to wander and seek their fortunes, women to stay home and look after houses and property, engaging in local rather than long-distance trade. Turning to Indonesia, we find among the Acehnese and Minangkabau a very similar 'social structural dominance' of women, linked with implicit or explicit matrilineal principles of organization. Is this reflected in spatial patterns within the house? I believe that it is.

A great deal has been written both about Minangkabau matriliny and their custom of *merantau*, the habit of young men to leave home and seek their fortunes far afield. Again, the pattern of men as mobile, women as fixed appears strongly entrenched, with women inheriting and administering all ancestral property. In a village, each house is known by the name of its leading and most active woman. A married man divides his time between his natal home and that of his wife, but is expected to spend the day in public places. He remains always something of a guest in his wife's house, but neither is he fully at ease in his mother's. Although men are appointed to certain formal leadership roles in the clans, they have very little real authority over mothers, sisters, or wives (Tanner 1982; F. Errington 1984: 14). In a traditional multi-family house, the position of an in-marrying son-in-law was a tenuous one. He had to show a great deal of respect for his wife's elder male kin, as well as for his mother-in-law, and had to leave the house very early in the morning in order to avoid meeting her. The fragility of a marriage tie in the face of disapproval from the wife's family is reflected in the Minangkabau saying: 'When your mother-in-law frightens the cat in front of you, better be prepared to leave the house' (Naim 1971: 8).[7] The Minangkabau will be discussed at greater length in Chapter 10, so I shall refrain from saying more about them here, save to point out that the themes mentioned here find their reflection also in Acehnese culture.

Elements of Acehnese social structure and house construction have been touched on in earlier chapters, but spatial arrangements in the house have not yet been described in detail. Most of the following description is derived from Dall (1982). The house (Figure 155) is set in an open courtyard, generally neater

at the front, which is planted with flowering plants, and less tidy at the rear, where useful vegetables and fruit trees are planted, where the well is situated, and where rubbish may be thrown out from the kitchen, which is always at the back of the house. The front, male entrance is the formal, public one; female access is through a more private, rear area where work is done (Dall 1982: 36). The house is approached by a stairway, which (as among the Thai) must have an odd number of steps. This leads on to the front veranda, used by men and guests. A curtain may separate this space from a central passageway which gives on to the main bedrooms. This is the inner part of the house (*dalam*), which is entered only by family, women, or close intimates. On the far side of this is the back veranda, used by women, and beyond this again, the kitchen. Another set of entrance steps, leading to the kitchen, is used only by women. Beneath the house is a useful storage and work area, where fire-wood may be chopped, coconut oil pressed, and rice pounded, and where women may set up their looms. Rice may be stored here in bins, and animals and poultry penned. The space under the house can accommodate overflows of guests on ceremonial occasions, and at funerals the mourners receive the condolences of friends and relatives here. The most sacred spot in the house is a platform high up in the roof, beneath the gable, on which are stored family heirlooms and valuables (*peusaka*).

There are a number of ways in which spatial oppositions are prominent in the organization of the Aceh home. Vertical oppositions between 'high' and 'low' areas express distinctions between the sacred and the profane; the three-layered vertical division of the house and its correspondence with cosmological ideas was discussed in Chapter 5. The second major contrast is that between 'male' and 'female', expressed most obviously in the distinctions made between front and back parts of the house. Equally significant, it would appear, is a contrast between 'inner' and 'outer' areas, which alters somewhat depending on which part of the house is taken as a focus. Meaning, then, is derived not from a crudely fixed polarity (for example, of male/female), but from an interweaving of shifting sets of contrasts.

The back of the house, used by women, may be characterized as a female, private, and everyday area. By contrast, the front is male, public, and used for formal occasions. Distinctions between 'inner' and 'outer'

155. Acehnese house in the village of Lam Teun, North Sumatra, 1965. The entrance is to the left. Note the different floor levels: the house-holders' bedroom in the centre, being the most sacred room in the house, has the highest floor. (Dorothy Pelzer Collection, courtesy of ISEAS, Singapore)

areas are shifting. The Acehnese regard the outside world to some extent as a source of danger, from which the house provides a sanctuary; in this sense, the house as a whole is 'inside' to the world's 'outside'. The inner section of the house, called *dalam* ('inside'), is very important and by contrast both the male and female ends of the house are 'outer'. The floor level of this inner portion of the house is also the highest, appropriately enough since, next to the roof space, it is the most sacred. One may, at the same time, see the whole of the 'male' portion of the house, oriented to the outside world, as 'outer' or extrinsic to the house proper, which is 'inner'. The men's veranda is separated from the inner part of the house by a wall, which is usually elaborately carved and decorated—a distinctive boundary marker, like the carved skirting-

board which divides the floor level, occupied by humans, from the place of animals below the house. This particular aspect of the inner/outer division clearly reflects the close identification of the woman with the house, which is, in fact, hers. Dall puzzles over the apparent contradiction between the relegation of the female to the rear of the house, and the fact that she actually owns the house and controls the daily running of the household and its property. But, in fact, it is the dynamic bringing together of male and female elements in the centre of the house (the main bedroom) which can be identified as the most significant feature of its organization. Here are situated the two main house posts, called *raja* and *putròë* ('prince' and 'princess'), against which the groom and the bride are seated on their wedding day (Snouck Hurgronje 1906:

43; Dall 1982: 50). It is here, too, that the procreation of new life will take place. Within the context of South-East Asian gender symbolism, with its characteristic emphasis on creative fusion of male and female elements, the layout of the Aceh house makes perfect sense. Though Dall's analysis only touches upon this point, some close comparisons can be drawn with the way space is used in the Sundanese house, as analysed by Wessing (1978). Dall states that his male informants regarded their part of the house as the most important, as indeed might appear to be borne out by the amount of decoration lavished upon it. (He unfortunately had little opportunity to discuss with women their own views on the subject.) But, he wonders, is this decoration not perhaps intended to 'keep the guests happy'? He echoes the impressions of previous writers, such as Snouck Hurgronje and Siegel, that the man is, in fact, little more than a guest in the house of his wife (Dall 1982: 53; Snouck Hurgronje 1906; Siegel 1969: 55). For in spite of the respect accorded to him while he is at home, the house remains essentially the domain of the woman.

In another Sumatran society, the Rejang of Lampung, at the southernmost tip of the island, the association of uxorilocality with spatial restrictions on the in-marrying husband are even more explicit. The Rejang traditionally were shifting cultivators, living in fortified villages along river banks, and they were organized into patrilineal clans. However, as in most other Indonesian societies with this arrangement, there were two possible forms of marriage: virilocal, with the payment of bridewealth, or uxorilocal, in which case the groom made only a small bridewealth payment, but performed brideservice for the wife's parents. This form of marriage was quite common and was called *semendo*. The uxorilocally residing husband was confined like a guest to the veranda and the front room, and in particular was forbidden access to the compartments of his wife's sisters. During the 1930s, according to Jaspan (1964), Rejang kinship structure underwent a shift from patrilineal to matrilineal, due, it seems, to a combination of factors which made the payment of large bridewealths difficult. One of these factors was the effect of the world economic depression, and another was local Islamic opposition to the payment of bridewealth. As a result, uxorilocal marriages became the norm, and inheritance of lineage property passed from being the right of the eldest son to that of the youngest daughter. Here again, then,

rather than women being 'confined' to the back of the house, it is men who are 'confined' to the front—a dubious honour at best.[8]

Women, Rice, and the Granary

We are beginning to develop a picture of patterns of spatial organization and gender symbolism within the house in a range of South-East Asian societies, and we have seen that in some instances, the identification of women and houses is particularly strong. I shall now turn to examine another area in which there is a strong identification with the female: namely, agriculture, rice, and the storage of rice, whether this is in a separate granary or within the house itself.

The sacredness of the granary and its respectful treatment as the storage place of rice has already been mentioned.[9] It is certainly ancient, as is indicated by the depictions of granaries on ritual objects or as miniatures buried with the dead in bronze-age cultures, discussed in Chapter 1. The ancient temple of Ise in Japan, whose resemblance to architectural styles of the South-East Asian archipelago was also noted, is based upon a granary and the cult performed there is chiefly concerned with fertility of the earth. In present-day South-East Asia, rice is widely represented as a female deity: Lady Koosok in Thailand, Dewi Sri in Java and Bali, and other names elsewhere, often with the meanings of 'mother' or 'princess', for example, among the Toba and Karo Batak and the Sumbanese (Niessen 1985: 129). The auspicious positioning of the granary in the Northern Thai house compound, and the requirement that its floor level be higher than that of the house, reflect the respectful attitude to rice. Even where the granary is part of the house, this rule is followed, and the floor of the barn must rest on its own floor beams. Davis (1984: 50) notes:

This gives the rice added protection from floods and additional ventilation from below. People also say that this arrangement gives the rice goddess, Lady Koosok, an elevated position worthy of her godhead and prevents her from being disturbed by vibrations from the living and kitchen areas.

In order not to disturb the goddess, rice is only put into or removed from the granary on certain auspicious days, but a bin on the balcony may contain rice which can be taken at any time, in case of sudden need (Krug and Duboff 1982: 76–8).

In Sunda (West Java), where the feminine associations of rice cultivation are equally pronounced, rice is housed in a store (*goah*) built either inside or next to the kitchen, the most female part of the house. Only women enter the rice store, and it is they who make offerings there to Dewi Sri; men may enter the kitchen, but never the *goah* (Wessing 1978: 55). There is, however, a kind of balance between 'male' and 'female' spaces in the house, as there is expected to be between the occupants. Sundanese say that within the household, husband and wife should be 'equally strong' (*pada kawasa*). As in Aceh, the division between front, 'male' parts of the house and rear, 'female' ones is mediated by the fusion of male and female elements in the centrally located bedroom of the householders. At the same time, the house space can also be read in terms of an inner/outer progression from rice store to kitchen to the rest of the house to the outside world, a progression which is symbolically one from 'female' to 'male' (Wessing 1978: 62).

In South-central Java, the association of Sri, the rice goddess, with the most sacred, inner part of the house is also quite explicit (Figure 156). The most important building in a compound, and the one to be built first,

is an enclosed structure called the *dalem* ('inner') or *omah*. Within this are a row of three smaller store rooms (*senthong*). Those to the left and right contain agricultural produce, and sewing tools or sometimes weapons, respectively, while the central one (*senthong tengah*) is the domain of Sri and the place where incense was customarily burned to her once a week, and where a bride and groom are seated during their wedding ritual. Placentas of the newborn are buried in front of it. The *dalem* as a whole, states Gunawan Tjahjono (1988: 5–13), is 'mainly the female domain'. Men are more associated with the outside and the *pendopo*, a pavilion structure in front of the *dalem*, which differs from it in being open and light instead of enclosed and dark, but is often identical to it in its roof shape. The central *senthong* has a raised floor, and contains a decorated bed, a male and female doll, women's garments, family heirlooms, and sometimes a sacred kris. According to Gunawan Tjahjono (1988: 5):

The bed is the place for Sri, the rice goddess, who was also transformed into the South Sea Goddess, Nyai-Loro Kidul, the key holder of the earth. She represents fertility, prosperity

156. Farmer's house in traditional style at Jepara, on the north coast of Central Java, 1966. (Dorothy Pelzer Collection, courtesy of ISEAS, Singapore)

and stability. Hence, a wedding takes place in front of her in order to ensure a good fortune and [offspring]. Facing the senthong tengah, one may recall the most ancient living environment, the cave. The womb-like milieu also mysteriously manifests the reproductive power.

Here too, then, male and female are *brought together* and united within the *predominantly female* innermost space of the house.[10]

In Bali, according to Tan (1967: 456), 'The storage of rice is almost glorified', though the kitchen, its place of preparation, is a simple building and there is no particular place at all for eating it (Figure 157). Storage of rice after harvest involves the performance of special rituals dedicated to Devi Sri, the rice goddess. Tan (1967: 453) notes the probability that the cult associated with rice cultivation dates from the pre-Hindu period, although in recent times there have been efforts to incorporate the rice goddess into the Hindu pantheon as the spouse of Vishnu. He remarks (1967: 452) that 'even though there is no actual division of sexes in a Balinese dwelling, kitchen and granary would be the special domain of women.'

Moving east to the island of Sumbawa, Hitchcock (1986: 26) writes of the highland-dwelling Dou Wawo of Bima (eastern Sumbawa) that 'Women are completely responsible for the storage of the rice harvest because it is only they who are permitted under customary law to enter the rice store.' In Tana Toraja, although men are not prohibited from entering granaries, in the normal course of events it is women who remove the rice from the barn, and make decisions about daily consumption and disposal of the rice. An old-fashioned custom, now rarely observed, was that a woman should remove her blouse before entering the granary, as a gesture of 'respect' to the rice—one in which a symbolic equation is apparently drawn between women and rice as sources of fertility and nourishment. For a man to interfere in his wife's rationing of the rice is considered to be laughable and in poor taste; during my fieldwork in a Toraja village, a rare instance of this behaviour was pointed out to me and the man in question was stigmatized as stingy and weak for failing to trust the capabilities of his wife (who predictably left him and found herself another husband).

In Kédang, the district of eastern Lembata Island studied by Barnes, the link between women and rice is also explicit. In Lembata, elaborate rules are followed concerning who may remove grain from a granary. Barnes (1974: 76-7) observes:

A symbolic association between women and the granary ... is clearly seen in Lamaholot where the young girl acting the role of 'rice maiden' ... must spend a night of vigil in the granary prior to planting ... and where in a certain area a special building for young girls is called a 'granary'. In Kédang the association is shown most directly by the rule that only women may take the grain out of the inner compartments of the granary. This means a man's wife or mother may do so. His children, even if female, may not. If his mother is dead, but his father (an old man) still lives, his father may take the grain out. If the man stays at home by himself, his wife should take the grain out for him before she leaves. This can be left in the outer compartments of the granary where the man can then get it. I was told that if the granary is full, the prohibitions apply even to the outer compartments. If an old man or woman is living, the grain for their meal should be removed first. The old people may eat first ... most strongly affected are children, who may in no circumstances remove grain from the inner compartments.

This passage not only demonstrates the especially close association between women and grain, but also shows that, to some extent, a principle of seniority cuts across the gender rule. There is an implied equation between women/inside and men/outside, which partly coincides with a similar spatial association of elders/inside and children/outside. The sacredness of rice and the enormous respect with which it is treated are evident, but this theme is also made use of as a means of articulating social relations through the imposition of spatial rules.

Mashman (1986) provides an acute analysis of gender and the uses of space in an Iban longhouse, as well as showing the profound literal and symbolic connection between women and rice agriculture. She notes that rice is associated, both in language and in ritual, with women as the 'custodians of fertility'. Women not only take the predominant role in the private family ceremonies surrounding different stages of rice cultivation, they also have greater technical expertise, and often assume the entire responsibility for rice cultivation while their men are away on migratory journeys (*bejalai*), which these days often involve the search for wage work on coastal plantations or oil rigs, or in logging camps.[11] It is women, too, who take charge of the storage of rice in bins in the loft above the *bilek* or family compartment in the longhouse.

157. Balinese rice barn (*lumbung*) in the village of Celuk, Gianyar district, 1988. (Photograph: Garth Sheldon)

The Iban longhouse may be broadly divided into two key areas, the *ruai* or veranda, running its entire length, and the *bilek* or family rooms, which open off the veranda. The focus of the *bilek* is the hearth, where women cook and prepare food. Above it, and extending out over the *ruai*, is the loft (*sadau*), of which Mashman (1986: 38) notes:

It is where rice is stored in bark bins, where the sacred strain of rice *padi pun* is kept and it is where unmarried girls may sleep.... As the highest physical point of the longhouse it is also of special importance, as in certain rituals it is a point of entry to the spirit world through a specially constructed dream house.... It is also the place where the *manang* [a transvestite shaman] undergoes his initiation with the assumption of female dress. Through association of use, it is possible to suggest that the *sadau* is an area of 'feminine' space.

The *ruai* is the public area, and one writer, Sutlive, posits that this is a symbolically 'male' space, since it represents an outward orientation, formerly manifested by men in hunting and warfare, and today through 'wandering', migration, politics, and public affairs in a state society; the *bilek*, by contrast, represents the domestic sphere (Sutlive 1978; Mashman 1986: 4). Mashman, however, notes that while the *bilek* may clearly be identified as a female space, there is a certain ambiguity about the *ruai*, since women also use this area for the performance of tasks such as weaving and rice pounding; though men take pride of place in the discussions of public affairs which are held here, women from an early age also participate actively in these and have a great deal of influence in longhouse affairs. Mashman (1986: 50) notes:

Despite men's apparent control of public affairs, it is possible to argue that their outward orientation suggests that they are peripheral to the longhouse, and women retain power in the *bilek*. Women, on the other hand, are central to the survival of the longhouse [because] of their role in the subsistence economy.... Sutlive (1978: 53–55) suggests, on the basis of a horizontal reading of space, that the *tanju* or open porch is spiritually the highest point of the longhouse and the *bilek* is the lowest point. Against this it is possible to argue that the *bilek* is central to two planes, the horizontal plane which is discussed by Sutlive, and the vertical plane, that extends upwards through the loft, the sanctuary for the sacred rice, and the rice bins, an area of feminine influence, to the roof and the spirit world beyond. Thus the *bilek* can be seen to be central to two major orientations of the Iban

cosmic view: upwards to the sky, and outwards to the river. In addition to this, women have power in the invisible territory of the spirit world, through their role in the rituals of rice cultivation, and their weaving of potent designs.

In one final case, that of Savu (Plate 12; Figures 158 and 159), we find in the layout of the house a quite distinct emphasis on 'male' and 'female' areas, with the grain store again being housed within the innermost and most 'female' section.[12] Savunese social structure includes both patrilineal clans and matrilineal moieties, but it is worth noting that houses are normally inherited by the youngest daughter, so that uxorilocal marriage is common and the 'woman of the house' is very likely to be the owner of it. The following description is derived from Kana (1980).

Along the front of the house is a platform, divided into two parts, a 'male' or 'bow' section (*duru*) and a 'female' or 'stern' section (*wui*). Men sit and work, or receive guests, on the one side, women on the other. A second, higher platform forming the main house floor rests on the main beams of the structure. It, too, is divided into a 'male' and 'female' side. Finally, there is a third, 'loft' platform on the 'female' side of the house, closed off by a coconut leaf screen. The loft is a specifically female part of the house, dark, protected, and associated with prosperity, where women store equipment, food, and thread for making cloth. Only women (specifically the 'woman of the house' or wife of the householder) may enter. She performs certain rituals here which no one else sees. As in Sumba, house posts are also designated 'male' or 'female', and the two main house posts (*taru*) are the object of ritual attentions. The 'female' part of the house itself is screened down the middle to ensure that the 'female' post is not visible to the 'male' post. Cooking is done in the 'female' part of the house on the side that is not screened. This part is called the 'chest' of the house, which suggests that it is thought of as central and as containing the 'breath' or life of the building (*hemanga*).

The complementary opposition in the house between what is dark, female, and hidden and what is light, male, and open to the outside is but one reflection, suggests Kana, of a whole series of symbolic dualisms in Savu society, dualisms which are most vividly expressed in various kinds of ritual confrontations. These include cockfights and stone-throwing battles, which dramatize the oppositional relation between the island's two moieties. Like so many houses

158. House in Bodai village, Savu, 1987. It has the distinctive extended ridge line which the Savunese call *rukoko* or 'leaf-neck'. (Photograph: Garth Sheldon)

159. The 'male' or open section of a Savunese house; the wall in the left half of the photograph divides it from the enclosed 'female' section, symbolically associated with life, prosperity, and nourishment. Clan village of Namata, Seba district, 1987. (Photograph: Roxana Waterson)

of the archipelago, the Savu house is windowless, dominated by its enormous roof; the enclosed part of it is symbolically womb-like: 'dark, female and hidden'. What is striking about this description, however, is its strongly positive associations: with life, prosperity, nourishment, and the control of rituals for which the woman of the house alone is responsible.[13]

In all these examples, we find women playing key roles in the household economy, centred on rice cultivation, as well as controlling the stored crop and frequently the rituals associated with it. The profound symbolic tie between women and rice is a reflection not only of the important economic and productive role of women in South-East Asian societies, but of a deeper association between female fertility and that of agricultural crops, between the nurturing capacities of women as child-bearers and as farmers. Respect for this creative power is echoed in the spatial rules surrounding the rice store.

The Theme of Immobility

Our discussion thus far has begun to reveal several distinctive patterns in the definition of space in South-East Asian dwellings. The house, rather than representing a 'domestic' domain isolated from and opposed to a 'public' world of economic production, ritual, and politics, must rather be seen as central to these concerns. While it may still be argued that there is a special symbolic association of women with the house, this in no way indicates their exclusion from other spheres. The female associations of granary and hearth, in particular, are indicative of women's control over the sources of nourishment, and of the identification of their fertility with that of the crops they grow. The hearth, obvious physical focus of many smaller dwellings, can often, even in larger structures, more meaningfully be viewed as located in central or 'inner' portions of the house rather than in 'rear' or inferior ones. Given the apparently universal South-East Asian theme of creative complementarity between the sexes, we have seen that even where houses are divided into 'front' and 'back' areas, one must be especially cautious in assuming connotations of superiority or inferiority. We have also seen how complex may be the interplay between gender symbolism and that of age, rank, or kinship identity, in societies where gender is not necessarily the predominant source of symbolic contrasts. This underplaying of gender oppositions

is perhaps most evident in the ritual sphere, in the typical absence of ideas of female pollution, or of rites from which women are excluded. Ancestors, the focus of much ritual attention, are (as we shall see in the next chapter) usually treated as a group including both sexes. Instead of sharply defining a domain of the 'sacred' by opposition to a 'profane' realm, there is rather a sort of continuity of sacredness in these societies, which makes sense in terms of the monistic world view in which everything in the cosmos is imbued with vital force. This continuity is notably evident, for example, in the fact that both the Kédangese and the Atoni lack any concept of a 'profane' category at all, and have no word to express it (Barnes 1974: 141; Schulte Nordholt 1980: 247).

In the Atoni case, we find the symbolic association between house interior, navel, the 'root' end of trees, immobility, sacredness, and the female, reflected most vividly in the conduct of the sacred 'female lord' who remains inside his palace (called the 'root') at the 'navel of the land' (Schulte Nordholt 1980: 241). I now want to pursue further this chain of associations as they occur in other Indonesian societies, for I believe that they form a deeply significant complex of ideas which resonates through a number of these cultures. That these themes should be so widespread is less remarkable in view of the fact that the origins of some of the key terms involved are Austronesian, and there is thus a strong possibility that we are dealing here with a distinctively Austronesian set of ideas.[14]

Centres, navels, and root/trunk ends of plants may all be seen as metaphorical sources of vitality. In Rindi thought, life proceeds, according to the botanic metaphor, from trunk to tip, and death is conceived of as a reverse movement, from tip to trunk. Wife-givers, the source of continued life, are as 'trunk' to their wife-receivers' 'tip' (Forth 1981: 201, 288). E. D. Lewis (1983), writing of the matrilineal Tana Ai of Flores, notes the predominance in Tana Ai thought of images of growth derived from the bamboo. In their language, the honorific terms for 'woman' and 'man' are words of Austronesian origin, meaning 'old, ripe, back, trunk' and 'new, young, unripe, front, shoot, tip', respectively. (Note, in particular, the symbolic connotations of 'back' and 'front' here, where 'back' has the strongly positive associations of seniority, of the strong, seasoned wood that comes from the base of the tree and which is the source of new growth.) Lewis (1983: 36) speaks of the 'deep structural complementarity' of the meanings of these words denoting gender, with their senses of centre and periphery, older and younger. These, in turn, 'accord with the order of Tana Ai houses and clans', the clans segmenting as a result of marriages into older, more central houses and younger, more peripheral houses.

There is an ambiguity about centres, however, for it is, in fact, from the nodes or *boundaries* between sections of the bamboo that new growth sprouts. As Lewis (1983: 22) expresses it: 'In Tana Ai, all origins are associated with boundaries, and all boundaries, not just those of the bamboo ... are potentially sources.' New growth can be generated by bringing things together at their boundaries. We can perhaps make further sense of this by referring to what Wessing has to say of centre and periphery in Sundanese thought. The centre, for the Sundanese, is itself a boundary between this world and the other world; it is the point through which supernatural power can be tapped from the universe and redistributed. The centre of the Sundanese house, the bedroom, may likewise be seen as a border at which the creative union of male and female takes place. In Sunda and in Java, ritual gatherings, which are such an important feature of community life, are also thought of as centres, through which supernatural power can be tapped by prayer (Wessing 1978: 62; Gunawan Tjahjono 1988: 12).

Immobility, fertility, and the female recur again as a theme among the Toraja. Certain noble houses in Tana Toraja are the holders of particular ritual offices within their communities. One of the most important of these is that of the co-ordinator of the rice-growing cycle, the *Indo' Padang* or 'Leader of the Land'. The literal meaning of *Indo'* is 'Mother', though its sense here is of 'head' or 'leader', and I was generally told that the office was filled by a man. He must avoid eating meat from funerals during the growing season, and is not supposed to travel too far afield while the rice is ripening. If he must do so, he must not eat of other people's rice but carry a small quantity of uncooked rice with him and have it mixed in with the rice of his hosts; otherwise the harvest of the whole community will diminish. Women in the west Torajan village where I lived, however, stated that the office is actually held by a woman, because, as they put it, 'It is the woman who *stays put* (*mari'pik*) and doesn't go wandering about.' She therefore is better suited to observe the prohibitions associated with the rice-cycle,

and she in particular must carry her own rice with her if she needs to travel about. She needs her husband to slaughter the pigs and chickens which are offered to the deities, but she cooks the rice for these offerings and spoons it out. The statements of these women reflect the commonly expressed Toraja notion of men as mobile and women as fixed, an idea which fits with the predominant pattern of uxorilocal marriage, which means that women are often house owners and remain firmly attached to their communities of birth. By asserting the importance of their own part in following the observances of the *Indo' Padang*, they pointed up the fact that indeed the office requires both a man *and* a woman to carry out all the duties associated with it. This is true of most ritual titles which involve the making of offerings; generally, whichever of the spouses actually holds rights in the house to which the office is attached, will properly be named as the office-holder. This pairing of functions in the fulfilment of ritual duties is not uncommon in other Indonesian societies.[15] An even more notable example of ritual immobility occurs in Toraja in the context of the great life-enhancing rite of *ma'bua'*, when the eight young noblewomen called *to tumbang* remain within the 'pregnant' house for an entire year, leading up to the final day of the ceremony. In some regions of Toraja, they are then carried to the ceremonial ground in litters, where they spend the day in a house-like structure with walls of sacred cloths, built in a holy *waringin* (banyan) tree. Here they 'symbolize celestial beings, who stay in their heavenly *tongkonan* (origin-house)' (Nooy-Palm 1979: 91; see also Waterson 1984a).

Further examples of ritual specialists 'staying put' can be found in Central Sulawesi, in the Moluccan island of Tanebar-Evav, described by Barraud, and among the Minangkabau. Among the people of the Poso region in Central Sulawesi (formerly known by Dutch linguists as the Bare'e Toraja), a female shaman conducting a curing ceremony used to enter a trance during which she would undertake long 'soul journeys' while remaining enclosed within a sort of tent of bark cloth hanging from the roof of the house. During her performance all doors and windows had to be closed, and nothing could be allowed to disturb her (Adriani and Kruyt 1951: Vol. II, 120). The immobilized officiant need not always be female, however: in Tanebar-Evav, a ritual pig hunt marks the start of the harvest, and while it is underway, the 'Guardian of the Earth', a man, must remain inside the ritual house. It is as if, as Barraud (1979: 75) describes it, by his immobility he takes upon himself any transgressions that others may have committed. For the Minangkabau, immobility in ritual is associated with status, dignity, and refinement. At the ceremonial ascension to office of a Minangkabau matrilineage head or *panghulu*, F. Errington (1984: 129ff.) describes how all the *panghulu* of the community must gather, heavily dressed, inside a ceremonial enclosure erected within the ancestral house of the newly appointed office-holder. The curtains of the enclosure are intended to keep out the air, thus symbolizing the idea that no outside influence should affect the *panghulu*'s decisions. They remain seated stiffly cross-legged for hours in stifling heat, listening to long, refined speeches and prayers, the degree of their discomfort being apparently directly proportionate to the esteem in which they are held. Perhaps the most widespread of ritual customs featuring immobility is that of seating the bride and groom in state before the guests at weddings (as among the Malays, Bugis, and Minangkabau). 'Motionless and perspiring', as Errington (1984: 56) puts it, they remain enthroned, in all their finery, for hours at a time. It is interesting to note that the couple are often deemed to be 'king' and 'queen' for the day, and their dress imitates that of royalty.

Immobility, then, represents a concentration of fertility, or of supernatural or political power. Dressing the wedding couple in royal finery suggests a symbolic parallel between reproductive and political power. Remarkable, too, is the fact that this immobility is always within a house, or else there is a particular association between a house and the person for whom immobility is enjoined—the Atoni ruler and his palace, Toraja ritual specialists and the origin-house from which their office derives.[16] What unites all these contexts, we may surmise, must be underlying concepts of *semangat*, viewed in terms of which these different kinds of potency do really all derive from the same source. The particular association of the female with the house and the quality of fixedness, though by no means unvarying, is nowhere more explicitly elaborated than in Timorese societies, through organic metaphors of the house as womb. Traube, for example, writes of the Mambai (1986: 78, 80):

In designating the social units of ritual action as 'houses', Mambai implicitly make reference to the feminine principle of the cosmos. If Father Heaven personifies the qualities attributed to agnatic relations among houses, it is Mother Earth who presides over the house itself.... Father Heaven patrols open spaces, but to Mother Earth belongs the warm, dark, protected space of the house, the world of the interior, where human birth and growth unfold. She is the personified principle of life-giving *immobility* and constancy, a fixed point of orientation in a wider world of motion and change. Through its association with Mother Earth, the house assumes a manifestly maternal character.... The house is also metonymically associated with women, who 'follow Mother Earth' and preside over the inner realm of space (emphasis added).

Mother Earth is also closely associated with the cosmic navel (the site of which is believed to be the sacred village of Raimaus, an important ritual centre for the Mambai). In the underworld, the Mother holds fast to the navel-cord to steady the earth, and when she shifts her grip, earthquakes occur (Traube 1986: 41).[17]

Mambai symbolic patterns align female/male contrasts with those of elder brother/younger brother, of trunk/tip, and of ritual/political powers, for in myth it is the elder brother who elects to remain behind at the origin-place, tending the altars of 'rock and tree', while the younger brother leaves to wander far off, taking with him the house wealth and emblems of political power. Mambai stress the 'immobility, fixity and constancy' of the elder brother. According to Traube (1986: 73):

The eldest is associated with the stillness of the interior, symbolized by the origin house where he remains, and by the sacred rock and tree over which he watches. Younger brothers belong to the world of the exterior. Active, mobile, restless, they traverse wild, open territories to settle at the fringes of inhabited space.

Symbolically identified with the female and the elder brother, and yet at the same time acting as the mediator who presides over the conjoining of male and female spheres in rites, is the Ritual Lord, of whom Traube (1986: 105) notes: 'His manifestly female character as dark, nurturing life-giver stands for the totality of male and female that makes life possible.... At the center, Mambai thought places, not the solitary female, but the life-giving couple.' Once again the emphasis is on the conjoining of 'male' and 'female' into a whole which is represented as female.

Writing of the matrilineal people of Wehali, a small princedom of the southern Belu or Tetum people of

160. Belu (Tetum) house at Kewar, Central Timor, 1965. (Dorothy Pelzer Collection, courtesy of ISEAS, Singapore)

161. Finely carved door panels with breasts in relief, from a Belu (Tetum) house at Kewar, Central Timor, 1965. (Dorothy Pelzer Collection, courtesy of ISEAS, Singapore/Smithsonian Institution, Washington)

162. Two Belu house doors carved with female figures and geometric motifs. (From Vroklage 1953: Pl. 90)

Central Timor (Figures 160–162), Francillon (1980: 261) notes:

The house with its dark interior and the woman in her fixed residence imply centrality, *immobility*, passivity and 'stupidity' (see van Wouden 1968); but they also imply silent authority, sacred fear, and the threat of death, all of which assert the superiority and dominance of Wehali over the patrilineal princedoms of the periphery (emphasis added).

As in the Atoni case, we have here the association of immobility with the female, with political authority and ritual power. Though surrounding states show both feminine and masculine features, 'Wehali held a different status through its matriliny; it was the "mother" kingdom, not just of the Liurai but of the entire world' (Francillon 1980: 261).

The theme of the mother as source is an equally dominant one among the eastern Tetum, described by Hicks (1976). Tetum matriliny is reflected in the dominance of women and female themes in ritual and myth. Concepts of the earth as womb, giving birth to the first humans, have already been encountered in Chapter 6, as was the idea of the house as body, its main room (containing both hearth and 'ritual pillar') being called the 'house womb' (*uma lolon*). Hicks's description of the birth ritual (1976: 31) is of particular interest to us here because it illustrates the complete alignment of the house interior, the female and the sacred:

An experienced older woman acts as midwife. Her dexterity critically regarded by as many hamlet women as the room will hold, the midwife nips the umbilical cord to leave roughly three inches dangling from the belly. This cord is known by the same name as that denoting a descent group (*cain*), which also means 'stalk' or 'stem'.... The midwife stuffs that part of the cord she has cut off into a small pouch which the father has previously plaited from palm-leaves. She adds the afterbirth to it, and fastens the pouch to the ritual pillar, at a spot slightly above the altar. The stained birth cloths and other soiled material she drops on the ritual shelf itself. As a 'bridge' between the two worlds, the ritual pillar is an apt place for these symbols of the productive benefits which derive from humans and ancestral ghosts uniting.[18]

A few days after the cord drops off, a second, symbolic birth occurs when the father ritually carries his child out through the 'house vagina' (the rear door) into the hamlet plaza and the waiting world of kinsfolk and affines. In the Tetum world, we see that sacredness lies right at the heart of the 'domestic' sphere. This fact is demonstrated most dramatically by the dropping of the soiled birth cloths on to the altar—an act which would be an unthinkable desecration in any culture where 'male' and 'female' are polarized as 'sacred' and 'profane'.[19]

The House as Womb

The reader may complain that I have wandered very far from floor plans at this point; but, I believe, the attempt to grasp some of the more fundamental ideas which shape Indonesian world views is ultimately essential in order fully to understand the significance of the symbolism of space, as it is worked out within the house. Ironically, with the repeated recurrence of the idea of the house as womb, which clearly is explicit in some cases and implicit in others, we seem to have come full circle. What difference is there, if any, between the womb-house of the Tetum or the Savunese, and that of the Berber as described by Bourdieu? Are we faced here simply with a form of universal symbolism, so fundamental that it will tend to present itself to house dwellers anywhere in the world? In a sense this may be so; as Hicks (1976: 23) points out, 'rooms', 'wombs', and 'tombs' resemble each other only phonetically in English, but in many other societies they are symbolically equated. It is not, however, necessary to resort as he does to the idea of Jungian archetypes to explain these associations. What my analysis shows, if anything, is the very different routes by which peoples may arrive at such equations. Therein, I believe, lies the distinction between the Berber and the Indonesian case. The womb is observably, in any culture of the world, a source of life, in the purely physical sense that children are born from it. We may tend to view an equation of the house with the womb as the ultimate, irreducibly 'natural' symbol beyond which nothing can be said. But in the house-based societies of Indonesia, the fact of the womb as life-source merely serves as the starting-point for metaphorical chains of association linking women, houses, kin groups, ancestors, the earth itself, and so on. In all the rich variety of cultural systems which have evolved throughout the archipelago, the celebration of life and fecundity is one thing they share in common. But in other cultural contexts, the prestige attached to women's reproductive capacity, and indeed the very manner in which it is conceptualized, may be very different. In a patriarchal society, the dependence upon women for the furtherance of life may even appear as an uncomfortable anomaly. Rather than celebrating biological life processes as being the very stuff of religion, they instead come to be associated with sin, corruption, and mortality, intrinsically opposed to the life of the spirit in the world religions, with their transcendental, other-wordly orientations. Or else, motherhood may be elevated and ambiguously revered even at the same time as female sexuality, menstruation, and childbirth are deemed to be polluting. So far as one can judge from Bourdieu's account, within the official male-dominated world view of the Berber, women's reproductive powers apparently evoke disgust and associations with defilement, while male 'excellence' is associated with purity. They are also symbolized as passive in Bourdieu's schema, in which male : female :: 'fertilizing' : 'able to be fertilized'. There is a sense in which sex, reproduction, and death are all associated, since all such natural functions are grouped together within the hidden realm of the domestic.

Bourdieu's unitary picture of Berber house symbolism is not, however, without its problems: the authorial voice of the anthropologist largely conceals from us whether he is talking about the model held by Berber men, or his own interpretation of it. There is no indication of what women say about the house, or whether they would recognize his account of it. Women are described as if they were entirely isolated in separate households, yet they must have some occasion to meet each other, for he states that men fear women's gossip (Bourdieu 1977: 92). A male ethnographer would doubtless face extreme difficulties in trying to ascertain how far women's world views may diverge from men's in such a society.

In spite of the apparent similarity with the Berber case, I argue that the symbolism of house and womb in South-East Asia has radically different implications. Indeed, the tone of associations in the societies I have described could hardly provide a stronger contrast. The house, here, is not opposed to and isolated from the 'public' sphere of life. Social reality for women differs dramatically—immobility as a *symbolic* theme does not translate into literal confinement within the house, but rather, women play active roles in the economy, ritual, and, at times, political life. More than this, South-East Asian world views, celebrating the life-giving fusion of male and female rather than their polarization, exploit an apparently similar theme to a different end. The association of house with womb, rather than serving to hive off women's capacities as birth-givers and nurturers within the constricted domain of 'denigrated domesticity', is merely the starting-point for a wide-reaching web of ideas about life processes and the reproduction of social groupings which themselves are intimately identified with the house.

1. See also Bloch (1974, 1977) on the functions of ritual, and the language of ritual, in the reproduction of ideology.

2. A most sensitive portrayal of the separation of domestic and public domains in India may be found in Satyajit Ray's film of Rabindranath Tagore's novel, *The Home and the World*—the title of which itself is revealing. With regard to the restrictions on knowledge, Humphrey (1974: 275) states that Mongol women were forbidden to touch books (usually religious texts), which were kept on the men's side of the tent near the altar. According to a Mongol proverb, 'For a woman to look at a book is like a wolf looking at a settlement.'

3. The Victorian mystification of this domestication of women receives one of its most elaborate expressions in Coventry Patmore's egregiously long poem, significantly entitled 'The Angel in the House'.

4. G. Forth (personal communication).

5. The association of woman, ship, and house recurs in Tanebar-Evav, where house-building offerings are likened to bridewealth, and bridewealth payments are called 'keel and oars of the ship' (Barraud 1979: 58).

6. Just how typical the division of the house into a 'male' and a 'female' half is in prescriptive alliance systems may be judged by comparing Needham's description (1962: 80–90) of the division of house space among the Purum, a Tibeto-Burman speaking people of the Indo-Burmese border who have the same type of kinship system.

7. Kato (1982: 58) remarks that the son-in-law 'is sometimes likened to a bull buffalo borrowed for impregnation'. In other sayings he is described as being 'like a horse-fly on the tail of a buffalo or like ashes on a hearth [when a little wind blows, it is gone]'. Such sayings are indicative of the lesser concern shown in many matrilineal systems with integrating the in-marrying spouse. In patrilineal systems, incorporation of the woman may be more critical because of the need to establish and maintain claims over her offspring.

8. Traube (1986: 88) also notes that among the Mambai of Timor, a man who marries uxorilocally is associated with the 'walls and verandah' (that is, the periphery) of the house.

9. See Chapter 3.

10. Regarding the reference to caves, it is significant that in the Sundanese case, the word for the grain store (*goah*) also means 'cave'.

11. Mashman notes that the low status of subsistence farming in a changing economy, and women's lesser opportunities for entry into the cash economy, may be eroding their status in Iban society today. Formerly, women gained prestige through their skills in dyeing and weaving, which were thought to involve supernatural dangers and were symbolically complementary to men's head-hunting activities.

12. Some elements of Savunese house symbolism have already been described in Chapter 6.

13. 'Ship' symbolism, which appears particularly frequently in eastern Indonesian societies, also raises an interesting point about the possible status implications of a division into 'bow' and 'stern'. Superficially, one might be tempted to equate these divisions with 'front' and 'back' and to assume that the front is the superior section. Boats, however, are controlled from the stern. Once again, the essential complementarity of male and female is probably more important. The explicit 'marrying' of male and female sections of the boat (the stem and the hull) in canoe- and ship-building in Indonesia is described by Horridge (1986: 6, 15); widespread similarities throughout the Malayo-Polynesian world indicate that we are dealing with a pattern of ideas of ancient (Austronesian) origin.

14. See Chapters 5 and 6 on the Austronesian roots of terms for 'navel', and 'trunk' and 'tip' in Indonesian languages. I am grateful to Geoffrey Benjamin for first drawing my attention to this possibility. In particular, he notes that in Temiar, there is a fusion of the concepts of 'tree trunk' and 'mother' (Benjamin, personal communication).

15. Clamagirand (1980: 146) gives an example of symbolic pairing: each chiefly core house of the Ema has a 'hot' and a 'cold' chieftain, regarded as symbolically 'male' and 'female'. The duty of the former is to judge disputes, and of the latter to invoke rain. See also Bowen (1984: 24n.) on Gayo, and Geertz and Geertz (1975: 90) on Bali, for examples of the paired roles of actual men and women.

16. The association of royalty with images of containment, immobility, and accumulation (of wealth, and the bodies of previous dead kings) within a palace is a feature also among the Sakalava of Madagascar. Royalty reserved to themselves the privilege of fencing their compounds, of which Feeley-Harnik (1980: 582) remarks: 'The most important thing which is restrained behind the royal fence is the royal body, especially the bodies of dead royalty.... Sakalava royal ritual is essentially ritual involved with their fences and the doors with which they are penetrated.'

17. Sacred navel-centres are a particularly prominent feature in the symbolic geography of Timorese people. The Ema too, for example, consider their territory to be located at the sacred origin-centre of the world, the 'earth-navel' (Clamagirand 1980: 151).

18. The uniting of humans and ancestors to ensure fertility and health is the aim of most Tetum rituals (Hicks 1976: 30).

19. Note the role of the father in preparing the bag for the after-birth. In Toraja, Toba, and elsewhere the father is the one who buries the placenta beside the house—a task which, in societies with an ideology of female pollution, would be considered extremely polluting. The intimate association of the individual with the placenta (which is widely regarded as a sort of twin), and the house where it is buried, is also a noticeable feature in a number of Indonesian societies. Toraja say that, no matter how far an individual may roam, he or she will always be drawn back eventually to the house of their birth, because their placenta is buried there. Niessen (1985: 161) says of the Toba: 'An individual is eternally identified with the house in which he or she was born, because it was there that the afterbirth, believed to contain one of his or her souls, was buried.' See also Gunawan Tjahjono (1988: 6) on Java, and Feeley-Harnik (1980: 580) on the Sakalava of Madagascar.

CHAPTER 9
Houses of the Dead

She has gone south to the place of no smoke
There to the south where no fire is lit
She has joined the house of our grandparents
Now she lives in the village of her ancestors
Is it lively and crowded down there?
There in the south, in the village of the grave?
If so, no doubt
You will prefer it there....

Toraja funeral chant[1]

ANCESTORS share with deities a position of prime importance in indigenous religions of South-East Asia, and the elaboration of mortuary rituals, especially in Borneo and Indonesia, reflects this fact. Funerary rites, commonly falling into two distinct phases (particularly for high-ranking individuals in the more hierarchical societies), may continue for long after the actual death of the individual concerned. In a number of societies, the most important and expensive of all rites are those in which a group of relatives together exhume the remains of several long-deceased ancestors in order to make them the object of fresh attentions. The bones may be either cleaned or cremated before being re-interred in a new receptacle, which may be a jar, a stone urn, a carved wooden ossuary, or a mausoleum on more monumental scale. In the highlands of Sarawak may still be seen stone urns, formerly used by the Kelabit for secondary placement of the bones of chiefs, in a practice believed to date back to around 2500 BC (Chin 1980: 22). Huge dolmens and menhirs were also erected in connection with Kelabit funeral rites, up until their conversion to Christianity in the 1950s. The working of stone and erection of megaliths as memorials to the dead is, as we have seen (Chapter 1), a feature of societies in numerous other parts of the archipelago, including Nias, Toba, Toraja, Central Sulawesi, Flores, and Sumba (Figure 163).

The Berawan of the Lower Baram district of Sarawak celebrate secondary rites in which the bones of the dead are cleaned and placed in a fantastically carved group mausoleum called *salong*, or commonly, in some areas, a similar structure called *lijeng*, raised on a single great post and intended for only one individual (Metcalf 1977, 1982). Similar mausoleums, with their great swirling baroque ridge decorations, are also a feature among the Kenyah, Kayan, Kajang, and Punan Ba peoples of Sarawak (Figures 164–166), while the Iban make small and elegantly carved 'burial huts' called *sungkup* (Figure 167), bearing winged roof finials much like the 'crossed horn' house finials which are such a widespread feature in the architecture of South-East Asian peoples (Sandin 1963). The Ma'anyan, to choose an example from Indonesian Borneo, celebrate secondary rites called *idjambe*, at which the remains of a number of related deceased persons are cremated in specially constructed coffins, and the ashes relocated in a collective mausoleum carved of ironwood, which is called *tambak*.[2]

The scale and importance of communal secondary rites is graphically described in many ethnographies. Metcalf (1982: 19), for example, describes Berawan funerals and secondary rites as 'the largest events in the life of the longhouse—the most prolonged, the most costly, and the most crowded ... the most ritually complex and symbolically dense of all communal celebrations'. They are also the grandest events staged

163. Funeral ground (*rante*) at Bori', Tana Toraja, with standing stones erected as memorials to deceased aristocrats, 1977. (Photograph: Roxana Waterson)
164. Kayan or Kenyah mausoleums (*salong*), photographed by Jean Demmeni in the Apo-Kayan region of Central Borneo, 1900. These magnificently carved monuments contained the bones of deceased aristocrats. (Photograph: Jean Demmeni, courtesy of Times Editions, Singapore)

165. *Salong* mausoleum at Sekapan on the Rejang River, Sarawak, 1968. It is made from a single huge tree trunk, decorated with gongs and enamel plates. (Dorothy Pelzer Collection, courtesy of ISEAS, Singapore)

166. *Salong* mausoleums are often placed at some distance from human habitation and may rapidly become engulfed by forest vegetation. This fantastically carved example, already half lost in the jungle, was photographed by Dorothy Pelzer near Rumah Laseh, Kejaman, Sarawak, in 1968. (Dorothy Pelzer Collection, courtesy of ISEAS, Singapore)

167. Iban *sungkup* burial hut and a stand hung with *garong* baskets, made for the Gawai Antu, the great festival to entertain the dead. (From Sandin 1963: Pl. 30)

by leaders to consolidate their positions. After the nine-day Ma'anyan rites of *idjambe*, says Hudson, (1972: 127), 'all the participants in the ceremony are mentally, physically, and, perhaps, economically exhausted'. Sandin (1980: 51), who gives a detailed description of the Iban festival for the spirits of the dead, the *Gawai Antu*, calls it 'one of the greatest and merriest'. It is held by the Iban at least once every fifteen years, and involves great expense, with much feasting and drinking, songs, and music. Iban bards sing songs describing the long journey of the ancestors' spirits as they arrive from the land of the dead, led by past chiefs and their wives who are all named in the chants. The spirits are believed to be present in the longhouse during the festival, enjoying all the feasting, dancing, cockfighting, and other entertainments prepared for them, and in exchange blessing their descendants with health, prosperity, and good luck. The festival ends with a journey to the cemetery; here the *sungkup* tomb huts which the men have made are placed over the graves of the dead. Women weave special baskets for each of the dead relatives to be honoured, and these are hung inside the huts or from carved poles planted close by (Sandin 1980: 62). Those sponsoring the feast now feel that they have fulfilled their responsibility to the dead, and in return the blessings of the ancestors are assured.

From the early work of Robert Hertz (1907), Borneo has long been famous among anthropologists as the classic region of secondary funeral rites, but indeed the pattern extends far into Indonesia, where funerals are likewise elaborate and costly. Among the Toba Batak of northern Sumatra, in spite of their almost total conversion to Christianity, the most important and expensive of all rites are still those in which a family regroups the bones of dead ancestors in a specially constructed mausoleum. Formerly of stone, these structures today are commonly made of painted concrete, in shape an elaborate replica of the traditional house. House-shaped tombs are dotted all over the Toba landscape, especially on the island of Samosir in the centre of the great Toba lake. Frequently, the money to finance these ceremonies and the building of tombs comes from Toba migrants living outside their homeland. Migrants will make every effort to return to Toba in order to be present at such rites. In Tana Toraja, the bodies of wealthy nobles may be stored for a year or more in the house while elaborate preparations are made for the great final ceremony of the funeral, which may be attended by thousands of people

and involve the sacrifice of hundreds of buffaloes and pigs. In many parts of Toraja, further expensive ceremonies may be held at long intervals to enable the ancestors to become deified. The dead thus enter a purified state, in which they move beyond the afterlife to become one with the deities, the stars, and the heavens. These rites are (or used to be) the prerogative of the nobility, so that only they may accede to this superior status.[3] Rites in which the tomb is opened to allow rewrapping of bones and communication with the ancestors, and at which further sacrifices are made for the deceased, occur annually in some areas (particularly Sesean), and at prolonged intervals in others (Figures 168 and 169). Sometimes, the opening of a grave to admit a new corpse provides the occasion for these attentions to be paid to those already there. Torajans have such strong feelings about the need to preserve and care for the bones of the dead that the idea of cremation is abhorrent to them. They believe, like the Toba, that it is this duty of the living to their deceased relatives which ensures the beneficence of the ancestors.

In all these societies, it is through the celebration of protracted mortuary rites that the living claim to ensure (or at least, give ceremonial recognition to) the transformation of the dead into beneficent ancestors, who have the power to influence the prosperity and fertility of their descendants. At the same time, the descendants enjoy the enhanced prestige which accrues to those who succeed in celebrating such important and expensive rites. Where traditional beliefs have been supplanted to greater or lesser degree by new religions such as Christianity (as, for example, among the Toba or Toraja), ideas about the status enjoyed by the deceased in the afterlife may cease to be of obvious importance. None the less, people still have very strong feelings about the proper tending of ancestral bones, and funeral celebrations are still major occasions on which the living may display and negotiate their own status. Whatever the influence of new beliefs, however, it is difficult to underestimate the intimacy which characterized relations with the ancestors in many indigenous Austronesian religions. It is not so much a question of 'worshipping' the ancestors as of maintaining a fruitful relationship with them.

168. Graves (*liang*) cut into a cliff at Lemo, Tana Toraja, with their ▶ rock balconies filled with effigies of the dead, 1977. (Photograph: Roxana Waterson)

169. Cleaning and giving new clothes to the *tau-tau* or effigies of the ancestors at a ceremony held for the dead in Malimbong district, Tana Toraja, 1979. (Photograph: Roxana Waterson)

Given the importance of exchange relationships among the living (for example, the prestations and counter-prestations accompanying marriage among the Toba, and the all-important giving of pigs and buffaloes at a Torajan funeral), the relationship with the ancestors may also be best conceived as one of exchange. The living provide the dead with food, wealth, and entertainment in the other-world, and in exchange expect the supernatural blessings of increased fertility, happiness, and prosperity. Typically, the ancestors soon cease to be remembered by name, but are thought of as a group (of both sexes) and are generally summoned—for example, when offerings are made—to be present as a group. This group has continuity with a group of the living, though in bilateral societies such as the Sa'dan Toraja, the boundaries of either are never clearly defined. Just as the Toraja remember membership of houses even when they may have forgotten exact genealogies, so Bloch says of the Merina of Madagascar that the dead become merged in people's minds with the tomb. The names of particular ancestors are forgotten, and ultimately one finds that 'the group of unnamed *ambiroa* [the aspect of the deceased's soul which is associated with the tomb] has merged with the actual tomb building' (Bloch 1971: 126). Ceremonies which involve the ritual regrouping of the dead in the tomb create, suggests Bloch, *ideal groups*, whose unity is something that can never be achieved by the living, for Merina kinship groupings are not clearly bounded, and people, being human, do not always get on as well as they properly should with their kinsfolk.

Membership of tomb groups may be more or less clearly defined. In Tana Toraja, for example, any individual has a choice of several possible burial places, just as he or she may also trace ties with a number of origin-houses on both the mother's and the father's side. In other bilateral kinship systems, residence or other criteria may be used to limit one's responsibilities for the upkeep of tombs. In the Ma'anyan case, as described by Hudson, individuals belong to descent groupings consisting of a male or female founder, his or her descendants living in the same village, and their spouses. These groupings are each associated with their own *tambak* or ironwood receptacle in which the ashes of the dead are placed. The founding of one's own *tambak* group means that one has achieved the highest possible social and economic status. Occasionally, an individual's children found a new *tambak*

group for him, to do him honour after his death. But sometimes the costs of maintaining a new group become too great, and after a time it will lapse again. Individuals begin by belonging to their natal *tambak* group, but may change membership at marriage. Most men move to their wife's house at marriage, performing brideservice for her parents for several years before the couple establish their own household. The in-marrying husband or wife takes up membership in the spouse's *tambak* group, although if the marriage is childless, a person's ashes may be taken back and buried in his own family *tambak*. Hudson (1972: 92) points out that, where some individuals may marry as many as ten times, the choice of *tambak* group for their children may become a little confusing, and if such a child were to die, a decision as to which *tambak* will receive the ashes must be reached by the discussion of the interested parties. Membership of *tambak* groups involves considerable expense because of the ceremonies performed, and some groups after flourishing for a while may become defunct if their members find the financial strain too great. They will then merge again with an older family *tambak* group.

In Tana Toraja, there are less well-defined groups associated with the upkeep of tombs, but strong emotions still attach to the choice of tombs and to the subject of the proper tending of ancestral remains. Residence during one's lifetime is a less strict criterion for choice of a burial place. Most frequently, a person will be buried in a *liang* or grave of his or her family (but even here there may be several possibilities) (Figure 170). Exceptionally, a husband and wife who are very fond of each other may request to be buried together in the family tomb of one of them. Their children then feel obliged to carry out this request. But there is often some competition between two sides of a family over where a deceased relative should be buried; neither side wishes to appear indifferent nor to be accused of a lack of affection for the dead person. It has been known for one side of a family to attack the other on the way to the grave, carrying off the body for burial in their own location. Occasionally, where a person has been buried in the grave of a spouse, the body will be reclaimed years later by family members and returned to a family grave. The choice of burial places is complicated by the bilateral tracing of descent, which gives everyone a number of possible choices of burial place. If a couple has no children, however, the in-marrying spouse will almost certainly be taken home

170. Graves (*liang*) cut into egg-shaped granite boulders in Malimbong district, Tana Toraja, 1979. Every origin-house should also have its own stone grave, the chamber of which is quite large and is used over generations. (Photograph: Roxana Waterson)

for burial in a family grave. The maintenance of strong ties with one's own houses and tombs after marriage in Toraja contrasts with the situation in patrilineal systems, such as Toba and Nias, where a woman's husband and his family take all responsibility for her funeral on the grounds that they have paid bridewealth for her, and she is never returned to her own family for burial.

Among the Merina of Madagascar, again, we find that 'tomb groups' are of considerable importance in kinship organization. As among the Ma'anyan, although descent is traced bilaterally, a choice is made of membership in only a single tomb group. Deciding to be buried in a particular tomb means joining an association for the upkeep of the tomb, a duty which, given the size and magnificence of these monuments, involves considerable expense (Bloch 1971: 116). Tomb groups have recognized heads, generally prominent individuals who are either heads of local families, government employees, or people of wealth.

On the basis partly of one's alliances with such individuals, one may choose to become a member of the tomb group either of one's father's relatives, mother's relatives, or spouse's relatives. Residence also considerably influences the choice, since one will usually have a closer association with the senior person of the place where one is living. Anyone who fails to contribute to the upkeep of a monumental tomb, however, can never expect the honour of secondary burial within it, but will be left for ever in their temporary grave. The most commonly quoted Merina proverb, says Bloch (1971: 165), expresses the idea of the rightness of being together with one's kin in life and death: 'Those who live in one house should be buried in one tomb.' The obligation to hold secondary burial rites is so strong that people will sometimes even sell off the land which is their livelihood in order to pay for the ritual.

In some cases, the prestige to be gained by the erection of an expensive grave accrues more specifically to a single individual. Hoskins (1986: 41) describes how ambitious men in West Sumba society may further their careers as socially important feast-givers by having their grave stones cut and dragged into the village during their lifetime. The stones must be hauled several kilometres and floated across a treacherous estuary, and the man who holds a stone-dragging must be capable not only of mobilizing thousands of helpers but of feeding them with meat throughout the process, which demands sacrifice of numerous buffalo. There are, however, limits upon an individual's gathering of renown; if he makes too heavy demands upon his kinspeople, upon whose help he ultimately depends, they will resist, and it is not unknown for jealous enemies or resentful kin to sabotage a stone-dragging attempt by smashing the stone or letting it sink into the sea.

The tendency of ossuaries and tombs to look like houses is so marked that it deserves our closer attention. Coupled with the literal resemblance of tombs to houses (as among the Toba, the Mamasa Toraja, the Minahasans of North Sulawesi, and numerous Borneo peoples), we frequently encounter imagery in which the grave is described as the house of the dead (Figures 171 and 172). There is an inherent ambiguity about the location of ancestral spirits, for as well as being in the 'land of the dead', where life is generally thought of as being very similar to that of the living, they are also closely associated with the grave itself. Among the Berawan, 'graveyards are explicitly likened to villages of the dead. The great vaults are raised on tall pilings well above the ground just as houses are, and the names used to refer to parts of the structure are the same as those used for ordinary houses (Metcalf 1982: 235). Metcalf adds (1982: 256n.):

It was once suggested to me that the tombs that we see in this world are like the small farmhouses (*sulap*) that Berawan build. Usually farmhouses are flimsy, small structures. Just

171. House-shaped stone ossuaries (*waruga*) at Sawangan, Minahasa, North Sulawesi, 1986. They have been regrouped here from various original locations. (Photograph: Roxana Waterson)

172. Remarkable house-shaped grave (*simalao*) at Balöhili, western North Nias. Its carved and painted figures depict scenes from the life of the deceased, with an emphasis on fertility—one of the scenes shows the deceased having intercourse with a young woman. Other armed figures serve a protective function, and heads are carved on the roof beams. (From Schröder 1917: Pl. 213)

173. House-shaped mausoleum (*sandung*) of the Ngaju of South Kalimantan, Tengirang village, Koeroen River, 1937. (Photograph: Karl Helbig, courtesy of Rijksmuseum voor Volkenkunde, Leiden)

174. The Ngaju conceive of the afterlife as a settlement on a river bank, closely resembling the habitations of the living. This Ngaju painting depicts houses in the land of the dead, filled with heirloom valuables such as gongs and jars. (From Schärer 1963: Pl. 12)

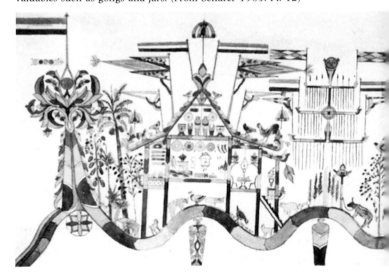

as Berawan have two places to live, so do the spirits of the dead. The implication was: Look how grand even their farmhouses are, imagine how splendid their longhouse is!

Miles writes of the Ngaju of Kalimantan that they conceptualize the afterlife as a settlement with the same structure as an ordinary village, with a core on the bank of a river surrounded by farm hamlets (Figures 173 and 174). Expenditure during secondary burial rites—varying according to the type of ossuary provided and the number of specialist priests engaged—determines the place of the deceased in this afterlife. 'Sacrifice of many or few bulls, oxen and chickens provides graded residential benefits. Until recently human sacrifices gained the departed soul the most favoured of all locations, a hill-top estate' (Miles 1976: 50). In Sumba, stone graves are arranged in rows within the village plaza, oriented in the same way as the houses of the living; the grave is called 'a house that does not rot, a floor that does not break' (Forth 1981: 50n.). In Sa'dan Toraja ritual poetry, it is referred to as 'origin-house without smoke, village where no fire is lit' (the afterlife being envisaged as a cold and fireless version of this life). A Toraja chant expresses sorrow that the deceased should have turned her (or his) back on the living and left her 'fine barn and house with long eaves', but goes on to hope that she will find it so crowded and lively in the 'village of the grave' that she will not want to return.

In Madagascar, the association of houses and tombs is so marked that Bloch (1971) has dedicated an entire book to the subject as part of his work on the Merina. Among the Sakalava, too, Feeley-Harnik (1980: 563n.) notes that coffins are categorized as a kind of 'house' (trano), the cover being the roof. She also adds:

Among the Merina, a coffin or bier may be called tranovorona, 'bird house'. Trano is also used to refer to the little replicas of houses placed on top of royal tombs (trano masina, 'sacred house') and the tombs of certain noble groups (trano manara, 'cold house', so-called because a hearth fire is never lit there.

The Mahafaly and other groups erect elaborately carved grave posts on top of impressively large stone graves (Feldman 1985: 190).

In a few societies, particularly in Borneo and high-land South Vietnam, the living may be fearful of the spirits of the dead, and graveyards are situated well away from the village. Dournes (1971: 307–8), noting the importance of funerary rites among the Jörai of South Vietnam, mentions that here, family tombs are commonly grouped together under a single roof. These cemetery buildings often exceed ordinary dwellings in the quality of their construction, as well as their sculptures, carvings, and paintings. All the same, they provide only temporary accommodation for the dead, who subsequently pass beyond the tomb to an afterlife in the west—the place of the dead, night, and white people. The cemetery is here a place of transit; tombs are always oriented north–south, as houses are, with the dead person facing to the east, like the living when they sleep. Their living descendants experience relief once the final rite of separation has been enacted, and the tomb can then be abandoned. Ancestors from the long distant past eventually become identified in Jörai thought with the yang or spirits of the wild.

But much more usually, relations between the living and their ancestors are characterized by a sense of closeness. The houses of the dead and the living may even be found side by side within the boundaries of the village itself, as in parts of Flores, Sumba, and among the Kalinga of the Philippines (Figures 175 and 176). Barbier (1983: 120) suggests that Toba tombs were sometimes in the middle of villages; as sites have shifted, this is now apparent only in a very few cases. It perhaps was true only of the most important tombs, which served as imposing memorials for deceased chiefs. These great stone receptacles with their curved lids and carved faces echo the shape of houses, and commonly contained the bones of a ruler's wife, and possibly other family members, as well as his own. They are called parholian (from holi, 'bones'). Two famous tombs at Tomok on the island of Samosir

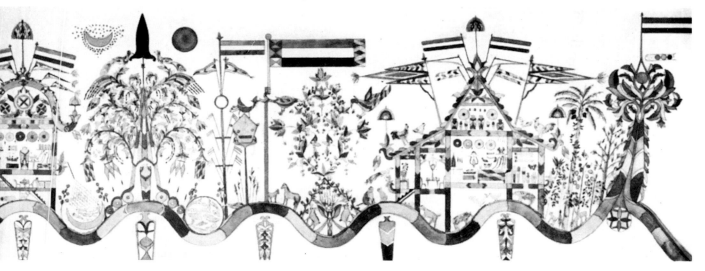

175. In Sumba villages, graves occupy prominent positions in front of the houses, suggestive of the close relations which exist, in the traditional world view, between the dead and the living. Tarung village, Loli district, 1987. (Photograph: Roxana Waterson)

176. Christian graves, now built in concrete, are still situated close to houses in North Nias. Bawödesölö village, 1986. (Photograph: Roxana Waterson)

belong to the chief Raja Ompu Soribuntu and his son, Raja Nai Batu, of the Sidabutar clan, who ruled Tomok about a century ago (Plate 18). Beside them are the smaller stone ossuaries of their younger siblings, their shape again reminiscent of the Toba house. But the Toba formerly constructed even more elaborate miniature houses of wood over some graves. These structures, called *joro*, no longer exist, but they were photographed by Bartlett in the 1920s, and he has left us an interesting record of them (Bartlett 1934) (Figures 177 and 178). These miniature houses, built on piles, had a tiny ladder leading up into them, and inside a miniature hearth. They were topped with an elaborate ridge-peak ornament shaped like a boat, and sometimes containing a carved human figure in the centre, representing the soul travelling to the afterlife,

177. House-shaped tomb (*joro*) at Tangga Batu, near Balige, Toba, photographed by Bartlett in the 1920s. It was finely decorated with carvings exactly like those on dwelling houses, and a frieze painted in red, white, and black. (From Bartlett 1934: Pl. 12)

178. House-shaped tomb (*joro*) at Lumban Silambi, Toba. The carving on the ridge represents the deceased travelling to the afterlife in a boat, protected by bird companions. (From Bartlett 1934: Pl. 11)

accompanied by bird companions called *manuk-manuk*, which were supposed to protect the soul on its journey.[4] As well as its location in the afterlife, the dead person's spirit was also supposed to take up residence in the grave house, and people would go to the grave and make offerings when seeking the ancestors' advice (Bartlett 1934: 6, 25).

It is particularly striking that among the Toba, whose traditional religion almost completely disintegrated under the impact of mission activity, it is precisely the collective rites associated with the regrouping of ancestors in the tomb which, in a now enthusiastically Christian society, have retained a special importance.[5] Bartlett, who noted the efflorescence of a new art form in the construction of concrete tombs during the 1920s (Figure 179), guessed that the trend might prove short-lived, but in fact he was wrong, for today, sixty years later, they are still being built. The tombs are called *tambak*, or sometimes simply *simen* (meaning 'cement'). Let us look a little more closely at these tombs and the rites associated with them. Since the remains of a number of clan ancestors are brought together in the new mausoleum, the rite is only held at prolonged intervals by any one group of clan descendants; an individual would be unlikely to witness more than one celebration of the rite in his lifetime. After the rite, in future years, other clan members may also be buried here when they die (the tomb now becoming a site of additional primary, rather than secondary, burials). Some tombs are shaped like churches with steeples, rather than houses, while yet others cunningly combine house with steeple, reflecting perhaps the changed images of the afterlife. Wives are generally included in a clan's tombs; they are not taken back by their own families for burial in their own clan tombs. The major criterion for incorporation in a communal tomb is whether one has had many children. Neither a childless person, nor his wife, will be included, for they are not seen as having fulfilled their contribution to the continuity of the descent line.

It is a source of some regret if one dies outside of one's homeland, though feelings on this subject are not nearly so strong as among the Toraja. Toraja will

179. Concrete tomb near Balige, Toba, photographed by Bartlett, *c.*1920. He admired the artistic vigour of Toba sculpture in this new medium, while predicting (wrongly, as it turned out) that the development might prove short-lived. (From Bartlett 1934: Pl. 28)

213

sometimes expend huge amounts of money in order to bring a corpse home for burial in a family tomb, but this is only occasionally done by the Toba. However, it is quite likely that at some point, the bones of a person buried away from Toba may be exhumed and brought home for ceremonial incorporation in a communal tomb. This is, from a practical point of view, much easier, since it can be done discreetly; very few bus drivers or boat owners are prepared to carry a corpse without a strong monetary incentive. As one Toba man explained to me, sometimes a person may express a last wish with regard to his burial site, or may say: 'Put me together with my grandparents, and my parents, bring my younger brother from his grave, and put us all together. Later on, if you want to come into this tomb too, you will be welcome—if not, that's your affair.' Such a last request places an obligation upon the children, and they will try their best to arrange a secondary burial ceremony in order to fulfil it. If the person was originally buried outside Toba, then his remains will be exhumed and finally returned to a communal resting place in his village of origin, where he will be united with his kin in death as in life.

Some people even have a tomb built during their lifetime, though this can be used simply for primary burial. On Samosir, in the vicinity of Tomok, a professor of theology who resides in Jakarta has reconstructed for himself a beautiful old house and barn which he bought from relatives on the far side of the island. Behind the house, at a corner of the house compound, there also stands a brand new concrete tomb in the shape of a house, not yet used. Though absent for years from his home village, except for regular visits, this man's attachment to his place of origin and to traditional house styles as an expression of his Toba identity are obvious. I shall have more to say on the role of migrants in building Toba tombs in the next chapter.

In the Ngada region of Flores, miniature houses in the village plaza are specifically the abode of female ancestors, male ones being provided with a post topped by a conical thatch roof (Figure 180).[6] Miniature houses may sometimes be seen here perched on the roofs of larger ones, a form of decoration which in other regions may likewise be intended to provide a resting place for the spirits of ancestors. Forth, however, found that present-day Ngada villagers have no explanation

180. Village plaza of Wogo Baru, Ngada, West Central Flores, 1965, showing a row of offering posts (ngadu) commemorating male clan ancestors, with, beside them, miniature houses (baka) representing female ancestors. (Dorothy Pelzer Collection, courtesy of ISEAS, Singapore/Smithsonian Institution, Washington)

to offer of them.[7] In Sumatra, Singarimbun (1975: 56) claims of the Karo that the miniature structures which are erected on some Karo roof ridges are 'purely decorative'; but in neighbouring Simalungun, an explicit connection with the ancestors is made. At Pematang Purba, I met an elderly man, E. Pesta Purba, who acts as guide at the great longhouse of the Rajas of Simalungun. This man was a son of the last Raja, and was born in the house, in which his father lived until 1945, together with ten of his twelve wives (Figures 181–184). Next door to the palace stands the council house, or *balai adat* (Figures 185–187), where the Raja used to meet with his councillors and pass judgement on those who had broken the law. A finely carved pillar, which bears an incised calendar for determining auspicious days for undertakings, runs from the floor right through the roof to support a miniature pyramidal house on the roof ridge. Purba confirmed that this miniature structure, which is called *rumah manik*, was intended to provide a resting place for the spirits of the ancestors. The Raja sat at the base of the pillar while giving judgements. The pillar might thus be viewed as a sort of lightning conductor by which the powers of the ancestors, who established the *adat* and have supernatural power to punish wrongdoers, might be conveyed through the Raja, and at the same time effectively symbolized and legitimized his authority.

Sometimes it is the head of the deceased which becomes the object of special attentions. This is not surprising when we note the importance ascribed by these societies to the head as a locus of power, as evidenced by the formerly extremely widespread custom of headhunting. Furthermore, the skull is the most durable part of the body, and as we have seen, great importance is attached to the endurance of an ancestor's mortal remains. The Karo Batak had a special structure, the *geriten* or 'head-house', in which they would put the skulls of chiefs and important individuals, several years after their death (Figure 188). The skulls would sometimes be elaborately decorated with gold and silver and wrapped in precious cloths (Bartlett 1934: 15). Some of these structures still exist in Karo villages. They are built on a square plan with tiered pyramidal roof, and on them are lavished the finest decoration of any Karo structure. The Naga of Northeast India paid special attention both to the heads of

181. Palace of the former rajas of Simalungun at Pematang Purba, on the northern shore of Lake Toba, 1986. It has now been restored as a museum. At the front the ridge ends in a realistically moulded buffalo head made of *ijuk* (sugar palm) fibre; a tail of the same material hangs from the rear end of the ridge. (Photograph: Roxana Waterson)

182. Undercroft of the raja's palace, Pematang Purba, 1986. Note the crossed-log structure of the foundations and the scooped joints. The massive piles are painted with designs in black and white. (Photograph: Roxana Waterson)

183. Detail of the raja's palace, Pematang Purba, 1986. The walls are made from woven and painted split bamboo. (Photograph: Roxana Waterson)

enemies (stored in the *morung* or men's house) and to those of departed relatives; the latter were placed, after initial exposure of the corpse and subsequent burial of the rest of the body, in stone urns along village pathways, where they were, for a few years at least, given offerings of food and drink on important ritual occasions (Fürer-Haimendorf 1976: 62).

Not only may miniature structures be specially provided as homes for the dead, but the ancestral spirits are commonly also thought to be present in, or to visit, the houses of the living. This may be reflected in the practice of 'feeding the ancestors' at mealtimes, as used to be the habit of the Sakuddei of Siberut Island, who dropped a few grains of rice through the floor of the longhouse, with a request for blessing, before eating (Schefold 1980: 85). The Toraja also kept a special basket over the hearth, in which small offerings of food would be placed at mealtimes—a custom which has now almost disappeared. A name commonly used for the Toraja traditional religion is, indeed, 'feeding the ancestors' (*pa'kandean nene'*). In Toba houses, small amounts of food might sometimes be laid out for the ancestors on the shelf called *pangombare* which runs along the side wall of the house. This, I was told, was done on occasions when a married daughter and her husband were visiting her parents bringing food with them for a meal (a custom which is regularly followed by the Toba). A prayer would be said to summon the spirits of parents, grandparents, and any other ancestors whose names might have been forgotten. In Tanimbar, morsels of food were placed on a plate beside the house ancestor image at every meal; Forbes (1885: 318) made the observation that 'Every time they drink they dip their finger and thumb in the fluid, and flick a drop or two upward with a few muttered words of invocation.' In such cases, we see that the ancestors are not only called to be present at feasts, but are thought to be close at hand even in the everyday. Toraja used even to take 'food for the ancestors' to the fields with them, for they felt that their spirits aided them in the important tasks of planting and harvesting the rice.

The idea that the dead may occupy various locations simultaneously, although apparently contradictory, is typical of the flexibility of indigenous religious concepts in South-East Asia. The Toraja, for example, traditionally think of the dead person's spirit as being both in the afterlife, and in some way attached to the grave or the wooden effigy (*tau-tau*) placed by it. At the

217

184. Interior of the raja's palace, Pematang Purba, 1986. The raja had his own enclosed compartment near the front; each of ten wives had her own hearth, with a rack suspended above, and a bamboo tube for water. Waste was disposed of through the central gulley. The panels suspended from the centre of the ceiling are carved in a shape representing pumpkin tendrils, which symbolize fertility. (Photograph: Roxana Waterson)

same time, the dead may also visit the living in their homes, searching for food, and their shades are thought to come and rest from time to time on the platform under the rice barn, enjoying the cool of the day just as humans do. The Mambai of Timor, too, envisage death as a protracted process, during which the dead may occupy various locations—all of which, significantly, seem to be thought of as houses. Traube (1986: 200) writes:

Before the dead can attain the status of nameless, returning shades, they must undergo a transitional period of indeterminate length, during which they retain their individual identities. According to the commonest conception, they pass the interim on the top of Nama Rau [the original first mountain] in the ultimate house of origins. In another conception, they take up residence in the cult houses of the groups to which they belong. Still another version locates them on the mountain, but in invisible spirit houses associated with their own groups.

The Padju Epat Ma'anyan believe that a deceased person's spirit (or rather, that particular aspect of it which survives his death) is conveyed to the afterlife by the holding of the *idjambe* cremation ceremony. But not all the dead are satisfied to remain there, and some, by means of a dream or sign, make known their intention to return in order to look after their living descendants. Such a returned ancestral spirit is called *nanyu'*, and a special spirit house will be prepared for it in the rafters of his (or her?—Hudson does not elucidate) former village house. Here the spirit gives its special protection to all descendants who honour it with food at the time of an annual ceremony which is held after the harvest. Newer houses may not have such a resident ancestral spirit, while prominent and long-established ones may have several. As extended family groups gradually grow and fission, a breakaway branch may found a new house but, having as yet no *nanyu'* of its own, it will continue to join with

185. The council house (*balai adat*) at Pematang Purba, 1986, with a miniature house on the roof ridge, surmounting the central pillar which runs right through the building. This miniature house is intended to provide a resting place for the ancestors. The gable-ends are decorated with modelled buffalo heads and the vertical wall planks are bound with *ijuk* (sugar palm) fibre in a lizard design similar to that found among the neighbouring Karo Batak. (Photograph: Roxana Waterson)

187. Calendar carved upon the central pillar of the *balai adat*, Pematang Purba, 1986. (Photograph: Roxana Waterson)

the older family group for the harvest celebration (Hudson 1972: 98–9).

Identification of both the living and the dead with the house is particularly marked in Roti. Here the dead were buried under the floor, while their spirits (*nitu*) took up residence in the loft, represented by three-pronged lontar leaf shapes called *maik*, hung in the rafters. Babies were buried under the house stairs, to facilitate the easy return of their spirits in a new body. As among the Toraja, the issue of choosing a burial site can lead to fierce fighting over a body. One is not necessarily buried in the house one has lived in, but in

◄ 186. Interior of the *balai adat*, Pematang Purba, 1986, showing the finely carved central pillar which runs up through the roof to support the miniature house on the ridge. The raja sat at the front of this pillar to give judgement, the power of the ancestors being thereby communicated to him as he did so. (Photograph: Roxana Waterson)

a clan house already designated as an *uma nitu* or 'spirit house', that is, one in which other burials have already taken place and which has therefore accumulated ritual power and is regarded as a sort of temple (Wetering 1923: 479; Fox 1987). For the individual, social identity is not fixed at birth, since one may associate with several houses over the course of a lifetime, and indeed one's final identification with a house is not determined until after one's death, when one's relatives reach an agreement about the burial site. Whoever succeeds in claiming a corpse not only strengthens the powers of that house but also their right to inherit from the individual concerned (Fox 1987: 175). This practice of incorporating the dead within the house greatly exercised the Dutch, who tried to abolish it on grounds of hygiene and forced people to bury their dead outside. The Rotinese responded by building little houses (*uma late*) over the graves.[8]

In exactly the same way, Kaudern (1925: 372) writes of the peoples of Central Sulawesi:

Formerly the natives at many places used to bury their dead underneath the house where they had lived. Especially at the village of Kantewoe I saw the skulls and bones of the dead issuing out of the ground. When the Dutch became masters of the country they forbade the old habit of burying the dead underneath the houses. At present the dead as a rule are buried outside the village where a little house is put up on the spot where they have found their last rest.

A similar practice can be traced as far away as Taiwan, where the Austronesian-speaking Paiwan also buried their dead in the house floor, either beneath the hearth or the central living area. Each deceased noble descendant of a family has a wooden panel carved and named for him or her. Male and female ancestor images are also carved on the door posts on either side of the entrance to the house, and on upright slate slabs erected in the courtyard, which are considered a sign of the family's social status (Cameron 1985) (Figure 189).

A final example of the presence of ancestors among the living comes from Tanimbar. Here we have to rely on older accounts of indigenous beliefs relating to the ancestors, since present-day Tanimbarese are all either Catholic or Protestant, and retain little memory of earlier practices. The evidence is usefully summarized by McKinnon (1983: 136–41). Some houses (probably only important named houses of the nobility) used to contain exquisitely carved ancestor statues, of which one or two examples survive in European museum

188. Karo Batak head-house (*geriten*) in the village of Lingga, 1986. Here were customarily stored the skulls of important clan ancestors. (Photograph: Roxana Waterson)

189. Paiwan nobleman outside his house. He is standing beside an upright slate slab carved with the figure of a female ancestor, signifying the social standing of his family. The Paiwan maintain an intimate relation with their dead, who are traditionally buried inside the house. Images of ancestors are also carved on the door posts. (From McGovern 1922: 134)

collections (Figures 190–192). The statue was placed opposite the trapdoor by which one entered the house. It was shaped from a broad upright plank of wood which, sometimes in highly abstract and sometimes more realistic form, represented a human figure, with two arm-like extensions curving upwards as if to support the roof beams. On a shelf above the figure, the skulls of the ancestors were placed on a plate, on which offerings of betel-nut would be made. Offerings were also made to the supreme deity, Ubila'a, on a plate kept on the seaward side of the house loft. Here, as among the Ma'anyan, we find that the ancestors are situated high up in the house, and that they are more closely associated with old-established and important origin-houses, which functioned as cult centres (McKinnon 1983: 147). The ancestors not only gave their protection to their living descendants, but more specifically, descendants of a certain house inherited the knowledge of particular kinds of magic plants or 'roots', ensuring success in curing, black magic, hunting, fishing, competitive singing, or warfare. Some skills were also inherited within particular houses, such as house and boat building, metal and ivory working, and spirit possession (a calling open to both male and female members of a house). Important houses were also distinguished by the possession of heirloom valuables and of finely carved horn-shaped ridge decorations which the Tanimbarese compare to the carved prow- and stern-boards of ships. At harvest each year, the Tanimbarese still hold a first-fruits festival which they call 'feeding the dead', although today this consists simply of the living sharing a ritual meal (McKinnon

190. Ancestral altar in a Tanimbar house, date unknown. At the base of the figure is a bench on which the head of the house would sit while pronouncing upon *adat* matters; above is the altar shelf on which offerings were made to the skulls of the ancestors. (VIDOC, Koninklijk Instituut voor de Tropen, Amsterdam)

1983: 117, 152). For the Tanimbarese, as for the Toraja, the Ma'anyan, or many of the other peoples of the archipelago, the ancestors had the power to ensure the continued fertility of the land and of human beings. A further interesting feature of the ancestor statue is that in front of it was placed a wooden bench, on which the head of the house sat while 'talking *adat*', and the ancestors were thought to descend along the statue to sit beside him. The house head is said to 'lean against the statue', that is, to draw strength and authority from the status of his ancestors, represented by the statue, and their supernatural presence, transmitted by the statue (McKinnon 1983: 137).[9] We are reminded of the council house of Simalungun, with its carved pillar connecting the king to the miniature house on the roof ridge. In Nias, too, the ancestors used to occupy a prominent position within the house-

hold, where their presence was signified by altars and by numerous carved wooden figures which now survive only in the museums of the West (Schröder 1917; Feldman 1977). Among the Atoni, as we have seen, it is the front left house post or 'head mother post' which is regarded as especially sacred, being closest to the attic entrance. A flat stone altar is placed at its base and sacred ancestral objects may be attached to it (Cunningham 1964: 42). We might note, also, the sacredness of the front right-hand house post in the Sumba house, on the symbolically 'male' side of the house, at the foot of which the priest sits to make offerings; this also acts as a sort of transmitter of power from the ancestors, who are associated with the heirloom valuables stored in the tall roof peak (Adams 1974: 336). In all these cases, not surprisingly, it is the highest parts of the house which we find associated with the ancestors or the sacred, while their powers are safely channelled and transmitted to the living by means of a statue or post.

Hoskins (1987: 147, 150) provides some intriguing information on the traditional Sumbanese mode of divination:

The spirits concerned were questioned though the medium of a sacred spear and made to reply at the base of the central house pillar ... questions could be asked directly of the housepost ... with yes or no answers provided by whether or not the diviner's thumb reached its mark at the tip of the spear.

This practice of communicating with the dead was stigmatized by Christian missionaries and teachers, but in the 1950s it came to be at the centre of a controversy over the burial of the dead. The spirits of some of the few early converts to the Christian faith, who had been interred in a church cemetery, at that time began asking in divination sessions to be transferred to the more prestigious stone graves which their relatives had in the meantime succeeded in erecting in their own villages. Local ritual practitioners blamed various illnesses and misfortunes on the fact that the dead were unhappy about their burial locations. To most Sumbanese, Christian burial was seen as only a temporary arrangement, but the church leaders viewed reburial as an attempt to 'steal back' hard-won souls into paganism (Hoskins 1987: 147).

In a number of societies, ancestors are closely identified with the heirloom treasures stored within the house. These treasures themselves may be regarded as imbued with supernatural power. In Rindi, East

191. Exquisitely carved ancestor figure from a house altar, Tanimbar. It represents in highly stylized form a human torso with outstretched arms, all of the design being geometric save for the small human face in the centre and two fish at the top. Collected before 1913 by W. Müller-Wismar. (Rautenstrauch-Joest Museum, Cologne)

192. An outstandingly beautiful altar carved in hardwood, from the island of Leti, South-west Moluccas. It represents the female ancestor Huchtalinna-Huchrainna, ancestor of the Halupnu lineage, also identified with the supreme deity. Around her neck is an ornament in the shape of a crescent moon, with tendrils of plants sprouting from it. The tall head-dress, possibly representing the tree of life, is ornamented with birds. Collected before 1913 in the village of Luhuleli, by W. Müller-Wismar. (Rautenstrauch-Joest Museum, Cologne)

Sumba, Forth mentions that the spirit of the clan's founding ancestor is considered to be present in the tall roof peak of the clan's origin-house, where it is also symbolized by the house treasures stored there. Such houses are so hedged about with prohibitions, and the heirlooms themselves (particularly certain classes of gold and metal ornaments) so charged with sacred power, that living in them becomes too burdensome for the owners. The danger of breaking a rule and incurring fatal supernatural sanctions is considered so great that the owners install more expendable house slaves as caretakers while themselves preferring to reside in ordinary, less sacred houses elsewhere (Forth 1981: 255; Hoskins 1987: 152). In rituals, the heirlooms may be used as 'altars' as a means of summoning the ancestors (Forth 1981: 195). Rodgers (1985: 216) notes that in Lio (Flores), heirloom jewellery and gold regalia may be taken out and worn by the female descendants of a house on the occasion of the roofing of a new clan house. Gathering in the space beneath the house floor, they go into trance in order to summon the ancestors. Volz (1909), writing on the Karo Batak of North Sumatra, describes how a female medium (*sibaso*) would dance inside the house until she entered a trance, and then by raising her hands to clasp the main beam of the roof, would be entered by ancestral spirits who would then speak through her. (Volz 1909: 108–13; cited by Domenig 1980: 140) (Figure 193). It may be concluded that the dance itself served the purpose of summoning the ancestors to be present in the roof space, the most sacred part of the house, from whence by contact with the beam their spirits could be transmitted into the medium's own body.

Relations with the ancestors are similarly a dominant theme of the indigenous religions of the South-East Asian mainland. The ancestors and spirits are typically accorded the place of honour within the house, and are kept informed of the doings of their descendants. In North Thailand, the ancestors' shelf, where offerings are placed, is situated above the head of the householders' bed, and no guest may sleep in the house without first being introduced to them and asking their permission (Charernsupkul and Temiyabandha 1979). Spirits, too, may have their houses: to avoid giving offence, the spirit of the land on which a house is built is commonly provided with a small 'spirit house' near the entrance to the compound. Among hill tribes such as the Akha, Lisu, and Hmong, the house

193. Karo Batak priestess (*sibaso*) dances in trance to summon the spirits of the ancestors. The spirits enter her body as she grasps the supporting beam of the house roof. (From Volz 1909, Vol. I: 111)

also contains its ancestral altar, generally positioned opposite the main door so that the spirits may move unobstructedly in and out (Lewis and Lewis 1984).

The providing of food and houses for the ancestors accords with the idea that their life in the other-world is basically similar to life on earth, and at the same time it reflects the closeness of the relation which continues to exist between them and their still living descendants. But the recurrence of house-shaped tombs must also be seen as yet another reflection of the vital role of houses themselves in the social organization of South-East Asian societies. We see here a continuity of ideas which leads to the modelling of the society of the dead upon that of the living, and the maintenance of a particularly close bond between ancestors and their descendants. Ties with the ancestors demonstrate an important aspect of Austronesian world views in which life and death are seen not as totally separate states, but as integrated aspects of a continuously recurring cycle. Living humans have a commitment to help the dead through stages of the afterlife, so that they may achieve deification and, in their turn, provide supernatural enhancement to the life forces of their descendants.

1. The Toraja verse runs as follows:

Male sau' tangmerambu
Lolo' tangdukku apinna
Sangbanua mo nene'ta
Sangtondok mo to dolona
Marua' raka i lolo'?
Ilo' bamba kaburu
Anna ia ra
Mukabuda-buda....

2. The words *lijeng*, *liang*, and related forms (including variants of *lubang*) recur in many Indonesian languages as well as in reconstructions of Proto-Austronesian. Their primary meaning is 'hole', but they very frequently refer to graves, carved wooden coffins, or ossuaries, as here. Among the Sa'dan Toraja, *liang* refers to family tombs carved out of solid rock faces. *Tambak* likewise features in Proto-Austronesian reconstructions, having the primary meaning of 'a mound of earth', but also being used (as in Ngaju and Toba languages) to refer to tombs or grave mounds. See Wurm and Wilson (1975) for reconstructions of Proto-Austronesian; see also King (1980: 143–5) for a discussion of Maloh tomb huts, and the distribution of terms for tombs in Borneo.

3. See, for example, Volkman (1985: 53–6) on the *maro* rite in the Sesean area. Near Ma'kale in 1979 I witnessed a rite for the transformation of ancestors, which is there called *pembalikan gandang*, or 'the turning over of the drum'. In the more westerly district of Saluputti, social hierarchy is less rigid and theology less specific; the dead stay in the afterlife, though they still have a deified status; a rite called *ma'paundi* ('to send after') may be held to 'send' further sacrifices for their use in the beyond.

4. This idea of a 'ship of the dead' is extremely widespread in the archipelago, providing perhaps the most dramatic instance of 'ship' symbolism associated with states of transition (see Gittinger 1976; Manguin 1986).

5. A German Protestant mission was first established here in 1860. See Castles (1975) for an analysis of pre-colonial Toba society. Today the old religion, *Parmalim*, still exists but perhaps claims no more than 10,000 adherents; exact numbers are difficult to estimate (B. Pasaribu, personal communication).

6. Miniature houses as the abode of female ancestors may also be seen in some West Sumba clan villages.

7. Forth, personal communication (1985).

8. This was, however, the first step towards the destruction of the Rotinese house as a social unit. Sadly, since Independence, Indonesian local government has kept up its pressure against the traditional house, which is regarded as 'old-fashioned'. In the space of the last twenty years, almost every traditional house on the island has been destroyed (Fox (1987: 176) and personal communication).

9. Slaves, by contrast, were said to 'come from the space beneath the house' (like animals). They were 'light' where nobles were 'weighty' and fixed in their houses (McKinnon 1983: 275). Hierarchical social relations were thus cast in terms of the 'house' idiom.

CHAPTER 10
*Migrations**

Satingi-tingi tabang bangau
Baliak ka kubangan juo

(*However high the egret flies*
It will still return to its pond)

Minangkabau saying

THE ancient migrations of the Austronesian peoples are woven like a linking thread through the story of the Indonesian archipelago and its architectures. We have seen how, in the rich diversity of contemporary island cultures, concepts and styles which are ultimately traceable to Austronesian origins have persisted with remarkable vigour, constantly being reshaped, abandoned, recovered, altered, and adapted over time. Given how closely elements of material and symbolic culture are interwoven in these cultures—objects, like the house, being used to express ideas and relations as much as to serve functional purposes—one must conclude that it is not only things, but more abstract cultural themes that have endured in this way.[1] We have had occasion to examine a number of these themes, from the immanence of cosmic power, to metaphors of growth and the joining of life and death in a continuously repeating cycle, to the social concerns of rank or the importance of secondary rites for the dead. The idea of migrating itself might be described as another such theme, for it has for thousands of years provided a constant impetus for exploration, expansion, cultural exchange, and economic activity throughout the archipelago.

What effect are present-day migrations having on local cultures and the vitality or otherwise of their architectural traditions? What, if anything, can we say about the possible future of these traditions? These questions provide the theme of this concluding chapter. In times of unprecedentedly rapid change, traditional styles of architecture in many parts of the world are under threat or have already disappeared. There are undoubtedly parts of South-East Asia, too, where such loss is currently threatened. Yet the picture is not all gloomy. Against all predictions of decline, there appears even to be a resurgence of building activity in some regions. Any assessment of the directions of change requires one to examine, not just external pressures, but the pattern of internal forces in a particular society, which may act upon the continuance or demise of its building traditions. Rather than dwell solely upon outside influences (such as administrative interventions or the effects of Westernization), I shall select a few examples and seek to show something of the internal dynamics of these societies. I shall argue that the phenomenon of migration is one particularly significant feature of these dynamics, which will repay our careful investigation.

But beyond this, raising the question of the future must lead us to consider what really is the nature of 'tradition' in any case, and what the *idea* of 'tradition' may be supposed to mean, not just to an English speaker but to South-East Asian peoples themselves. 'Tradition', I shall argue, remains a problematic notion, and one that needs to be carefully addressed in any attempt to understand the forces that may help or hinder the survival of indigenous architectures.

---

* An earlier version of this chapter first appeared in J. P. Bourdier and N. Al Sayyad (eds.), *Dwellings, Settlements and Tradition*, New York: University Press of America, 1989.

229

Migration in Contemporary South-East Asia

It is clear that the tradition of migration as a young man's ideal adventure is very long established in a number of today's Austronesian-speaking societies, both of island South-East Asia and of Oceania.[2] Familiar in Indonesian as *merantau* ('to leave one's home area, go abroad'; *rantau* means literally the estuary of a creek, figuratively, 'a foreign land'), the concept of migration is here particularly closely associated with the Minangkabau people of West Sumatra, who, as historical records show, have made a habit of it for centuries. It is considered particularly desirable for young men seeking opportunity, experience, and a path to maturity. Though less renowned for it, the Acehnese, too, migrate in large numbers, gaining a livelihood in small-scale trade and formerly often returning home each year at the end of the fasting month—though nowadays it is increasingly common for whole families to live permanently on the *rantau* (Siegel 1969; Wessing 1984). But *merantau* is equally long established among other groups, such as the Bugis, the Baweanese, and the Banjarese (Castles 1967; Lineton 1975; Persoon 1986). Castles (1967: 167), indeed, describes the people of Bawean—a small island off the North Java coast—as 'the Indonesian *suku* [people] in whom the urge to *merantau* is most pronounced'; their favoured destinations have long been outside of Indonesia itself. Today there are, according to the 1980 census, 28,584 people identifying themselves as Baweans in Singapore (the preferred destination until authorities there placed restrictions on entry a few years ago), while in Malaysia (currently the favoured destination) there are another 10,000 or so in Kuala Lumpur alone (Vredenbregt 1964; *Kompas* 2 April 1985).[3] The group which has spread itself the most widely, however, is probably the Buginese, who over the centuries established themselves not only among the eastern Indonesian islands, but in Riau, Singapore, Malaysia, and Thailand, as well as sailing regularly with the monsoon winds as far south as the north coast of Australia, where they went in search of *trepang* or sea slugs, which the Chinese prize as a delicacy. For the eastern Indonesians, 'circular' or seasonal migration between nearby islands is also a well-established pattern, especially for young men in the dry season, when there is little agricultural work to be done.[4] The goldsmiths of Ndau are a well-known example, leaving home yearly to fulfil commissions for people in other islands like Sumba, Roti, and Savu, all of whom rely on these craftsmen for supplies of their own preferred styles of jewellery and ritual ornaments.

Among the Iban, migration or the mounting of trading expeditions is termed *bejalai*; in the past it provided, along with head-hunting, the main opportunity for youth to distinguish themselves and win prestige. Now that warfare is no longer an option, downriver journeys to trade, or in search of wage labour, assume an even greater importance, and interestingly, some of the imagery associated with head-hunting has today retained its salience in Iban culture by being transferred into the context of *bejalai*. Mashman (1986: 5-6) notes that Lang, the god of war (symbolized by a hornbill), is still the object of invocatory chants sung at *gawai* festivals. But today

the Iban at the gawai ceremony call on the spirit of the hornbill to seek for wealth in far-off lands, rather than to attack their enemies.... The trophy head, formerly the ultimate symbol of success, is replaced by material goods, money, or academic achievement. References to the Kayan and the Ukit as enemies of the Iban in the oral narratives sung at the festival take on a figurative significance: they are no longer foes in themselves, but represent obstacles to material success.

In the Philippines, the Ilongot, another former head-hunting people, similarly idealize travel as a source of knowledge and awareness (Rosaldo 1980).

For the Muang or Northern Thai, migration is called *aew*, and for the Central Thai, *thiaw*. Davis (1984: 68) explicitly likens the custom to Sumatran *merantau* as 'a typically South-East Asian pattern'. The Northern Thai image of man as mobile and woman as sedentary (which we linked in an earlier chapter to matrifocality and female ownership of houses) is reflected in the proverb: 'Husbands are fishnets, wives are creels.' Men are expected to wander off and gain their income from diverse sources, handing over what they earn to their wives, who manage domestic finances. A reflection of the pattern may be seen, too, in the custom of 'mother roasting' by which a newly delivered mother must be warmed by a fire for a certain number of days after birth.[5] According to traditional Muang practice, the period of 'lying by the fire' should last twenty-nine days after the birth of a son and thirty days or more after the birth of a daughter. Davies (1973: 55) notes:

It is believed that if the recovery period were longer than 29 days in the case of a male birth, the son would not be able to wander abroad when he matured. A period shorter than 30 days after the birth of a daughter would make her reluctant to remain at home when she reached a marriageable age.

During the Dutch colonial period in Indonesia, even the more isolated hill peoples such as the Batak and the Toraja began to develop a more centrifugal orientation, as education, improved communications, and the introduction of a money economy opened up new opportunities for them beyond their homelands.[6] In modern Indonesia, the extent of migration is much greater than ever before, though exact figures are impossible to come by. Census data since 1960 have not included information about ethnic origins, but some rough estimates have been offered. Castles (1967: 185), for example, estimated there were 60,100 Minangkabau in Jakarta in 1961, but the present head of the population department of the provincial government (himself a Minangkabau) believes that a more accurate estimation would be 10 per cent of Jakarta's population of 6 million, that is, 600,000 (Persoon 1986: 181). Kato (1982: 131) estimates that as many as 1 million, or approximately 30 per cent of the total population of Minangkabau, are to be found on the *rantau*.[7] The proportion of Bataks on the *rantau* is not known but they are very strongly represented, particularly in Medan, Jakarta, and other Javanese cities such as Bandung. Again, no exact figures are available for Torajan migrants, but they are so numerous that in some districts where land shortages are most acute, almost no young people are left in the villages at all. Every family hopes to have at least one member working on the *rantau*, whose remittances will assist those left at home to work the land. As well as the cities, they are drawn to Kalimantan and Malaysia where work is to be found with oil and timber companies or on plantations. The amount of money entering Toraja in the form of remittances, through the bank, the post office, and informal channels, is perhaps the single biggest factor affecting the development of the Toraja economy today. Minahasans of North Sulawesi, too, are frequent migrants, and maintain a sense of identity in far-off cities and overseas by forming associations (modelled on village associations at home), sending home money and goods and returning for periodic visits (Lundstrom-Bürghoorn 1981: 124). It is noticeable that, where older *merantau* traditions tend to depict migration as a masculine activity, these newer patterns of migration typically involve both sexes. Young Toraja women, for example, travel by themselves to Ujung Pandang or further afield in search of work as household servants, seamstresses, or bar hostesses, and there is no prejudice against women seeking higher education if they can afford it. Vredenbregt's figures (1964: 115) on the Baweans of Singapore show a steady increase since the mid-nineteenth century in the ratio of women to men on the *rantau*, from 60 per 1,000 in 1849 to 914 per 1,000 by 1957. Today, even Minangkabau migrants, who formerly would have left their wives at home in charge of ancestral houses and lands, now frequently take their families with them on the *rantau*. Castles' figures for 1960 (1967: 190) showed a ratio of 78 : 100 Minangkabau women to men in Jakarta, compared to 52 : 100 in the 1930 census, and it has almost certainly equalized further in the intervening period. Persoon (1986: 183) remarks that Minangkabau women on the *rantau* often take the initiative of setting up their own businesses in order to gain an income independent of their husband. They apparently play an important role in chemist's shops among other enterprises.

At least 40 per cent of Jakarta's population are migrants (Sundrum 1976: 90); as the major destination of migrants from all over Indonesia, the city is so ethnically mixed that it has been described as 'a city of minorities' (Persoon 1986: 180). Much the same could be said of some other major cities, like Medan in Sumatra. Though some Javanese peasants are driven to Jakarta because of sheer overwhelming poverty at home, most migrants from the outer islands are drawn to the capital in search of education, careers, and the thrill of city life. Castles (1967: 192) notes:

In migration from the more distant areas, the quest for education, excitement and power seems to be more important than narrowly economic considerations. There is a marked correlation between the areas where education was more advanced in the late colonial period and those from which large numbers of migrants have come to Jakarta since independence.

The concentration of higher educational institutions, not just in Jakarta but in Java as a whole, draws many young people from other provinces as students (Sundrum 1976: 88). But migration is not restricted to destinations within Indonesia itself; 80,000 Indonesians currently work in Saudi Arabia, and an uncertain number in Malaysia, as well as others scattered in countries further afield.

231

Migration, it might be thought, would be likely to have a negative impact on the continuity of 'traditional' cultures, either because it is assumed to be the most enterprising people who leave, or because migrants become exposed to new fashions and come to regard their old styles as unsatisfactory. But, in fact, migration is by no means simply a drain upon local cultures. Those who migrate often maintain very strong ties with their places of origin, while at the same time experiencing a heightened sense of ethnic identity in the context of a strange city where they are constantly meeting people of different cultural backgrounds.[8] Rather than simply becoming urbanized and acculturated in the cities, migrants may be feeding back into the home community not only considerable amounts of money but of cultural energy, as they seek for a way to reassert their cultural identity or to convert new wealth into prestige at home. Since, in so many Indonesian societies, it is precisely the house through which descent is traced and to which one feels a special attachment as origin-site, it is not surprising that houses should continue to attract the attention and loyalty of migrants.

When doing fieldwork in Tana Toraja, I was struck by the frequency with which houses of origin are renewed or rebuilt, and the importance of this activity in enhancing the status of the house's descendants. The rebuilding of a house is not solely determined by whether its physical state requires it, but rather by a decision on the part of its descendants to co-operate in upgrading its status as origin-house. The more times a house has been rebuilt, the more prestige attaches to it, especially since the completion of the work is celebrated by a large feast at which many pigs will be slaughtered. In the last two decades or so there has been a spate of rebuilding, much of it funded by emigrant Torajans who live outside of their homeland. I later became aware of similar attitudes to houses and their renewal in other parts of the archipelago, in areas where migration is also a prominent feature. The same motives for house building appear to apply in parts of mainland South-East Asia, too, for Turton (1978: 114) says of the Northern Thai:

A householder's strategy is to build a bigger and better house as soon and as often as he can. Houses are not replaced when physically necessary but according to certain social requirements and processes. Building a house can also be an important statement about status and a claim to prestige.

In what follows I have chosen to focus upon three main examples: Toraja, Toba, and Minangkabau. The case of the Toba Batak is of particular interest because here, as we have seen, it is not necessarily on houses that the most money is spent, but on elaborate house-shaped tombs which are the sites of secondary burial for the bones of a whole group of ancestors. The ceremony for the construction of such a tomb is the greatest and most expensive of Toba ritual occasions, and is sure to be attended by many emigrant as well as locally resident kinspeople. As for the Minangkabau, there is currently here, too, a considerable interest in the renewal of houses, very often funded by migrants. I shall argue that houses at the present time continue to be regarded as deeply significant structures, even as shifts take place in *what* exactly it is that the house is held to signify (Figure 194). It is this reflexive link between migrants and their home communities, and the shifts and continuities taking place in cultural practices and meanings, which I shall discuss below.

'Tradition' versus 'Modernity'

Before going further, it is important to address the question of 'tradition' and what it really means, both to the investigator and the subjects of investigation. This will always be a difficult question, I suggest, because the concept itself is inherently ambiguous. It is not only in Western cultures that a bias is evident toward an understanding of tradition as something deserving of reverence, which ought to be upheld without change. It has a tendency to become equated with stasis, whereas its implied opposite—'modernity' or 'modernization'—is just as indissolubly equated with change. But 'tradition' really describes a process of handing down, and as such is just as dynamic and as historical as any other social process. The *idea* of tradition, however (and its clash with the ideology of modernization, as this is translated into action in the form of national policies, for example) are also a part of the total social dynamic and need to be considered as such. Tradition, like history, is something that is continually being recreated and remodelled in the present, even as it is represented as fixed and unchangeable.

Telling insights into the history of the word are provided by Raymond Williams. Observing 'tradition' to be 'a particularly difficult word' (in the sense of one

194. Minangkabau *madrasah* or Islamic school, photographed by Jean Demmeni around the turn of the century, draws strongly on traditional architectural themes while also utilizing modern zinc as a roofing material. Zinc has been used by the Minangkabau at least since 1905, raising a query in the mind about when a particular item may be said to have become 'traditional'. (Photograph Jean Demmeni, courtesy of Times Editions, Singapore)

whose meanings have shifted over time), he notes that it came into English via old French in the fourteenth century, its root being the Latin *traditionem*, from *tradere*—to hand over or deliver. Williams writes (1976: 269):

The Latin noun had the senses of (i) delivery, (ii) handing down knowledge, (iii) passing on a doctrine, (iv) surrender or betrayal. The general sense (i) was in English in mC16, and sense (iv), especially of betrayal, from lC15 to mC17. But the main development was in senses (ii) and (iii).... Tradition survives in English as a description of a general process of handing down, but there is a very strong and often predominant sense of this entailing respect and duty....

It is sometimes observed, by those who have looked into particular traditions, that it only takes two generations to make anything traditional: naturally enough, since that is the sense of tradition as active process. But the word moves again and again towards *age-old* and towards ceremony, duty and respect. Considering only how much has been handed down to us, and how various it actually is, this, in its own way, is both a betrayal and a surrender.[9]

Ambiguities are likely to arise wherever the concepts of 'tradition' and 'modernization' form part of local discourse, particularly due to the difficulty of reconciling their implications. In today's world, it has become virtually impossible to separate the idea of modernization from industrialization and, in most instances, colonial and post-colonial Western influences. However, it is also likely to be identified with the goals of nationalist development. Traditions, particularly in a nation like Indonesia with its enormous diversity of cultures, have to be thought of as multiple, but 'modernization' is more likely to be conceived of as a unitary goal to which the whole nation aspires. Most of the peoples of modern Indonesia are engaged in a lively debate among themselves about what exactly should constitute the enduring and unchangeable elements of their own particular *adat* or customs. The Constitution itself is designed to uphold respect and tolerance for different customs and religious beliefs within the nation, and 'Unity in Diversity' is the national motto. At the same time, 'Development' and 'Modernization' are powerful keywords in current Indonesian administrative ideology, which inevitably has practical impacts on local cultures.[10]

Clearly, the potential impact of administrative policies and attitudes upon the maintenance of indigenous architectural styles is very great, and can be either drastic or benign. We have seen how both colonial Dutch and post-Independence administrations have had their effects on a number of indigenous architectural traditions, particularly where concepts of modernization and related ideas (for example, hygiene) are brought into play. At the local level, policy applications can be very uneven and have not always reflected the more sophisticated opinions of higher echelons of the administration about the desirability of preserving Indonesia's diversity of cultural traditions. 'Modernization' has sometimes been interpreted very literally in terms of preferences for—even an insistence upon—a particular building style (or mode of dress, or type of religious belief) over another. Fox, for example, reports that, up until the late 1960s, almost all houses on the island of Roti were built in traditional style. Dutch insistence on ending the custom of burying the dead under the floor (which we encountered in the previous chapter) had thus apparently not affected actual house-building practices very much. Objections of the post-Independence administration appear to have focused on the keeping of livestock in the space beneath the house floor. Between 1968 and 1975, rather than suggesting that the animals be moved elsewhere, local officials decreed that these houses should be pulled down and replaced with more 'modern' and 'hygienic' houses built on the ground, following what is basically a Dutch bungalow model. There are now scarcely any traditional houses left on the island at all, though on a brief visit in 1987 I did succeed in visiting one. I also heard of one remaining village of clan origin-houses, now probably the oldest houses surviving on the island.

In complete contrast with this tragic local aberration, the Government has in other places given generously of funds to aid in the preservation of outstanding traditional buildings—as in the case of the Minangkabau royal palace at Pagarruyung (Figure 195), rebuilt as a museum after it was destroyed by a fire, the great house of the Raja of Simalungun and associated buildings at Pematang Purba on the northern shore of Lake Toba (Sumatra), and some traditional origin-houses in Tana Toraja which have also been designated as National Monuments. We must, therefore, consider the possibility that part of the reason for the continued vitality of architecture in the regions I am considering has to do with the fact that people have not been demoralized by interventions leading them to devalue their traditional forms. At the same time, we may note that a major motive

195. The Minangkabau royal palace of Pagarruyung, recently rebuilt after a fire with the aid of government funds. It is now a museum. (Photograph: Roxana Waterson)

behind government support is to boost tourism, which is a significant income earner in the three regions I have mentioned, but as yet very insignificant in remoter islands of eastern Indonesia like Roti. The restored buildings, as well as being part of the nation's cultural heritage, become designated 'Tourist Objects'. But clearly it is easier to destroy a tradition than to bring it back, or to legislate against its disappearance. Admirable as it is, the preservation of a few outstanding buildings would not in itself ensure the maintenance of a tradition among the populace at large. Neither would the use of traditional architectural idioms in new municipal buildings or hotels, popular as this device is throughout South-East Asia. It is noticeable how often traditional roof forms, in particular, are incorporated as elements in new buildings. The results can be, at best, creative, sensitive, and culturally and climatically appropriate new structures, or at worst, merely a poor pastiche in which a particular shape is used as a signal of cultural identity. Whether the culture itself really retains its dynamism, however, is a more complex matter. Even from this brief discussion, a multiplicity of factors can be seen to be interacting with each other in determining the fate of an indigenous style. Below, I aim to reveal some other aspects of the social process affecting the survival of architectural 'traditions', in the genuinely active sense of the word.

Toraja

The present-day administrative district of Tana Toraja, in the northern highlands of South Sulawesi, has a population of around 350,000—largely subsistence farmers growing wet rice in rain-fed hill terraces. They rear buffaloes and pigs, destined for sacrifice in one of the many ceremonies which are a major focus of Toraja social life—even for those (60 per cent or more) who today have become Christian. Most of the remaining percentage adhere to their traditional religion, which has official status as one of Indonesia's recognized religions. In Tana Toraja today, the spread of Christianity, the forces of modernization, and another, very different kind of 'migration' in reverse—tourism—all raise questions about what, in Torajan traditions, should be maintained and what should be altered. At the same time, the flow of new wealth from the *rantau* has created a boom in ritual expenditure, so that there has been what Volkman (1985: 43) aptly terms 'a

simultaneous blossoming of ritual activity and doubt'.

It might be imagined that all this exposure to city sophistication, on the one hand, and invasion by tourists, on the other, bodes ill for the survival of any cultural traditions, including architectural ones. But it is not that simple. Although tourism certainly poses its problems, it is by no means a wholly negative influence. To the contrary, when tourism first took off in the early 1970s, the arrival of foreigners who had travelled thousands of miles purely in order to admire Toraja houses and witness their funeral ceremonies genuinely caused many Torajans to ponder on the worth and value of their traditions at a time when most of these traditions were in decline or actively under attack from the more fundamentalist members of the (Calvinist) Toraja Church. In the same way, as I have suggested, emigration may have its positive aspects for the vitality of the home culture. Migrants from Toraja maintain remarkably strong ties with their homeland, to which they typically make periodic visits, even from great distances and at heavy expense, in order to participate in ceremonies. Such visits are an occasion for the renewal of links with kin, and a re-affirmation of one's Torajaness through the exchange of pigs and distribution of meat which is so much a part of Toraja rituals, and consequently of social life. The link with one's home village is, however, even more importantly expressed through ties with the *tongkonan* or family origin-houses. These are the houses where one's parents, grandparents, or more distant ancestors were born. At birth, a baby's placenta (which is regarded as a sort of twin) is buried on the east side of the house; Torajans say that, however far they may roam, in the end the placenta will always draw them back to their birthplace. In the past, commoners were not permitted to build the grandest style of house, complete with carved panels and enormous roof, but with the erosion of rules about rank, many families today have built themselves finer houses than would formerly have been allowed them. One of the most prominent ways in which migrant money is being spent is on the renewal and ceremonial reinauguration of origin-houses (Figure 196). Nothing adds more visibly and

196. Origin-house (*tongkonan*) at Kata, Malimbong district, Tana ►
Toraja, 1983, whose recent rebuilding was funded by a wealthy descendant of the house who is now a civil servant in Jakarta. The new house is considerably larger than the previous one on the site, and follows the now general 'Rantepao' style with sharply extended points to the eaves. (Photograph: Roxana Waterson)

enduringly to a family's prestige, or is better appreciated by fellow Torajans, than this type of expenditure. The idea that one should return some of the product of one's labours to one's home community is expressed in the saying, 'Eat in other people's villages, but shit in your own' (*ke kumande ko dio padangna tau, sittai ko dio tondokmu*). It is indeed considered despicable to have a fine house in the city if one's own origin-houses in Tana Toraja are left in a dilapidated state.[11]

Torajans recognize the changes taking place in their society, yet often express the opinion that there is an unchanging core of tradition that will never change. When I asked people of what this core consisted, the things most frequently mentioned were the ritual cycle, the ceremonial division and distribution of meat, and the *tongkonan*. In many respects, however, the role of the *tongkonan* has changed. In the past, the noble ruler of a community lived in his family's origin-house, which physically dominated all the houses around it by its size and magnificence. The number of these ruling houses became fixed at some time in the past, and there are no new ones today. But the house as a concrete representation of the political power of an aristocracy ceases to be very relevant in the context of the modern national administration. The resident of a noble *tongkonan* used also to hold certain ritual offices in the community, but those who are now Christian have for the most part ceased to function as ritual leaders. In terms of everyday life, ideas about comfort may also undergo some change. Although huge on the outside, the interior space of the traditional house is actually surprisingly small, consisting of three narrow rooms with no furniture and only very small window openings to admit light during the day. The doorway is a small square opening at knee height, closed by a heavy door carved from a solid slab of wood. Many people find the old houses too cramped and uncomfortable for modern living; even those who have the right to inhabit an ancestral house often prefer not to. New houses today are often built in an imitation of the Bugis style, with a very open plan, and large windows and doors. Most modern of all, for those who can afford it, is to build a bungalow house of stone and concrete, in a style first introduced by the Dutch. At a seminar held in the early 1980s to discuss Torajan culture, a number of speakers expressed the opinion that builders and architects were much to blame for departing from traditional styles and were 'ruining the *adat*'. One individual then got up and asked whether anyone present would be prepared to live in a house of the traditional style, but no one could bring themselves to reply in the affirmative (Setiono 1983: 4). One acquaintance who feels particularly strongly about what he perceives as Torajan cultural decline expressed scorn for those who claim that traditional houses are too uncomfortable. As he put it, it all depends on the will: if people choose to, they are able to live in submarines without complaining of discomfort, and the same should be true of the traditional house!

Those who are sufficiently wealthy may seek a compromise which enables them to enhance their social prestige in terms of both 'tradition' and 'modernity'. They may rebuild a traditional origin-house at great expense and with all the attendant ceremonies and then leave it empty, preferring to live in a modern stone-built house alongside. In one district not far from the town of Rantepao stands a newly constructed *tongkonan* and a line of six rice barns, with a large stone bungalow beside it (Plate 23). The house is actually on a new site, and not the site of an old ruling house, but its builder is of noble descent. He organized the construction as part of the preparations for a large double funeral held some years ago for his father and grandfather. He himself lives in Jakarta and rarely visits Tana Toraja, but when he does, he and his family stay in the stone house. The rest of the time a caretaker lives there, and looks after the *tongkonan*. A generator behind the house supplies electricity, and each of the rice barns is fitted with a light bulb. The caretaker is instructed to turn on the lights at dusk every night and leave them on until about 2 a.m., impressing upon the local populace the heights to which his absent employer's fortunes have risen on the *rantau*.

Another innovation in style is the two-storey wooden house. The first floor is in 'Bugis' style, with a roughly square plan, spacious rooms, and large doors and windows. The second floor is built in entirely 'traditional' style complete with wall carvings and saddle roof (Plate 22). Although at first sight its appearance is strange, this style represents a particularly clever compromise between the desire for a more 'modern' and convenient living space, and the high value which is still placed upon the traditional form. Needless to say, it is this new creation, in particular, which is decried by purists as a devaluation of the original style. But there are other more subtle changes, too.

One of these has to do with the standardization of carving styles.[12] An examination of the oldest surviving houses in different regions of Tana Toraja reveals considerable differences in the exact proportions of houses, the carving motifs most commonly used, and to some extent their style of execution and colouring. Only four colours are used—black, white, red, and yellow—but in some areas, such as Saluputti, one finds in the older houses a heavier predominance of black, or greater use of yellow rather than red, and so on. Furthermore, some of the carpenters no longer use natural earth colours but commercial paint. What seems to be happening is a centralization of the carpenters in the main town of Rantepao and the growing predominance of a 'Rantepao' style of house whose proportions are rather more elongated, the ridge of the roof being exaggerated into longer and longer points at each end. A certain amount of rigidity seems to creep into the execution of carving motifs at the same time. With improved roads and communications, the carpenters can easily move about to other areas to take commissions, and those who want to learn the trade are more likely to go to Rantepao to do so.

In spite of these changes, there is no doubt that 'traditional' architecture in Tana Toraja is still very much alive. The 1950s and 1960s in South Sulawesi were times of considerable economic hardship and social disturbance. The Second World War and the deprivations caused by the Japanese Occupation were followed by the struggle for Independence and then the incursions of Islamic guerrillas into the Toraja highlands during the 1950s. They burned villages (destroying a number of old *tongkonan* in the process) and conscripted some Torajans into their forces.[13] Not surprisingly in these circumstances, hardly anyone was in a position to carry out building projects, and there was almost no renewal of origin-houses. The 1950s and 1960s also saw the emergence of the Indonesian Christian Party (Parkindo) as the dominant force in Toraja politics. Its members, together with the Torajan Church, were hostile to many aspects of traditional culture, including the ceremonies associated with house building. Anyone attempting to make a prediction at this time about the future of Toraja architecture would have painted a gloomy picture indeed. However, by 1969, the traditional religion had received official government recognition as an approved religion, and Parkindo suffered an overwhelming defeat in the elections of 1971 as Torajans

voted for the government party, Golkar.[14] With the return of more peaceful and prosperous times, there was an immediate resurgence of building activity. I attribute this, firstly, to the continued centrality of the house within the Toraja kinship structure and, secondly, to its continued importance as a ritual site.

Toraja ceremonial life is too culturally specific to translate easily to areas outside the homeland, just as houses outside of Toraja are never thought of as 'origin-houses', and a house in traditional style would not really 'mean' the same thing elsewhere. Hence, the compulsion to return to celebrate rites where people can understand and appreciate what one is doing. Visits home are not just for the sake of a reaffirmation of identity, however. Wealthier migrants often maintain considerable landholdings in Toraja, and use the occasion of their return for a ceremony to check on their affairs or make new deals. They may take land in pawn in exchange for loans, and arrange for relatives or others to share-crop it for them. At the same time, when they come home they want to make an impression, and the family origin-house is essential to family prestige.[15]

In a broader sense, the house lends itself as a convenient cultural symbol, as the issue arises of defining an ethnic identity in the context of the modern nation with all its cultural diversity. In spite of its close connections with ritual, most people are able to agree in viewing the house as a 'secular' element of culture, and therefore less contentious than are some other items such as funeral ceremonies, the rectitude of which is still debated by some Toraja Christians. Even as some of the older significances of the house are lost, then, it still continues to function as a vivid and condensed symbol, with which all can identify, of what it means to be Toraja.

Minangkabau

The Minangkabau occupy the province of West Sumatra, whose population in 1980 numbered 3.4 million. This figure does not include the probably 1 million or more Minangkabau who have left their homeland to trade or seek city jobs in other parts of Indonesia or beyond. Minangkabau, even more than other peoples of Indonesia, are much given to discussion and analysis of their own *adat* and social patterns, and they are not at all surprised when outsiders show interest in their unusual customs. Though they may tend to view their *adat* as fixed and unchanging, that which 'neither rots in the rain nor cracks in the sun', in fact historical changes have constantly shaped and reshaped Minangkabau society, making it necessary to be especially cautious in speaking of a 'traditional' Minangkabau society. Although they have been Muslim for several centuries, they have maintained their matrilineal system of inheritance; Islamic and *adat* traditions are so integrated that (notwithstanding the efforts of various Islamic reform movements in Minangkabau history) most Minangkabau do not perceive any contradiction between the two.[16] The centrality of the house in Minangkabau social organization has been described already in earlier chapters.

The Minangkabau view their world, the *Alam Minangkabau*, as divided essentially into two areas, the *darek* or inner highlands of Minangkabau territory and the *rantau*, or outlying frontier areas. Kato suggests that in earliest times, *merantau* must have represented the movement of population into new areas of West Sumatra as villages grew and split to form new settlements. Later, a 'circulatory' pattern developed as men oscillated between their home villages and various relatively close destinations, mostly cities within Minangkabau itself or in other regions of Sumatra. But some went further afield, to Java, Malaya, eastern Indonesia, and the Middle East. Even from an early date, however, there were also movements of a more permanent nature, for example of settlers to the Negeri Sembilan area of the Malay Peninsula during the seventeenth and eighteenth centuries. Nowadays, many whole families reside permanently on the *rantau*, especially in Java. They maintain ties with their homeland through occasional visits home, and through the activities of the vigorous Minangkabau associations which exist in these cities.

As more and more Minangkabau settle in *rantau* cities, Minangkabau associations have increased rapidly in number. Persoon (1986: 186) calculates that there are hundreds in Jakarta alone. There are several kinds of association, from those which are open to all Minangkabau, to those based on district, sub-district, or local village (*nagari*) membership. Some cater especially to particular groups, such as students or women; others specialize in artistic activities. Those forming art, dance, and theatre groups often make periodic return visits to the homeland to give performances and thus inject new energy into various uniquely Minangkabau art forms; others publish Minangkabau newspapers and magazines. As numbers have grown, there has been a proliferation especially of the smaller-level associations and a fading out of original pan-Minangkabau groups. Persoon (1986: 187) describes it as 'no exception' that at present, 1,000 out of a total of 1,500 people from one village in West Sumatra are living in Jakarta. As well as providing help with accommodation and mutual assistance in the city, and channelling funds back home to assist in the maintenance of their villages, associations also help to arrange important ceremonies, especially weddings, for their members. It appears that certain ceremonies, such as weddings, funerals, or the Lebaran festivities at the end of Ramadan, can now very well be celebrated on the *rantau* and are less likely to provide the occasion for a visit home. Others, such as the appointment of a new clan leader, would still have to take place in the house and village of origin.

Thus the concept of an 'inner' and 'outer' territory of Minangkabau, and the practice of migration itself, have always been part of the Minangkabau world view. Returning migrants have always been a source of new ideas and information about the outside world; the sense of Minangkabau identity itself is partly shaped by experiences on the *rantau*.[17] Several writers have suggested that an attitude of 'romantic conservatism' characterizes those who settle permanently on the *rantau* (Taufik Abdullah, cited in Kato 1982: 232; Persoon 1986: 189). Even though they have no desire to remain at home, the knowledge that their home villages continue to adhere to *adat* patterns is reassuring for migrants. Persoon even suggests that permanent migrants are in some ways *more* traditional than those who regard their stay on the *rantau* as temporary; it is precisely the former group, for example, who show an increased interest in traditional literature, music, and dance.

The dynamic relationship between home-based and migrant Minangkabau is further reflected in the fact that migrants often fund the rebuilding of origin-houses, either for the sake of their own matrilineal kin or those of their wives. In the past, there was a strong resistance in Minangkabau custom to the husband having anything to do with the building of his wife's family *adat* house. One of the effects of more long-term migration, however, where couples are living together on the *rantau*, is a strengthening of the previously fragile bond between spouses. The result has been, not a decline in the matrilineal principle (as has often been predicted) but an increasing involvement of men in their wives' matrilineages as well as their own. Nowadays, according to Kato (1982: 177), a man often helps his wife to build a house, but this will nearly always not be an *adat* house: it will not have a horned roof, for example. Tanner (1976: 11) notes that

... newer style houses tend to be more square than long and do not have the distinctive Minangkabau roof; however, the internal space of the larger newer houses is also divided into a large central common room and bedrooms for married daughters. In each case a kitchen is usually found at the back.

Rebuilding the house of one's origin for the sake of one's *kemanakan* (sisters' children) remains, none the less, one of the major means by which a migrant may maintain active ties with his home village, as well as demonstrate his success on the *rantau*. Others include remittances of money (as in Toraja, huge amounts of money are transmitted via the post office); contributions to public building projects, such as mosques and schools, in the home village; return visits to attend weddings or other ceremonies; and efforts to redeem pledged ancestral land (Kato 1982: 232). Like the Toraja, Minangkabau feel the urge to hold on to land in the home village, as a genuine proof of one's origins there (Kato 1982: 228).

As in the Toraja case, interest in the maintenance of origin-houses appears to have fluctuated but is currently enjoying a resurgence. During this century, various disasters have caused the destruction of a great many older houses. In 1926, for example, there was a serious earthquake in Padang Panjang which toppled houses. During the 'Padri War' of 1821–38, a number of villages, or their mosque or *balai*, were burned down. Thousands more were destroyed by the Dutch in the war for Indonesian Independence (1945–9), and again by warring factions during the unsuccessful PRRI Rebellion of the 1950s. Of this period, Tanner (1976: 53) remarks: 'Both Government troops and local guerillas utilized selective house, house cluster, or village burning and looting to retaliate [against] "lack of loyalty".' Subsequently, it was simply too expensive to rebuild these houses and finance the necessary rituals accompanying their construction. In addition, deforestation has made it increasingly difficult to find the trees large enough to furnish the great central pillars of the *rumah gadang* ('great house').

Figures compiled by Kato (1982: 176) suggest that in the early decades of this century there was still a very high proportion of buildings in '*adat*' style, while within the last generation or so the percentage has declined dramatically.

In recent years, there has been a proliferation of individual family dwellings. In part this also reflects a growing preference for the greater privacy such houses afford, compared to the intense interaction of life in the multi-family *rumah gadang*. Nowadays, one may even come across a large *rumah gadang* standing empty, with the descent group occupying a number of smaller houses around it. In 1986, I stayed in a small village near Payakumbuh, in a compound of seven houses built around a beautiful old traditional house (Plates 20 and 21). The houses were occupied by a group of married sisters and daughters. Those who were better off had built themselves new, modern houses in stone and concrete, the latest of which was the pride of the compound, complete with Corinthian columns, net curtains and purple lamps. The old house was still occupied by the eldest sister, but the others privately felt sorry for her, because she and her husband had not been able to afford to build a new house.

Swift (1971: 259-60), writing on social change among the Minangkabau in the 1960s, suggested that to be able to fund the building of a new stone house was regarded as very prestigious, and some houses were being built, with money earned on the *rantau*, even if no one wanted to live in them and they were left standing empty. He noted, however, that people were becoming unwilling to spend large sums on the maintenance of traditional houses, since this might mean having to forego the status to be gained by building a modern house, and instead merely adding to the prestige of *adat* superiors and elders. This was resented and, moreover, people were beginning to find the traditional houses uncomfortable. Furthermore, he suggested that the *rantau* was tending to become a permanent, rather than an episodic, form of migration, which caused a loosening of ties to the home area, accentuated in second-generation migrants born in cities outside of Minangkabau. His predictions do not appear to have been fully borne out, however. We have already mentioned the apparently strong continuation of ties to the home area even among permanent migrants. Houses are still important as the proper sites for rituals and gatherings of the kin group, and people emphasized to me that one would feel shame if the group were without such a gathering place. A number of researchers more recently have commented on the definite upsurge of renewed interest in the re-building of traditional houses, or at least in building houses with traditional roof styles, though as yet this may be more obvious in some areas than others (Plate 24). Persoon (1986: 188), for example, notes: 'Many traditional adat houses of typical Minangkabau design have been nicely restored during the last 10 or 15 years with money earned somewhere in the rantau.'[18] Similarly, the matrilineal system, though its demise has often enough been predicted, has proved itself resilient in the face of changing circumstances.[19] One may yet be justified in hoping that Minangkabau architecture will remain an active and living tradition.

Toba Batak

The Toba are by far the most numerous of the Batak peoples. They occupy the heart of the Batak homelands in North Sumatra, centring around the island of Samosir in Lake Toba. The Toba region is a great mountain plateau with an altitude of 900 metres. In this wild and beautiful landscape may still be seen large numbers of the traditional finely decorated houses and sculpted stone tombs of the Toba (Plate 14).

During the late nineteenth century, Toba culture began to be drastically altered by missionary activity and Dutch administration. In 1860, a German Protestant mission was established and there were mass conversions. Subsequently, the Dutch took over the area, though they did not succeed in pacifying all the Batak lands until early this century. Improved communications, education, and the introduction of a money economy changed Toba society from an inward-looking one, distrustful of outsiders, to a centrifugal one from which many migrants began to move to cities in other parts of Indonesia to live and work. The traditional religion disintegrated under the impact of Christianity and was abandoned. Yet elements of Toba culture have survived in a changed configuration, and the dynamic relationship between the Toba homeland and Toba emigrants in Indonesian cities has fostered the growth of a new and vigorous ethnic awareness among the Toba.

Toba are particularly numerous in Medan, as well as in Jakarta and other Javanese cities. Sjahrir (1983: 77) gives a figure of 60,566 Toba resident in Jakarta

in 1973; although smaller than many ethnic groups in the city, they are among those that have grown most rapidly. They are extremely enterprising and hard-working, and some have built up highly successful businesses. Numerous clan, district, and church associations provide points of contact for Toba in the cities; these are well described by Bruner (1970, 1972) for the 1950s and 1960s, and are still very much a part of the scene in Medan today. One woman, for example, told me that she attends a meeting of her clan association once a fortnight, as well as being a member of two local ward groups who meet regularly for prayer meetings and choral practices, so that at least once a week she would be meeting with groups of fellow Toba. A wealthy Toba businessman and newspaper owner in Medan recently endowed a Batak university, the Universitas Sisingamangaraja, which includes a 'Centre for Batakology', with a small museum and many plans for encouraging the preservation of Batak culture and stimulating a sense of Batak identity, not only among migrants but in the homeland. When the inaugural ceremony for the university was held in 1984, efforts were made to trace and invite all known Toba clan associations in Medan, and around eighty groups responded; it is possible that there are even more. The Rector's Representative at the University, in describing all these developments, himself remarked that his own interest in Batak culture had only really developed when he left the homeland and came to the city!

On the rantau, a strong element of continuity in Toba identity is made possible by the maintenance of ties between wife-giving and wife-taking clans, the hula-hula and boru. Wife-givers, as we have seen, are ritually superior to wife-takers. The major context for the expression of these ties is at ceremonies. Traditionally, the house provides the setting and the backdrop for these ceremonies, at which the hula-hula and the boru exchange gifts. On the rantau, attendance of both wife-giving and wife-taking clans at weddings is still regarded as essential. A sense of clan identity is kept alive through membership of clan associations. As in the Minangkabau case, earlier associations based on wider territorial origins have tended to give way to those based on clan membership as an increase in numbers has made this feasible (Sjahrir 1983: 79). What is distinctive about these associations is that, although the clans themselves are patrilineal, membership in the associations appears to follow a bilateral pattern. My own inquiries in Medan concord on this point with the picture given by Sjahrir (1983) of clan associations in Jakarta. Any Toba individual will belong to a minimum of two associations, those of his mother's and his father's clan. Moreover, married people also join in the activities of the clan associations of their spouses, which will also be two in number. Thus, membership in city associations creates a wider network of organized inter-clan participation than would normally exist in the village. As in Medan, the Jakarta clan associations assist in the celebration of births, marriages, and funerals, may intervene to settle marital disputes, and will provide temporary accommodation, loans, and assistance to newcomers to the city (Sjahrir 1983: 79–80).

In the previous chapter, we saw how an ancient tradition of stone tomb building is today carried on in a new medium, concrete. These elaborate and expensive tombs may imitate in every detail the shape of the traditional Toba house (Figures 197–199). The use of concrete began very early this century, for Bartlett comments on it, but the examples he recorded mostly pre-dated the First World War, and he noted few had been erected in the period 1918–1927. He warmly admired the quality of their design, but interpreted it as only a last burst of artistic energy in a culture that was inevitably dying. His comments are interesting now that we have the advantage of hindsight. He wrote (1934: 29):

It is seldom that one has an opportunity to see what effect the introduction of an entirely unfamiliar material (such as concrete) will have on the art expression of a primitive people. These concrete tombs show very conclusively that, in spite of the disintegrating effect of European contact, the Batak retained for a time the capacity for development of their own peculiar art through the adoption of materials and technical processes from outside. It appears that the movement to create a new art in the spirit of the past was abortive. The forces bringing about cultural disintegration are too strong.

197. House-shaped tomb at Sangkal, Samosir Island, Lake Toba, 1986. Such tombs are used for the secondary burial of the bones of a group of deceased ancestors. (Photograph: Roxana Waterson)

198. Forms of house and tomb echo each other at Sangkal, Samosir Island, Lake Toba, 1986. (Photograph: Roxana Waterson)

As it turns out, this prognostication was overly pessimistic, since one now sees concrete tombs all over the area. Some, moving away from the imitation of house forms, incorporate new views of the afterlife with the inclusion of features such as church steeples. The tombs, called *tambak* or *parholian*, are constructed by a group of patrilineally related kin who co-operate to meet the expense and to hold a special ceremony in which the bones of a number of ancestors of several generations will be exhumed, regrouped, and transferred into the new tomb. This ceremony, today somewhat Christianized, will be attended by both the wife-giving and the wife-taking clans of the hosts. The survival of secondary burial practices in this form provides modern-day Toba with the opportunity to assert their continuity with their clan ancestors as well as to gain prestige in the eyes of the community by the celebration of this much-valued ceremony. The great expense of the ceremony, as well as the construction of the tomb itself, is frequently met by migrant clan members, who will return long distances to attend this most important of Toba ceremonies. Certain craftsmen specialize in making the tombs, which I was told may cost up to Rp 1 million (at 1986 rates, nearly US $700).

Even more expensive, and demanding an even bigger ceremony, is a kind of mausoleum or memorial monument, which commemorates the founding ancestors of an entire clan. It may, in fact, have no bones inside it at all; if the grave of the ancestors concerned is already lost without trace, some earth may be taken from a likely spot and placed inside. In the past, a stone urn sometimes served this commemorative function, but the monument is a new development dating from the 1960s. It is called *tugu*, an Indonesian word which refers to national monuments and obelisks, such as were erected in large numbers in the post-Independence period. A *tugu*, I was told, should be tall, and indeed some are of impressive size, reached by flights of steps. They often incorporate imaginative 'portrait' figures

199. Elaborate concrete tomb at Sangkal, Samosir Island, Lake Toba, 1986, combines the forms of house and church steeple, reflecting changing concepts of the afterlife. (Photograph: Roxana Waterson)

245

of the ancestors being commemorated, worked in painted concrete, and sometimes an original urn is visible as well (Plate 19; Figure 200). I was told of one *tugu* which had cost Rp 10 million. Being something of an innovation, not all clans as yet have a *tugu*. The *tugu* is an interesting example of a highly traditional and distinctively local idea recast in a modern, nationalist idiom. That this form of commemorating a larger clan group should have emerged at this particular time is no mere coincidence, but appears to be directly related to the role of clan associations on the *rantau*; it is they who apparently are responsible for this new idea. Sjahrir (1983: 80) links *tugu* building to an increased intensity of ritual performance as part of a 'new social phenomenon' such as has never been seen before in the homeland, but which on the contrary has grown directly out of the urban experience of migrants. The particular architectural idiom selected reflects the process by which ethnic identity is being self-consciously redefined in

the new and wider context of the nation state. Toba investment of money, effort, and artistic creativity in tomb building is a remarkable example of the way a society undergoing far-reaching economic, political, and religious changes may yet succeed in maintaining a thread of continuity through the creative reassembly of elements of its traditional culture.

*   *   *

In selecting these three examples I have attempted to give a picture of some architectural traditions which are truly active, in Williams's sense of the word. They are not fixed and immutable, and the societies which produce them are experiencing many forces of change, but they have an undeniable vitality. In all three cases, what keeps such a tradition vital has as much to do with the ritual importance of houses or tombs, and their important place within kinship systems, as with any purely functional considerations. Migration, a

200. Toba *tugu* or clan monument, erected by the descendants of Raja Namora Titip Manurung at Lumban Ganjang in 1983. These monuments are a relatively new invention, apparently made popular by emigrant Toba, which demonstrate in a modern idiom an entirely traditional concern to honour the ancestors. (Photograph: Roxana Waterson)

246

major factor affecting all three societies, is one source of change and new ideas, but it also gives birth to a new search for ethnic identity, in which the house (or tomb), even as its traditional functions change, can apparently become more important than ever as a symbol of what it means to belong to that society. Migration channels energy and resources back in to the sending society as well as out into a wider world.

In all three cases, two decades or more ago it appeared that the decline of their vernacular styles was irrevocable. In fact, this has not happened and the cultures have shown more resilience than would have been expected. They have flourished while adapting themselves to new circumstances, and there has been a resurgence of building in traditional styles. In all three cases, it is significant that those who have been most successful on the *rantau*, and who now form part of a new national élite, still find it important and desirable to maintain close ties with their places of origin, and often go to enormous lengths to build up their reputations both with villagers at home, and with their ethnic associations on the *rantau*, as generous and prominent members of the ethnic community. The ways in which they seek recognition are partly very traditional ones, such as the funding of houses, tombs, or ceremonies; but the arena in which status is demonstrated has actually grown larger. All the evidence is indicative of the heightened intensity of ethnic feelings among those who, in the cities, become increasingly aware of the need to define an identity in relation to the multiplicity of other cultural groups with whom they come into contact. Finally, one may ask, what of second-generation migrants? While everyone seems to be agreed that children born in cities outside of the homeland do not experience the same feelings toward the place of origin, and the same searching for identity as their parents do—indeed, they may often feel uncomfortable in the villages and may not even speak the language of origin—none the less the effects of this on the overall dynamic should not be overestimated. There will always be a new generation of first-time migrants over whom the origin-place will exercise its pull.

We have now seen the many facets of the role played by houses and other built forms in Austronesian societies. We have discovered the reasons why the house should resonate with so many levels of meaning in these societies, and perhaps gained a clue as to the incredible persistence, over thousands of years and

hundreds of variations, of an ancient style and aesthetic. The continuing vitality of the magnificent indigenous architectures of South-East Asia depends, clearly, on many things: it depends on sensitive assistance and encouragement from governments; it depends on the continued self-confidence of these traditions, their ability to resist the homogenization of Western influences and the lures of an indiscriminately standardizing 'modernization'; but not least, we have seen that it may depend on certain intangible significances of the house, its continued importance within kinship and ritual systems. As these systems rework themselves and adapt to the circumstances of the modern world, they yet find ways to preserve threads of continuity with the past. Old patterns of social relationships, once mirrored in the house, may change, yet houses continue to offer themselves as symbols of a cultural identity, and as sites where that identity can be made real through the celebration of rituals. All of these things have their contribution to make to the maintenance of indigenous architectural forms. If this book, by paying homage to these creations, can make any contribution to an appreciation of their beauty, it will have served some purpose. Once destroyed, these traditions can never be re-created; let us hope that on the contrary, the house will go on living for the next few thousand years!

1. For further explorations of this idea, see Barnes (1977), Esterik (1984), King (1985), and Waterson (1988a). I am grateful also to James Fox for his comments on the persistence of certain Austronesian cultural themes.

2. On the 'mental mobility' of Micronesian and other Polynesian navigators, see D. H. Lewis (1972) and Alkire (1972). In the Melanesian world, the ocean voyages connected with the Kula trade ring are especially famous.

3. Census figures may be an underestimate, since many people of Indonesian origins choose to define themselves simply as 'Malay' for census purposes. The head of Singapore's Bawean Association estimates that numbers may be as high as 100,000.

4. James Fox (personal communication).

5. Versions of this custom are very widespread in South-East Asia (Davis 1973: 55).

6. See Viner (1979) on changes in Batak society.

7. Naim (1973) suggests a much higher figure which Kato points out is inflated by the inclusion of neighbouring districts such as Kerinci, which are only distantly related to Minangkabau.

8. A great deal of literature has shown how ethnicity operates as a boundary-defining mechanism, and as such is likely to become important where ethnic groups most often come into contact with

each other, as is usually the case in cities. See particularly Barth (1969) and Cohen (1974).

9. In very much the same way, the shades of meaning attaching to the terms 'modern' or 'modernization' have shifted over time, and from a primary sense of 'contemporary', have acquired tones both favourable and unfavourable. Interestingly, Williams (1976: 174) notes that the majority of pre-nineteenth century meanings were *unfavourable*, while throughout the nineteenth and still more noticeably in the twentieth century, 'there was a strong movement the other way, until *modern* became virtually equivalent to improved, or satisfactory or efficient'.

10. Williams (1976); van Langenberg (1986). The concept of 'keywords' was developed by Williams (1976: 13) to refer to words which denote important cultural concepts whose meanings, although often taken for granted, have typically shifted over time; they are defined by him as 'significant, binding words in certain activities and their interpretation; they are significant, indicative words in certain forms of thought'.

11. See also Waterson (1984b, 1986) on the role of the house in the construction of Toraja identity, and on its significance within the kinship system and the manner in which rebuilding projects are organized. Torajans disagree about the length of time necessary for a house to come to be viewed as an 'origin-house' by its descendants, but the basic rule seems to be that one rebuilding (that is, two generations) is enough. This is fully in accord with Williams's definition of tradition as an active process.

12. See Waterson (1988a, b) on house carvings of the Toraja.

13. In Buginese areas themselves, the loss of old houses due to guerrilla action was apparently far more severe. So many were burned by Islamic rebels, on the grounds of their association with 'superstitions', that, writes Pelras (1975: 95), 'as a result, almost no evidence is left of the architecture of earlier times'.

14. Prominent Torajans from Jakarta, whom I had occasion to meet in Tana Toraja during my fieldwork when they returned home for ceremonies, showed a great concern to maintain a sense of Toraja identity in the city, especially among the children of migrants who

had been born there. In 1983, they had held a seminar to discuss these matters, and one man was eager that I should address their young people in Jakarta in order to impress upon them the importance of their culture! Unfortunately, I have no information on whether there are organized associations of Torajans in Jakarta, but they certainly maintain informal contacts. There is a small association in Medan, which was founded in 1974 and is called, significantly enough, 'Tongkonan' (origin-house). Membership in 1986 totalled about fifty families, who paid small monthly fees and met for regular prayer meetings. Since a significant proportion of Torajans in Medan are there as students or on official postings, the composition of the association is somewhat shifting, and it is much smaller in scale than the very numerous Batak associations.

15. See Crystal (1974) for a fuller discussion of these events.

16. See Taufik Abdullah (1966) for an excellent analysis by a Minangkabau writer of the historical interweaving of *adat* and Islam in Minangkabau.

17. The percentage of 'return migrants' in West Sumatra (those who are living in their province of birth but who have lived elsewhere prior to that) is about 35 per cent, higher than the national average of 21 per cent (Sundrum 1976: 77).

18. The renewed interest in restoring old houses or building new ones in traditional style has been noted also by others (Audrey Kahin, Anton Alers, personal communications). The popularity of Minangkabau roof forms in municipal buildings also reflects the appeal of this building element, in particular, as an 'instant' statement of Minangkabau identity (although in these cases, the roofs are usually made in zinc and not necessarily constructed according to traditional methods). In a development rather similar to that on which I have remarked in Toraja, Alers notes that the centralization of carpenters in the village of Pandai Sikat, near Bukittinggi, may be leading to a certain standardization of carving styles. Some of the carpenters work from stencils rather than freehand, which tends to introduce a certain rigidity to the style. They can now travel easily to other districts to execute commissions.

19. See Kato (1982) and Tanner (1982).

Bibliography

Abidin, W. B. B. Wan (1981), *The Malay House: Rationale and Change*, Cambridge, Mass.: MIT Press.

Acciaioli, G. (n.d.), 'Searching for Good Fortune: Knowledge and Fate among the Bugis of Lake Lindu' (unpublished paper), Canberra (ANU).

Adams, M. J. (1974), 'Symbols of the Organised Community in East Sumba, Indonesia', *Bijdragen tot de Taal-, Land- en Volkenkunde*, 130(4), pp. 324–47.

_____ (1980), 'Structural Aspects of East Sumbanese Art', in J. J. Fox (ed.), *The Flow of Life: Essays on Eastern Indonesia*, Cambridge, Mass.: Harvard University Press, pp. 208–20.

Adriani, N. and Kruyt, A. C. (1951), *De Bare'e-Sprekende Toradja's van Midden-Celebes* (The Bare'e-speaking Toraja of Central Celebes) (2nd edn.), 3 vols., Amsterdam: North-Holland.

Alkire, W. H. (1972), 'Concepts of Order in South-East Asia and Micronesia', *Comparative Studies of Society and History*, 14(4), pp. 484–93.

Anderson, B. R. O'G. (1972), 'The Idea of Power in Javanese Culture', in C. Holt (ed.), *Culture and Politics in Indonesia*, Ithaca: Cornell University Press, pp. 1–69.

Arndt, P. (1951), *Religion auf Ostflores, Adonara und Solor* (Religion in East Flores, Adonara and Solor), Studia Instituti Anthropos, Vol. 1, Wien-Mödling: Missionsdruckerei St. Gabriel.

Austin, M. R. (1988), 'The Gable End in Oceania', Paper presented to the International Symposium on Traditional Dwellings and Settlements in a Comparative Perspective, University of California, Berkeley (April).

Avé, J. B. and King, V. T. (1986), *The People of the Weeping Forest: Tradition and Change in Borneo*, Leiden: National Museum of Ethnology.

Bambowo Laiya (1980), *Solidaritas Kekeluargaan dalam salah satu Masyarakat Desa di Nias—Indonesia* (Kinship Solidarity in a Village Community in Nias—Indonesia), Yogyakarta: Gadjah Mada University Press.

Barbier, J. P. (1983), *Tobaland: The Shreds of Tradition*, Geneva: Barbier-Müller Museum.

Barnes, R. (1974), *Kédang: A Study of the Collective Thought of an Eastern Indonesian People*, Oxford: Clarendon Press.

_____ (1977), 'Mata in Austronesia', *Oceania*, 47(4), pp. 300–19.

Barraud, C. (1979), *Tanebar-Evav: Une Société de Maisons tournée vers le Large* (Tanebar-Evav: A Society of Houses Oriented Towards the Sea), Cambridge: Cambridge University Press/Editions de la Maison des Sciences de l'Homme.

Barth, F. (1969), *Ethnic Groups and Boundaries*, London: Allen and Unwin.

Bartlett, H. H. (1934), *The Sacred Edifices of the Batak of Sumatra*, Ann Arbor: University of Michigan Press.

Bateson, G. (1973) (1949), 'Bali: The Value System of a Steady State', reprinted in G. Bateson, *Steps to an Ecology of Mind*, St. Albans: Paladin, pp. 80–100.

Beauclair, I. de (1958), 'Fighting and Weapons of the Yami of Botel Tobago', *Bulletin of the Institute of Ethnology (Academia Sinica)*, 5, pp. 87–109.

_____ (1969), 'Gold and Silver on Botel Tobago: The Silver Helmet of the Yami', *Bulletin of the Institute of Ethnology (Academia Sinica)*, 27, pp. 121–7.

Beccari, O. (1902), *Nelle Foreste di Borneo: Viaggi e Ricerche di un Naturalista* (In the Forests of Borneo: Travels and Researches of a Naturalist), Florence: Landi.

Becker, A. and Yengoyan, A. (eds.) (1979), *The Imagination of Reality: Essays in Southeast Asian Coherence Systems*, Norwood: Ablex.

Bekkum, W. van (1946), *Manggaraische Kunst* (Manggarai Art), Koninklijke Vereeniging Indisch Instituut Te Amsterdam, Leiden: Brill.

Bellwood, P. (1978), *Man's Conquest of the Pacific: The Prehistory of South-East Asia and Oceania*, Auckland: Collins.

_____ (1985), *Prehistory of the Indo-Malaysian Archipelago*, North Ryde, New South Wales: Academic Press.

Benedict, P. (1975), *Austro-Thai Language and Culture: With a Glossary of Roots*, New Haven: Human Relations Area Files Press.

_____ (1986), *Japanese/Austro-Thai*, Michigan: Karoma.

Benjamin, G. (1979), 'Indigenous Religious Systems of the Malay Peninsula', in A. Becker and A. Yengoyan (eds.), *The Imagination of Reality: Essays in Southeast Asian Coherence Systems*, Norwood: Ablex, pp. 9–27.

_____ (1980), 'Semang, Senoi, Malay: Culture-History, Kinship and Consciousness in the Malay Peninsula' (unpublished paper), Singapore.

_____ (1987), 'Notes on the Deep Sociology of Religion', National University of Singapore, Department of Sociology Working Paper No. 85.

Bernatzik, H. A. (1947), *Akha und Meau* (Akha and Miao), 2 vols., Innsbruck: Wagner'sche Universitätsbuchdruckerei.

_____ (1958), *The Spirits of the Yellow Leaves*, London: Robert Hale.

Bird, I. (1883), *The Golden Chersonese, and the Way Thither*, London: John Murray; reprinted Kuala Lumpur: Oxford University Press, 1980.

Bloch, M. (1971), *Placing the Dead: Tombs, Ancestral Villages, and Kinship Organisation in Madagascar*, London: Seminar Press.

_____ (1974), 'Symbol, Song, Dance and Features of Articulation: Is Religion an Extreme Form of Traditional Authority?', *European Journal of Sociology*, 15, pp. 15–81.

_____ (1977), 'The Past and the Present in the Present', *Man*, 12, pp. 278–92.

Blust, R. (1976), 'Austronesian Culture History: Some Linguistic Inferences and their Relations to the Archaeological Record', *World Archaeology*, 8, pp. 19–43.

_____ (1980), 'Early Austronesian Social Organisation: The Evidence of Language', *Current Anthropology*, 21(2), pp. 205–47; 21(3), pp. 415–19; 22(2), pp. 184–5.

Boer, D. W. N. de (1920), *Het Niassche Huis* (The Nias House), Mededeelingen van het Encyclopaedisch Bureau Betreffende de Buitengewesten 25, Batavia: G. Kolff.

_____ (1946), 'Zeden, Gewoonten en Wetten van Nai Pospos' (Manners, Customs and Laws of Nai Pospos), *Bijdragen tot de Taal-, Land- en Volkenkunde*, 103, pp. 339–457.

Bonneff, M. and Voisset, G. (1980), ' "Guide Archipel" IV: L'Ile de Sumba' ('Archipel Guide' IV: The Island of Sumba), *Archipel*, 19, pp. 119–41.

Bourdieu, P. (1973) (1971), 'The Berber House', in M. Douglas (ed.), *Rules and Meanings*, Harmondsworth: Penguin, pp. 98–110.

_____ (1977), *Outline of a Theory of Practice*, Cambridge: Cambridge University Press.

Bowen, J. (1984), 'Death and the History of Islam in Highland Aceh', *Indonesia*, 38, pp. 21–38.

Brody, H. (1987), *Living Arctic*, London: Faber and Faber.

Bruner, E. (1970) (1963), 'Medan: The Role of Kinship in an Indonesian City', in W. Mangin (ed.), *Peasants in Cities: Readings in the Anthropology of Urbanization*, Boston: Houghton Mifflin, pp. 122–34.

_____ (1972), 'The Expression of Ethnicity in Indonesia', South-East Asia Development Advisory Group, Papers on Problems of Development in South-East Asia, 72(9), New York: SEADAG/The Asia Society.

Cameron, E. (1985), 'Ancestor Motifs of the Paiwan', in J. A. Feldman (ed.), *The Eloquent Dead: Ancestral Sculpture of Indonesia and Southeast Asia*, Los Angeles: UCLA Museum of Cultural History, pp. 161–70.

Cameron, E. and Sumnik-Dekovich, E. (1985), 'Magamaog: Benevolent Ancestor of the Yami', in J. A. Feldman (ed.), *The Eloquent Dead: Ancestral Sculpture of Indonesia and Southeast Asia*, Los Angeles: UCLA Museum of Cultural History, pp. 171–4.

Carey, I. (1976), *Orang Asli: The Aboriginal Tribes of Peninsular Malaysia*, Kuala Lumpur: Oxford University Press.

Castles, L. (1967), 'The Ethnic Profile of Jakarta', *Indonesia*, 3, pp. 153–204.

_____ (1975), 'Statelessness and Stateforming Tendencies among the Batak before Colonial Rule', in L. Castles and A. Reid (eds.), *Precolonial State Systems in South-East Asia*, Kuala Lumpur: Malayan Branch of the Royal Asiatic Society, pp. 67–76.

Cederroth, S. (1981), *The Spell of the Ancestors and the Power of Mekkah: A Sasak Community on Lombok*, Göteborg: Acta Universitatis Gothoburgensis.

Charernsupkul, A. and Temiyabandha, V. (1979), *Northern Thai Domestic Architecture and Rituals in House Building*, Bangkok: Fine Arts Commission of the Association of Siamese Architects.

Charles, M. (1973), 'Additional Reconstructions to be added to Zorc and Charles (1971) "Proto-Philippine Finder List" ' (typescript), Ithaca: Cornell.

Chin, L. (1980), *Cultural Heritage of Sarawak*, Kuching: Sarawak Museum.

Clamagirand, B. (1975), 'La Maison Ema (Timor Portugais)' (The Ema House (Portuguese Timor)), *Asie du Sud-Est et Monde Insulindien*, 6(2–3), pp. 35–60.

_____ (1980), 'The Social Organisation of the Ema of Timor', in J. J. Fox (ed.), *The Flow of Life: Essays on Eastern Indonesia*, Cambridge, Mass.: Harvard University Press, pp. 134–51.

_____ (1982), *Marobo: Une Société Ema de Timor* (Marobo: An Ema Society of Timor), Paris: SELAF.

Clément, P. and Charpentier, S. (1974), 'Notes sur l'Habitation sur Pilotis en Asie du Sud-Est' (Notes on the Pile Dwelling in South-East Asia), *Asie du Sud-Est et Monde Insulindien*, 5(2), pp. 13–24.

_____ (1975a), 'Pour une Approche Ethno-architecturale de l'Habitation' (Towards an Ethno-architectural Approach to the Dwelling), in *Histoire et Theories de L'Architecture*, Paris: Institut de l'Environnement, pp. 127–30.

_____ (1975b), 'Deux Systemes de Construction Lao: Contribution a l'Etude des Charpentes en Asie du Sud-Est' (Two Lao Systems of Construction: A Contribution to the Study of House-framing Methods in South-East Asia), *Asie du Sud-Est et Monde Insulindien*, 6(2–3), pp. 101–32.

Cohen, A. (1974), *Urban Ethnicity*, London: Tavistock.

Condominas, G. (1977) (1957), *We have Eaten the Forest: The Story of a Montagnard Village in the Central Highlands of Vietnam*, New York: Hill and Wang.

Conklin, H. C. (1980), *Ethnographic Atlas of Ifugao: A Study of Environment, Culture and Society in Northern Luzon*, New Haven: Yale University Press.

Cooley, F. L. (1962), *Ambonese Adat: a General Description*, New Haven: Yale University Press.

Coulaud, D. (1982), 'The Zafimaniry House: A Witness of the Traditional Houses of the Highlands of Madagascar', in K. Izikowitz and P. Sørensen (eds.), *The House in East and Southeast Asia: Anthropological and Architectural Aspects*, London: Curzon, pp. 188–97.

Covarrubias, M. (1937), *Island of Bali*, New York: Knopf; reprinted Singapore: Oxford University Press, 1987.

Crocker, W. M. (1881), 'Notes on Sarawak and Northern Borneo', *Proceedings of the Royal Geographical Society*, pp. 193–216.

Crystal, E. (1974), 'Cooking Pot Politics: A Toraja Village Study', *Indonesia*, 18, pp. 119–51.

_____ (1979), 'Mountain Ikats and Coastal Silks: Traditional Textiles in South Sulawesi', in B. Solyom and G. Solyom (eds.), *Threads of Tradition: Textiles of Indonesia and Sarawak*, Berkeley: University of California Press.

Cunningham, C. (1964), 'Order in the Atoni House', *Bijdragen tot de Taal-, Land- en Volkenkunde*, 120, pp. 34–68.

Dall, G. (1982), 'The Traditional Acehnese House', in J. Maxwell (ed.), *The Malay-Islamic World of Sumatra*, Melbourne: Monash University Centre of South-East Asian Studies, pp. 34–61.

Danandjaja, J. (1971), 'Acculturation in Tano Niha', *Kroeber Anthropological Society Papers*, 44, pp. 1–29.

Davis, R. (1973), 'Muang Matrifocality', *Journal of the Siam Society*, 61(2), pp. 53–62.

_____ (1984), *Muang Metaphysics: A Study of Northern Thai Myth and Ritual*, Bangkok: Pandora.

Djauhari Sumintardja (1973), 'Looking for a Traditional House of West Java', *Masalah Bangunan*, 18(1), pp. 10–13.

_____ (1979), 'The Badui of West Java: On the Crossroads of Development', *Prisma*, 12, pp. 34–45.

Domenig, G. (1980), *Tektonik im Primitiven Dachbau* (Tectonics in Primitive Roof Construction), Zürich: Institut Gaudenz/ETH.

Douglas, M. (1972), 'Symbolic Orders in the Use of Domestic Space', in P. Ucko *et al.* (eds.), *Man, Settlement and Urbanism*, Cambridge, Mass.: Schenkman, pp. 513–21.

Dournes, J. (1971), 'Aspects de l'Habitat et Techniques de Construction des Sré aux Jörai' (Aspects of Habitat and Techniques of Construction from the Sré to the Jörai), *Objets et Mondes*, 11(3), pp. 281–320.

Drabbe, P. (1940), *Het Leven van den Tanembarees: Ethnografische Studie over het Tanembareesche Volk* (The Life of the Tanimbarese: Ethnographic Study of the Tanimbarese People), Internationales Archiv für Ethnographie, Supplement to Vol. 37, Leiden.

Drexler, A. (1955), *The Architecture of Japan*, New York: Museum of Modern Art.

Duly, C. (1979), *The Houses of Mankind*, London: Thames and Hudson.

Dumarçay, J. (1981), 'La Faitière Tendue (Histoire d'une Technique)' (The Extended Ridge (History of a Technique)), *Bulletin de l'Ecole Française d'Extrême-Orient*, 70, pp. 231–51.

_____ (1985), *The House in South-East Asia*, Singapore: Oxford University Press.

Ellen, R. (1978), *Nuaulu Settlement and Ecology*, The Hague: Nijhoff.

_____ (1986), 'Microcosm, Macrocosm and the Nuaulu House: concerning the Reductionist Fallacy as applied to Metaphorical Levels', *Bijdragen tot de Taal-, Land- en Volkenkunde*, 142(1), pp. 2–30.

Endicott, K. (1970), *An Analysis of Malay Magic*, London: Cambridge University Press; reprinted Kuala Lumpur: Oxford University Press, 1981.

Errington, F. (1984), *Manners and Meaning in West Sumatra: The Social Context of Consciousness*, New Haven: Yale University Press.

Errington, S. (1979), 'The Cosmic House of the Buginese', *Asia* (January–February), pp. 8–14.

_____ (1983a), 'Embodied *Sumange* in Luwu', *Journal of Asian Studies*, 42(3), pp. 545–70.

_____ (1983b), 'The Place of Regalia in Luwu', in L. Gesick (ed.), *Centers, Symbols and Hierarchies: Essays on the Classical States of South-East Asia*, New Haven: Yale University Centre for South-East Asian Studies, pp. 194–241.

_____ (1984), 'The Construction of Gender in Southeast Asia: A Call for Papers' (unpublished paper), University of California, Santa Cruz.

Esterik, P. van (1984), 'Continuities and Transformations in Southeast Asian Symbolism: A Case Study from Thailand', *Bijdragen tot de Taal-, Land- en Volkenkunde*, 140(1), pp. 77–91.

Etienne, M. and Leacock, E. (eds.) (1980), *Women and Colonization: Anthropological Perpectives*, New York: Praeger.

Evans, I. H. N. (1951), 'Dusun and Other "House-horns"', *Journal of the Malayan Branch of the Royal Asiatic Society*, 24(1), pp. 165–8.

Feeley-Harnik, G. (1980), 'The Sakalava House (Madagascar)', *Anthropos*, 75, pp. 559–85.

Feldman, J. A. (1977), 'The Architecture of Nias, Indonesia, with Special Reference to Bawömataluo Village', Ph.D. thesis, Columbia.

_____ (1979), 'The House as World in Bawömataluo, South Nias', in E. Bruner and J. Becker (eds.), *Art, Ritual and Society in Indonesia*, Athens, Ohio: Ohio University Centre for International Studies.

_____ (1984), 'Dutch Galleons and South Nias Palaces', *RES*, 7(8), pp. 21–32.

_____ (1985), *The Eloquent Dead: Ancestral Sculpture of*

Indonesia and Southeast Asia, Los Angeles: UCLA Museum of Cultural History.

Fischer, H. Th. (1931), 'Het Begrip "mana" bij de Toba-Bataks' (The Concept of 'Mana' among the Toba Batak), *Koloniaal Tijdschrift*, 20, pp. 592-604.

Forbes, H. O. (1885), *A Naturalist's Wanderings in the Eastern Archipelago*, London: Sampson Low, Marston, Searle and Rivington; reprinted Singapore: Oxford University Press, 1989.

Forth, G. (1981), *Rindi: An Ethnographic Study of a Traditional Domain in Eastern Sumba*, The Hague: Nijhoff.

Fox, J. J. (1977), *Harvest of the Palm: Ecological Change in Eastern Indonesia*, Cambridge, Mass.: Harvard University Press.

_____ (1980), *The Flow of Life: Essays on Eastern Indonesia*, Cambridge, Mass.: Harvard University Press.

_____ (1985), 'Possible Models of Early Austronesian Social Organisation', Paper presented at 12th Congress of the Indo-Pacific Prehistory Association, Penablanca, Philippines.

_____ (1987), 'The House as a Type of Social Organisation on the Island of Roti', in *De la Hutte au Palais: Sociétés 'à Maison' en Asie du Sud-est Insulaire* (From Hut to Palace: 'House Societies' in Island South-East Asia), Paris: CNRS, pp. 171-8.

Francillon, G. (1980), 'Incursions upon Wehali: A Modern History of an Ancient Empire', in J. J. Fox (ed.): *The Flow of Life: Essays on Eastern Indonesia*, Cambridge, Mass.: Harvard University Press, pp. 248-65.

Fraser, D. (1966), *The Many Faces of Primitive Art: A Critical Anthology*, Englewood Cliffs: Prentice-Hall.

_____ (1968), *Village Planning in the Primitive World*, New York: Brazilier.

Freeman, D. (1970), *Report on the Iban*, London: Athlone.

Fürer-Haimendorf, C. von (1976), *Return to the Naked Nagas*, New Delhi: Vikas.

Geddes, W. R. (1957), *Nine Dayak Nights*, London: Oxford University Press; reprinted Singapore, Oxford University Press, 1985.

Geertz, C. (1959), 'Form and Variation in Balinese Village Structure', *American Anthropologist*, 61, pp. 991-1012.

_____ (1980), *Negara: The Theatre State in 19th-century Bali*, Princeton: Princeton University Press.

Geertz, H. and Geertz, C. (1975), *Kinship in Bali*, Chicago: University of Chicago Press.

Gelman Taylor, J. (1983), *The Social World of Batavia: European and Eurasian in Dutch Asia*, Madison: University of Wisconsin Press.

Gibbs, P. (1987), *Building a Malay House*, Singapore: Oxford University Press.

Gittinger, M. (1976), 'The Ship Textiles of South Sumatra: Functions and Design System', *Bijdragen tot de Taal-, Land-en Volkenkunde*, 132(2-3), pp. 207-27.

_____ (1979), *Splendid Symbols: Textiles and Tradition in Indonesia*, Washington, DC: The Textile Museum; reprinted Singapore: Oxford University Press, 1985.

Glover, I. (1979), 'The Late Prehistoric Period in Indonesia', in R. Smith and W. Watson (eds.), *Early South East Asia*, Oxford: Oxford University Press, pp. 167-84.

Glover, I., Bronson, B., and Bayard, D. (1979), 'Comment on "Megaliths" in Southeast Asia', in R. Smith and W. Watson (eds.), *Early South East Asia*, Oxford: Oxford University Press, pp. 253-4.

Gonda, J. (1973) (1952), *Sanskrit in Indonesia*, New Delhi: International Academy of Indian Culture.

Gordon, J. (1980), 'The Marriage Nexus among the Manggarai of West Flores', in J. J. Fox (ed.), *The Flow of Life: Essays on Eastern Indonesia*, Cambridge, Mass.: Harvard University Press, pp. 48-67.

Griaule, M. (1965), *Conversations with Ogotemmêli*, Oxford: Oxford University Press, for International African Institute.

Guidoni, E. (1978), *Primitive Architecture*, New York: Abrams.

Gunawan Alif, M. (1985), 'Bangunan Tradisional Sasak' (Traditional Sasak Architecture), *Asri*, 32, pp. 43-5, 61-4.

Gunawan Tjahjono (1988), 'Center and Duality in Javanese Dwellings', Paper presented to International Symposium on Traditional Dwellings and Settlements in a Comparative Perspective, University of California, Berkeley (April).

Guy, J. (1987), 'Commerce, Power and Mythology: Indian Textiles in Indonesia', *Indonesia Circle*, 42, pp. 57-75.

Hanbury-Tenison, R. (1975), *A Pattern of Peoples: A Journey among the Tribes of Indonesia's Outer Islands*, London: Angus and Robertson.

Hauser-Schäublin, B. (1985), 'Blockbauten der Sa'dan Toraja: Materialen zur Geschichten der Toraja aufgrund von frühen Hausformen' (Log Constructions of the Sa'dan Toraja: Contributions to the History of Toraja Based upon Early House Forms), *Ethnologica Helvetica*, 10, pp. 59-82.

Heine-Geldern, R. von (1942), 'Conceptions of State and Kingship in South-East Asia', *Far Eastern Quarterly*, 2, pp. 15-30.

_____ (1947), 'The Drum Named Makalamau', *India Antiqua*, pp. 167-79.

_____ (1966), 'Some Tribal Art Styles of South-East Asia: An Experiment in Art History', in D. Fraser (ed.), *The Many Faces of Primitive Art: A Critical Anthology*, Englewood Cliffs: Prentice-Hall, pp. 165-221.

Henriksen, M. (1982), 'The First Excavated Prehistoric House Site in South-East Asia', in K. Izikowitz and P. Sørensen (eds.), *The House in East and Southeast Asia: Anthropological and Architectural Aspects*, London: Curzon, pp. 17-24.

Hertz, R. (1907), 'Contribution à une Etude sur la Représentation Collective de la Mort' (Contribution to a Study of the

Collective Representation of Death), *Année Sociologique*, 10, pp. 48-137.

Hicks, D. (1976), *Tetum Ghosts and Kin*, Palo Alto: Mayfield.

_____ (1984), *A Maternal Religion: The Role of Women in Tetum Myth and Ritual*, Northern Illinois University, Centre for Southeast Asian Studies: Special Report 22.

Hilton, R. N. (1956), 'The Basic Malay House', *Journal of the Malayan Branch of the Royal Asiatic Society*, 29, pp. 134-55.

Hitchcock, M. J. (1983), 'Technology and Society in Bima, Sumbawa, with Special Reference to House Building and Textile Manufacture', D.Phil. thesis, Oxford.

_____ (1986), 'Basket Makers of the Highlands: The Dou Wawo of Bima, Sumbawa', *Expedition*, 28(1), pp. 22-8.

Hobart, M. (1978), 'The Path of the Soul: The Legitimacy of Nature in Balinese Conceptions of Space', in G. Milner (ed.), *Natural Symbols in South-East Asia*, London: School of Oriental and African Studies, pp. 5-28.

Hobhouse, H. (1985), *Seeds of Change: Five Plants that Transformed Mankind*, London: Sidgwick and Jackson.

Hoffman, C. L. (1981), 'Some Notes on the Origins of the "Punan" of Borneo', *Borneo Research Bulletin*, 13(2), pp. 71-4.

Horridge, G. A. (1986), 'A Summary of Indonesian Canoe and Prahu Ceremonies', *Indonesia Circle*, 39, pp. 3-17.

Hoskins, J. A. (1986), 'So My Name Shall Live: Stone-Dragging and Grave-Building in Kodi, West Sumba', *Bijdragen tot de Taal-, Land- en Volkenkunde*, 142(1), pp. 31-51.

_____ (1987), 'Entering the Bitter House: Spirit Worship and Conversion in West Sumba', in R. Kipp and S. Rodgers (eds.), *Indonesian Religions in Transition*, Tucson: University of Arizona Press, pp. 136-60.

Howe, L. (1983), 'An Introduction to the Cultural Study of Traditional Balinese Architecture', *Archipel*, 25, pp. 137-58.

Hudson, A. (1972), *Padju Epat: The Ma'anyan of Indonesian Borneo*, New York: Holt, Rinehart and Winston.

Huender, W. (1929), 'Het Karo-Bataksche Huis' (The Karo Batak House), *Bijdragen tot de Taal-, Land- en Volkenkunde*, 85, pp. 511-23.

Hugh-Jones, C. (1978), 'Food for Thought: Patterns of Production and Consumption in Pira-Parana Society', in J. La Fontaine (ed.), *Sex and Age as Principles of Social Differentiation*, London: Academic Press, pp. 41-66.

_____ (1979), *From the Milk River: Spatial and Temporal Processes in Northwest Amazonia*, Cambridge: Cambridge University Press.

Hugh-Jones, S. (1979), *The Palm and the Pleiades: Initiation and Cosmology in Northwest Amazonia*, Cambridge: Cambridge University Press.

_____ (1985), 'The Maloca: A World in a House', in E. Carmichael *et al.*, *The Hidden Peoples of the Amazon*, London: Museum of Mankind, pp. 78-93.

Humphrey, C. (1974), 'Inside a Mongolian Tent', *New Society* (31 October), pp. 273-5.

_____ (1978), 'Women, Taboo and the Suppression of Attention', in S. Ardener (ed.), *Defining Females: The Nature of Women in Society*, London: Croom Helm, pp. 89-108.

Iijima, S. (1979), 'Ethnic Identity and Sociocultural Change among Sgaw Karen in Northern Thailand', in C. Keyes (ed.), *Ethnic Adaptation and Identity: The Karen on the Thai Frontier with Burma*, Philadelphia: Institute for the Study of Human Issues, pp. 99-118.

Izikowitz, K. and Sørensen, P. (eds.) (1982), *The House in East and Southeast Asia: Anthropological and Architectural Aspects*, London: Curzon.

Jaspan, M. (1964), *From Patriliny to Matriliny*, Ph.D. thesis, Canberra.

Jeffery, P. (1979), *Frogs in a Well: Indian Women in Purdah*, London: Zed.

Jenks, A. (1905), *The Bontoc Igorot*, Philippine Islands, Department of the Interior, Ethnological Survey Publications.

Josselin de Jong, J. P. B. de (1952), *Lévi-Strauss's Theory on Kinship and Marriage*, Leiden: Brill.

Josselin de Jong, P. E. de (1951), *Minangkabau and Negri Sembilan: Socio-Political Structure in Indonesia*, Leiden: Ijdo.

_____ (ed.) (1975), *Social Organisation of Minangkabau*, Publication No. 8, Instituut voor Culturele Antropologie en Sociologie der niet-Westerse Volken, University of Leiden.

_____ (ed.) (1977), *Structural Anthropology in the Netherlands*, The Hague: Nijhoff.

Jumsai, S. (1988), *Naga: Cultural Origins in Siam and the West Pacific*, Singapore: Oxford University Press.

Just, P. (1984), 'Houses and House-Building in Donggo', *Expedition*, 26(4), pp. 30-46.

Kana, N. (1980), 'The Order and Significance of the Savunese House', in J. J. Fox (ed.), *The Flow of Life: Essays on Eastern Indonesia*, Cambridge, Mass.: Harvard University Press, pp. 221-30.

Kano, T. and Segawa, K. (1956), *An Illustrated Ethnography of Formosan Aborigines, Vol. I: The Yami*, Tokyo: Maruzen.

Kartomi, M. (1981), 'Lovely when Heard from Afar: Mandailing Ideas of Musical Beauty', in M. Kartomi (ed.), *Five Essays on the Indonesian Arts*, Melbourne: Monash University Press, pp. 1-16.

Kato, T. (1982), *Matriliny and Migration: Evolving Minangkabau Traditions in Indonesia*, Ithaca: Cornell University Press.

Kaudern, W. (1925), *Ethnographical Studies in Celebes: Results of the Author's Expedition to Celebes 1917-1920. Vol. I: Structures and Settlements in Central Celebes*, Göteborg: Elanders Boktryckeri Aktiebolog.

_____ (1944), *Ethnographical Studies in Celebes: Results of the Author's Expedition to Celebes 1917-1920. Vol. VI: Art in Central Celebes*, Göteborg: Elanders Boktryckeri Aktiebolog.

King, V. T. (1976a), 'Punan—Borneo', *Family of Man Encyclopaedia*, 6(81), pp. 2252-4.

_____ (1976b), 'More on Maloh Designs', *Sarawak Museum Journal*, 24, pp. 165-72.

_____ (ed.) (1978), *Essays on Borneo Societies*, Oxford: Oxford University Press.

_____ (1980), 'Symbols of Social Differentiation: A Comparative Investigation of Signs, the Signified and Symbolic Meanings in Borneo', *Anthropos*, 80, pp. 125-52.

_____ (1985), 'Symbolism and Material Culture: A Footnote for Penny van Esterik', *Bijdragen tot de Taal-, Land- en Volkenkunde*, 141(1), pp. 142-7.

Kis-Jovak, J. (1980), *Autochthone Architektur auf Siberut* (Indigenous Architecture of Siberut), Zürich: ETH.

Komanyi, M. (1972), 'The Real and Ideal Participation in Decision Making of Iban Women', Ph.D. thesis, New York.

Kompas (1985), 'Kampung Orang Bawean di Kuala Lumpur' (A Bawean Community in Kuala Lumpur) (2 April).

Kooijman, S. (1942), 'Sahala, Tondi: De Begrippen "Mana" en "Hau" bij enkele Sumatraanse Volken' (Sahala, Tondi: The Concepts of 'Mana' and 'Hau' among Some Sumatran Peoples), Ph.D. thesis, Utrecht.

Kraisri Nimmanahaeminda (1979), 'Ham Yon, the Magic Testicles: Aspects of Northern Thai Architecture', in *The Artistic Heritage of Thailand*, Bangkok: National Museum Volunteers and Sawaddi Magazine, pp. 127-30.

Kroeber, A. (1925), *Handbook of the Indians of California*, Bureau of American Ethnology, Bulletin 78, Washington, DC.

Krug, S. and Duboff, S. (1982), *The Kamthieng House: Its History and Collections*, Bangkok: Siam Society.

Kruyt, A. (1938), *De West-Toradja's op Midden-Celebes* (The West Toraja of Central Celebes), 5 vols., Amsterdam: Verhandelingen der Koninklijke Nederlandse Akademie van Wetenschappen.

La Fontaine, J. (1981), 'The Domestication of the Savage Male', *Man*, 16, pp. 333-49.

Langenberg, M. van (1986), 'Analysing Indonesia's New Order State: A Keywords Approach', *Review of Indonesian and Malaysian Affairs*, 20(2), pp. 1-47.

Lansing, J. (1974), *Evil in the Morning of the World*, Michigan Papers in South and South-East Asia, 6.

Leach, E. R. (1950), *Social Science Research in Sarawak*, London: HMSO.

Lebar, F. (ed.) (1972), *Ethnic Groups of Insular South-East Asia, Vol. I: Indonesia, Andaman Islands and Madagascar*, New Haven: Human Relations Area Files Press.

Lévi-Strauss, C. (1963), 'Do Dual Organizations Exist?', in his *Structural Anthropology*, Harmondsworth: Penguin, pp. 132-63.

_____ (1969), *The Elementary Structures of Kinship*, London: Eyre and Spottiswoode.

_____ (1983), *The Way of the Masks*, London: Cape.

Lewcock, R. and Brans, G. (1975), 'The Boat as an Architectural Symbol', in P. Oliver (ed.), *Shelter, Sign and Symbol*, London: Barrie and Jenkins, pp. 107-16.

Lewis, D. H. (1972), *We, the Navigators: The Ancient Art of Landfinding in the Pacific*, Canberra: Australian National University Press.

Lewis, E. D. (1983), 'Opposition, Classification and Social Reproduction: Gender as Operator in Tana Ai Thought', Working Paper presented to the Research Seminar on Gender, Ideology and Social Reproduction, Canberra: Department of Anthropology, Research School of Pacific Studies, Australian National University (August).

Lewis, P. and Lewis, E. (1984), *Peoples of the Golden Triangle: Six Tribes in Thailand*, London: Thames and Hudson.

Li Yih-Yuan (1957), 'On the Platform-House found among some Pingpu Tribes in Formosa', *Bulletin of the Institute of Ethnology (Academia Sinica)*, 3, pp. 139-44.

Lim Jee Yuan (1987), *The Malay House: Rediscovering Malaysia's Indigenous Shelter System*, Penang: Institut Masyarakat.

Lineton, J. (1975), 'The Bugis of South Sulawesi: An Indonesian Society and its Universe', Ph.D. thesis, London, School of Oriental and African Studies.

Ling Shun-Sheng (1958), 'Ancestor Temple and Earth Altar among the Formosan Aborigines', *Bulletin of the Institute of Ethnology (Academia Sinica)*, 6, pp. 1-57.

Linzey, M. (1988), 'Speaking to and Talking about: Maori and European-educated Comportments towards Architecture', Paper presented at the International Symposium on Traditional Dwellings and Settlements in a Comparative Perspective, Berkeley (April).

Loeb, E. (1935), *Sumatra: Its History and People*, Vienna: University of Vienna Institut für Volkenkunde; reprinted Singapore: Oxford University Press, 1989.

Lovric, B. (1987), 'The Art of Healing and the Craft of Witches in a "Hot Earth" Village', *Review of Indonesian and Malaysian Affairs*, 21(1), pp. 68-99.

Lundstrom-Bürghoorn, W. (1981), *Minahasa Civilization: A Tradition of Change*, Göteborg: Acta Universitatis Gothoburgensis.

MacCormack, C. and Strathern, M. (eds.) (1980), *Nature, Culture and Gender*, Cambridge: Cambridge University Press.

McGovern, J. (1922), *Among the Headhunters of Formosa*, Boston: Small.

McKinnon, S. (1983), 'Hierarchy, Alliance and Exchange in the Tanimbar Islands', Ph.D. thesis, Chicago.

Manguin, P. (1986), 'Shipshape Societies: Boat Symbolism and Political Systems in Insular Southeast Asia', in D. Marr and A. Milner (eds.), *Southeast Asia in the 9th to 14th Centuries*, Singapore: Institute of Southeast Asian Studies/ Australian National University.

Marshall, L. (1973) (1960), 'Each Side of the Fire', in M. Douglas (ed.), *Rules and Meanings*, Harmondsworth: Penguin, pp. 95–7.

Marsden, W. (1966) (1811), *The History of Sumatra*, Kuala Lumpur: Oxford University Press; reprinted Singapore: Oxford University Press, 1986.

Mashman, V. (1986), 'Warriors and Weavers: A Study of Gender Relations among the Iban of Sarawak', MA thesis, Kent.

Matras-Troubetzkoy, J. (1975), 'Eléments pour l'Etude du Village et de l'Habitation Brou (Cambodge—Province de Ratanakiri)' (Elements for the Study of Brou Villages and Dwellings (Cambodia—Province of Ratanakiri), *Asie du Sud-Est et Monde Insulindien*, 6(2–3), pp. 201–28.

Mernissi, F. (1975), *Beyond the Veil: Male–Female Dynamics in a Modern Muslim Society*, New York: Schenkman.

Metcalf, P. (1977), 'Berawan Mausoleums', *Sarawak Museum Journal*, 24, pp. 121–36.

_____ (1982), *A Borneo Journey into Death: Berawan Eschatology from its Rituals*, Philadelphia: University of Pennsylvania Press.

Miles, D. (1964), 'The Ngadju Longhouse', *Oceania*, 35(1), pp. 43–57.

_____ (1976), *Cutlass and Crescent Moon: A Case Study of Social and Political Change in Outer Indonesia*, Sydney: Centre for Asian Studies, University of Sydney.

Moertono, S. (1968), *State and Statecraft in Old Java*, Ithaca: Cornell University Press.

Morgan, L. H. (1965) (1881), *Houses and House Life of the American Aborigines*, Chicago: University of Chicago Press.

_____ (1877), *Ancient Society; or, Researches in the Lines of Human Progress from Savagery through Barbarism to Civilization*, Chicago: Kerr.

Mubin Sheppard, Tan Sri Haji (1969), 'Traditional Malay House Forms in Trengganu and Kelantan', *Journal of the Malayan Branch of the Royal Asiatic Society*, 42(2), pp. 1–28.

_____ (1972), 'Palaces and Wood Carving', in his *Taman Indera (A Royal Pleasure Ground): Malay Decorative Arts and Pastimes*, Kuala Lumpur: Oxford University Press, pp. 28–41; reprinted Singapore: Oxford University Press, 1986.

Naim, M. (1971), *Merantau: Causes and Effects of Minangkabau Voluntary Migration*, Singapore: Institute of Southeast Asian Studies, Occasional Paper No. 5.

_____ (1973), 'Merantau: Minangkabau Voluntary Migration', Ph.D. thesis, Singapore.

Nas, P. (ed.) (1986), *The Indonesian City: Studies in Urban Development and Planning*, Dordrecht: Foris.

Navis, A. (1984), *Alam Terkembang Jadi Guru: Adat dan Kebudayaan Minangkabau* (The World of Nature Becomes our Teacher: Minangkabau Traditions and Customs), Jakarta: Grafitipers.

Needham, R. (1962), *Structure and Sentiment: A Test Case in Social Anthropology*, Chicago: University of Chicago Press.

Nguyen Van Huyen (1934), *Introduction A L'Etude De L'Habitation Sur Pilotis Dans L'Asie Du Sud-Est* (Introduction to the Study of Pile Dwellings in South-East Asia), Paris: Librairie Orientaliste Paul Geuthner.

Niessen, S. (1985), *Motifs of Life in Toba Batak Texts and Textiles*, Dordrecht: Foris.

Nieuwenhuis, A. (1904, 1907), *Quer durch Borneo: Ergebnisse seiner Reisen in den Jahren 1894, 1896–97, und 1898–1900* (Across Borneo: An Account of His Journeys in the Years 1894, 1896–97, and 1898–1900), 2 vols., Leiden: Brill.

Nooteboom, C. (1939), 'Versieringen van Manggaraische Huizen' (Manggarai House Decorations), *Tijdschrift voor Indische Taal-, Land- en Volkenkunde*, 79, pp. 221–38.

Nooy-Palm, C. H. M. (1979), *The Sa'dan Toraja: A Study of Their Social Life and Religion*, Vol. 1, The Hague: Nijhoff.

_____ (1980), 'De Rol van Man en Vrouw in Enkele Rituelen van de Sa'dan-Toraja (Sulawesi, Indonesie)' (The Role of Man and Woman in Some Rituals of the Sa'dan Toraja (Sulawesi, Indonesia)), in R. Schefold *et al.* (eds.), *Man, Meaning and History: Essays in Honour of H. G. Schulte Nordholt*, The Hague: Nijhoff, pp. 140–78.

Nooy-Palm, C. H. M. *et al.* (1979), 'The Sa'dan Toraja in Ujung Pandang (Sulawesi, Indonesia): A Migration Study', Amsterdam/Ujung Pandang: Koninklijk Instituut voor de Tropen/University of Hasanuddin Press.

Oliver, P. (ed.) (1969), *Shelter and Society*, London: Barrie and Rockliff.

_____ (ed.) (1971), *Shelter in Africa*, London: Barrie and Jenkins.

_____ (ed.) (1975), *Shelter, Sign and Symbol*, London: Barrie and Jenkins.

_____ (1987), *Dwellings: The House Across the World*, London: Phaidon.

Onvlee, L. (1980), 'The Significance of Livestock on Sumba', in J. J. Fox (ed.), *The Flow of Life: Essays on Eastern Indonesia*, Cambridge, Mass.: Harvard University Press, pp. 195–207.

Ortiz, A. (1969), *The Tewa World: Space, Time, Being and Becoming in a Pueblo Society*, Chicago: University of Chicago Press.

Ortner, S. (1974), 'Is Female to Male as Nature is to Culture?', in M. Rosaldo and L. Lamphere (eds.), *Woman, Culture and Society*, Stanford: Stanford University Press, pp. 67–88.

Ossenbruggen, F. D. E. van (1977) (1918), 'Java's Moncapat: Origins of a Primitive Classification System', in P. E. de Josselin de Jong (ed.), *Structural Anthropology in the Netherlands*, The Hague: Nijhoff, pp. 32–60.

Padtbrugge, R. (1866) (1679), 'Beschrijving der Zeden en Gewoonten van de Bewoners der Minahassa' (Description of the Manners and Customs of the Inhabitants of Mina-hassa), *Bijdragen tot de Taal-, Land- en Volkenkunde*, 13, pp. 304–31.

Parkin, H. (1978), 'Batak Fruit of Hindu Thought', D.Theol. thesis, Serampore College.

Pawley, A. and Green, K. (1975), 'Dating the Dispersal of the Oceanic Languages', *Oceanic Linguistics*, 12(1), pp. 1–67.

Pelras, C. (1975), 'La Maison Bugis: Formes, Structures et Fonctions' (The Bugis House: Forms, Structures and Functions), *Asie du Sud-Est et Monde Insulindien*, 6(2–3), pp. 61–100.

Persoon, G. (1986), 'Congelation in the Melting Pot: The Minangkabau in Jakarta', in P. Nas (ed.), *The Indonesian City: Studies in Urban Development and Planning*, Dordrecht: Foris, pp. 176–96.

Poirier, J. (1972), *Ethnologie Régionale* (Regional Ethnology), Vol. I. Collection Encyclopédie de la Pléiade, Paris: Gallimard.

Quaritch-Wales, H. G. (1959), 'The Cosmological Aspect of Indonesian Religion', *Journal of the Royal Asiatic Society* (3–4), pp. 100–39.

Raffles, S. H. (Lady) (1830), *Memoir of the Life and Public Services of Sir Thomas Stamford Raffles*, London: John Murray.

Rapoport, A. (1969), *House Form and Culture*, Englewood Cliffs: Prentice-Hall.

_____ (1975), 'Australian Aborigines and the Definition of Place', in P. Oliver (ed.), *Shelter, Sign and Symbol*, London: Barrie and Jenkins, pp. 7–37.

_____ (1982), *The Meaning of the Built Environment: A Nonverbal Communication Approach*, Beverley Hills: Sage.

Rassers, W. (1959), *Panji, the Culture Hero: A Structural Study of Religion in Java*, The Hague: Nijhoff.

Reid, A. (1980), 'The Structure of Cities in South-East Asia, 15th to 17th Centuries', *Journal of South-East Asian Studies*, 11(2), pp. 235–50.

Ricklefs, M. (1981), *A History of Modern Indonesia*, London: Macmillan.

Rodgers, S. (1985), *Power and Gold: Jewelry of Indonesia, Malaysia and the Philippines*, Geneva: Barbier-Müller Museum.

Rosaldo, M. (1980), *Knowledge and Passion: Ilongot Notions of Self and Social Life*, Cambridge: Cambridge University Press.

Roth, H. L. (1968) (1896), *The Natives of Sarawak and British North Borneo*, 2 vols., Kuala Lumpur: University of Malaya Press.

Rudofsky, B. (1964), *Architecture without Architects*, London: Academy Editions.

_____ (1977), *The Prodigious Builders*, London: Secker and Warburg.

Saber, M. and Madale, A. (eds.) (1975), *The Maranao*, Manila: Solidaridad.

Sandin, B. (1963), '"Garong" Baskets', *Sarawak Museum Journal*, 11(21–2), pp. 321–6.

_____ (1980), *Iban Adat and Augury*, Penang: Universiti Sains Malaysia.

Sarasin, P. and Sarasin, F. (1905–6), *Reisen in Celebes*, 2 vols., Wiesbaden: C. W. Kreidel's Verlag.

Sargeant, G. (1977), 'House Form and Decoration in Sumatra', in D. Jones and G. Michell (eds.), *Vernacular Architecture of the Islamic World and Indian Asia*, London: Art and Archaeology Research Papers, pp. 27–32.

Sargeant, G. and Saleh, R. (1973), *Traditional Buildings of Indonesia, Vol. 1: Batak Toba; Vol. 2: Batak Karo; Vol. 3: Batak Simalungun/Mandailing*, Bandung: REHOCE (Regional Housing Centre).

Savage, V. (1984), *Western Impressions of Nature and Landscape in Southeast Asia*, Singapore: Singapore University Press.

Schärer, H. (1963), *Ngadju Religion: The Conception of God among a South Borneo People*, The Hague: Nijhoff.

Schefold, R. (1976), 'Religious Involution: Internal Change, and its Consequences, in the Taboo System of the Mentawaians', *Tropical Man*, 5, pp. 46–81.

_____ (1980), 'The Sacrifices of the Sakuddei (Mentawai Archipelago, Western Indonesia): An Attempt at Classification', in R. Schefold et al. (eds.), *Man, Meaning and History: Essays in Honour of H. G. Schulte Nordholt*, The Hague: Nijhoff, pp. 82–108.

_____ (1982), 'The Efficacious Symbol', in P. E. de Josselin de Jong and E. Schwimmer (eds.), *Symbolic Anthropology in the Netherlands*, The Hague: Nijhoff, pp. 125–42.

Schröder, E. E. W. Gs. (1917), *Nias: Ethnographische, Geographische en Historische Aanteekeningen en Studien* (Nias: Ethnographical, Geographical and Historical Notes and Studies), Leiden: Brill.

Schulte Nordholt, H. G. (1971), *The Political System of the Atoni of Timor*, The Hague: Nijhoff.

_____ (1980), 'The Symbolic Classification of the Atoni of Timor', in J. J. Fox (ed.), *The Flow of Life: Essays on Eastern Indonesia*, Cambridge, Mass.: Harvard University Press.

Scott, W. H. (1966), *On the Cordillera: A look at the Peoples and Cultures of the Mountain Province*, Manila: MCS Enterprises.

Setiono, H. (1983), 'Arsitektur Tradisional Toraja sebagai Ungkapan Wadah Fisik Nilai Budaya Adat Toraja' (Traditional Toraja Architecture as an Expression in Physical Form of the Cultural Values of Toraja Adat), Paper presented to seminar on Toraja Adat, Ujung Pandang (April).

Sherman, D. (1982), 'Social Organisation of Samosir Batak Livelihood in Relation to their System of Beliefs and Values', 2 vols., Ph.D. thesis, Cornell.

Sherwin, D. (1979), 'From Batak to Minangkabau: An Architectural Trajectory', *Majallah Akitek*, 1(79), pp. 38–42.

Shih Lei (1964), 'The Family System of the Paiwan at Su-Paiwan Village', *Bulletin of the Institute of Ethnology (Academia Sinica)*, 18, pp. 89–112.

Shway Yoe (Sir J. G. Scott) (1963) (1882), *The Burman: His*

Life and Notions, New York: Norton.

Siegel, J. (1969), *The Rope of God*, Berkeley: University of California Press.

Singarimbun, M. (1975), *Kinship, Descent and Alliance among the Karo Batak*, Berkeley: University of California Press.

Sjahrir, K. (1983), 'Asosiasi Klan Orang Batak Toba di Jakarta' (Toba Batak Clan Associations in Jakarta), *Prisma*, 12(1), pp. 75–81.

Skeat, W. (1900), *Malay Magic: Being an Introduction to the Folklore and Popular Religion of the Malay Peninsula*, London: Macmillan; reprinted Singapore: Oxford University Press, 1984.

Snouck Hurgronje, C. (1906), *The Acehnese*, 2 vols., Leiden: Brill.

Soebadio, H. (1975), 'The Documentary Study of Traditional Balinese Architecture: Some Preliminary Notes', *Indonesian Quarterly*, 3, pp. 86–95.

Soelarto, R. (1973), 'Villages Balinais: Tradition, Restauration, Renovation' (Balinese Villages: Tradition, Restoration, Renovation), *L'Architecture D'Aujourd'hui*, 167, pp. 44–9.

St. John, S. (1862), *Life in the Forests of the Far East: Or Travels in Northern Borneo*, 2 vols., London: Smith, Elder and Co.; reprinted Singapore: Oxford University Press, 1986.

Stapel, H. (1914), 'Het Manggaraische Volk' (The Manggarai People), *Tijdschrift voor Indische Taal-, Land- en Volkenkunde*, 56, pp. 157–78.

Straits Times (1985), 'Rites Before Restoration' (26 June).

Strathern, M. (1984), 'Domesticity and the Denigration of Women', in D. O'Brien and S. Tiffany, *Rethinking Women's Roles: Perspectives from the Pacific*, Berkeley: University of California Press, pp. 13–31.

Suchtelen, B. C. M. M. van (1921), *Endeh (Flores)*, Weltevreden: Mededelingen van het Bureau voor de Bestuurszaken der Buitenbezittingen bewerkt door het Encyclopaedisch Bureau, No. 26.

Sundrum, R. (1976), 'Interprovincial Migration', *Bulletin of Indonesian Economic Studies*, 12, pp. 70–92.

Sutlive, V. (1978), *The Iban of Sarawak*, Illinois: AHM.

Suzuki, P. (1959), *The Religious System and Culture of Nias, Indonesia*, The Hague: Excelsior.

_____ (1973), 'Feasts among the Niasans of the Batu Islands, Indonesia', *Anthropos*, 68(3–4), pp. 597–603.

_____ (1984), 'The Limitations of Structuralism and Autochthonous Principles of Urban Planning and Design in Indonesia: The Case of Nias', *Anthropos*, 79, pp. 47–53.

Swellengrebel, J. (1960), 'Introduction', in W. Wertheim (ed.), *Bali: Studies in Life, Thought and Ritual*, The Hague: van Hoeve, pp. 1–53.

Swift, M. (1971), 'Minangkabau and Modernization,' in L. Hiatt and A. Jayawardena (eds.), *Anthropology in Oceania: Essays Presented to Ian Hogbin*, Sydney.

Tambiah, S. J. (1970), *Buddhism and the Spirit Cults in North-East Thailand*, Cambridge: Cambridge University Press.

_____ (1973) (1969), 'Classification of Animals in Thailand', in M. Douglas (ed.), *Rules and Meanings*, Harmondsworth: Penguin, pp. 127–66.

_____ (1976), *World-Conqueror and World-Renouncer*, Cambridge: Cambridge University Press.

Tan, R. (1967), 'The Domestic Architecture of South Bali', *Bijdragen tot de Taal-, Land- en Volkenkunde*, 123(4), pp. 442–75.

Tanner, N. (1976), 'Minangkabau', in F. Lebar (ed.), *Insular South-East Asia: Ethnographic Studies*, Vol I: Sumatra, New Haven: Human Relations Area Files Press, pp. 1–82.

_____ (1982), 'The Nuclear Family in Minangkabau Matriliny: The Mirror of Disputes', *Bijdragen tot de Taal-, Land-en Volkenkunde*, 138(1), pp. 129–51.

Taufik Abdullah (1966), 'Adat and Islam: An Examination of Conflict in Minangkabau', *Indonesia*, 2, pp. 1–24.

Tempo (1985), 'Istana-Istana Tanpa Tuah.... Membangun Keraton Menurut Kawruh Kalang' (Palaces That Have Lost Their Magic.... Building the Palace According to the *Kawruh Kalang* [a book of rules for construction of palaces]), 51 (16 February).

Tiffany, S. (1978), 'Models and the Social Anthropology of Women', *Man*, 13, pp. 34–51.

Tillema, H. (1938), *Apo-Kajan: een Filmreis naar en door Centraal-Borneo* (Apo-Kajan: A Film Journey To and Through Central Borneo), Amsterdam: Van Munsters.

Tischner, H. (1934), *Die Verbreitung der Hausformen in Ozeanien* (The Distribution of House Forms in Oceania), Leipzig: Verlag der Werkgemeinschaft.

Tobing, L. (1956), *The Structure of the Toba-Batak Belief in the High God*, Amsterdam: van Campen.

Traube, E. (1986), *Cosmology and Social Life: Ritual Exchange among the Mambai of East Timor*, Chicago: University of Chicago Press.

Turton, A. (1978), 'Architectural and Political Space in Thailand', in G. Milner (ed.), *Natural Symbols in South-East Asia*, London: School of Oriental and African Studies, pp. 113–32.

Tuuk, H. N. van der (1864–7), *Tobasche Spraakkunst* (Toba Grammar), 2 vols., Amsterdam.

Urry, J. (1981), 'A View from the West: Inland, Lowland and Islands in Indonesian Prehistory', Paper presented at the 51st ANZAAS Congress, Brisbane (May).

Vergouwen, J. (1964), *The Social Organisation and Customary Law of the Toba-Batak of Northern Sumatra*, The Hague: Nijhoff.

Viaro, A. (1980), *Urbanisme et Architecture traditionnels du Sud de L'Ile de Nias* (Traditional Urbanism and Architecture in the South of Nias Island), Paris: UNESCO.

_____ (1984), 'Nias: Habitat et Megalithisme' (Nias: Habitat and Megalithic Culture), *Archipel*, 27, pp. 109–44.

Viner, A. (1979), 'The Changing Batak', *Journal of the Malayan Branch of the Royal Asiatic Society*, 59(2), pp. 84–112.

Volkman, T. (1980), 'The Pig has Eaten the Vegetables:

Ritual and Change in Tana Toraja', Ph.D. thesis, Cornell.

_____ (1985), *Feasts of Honor: Ritual and Change in the Toraja Highlands*, Urbana: University of Illinois Press.

Volz, W. (1909), *Nord-Sumatra: Vol. I, Die Bataklander* (North Sumatra: Vol. I, the Batak Lands), Berlin: Dietrich Reimer (Ernst Vohsen).

Vredenbregt, J. (1964), 'Bawean Migration: Some Preliminary Notes', *Bijdragen tot de Taal-, Land- en Volkenkunde*, 120(1), pp. 109-37.

Vroklage, B. A. G. (1936), 'Das Schiff in den Megalithkulturen Sudostasiens und der Sudsee' (The Ship in the Megalithic Cultures of Southeast Asia and the South Seas), *Anthropos*, 31, pp. 712-57.

_____ (1940), 'De Prauw in Culturen van Flores' (The Ship in Cultures of Flores), *Cultureel Indië*, 2, pp. 193-9, 230-4, 263-70.

_____ (1953), *Ethnographie der Belu in Zentral-Timor* (Ethnography of the Belu of Central Timor), Leiden: Brill.

Wagner, W. (1981a), 'Present Tendencies in the Resettlement Policy on the Mentawai Islands from a Historical Perspective', Paper presented to the Symposium Mengenai Pembangunan Sosio-Ekonomi, Kebudayaan Tradisional dan Lingkungan Hidup Pulau Siberut, Andalas University, Padang (March).

_____ (1981b), 'Some Preliminary Remarks on the Social History of Mentawai', Paper presented to the Symposium Mengenai Pembangunan Sosio-Ekonomi, Kebudayaan Tradisional dan Lingkungan Hidup Pulau Siberut, Andalas University, Padang (March).

Walden, R. (ed.) (1977), *The Open Hand: Essays on Le Corbusier*, Cambridge, Mass.: MIT Press.

Wardi, P. (1981), 'The Malay House', *MIMAR: Architecture in Development*, 2, pp. 55-63.

Waterson, R. (1984a), 'Rites of East and West: Ritual, Gender and Status in Tana Toraja', in R. Waterson, *Ritual and Belief among the Sa'dan Toraja*, Occasional Paper No. 2, University of Kent Centre of South-East Asian Studies, pp. 3-33.

_____ (1984b), 'Taking the Place of the Ancestors: Ethnic Identity in Tana Toraja in the 1980s', in R. Waterson, *Ritual and Belief among the Sa'dan Toraja*, Occasional Paper No. 2, University of Kent Centre of South-East Asian Studies, pp. 34-72.

_____ (1986) 'The Ideology and Terminology of Kinship among the Sa'dan Toraja', *Bijdragen tot de Taal-, Land- en Volkenkunde*, 142(1), pp. 87-112.

_____ (1988a), 'Hornbill, Naga and Cock in Sa'dan Toraja Woodcarving Motifs', *Archipel* (forthcoming).

_____ (1988b), 'The House and the World: The Symbolism of Sa'dan Toraja House Carvings', *RES*, 15, pp. 35-60.

Weatherbee, D. (1981), 'The Indonesianization of East Timor', *Contemporary Southeast Asia*, 3(1), pp. 1-23.

Weiner, A. (1978), 'The Reproductive Model in Trobriand Society', *Mankind*, 11, pp. 175-86.

Wessing, R. (1977), 'The Position of the Badui in the Larger West Javanese Society', *Man*, 12(2), pp. 293-303.

_____ (1978), *Cosmology and Social Behaviour in a West Javanese Settlement*, Athens, Ohio: Ohio University Centre for International Studies.

_____ (1979), 'Life in the Cosmic Village: Cognitive Models in Sundanese Life', in E. Bruner and J. Becker (eds.), *Art, Ritual and Society in Indonesia*, Athens, Ohio: Ohio University Centre for International Studies.

_____ (1984), 'Acehnese', in R. Weekes (ed.), *Muslim Peoples: A World Ethnographic Survey*, Westport: Greenwood Press.

Wetering, F. H. van de (1923), 'Het Rotineesche Huis' (The Rotinese House), *Tijdschrift voor Indische Taal, Land- en Volkenkunde*, 62, pp. 445-95.

Whitmore, T. (1977), *The Palms of Malaya*, Kuala Lumpur: Oxford University Press.

Williams, R. (1976), *Keywords: A Vocabulary of Culture and Society*, London: Fontana.

Woolard, D. (1988), 'Traditional Dwellings of the South Pacific', Paper presented to the International Symposium on Traditional Dwellings and Settlements in a Comparative Perspective, University of California, Berkeley (April).

Wouden, F. A. E. van (1968) (1935), *Types of Social Structure in Eastern Indonesia*, The Hague: Nijhoff.

_____ (1977) (1956), 'Local Groups and Double Descent in Kodi, West Sumba', in P. E. de Josselin de Jong (ed.), *Structural Anthropology in the Netherlands*, The Hague: Nijhoff, pp. 184-222.

Wurm, S. and Wilson, B. (1975), *English Finderlist of Reconstructions in Austronesian Languages (post-Brandstetter)*, Canberra: ANU Press.

Zerner, C. (1983), 'Animate Architecture of the Toraja', *Arts of Asia*, September-October, pp. 96-106.

Zorc, R. and Charles, M. (1971), 'Proto-Philippine Finder List' (typescript), Ithaca: Cornell.

Index